Harmony Ideology

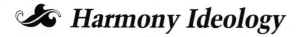 **Harmony Ideology**

Justice and Control

in a Zapotec Mountain Village

Laura Nader

STANFORD UNIVERSITY PRESS *Stanford, California*

Stanford University Press
Stanford, California
© 1990 by the Board of Trustees
of the Leland Stanford Junior University
Printed in the United States of America

Original printing 1990

Last figure below indicates year of this printing:

00 99 98 97 96 95 94 93 92 91

CIP data appear at the end of the book

To Immy and Bayee and
buIni rshidza'

Acknowledgments

I was introduced to Zapotec culture and civilization during my Smith College Junior Year Abroad at the Colegio de México (1950–51) in Mexico City by Pedro Armillas and through personal travels in southern Mexico. During my years as a graduate student at Harvard University, Gordon Willey and Evon Z. Vogt refined my knowledge of Mexican archaeology and ethnology. At Harvard, my interest in the Zapotec continued, and Clyde Kluckhohn encouraged me to undertake a serious study of contemporary and unstudied Zapotec peoples of the Sierra Madre mountains. That interest has been continuous since I went into the field in 1957.

Financial support for my initial fieldwork came from the Mexican government and covered 12 months during 1957–58. A grant from the Milton Fund at Harvard supported an additional three months in 1959–60. The Center for Advanced Study in the Behavioral Sciences at Stanford, California, where I was a Fellow during 1963–64, provided funding for further field research and for filming early in 1964. My first monograph, *Talea and Juquila: A Comparison of Zapotec Social Organization*, was published in 1964, and with a grant from the Institute for International Studies at Berkeley I was able to complete a film, *To Make the Balance*, in 1966. Between the years 1964 and 1969 and later in 1979 and early 1988, I visited the Rincón Zapotec for short periods, supported mostly by small grants from the University of California at Berkeley. A second film, *Little Injustices: Laura Nader Looks at the Law*, was completed during the fall of 1980 and supported through the Odyssey Program of PBS. Support for the writing of a book on Zapotec law was awarded by the Woodrow Wilson Center for International Scholars in Washington,

viii   *Acknowledgments*

D.C., where I was a Fellow during 1979–80. My time at the Wilson Center was indispensable to launching the bulk of the work and gave me time to think about new materials that changed the course of my work. My fall 1986 sabbatical from the University of California, Berkeley, made it possible for my thinking about harmony theory and Christian missionizing to take shape. The University also helped underwrite publication of the tables.

Several students have accompanied me in my research and received their first field experience in Talea: Penny Addiss, John Rothenberger, Gobi Stromberg, Richard Dillon, and others who passed through for shorter periods. However, there would be no study at all without the help and cooperation of the Talean people themselves. They helped me because I asked for help, and then they became interested in this study of their community. Although many of them did not live to see the results of their help, I remember them all with gratitude: Alfredo Bautista and Rodolfo Bautista in particular, but others as well, Rosa Vasconcelos, Constantino Hernández, León Vasconcelos, Chemu Vasconcelos, Adela Bautista, Elias González, Salomón León, and many other friends both in Talea and Juquila, made central contributions to this work. The Papaloapan Commission and in particular Annuar Abdala Luna and Lini de Vries helped with the logistics of studying in the mountains beyond Ixtlán before there was road communication and of surviving the illnesses I had to manage as a result of fieldwork.

I want to acknowledge my colleagues who read all or portions of the manuscript and who have encouraged this work while sometimes disagreeing with it: Elizabeth Colson, Beatrice Whiting, John Whiting, Woodrow Borah, Donald Black, Eugene Hammel, Nancy Howell, Paul Bohannan, and a very helpful anonymous reader. Elizabeth Colson's careful and critical reading was a model of collegiality rarely achieved. JoAnn Martin and Cathie Witty helped with the coding and organizing of case materials, and they and Saddeka Arebi, Laurel Rose, Suzanne Bowler, Jenny Beer, and Lori Powell read and commented on, or corrected errors in, the chapters. Others along the way helped with the tedious job of translating the cases: Penny Addiss, Jeanne Cooke, Betty Adams, Gobi Stromberg, and Rene Veron Golden. Grace Buzaljko bore with me over the editing during many years, and Barbara Quigley and others in the anthropology department at Berkeley lent me their skills. Bruce Gemmel and William DuVoll drew the maps. Patricia Marquez helped with the index.

Finally, I could not have completed any of this work without the support of my parents, my siblings, my husband, and my children.

I am particularly grateful that Rania Milleron worked on pulling together bibliographic sources, that Tarek Milleron extended his patience and intelligence to editing and proofreading the final manuscript, and that Nadia Milleron ensured that my preoccupation with this manuscript was not total.

L.N.

Contents

Part IV. Connections

Twelve pages of photographs follow p. 118

Tables and Figures

Tables

Figures

Preface

In the spring of 1957, I began fieldwork in the Sierra Madre mountains of Oaxaca, Mexico, in a village that was still recovering from a clash between a small group of Protestant converts and the majority group of Catholic parishioners. Feelings were running high because of the refusal of the Protestants to participate in the civil and religious responsibilities expected of all villagers. The Protestants were attacked by fellow villagers, their homes were burned, and the state intervened to restore order. The village was forced to pay compensation and a heavy fine. For the moment the Protestants receded into the background. The bitterness remained, and my arrival was greeted with suspicion that my purpose was evangelical. Upon every occasion I was informed of village unity. The contradiction between conflict and values of harmony was present from the beginning. A solid front was presented to outsiders, a not uncommon stance for Oaxacan villages embroiled in internal disputes (Paddock 1975; Dennis 1987).

I based my work on the villages of Talea de Castro and Juquila Vijanos, where Zapotec-speaking peoples were on the verge of major change. The Papaloapan Commission, a government development agency, was in charge of completing the road from Oaxaca City to Ixtlán, and on through the virgin mountains to the region known as El Rincón, where Talea and Juquila are located. The people of the region were living in anticipation of improved access to the capital, but they also feared increased and uncontrolled contact due to the developing road system that would open them to the "outside." Now some thirty years later, the best and the worst of their concerns are being realized: more Rinconeros can come and go; the government and outside business interests have more control and influence over village life; local cultural traditions are being eroded and reconstructed; and new ideas and values are traveling with new products and new agricultural technologies. The economic impact of increasing dependence on the cash crop of coffee has been widespread; perhaps even more striking are the demographic changes due to steady out-migration.

During my first field trip, I was interested in studying the social-organizational consequences of compact and scattered settlements (Schmieder 1930). As part of this work on space and social organization, I obtained a month's sample of court cases from the village of Talea, and through an analysis of this material (Nader 1964b), I began my exploration of the contextual study of Zapotec law (Nader 1964b, 1966a, 1969b). The data from the courts were rich in information on relations of power and on the values that Taleans fought to defend. I returned in 1959–60 for three months of concentrated field research on questions of law and social control that were to take me far beyond the courtroom.

In the late 1950's and 1960's, ethnographers of law were few (Nader 1965a), and there was little interest in "dispute resolution" in law and the social sciences. When Duane Metzger and I collaborated on analyzing Indian village law (1963), the literature on the subject was virtually nonexistent for Mexico. I remember E. Z. Vogt from Harvard University writing to ask for my early papers because his student Jane Collier was interested in studying the law of the Mexican Zinacantecans. Few American universities were training students in the anthropological study of law. Yet, by the 1960's, standards for ethnographies of law were strongly set in an empirical mode based on the publications of Malinowski (1926), Llewellyn and Hoebel (1941), Gluckman (1955), Bohannan (1957), Pospisil (1958), Moore (1958), Schapera (1959), and Gulliver (1963). Since then, ethnographies of law in non-Western societies have remained richly descriptive and are still few in number (Koch 1967; Fallers 1969; Collier 1973; Starr 1978; Rosen 1984; Moore 1986; Williams 1987).

In this book I analyze data collected by participation, observation, and interviewing techniques. I make central use of the dispute case: cases that were observed in court, reported to me, recorded in the archives, recorded on film, and elicited from hypotheticals. I followed cases out of the courtroom into the community using direct and indirect elicitation. In sampling I cast a wide net. With the help of Talean and student assistants, I took samples of court cases heard over the thirteen years from 1957 to 1969, while also collecting all the memory cases I could elicit under any circumstances outside the court.

This book includes what has emerged from an analysis of a full range of field material on the Talean Zapotec, only a part of which I have published previously. The book has had the benefit of more recent Berkeley studies of the Villa Alta district court (Parnell 1978a, 1989) and research on adaptation strategies of Zapotec migrants in Mexico City (Hirabayashi 1986). The book has also profited from the comparative study of dispute processing carried out by the Berkeley Village Law Project (*The Disputing Process*; Nader and Todd 1978), and from the Berkeley Complaint Project (1970–80), which dealt with American economic grievances about products and services (*No Access to Law*; Nader 1980). *Little Injustices* (Nader 1981), a film produced by the Public Broadcasting System as part of its Odyssey series, captured some of this material. Field experiences outside the Zapotec region and a visit to Talea in January 1988 have proved invaluable for understanding social transformation through law. The perspective that proves useful in understanding the microcosm is also supplemented by a comparative perspective on ideologies that have had worldwide impact on law evolving locally (Nader 1989a).

Different ways of knowing come in waves in anthropology, when they might be used simultaneously. The evolutionists concentrated on change in the law on a global scale (Maine 1861), the structural functionalists examined communities as microcosms of connected social activity as if they were autonomous and unconnected to global networks (Gluckman 1955; Bohannan 1957). Those interested in process, in power, and in multiple systems focus on the active individual, and those interested in the internal cultural logic of disputes add yet another dimension—all these and more are reflected in the ways of knowing employed by anthropologists (see also Nader 1979; Salzman 1988).

This work utilizes the *ethnographic, comparative,* and *historical* approaches to reveal how social organization in general and how the social organization of law in particular relate to control, to relative power, and to autonomy over an extended period of colonization. It is the story of justice and control through the uses of harmony. It seems obvious that the logic of disputes depends on conditions that evolve over extended periods of time.

Although a good portion of this book focuses on court disputation, knowing something about how Zapotecs act and think about law and controversy requires ethnography, a method that does not isolate the judicial from the rest of social control activity and organizations or from the wider social structure. From the start I have not been interested in law as an isolated social and cultural system, although it can be instructive to study the idea of law as autonomous—a form of hegemonic control (Gordon 1982).

Malinowski's work with the Pacific Trobriand Islanders (1926), a people without courts, was an early reappraisal of the place of law in social life and indirectly a critique of the Western idea of an autonomous law. In line with the Malinowskian approach, I searched for principles of association that order and disorder social life (Malinowski and de la Fuente 1982). Studies of societies with courts require an understanding of law as a system inextricably linked to social life. The study of law was to be something more than a description of an ideal, self-contained system of handling rights and wrongs. There was a dynamic that had to be grasped, sometimes through the transformation of social institutions, at other times by means of active individuals, or as a result of new systems of thought. Colson (1953) had already focused our attention on process in social control by utilizing extended cases of dispute, but explanation requires comparison.

Explanation by means of comparison has been fundamental to anthropology. History informs specific explanation, but several histories will lead to comparison and to general understanding. The specific and general intertwine, one informing the other. An examination of user patterns in different contexts has yielded the idea that law varies inversely with other kinds of social control (Colson 1953; Black 1976). And controlled comparisons have been helpful in delineating the relation between legal form and social morphology (Nader 1965a); the distribution of people in groups or networks acts as a constraint on the development of forums for the handling of conflict. Further comparison shifted attention from social structure to the relation between the elements of the disputing process and the style of disputing (Nader 1969b). Interest in the style of court proceedings, in the mode of expression, derived from filming a Zapotec law court in action (*To Make the Balance*; Nader 1966a). I was dealing with both cultural (El Guindi 1973) and sociological dimensions, intent on specifying that which generates the style of dispute handling. In this book I use comparison to understand internal variation and the global diffusion of legal ideas that form the core of disputing styles.

Variation can be explained first within a society like that of the Talean Zapotec and then between societies across continents, for it is sometimes true that "the more ethnohistory we know, the more clearly 'their' history and 'our' history emerge as part of the same history" (Wolf 1982: 19). It is at this point that the interest in small-scale and seemingly autonomous communities gives way to comparison between seemingly autonomous communities (Nader and Todd 1978) and later to an interest in the diffusion of ideas pertaining to law, a process that has us emerge as part of the same history as that of the contemporary Zapotec and that questions the degree to which any community may be treated as autonomous. The analysis of Talea gathers power when the particular is placed in a global context, one in which Christianity and colonialism and the resistances and adaptations to these global movements are incorporated and brought to bear on a broader understanding of the Zapotec (Young 1976; Laviada 1978).

There have been attempts to transcend the boundaries of the microcosm in anthropology. Sir Henry Maine (1861) was involved in understanding the impact on law of the transition from kinship to territorially based societies in two civilizations. More recently, Jane Collier (1973) examined law and politics among the Zinacantecans of Mexico, and Sally Falk Moore (1986) analyzed the social and economic transformation of the Chagga of Tanzania, who radically changed the context in which "customary law" was used. Carol Greenhouse (1986) also transcended the local community to understand how the historical events of the Civil War dramatically affected the way in which disputing is today perceived among the Georgia Baptists who pray for justice.

The search for configurations of culture, for cultural coherence, inspired me to move from local to global. To understand the meaning of harmony within a persistently litigious population, I had to examine the historical literature from the colonial period for data on missionary and civil practices in relation to law and had to look elsewhere in the world for information on the colonial and contemporary interaction between missionizing Christians, neocolonialism, and disputing processes. The worldwide distribution of Christian ideas of harmony and the way harmony values were and are used in different settings required a keen comparative consciousness and an awareness of the diffusion of idea systems and ideologies of control.

The isolation of the mountain Zapotec is only relative; they are part of the wider world. Contemporary villagers make special pleas for doctors to be sent to their area to perform the required term of medical service, thereby inviting individualistic ideas about cures. Large numbers of Taleans went to the United States as workers (*braceros*) during World War II, and returning braceros used their savings to buy coffee plants, to initiate the first large-scale cash cropping in the modern era; the idea of surplus connected them with world coffee markets. Compared with other native peoples of Mexico, the isolated geographic position of the Rinconeros has allowed them to partially control the degree, rate, and form of contact with the outside world. Numerous intrusions have occurred over the past several hundred years of colonization and development. Catholic priests and Protestant missionaries, teachers, tax collectors, judges, developers, and industrialists come with or without invitation. Long after they leave, their ideas remain.

In 1524 the respected elder men of the Rincón made contact with Spanish soldiers and Christian missionaries. Idea systems moved with the newcomers, who after all were there to convert and exploit. The Crown expended large sums in support of missions. There were two sets of laws and two sets of courts: the sacred and the secular. In sixteenth-century villages of converts, the clergy "administered justice, decided questions of succession, distributed the goods of the dead among the various heirs. . . . The missionaries thus became true political authorities" (Ricard 1966: 139). In the hinterland itinerant missionaries influenced local thinking and behavior. From the moment Crown policy created indigenous communities and their courts, the law has been used as a tool of political control to break insurgency and revolt. The colonization that began over 400 years ago continues today (Whitecotton 1977).

The contemporary clash of legal traditions in rural Oaxaca is one between a Spanish legal tradition stemming from the sixteenth-century ideals of Christian harmony and a more adversarial form of nation-state law. Villagers have a long history of relations with the district court, and they know the differences between contemporary village and district courts: fines paid to the village treasury of Talea are customarily translated into public works for public good, whereas the "fines" paid in the district court of Villa Alta commonly benefit local officials; local-level hearings are geared toward compensating victims or reconciling litigants, and an ideology of harmony permeates encounters between officials and litigants. State law as practiced in the district court concentrates on punishment rather than compensation.

Other observations about state and village law are striking: local-level hearings are a result of open participation and open access, and the activity in this arena is defined heavily by the action of plaintiffs and defendants; state hearings are the result of a professional definition of relevance based on an ideal of equal application of the law to all. Access to village courts is determined by how many people are waiting ahead of one; at the state level access is sometimes also limited by the content of the case and one's ability to pay a lawyer or other intermediary. Structure and action are reflected in different systems of thought at the local and state level.

State courts have brought some benefits to the Rincón. The most obvious is the third-party role they play in connection with intra- or inter-village feuds and factionalizing. Their safety-valve potential for handling local abuse of power is another important role. At the same time, Hunt and Hunt's study of a Oaxacan district court (1967) and Parnell's work (1978a, 1989) in the Villa Alta district court indicate that district courts discriminate; they apply the letter of the law to the indigenes and a more comfortable situational "law" to mestizos, who are more like themselves. Furthermore, the innocent and/or angry villager who goes to the district court for impartial mediation or adjudication of local politics often does not realize that the wealth of his opponent is a deciding factor.

Local preservation of autonomy using local legal practices has in great part encouraged solidarity and legal involution in the villages (Parnell 1978a). Local autonomy is exercised by means of law, and customary legal practices have evolved over the past hundreds of years of colonization. The Zapotec are a practical people who developed a civilization with a sophisticated division of labor long before contact with the Spaniards. Their pantheon included a set of gods who dealt with the administration of justice. Under foreign rule, the Zapotec continued to equate customary law with local administration. Thus, when village law is preferred, they make agreements (*convenios*) between parties because "there is no agreement where there are laws." When there is no agreement, they move the case into court and cross-examination (*careo*), but the Talean Zapotec prefer to make agreements. Administrative resolution is separate from judicial resolution in the minds of the villagers, and the administrative is preferable to a system of courts based on a law foreign to the social conditions of rural Mexico.

Another mechanism through which village law has evolved is the town meeting, to which I was decidedly not invited. It is at the town meeting where Zapotecs discuss their relations with the outside (*relaciones exteriores*) and where the norms of the village are stated and argued, usually in Zapotec. It is at the town meeting where village men agree that punishment of local violations of state law will be shared by all town citizens when they find it necessary to go against state law. This pursuit of unity and harmonious relations has prevented the devastation that might otherwise result from the interaction of state and local law. If there were no principle of unity in the face of outsiders—a unity that supports the pattern of shared guilt and punishment in the face of infractions of state law—the Rincón Zapotec, like the valley Zapotec of past centuries, would be in disorder (Gay 1881). As long as the village keeps its house in order, there is minimal interference; the Oaxacan judiciary has been laissez-faire in its judicial policy regarding the district of Villa Alta. Several of the highest state judges informed me that the judiciary is aware of a correlation between the penetration of the state legal system into the hinterland and an increased crime rate there. As long as there is no conflict of interest between the state and the local level, this live-and-let-live policy will probably continue. However, as geographic isolation disappears and as a fully monetized economy develops, the picture changes and legal professionals begin to participate in local-level law.

One consequence of professionalism in cultures of European origin has been the segregation of professionals from potential clients. In the 1960's about thirty lawyers were trained yearly in the law school at the University of Benito Juárez in Oaxaca, but there were no more than 200 practicing lawyers in the whole state. The rest migrated to Mexico City to work in offices. People go to the cities because they desire to be upwardly mobile, and mobility precludes returning to the rural areas, which are being denuded of people. A chief justice of the Oaxacan Supreme Court noted that appointment to a place like Villa Alta is like a punishment, and many officials would rather resign than go there. Qualified professional people do not frequent the rural areas, and in Villa Alta, we often find the posts of judge and *ministerio publico* (prosecutor) vacant, with experienced local secretaries of the court filling in for lack of a Oaxacan-trained judge or ministerio publico. Local self-sufficiency reigns. Indeed, villagers try to solve their problems without appeal to the district court and consciously avoid it. The contact of two systems of law, each with a different orientation, gives rise to a situation in which both systems tend to function to the exclusion of the other. As one chief justice expressed it: "Indigenous law is directed at satisfying the necessities of subsistence, whereas state law must follow the profit motive and the accumulation of capital." The state system, he said, is *más centrista*, more individualistic, and less community oriented.

Among the Talean Zapotec, village law works in the context of village social organization. The relation between the village court and villagers is mutually interactive, and insofar as citizens in this town actively participate in the court, they are defining the court agenda and the direction of law. Yet to understand the dynamic of law in a village requires an understanding of the social system wider than the Rincón. The world political economy is present in the village alongside and embedded in the local system. My interest in the Talean court is based on the interaction of local social relations and globally distributed traditions in the construction of law by means of harmony ideology.

The plan of the book is straightforward. In Part I, after introducing the village dispute settings in which harmony plays an important role, I deal with the organizations of social control and summarize the geographic, economic, historical, and political context in which law is found. In Part II, I describe the Zapotec court, court officials, litigants, and styles of court encounters. Part III deals with the substance of cultural control surrounding complaints relating to gender, property, and governance. Finally, in Part IV, by means of comparison and history, I hypothesize that harmony ideology has been an important part of social transformation through law under Western political and religious colonization and a key to counter-hegemonic movements of autonomy as well. The hegemonic forces that seek pacification and resocialization become the forces of resistance and accommodation.

This book has been written over many years and for that reason has been a pleasure intellectually. I have not been in a hurry to produce a work that fits into the latest mood in anthropology. Rather, I have been able to incorporate the wealth of insight that has come from each successive contribution: the structural-functionalists, the interest in process and power, a reflective style that has forced a consideration of paradigm and the place of a critical anthropology, the world-system theories, and the insight that comes from understanding cultural as well as social control. Anthropology, of all disciplines, should not be hampered by schools of thought or by subdivisions. When I began my analysis, it was law as social control that fascinated me. As I conclude this work, my focus is drawn to law as cultural control inseparable from political and religious colonization. Our understanding of hegemonic ideational control must be connected to our knowledge of social or institutional control. In the 1990's a composite approach, rather than attachment to any particular school of social or cultural theory, will add to the power of anthropological analysis of the microcosm in a global system.

Harmony Ideology

Chapter One

Introduction

When I began my studies among the Talean Zapotec of Mexico, my attention was claimed by the role of courts in systems of cultural and social control, a problem until then unstudied by anthropologists. To explain what I was observing and its uniqueness, I turned to comparison with other communities and posed the question "Why do the Talean Zapotec litigate so frequently in comparison with other American Indian groups or even in comparison with other groups I have studied, the Shias of southern Lebanon?" When I wished to explain the Talean ideology of harmony (seemingly contradictory with the high litigation rate), I found it difficult to find the answer in the particular conditions of the village without considering external forces, macro-scale phenomena that had impacted on Talea. Ideologies associated with harmony might have accompanied colonialism and the associated spread of Christian/Western missions—macro-processes that, as we shall see, utilize both conflict and harmony as controlling processes in disputing. The contours of the courts and court use in Talea had to be situated in a comparative and historical perspective.

The Zapotec observe that "a bad compromise is better than a good fight." Why? My research suggests that compromise models and, more generally, the harmony model are either counter-hegemonic political strategies used by colonized groups to protect themselves from encroaching superordinate powerholders or hegemonic strategies the colonizers use to defend themselves against organized subordinates. In the case of the Talean Zapotec, I have come to the conclusion that their harmony tradition stems from Spanish and Christian origin, an idea that leads me to propose that the uses of harmony are political. Legal styles are a component of political ideology that link harmony with autonomy or harmony with control.

The features of Talean court style have something in common with models presented by anthropologists and sociologists for people in other parts of the world, despite great organizational and cultural differences. James Gibbs (1963) observed a model of harmony while studying what he thought of as the therapeutic process of conciliatory dispute settlement used by the Kpelle of Liberia in Africa. Others, such as Gluckman (1955), Bohannan (1957), and Gulliver (1963), had also noticed the influence of models of conciliation or reasonableness among the African peoples they had studied. I published on the harmony model (not to be confused with mediation) among the Zapotec (1969b).

Elsewhere, others observed change in preferred law models. The harmony model was being replaced by the adversary model for dispute resolution with the development of new nation-states (see Nader and Todd 1978). Aubert (1969) reported that Norway had moved toward the harmony model and away from the adversarial one with the advent of the welfare state. A decade later, under the guise of alternative dispute resolution, the harmony model was replacing the adversarial model in the United States (Nader 1979, 1980, 1989b; Abel 1982). Were these changes in law models fortuitous or part of a common process?

In this book I address harmony as an inherent component of social organizations and of ideologies that evolved as a consequence of colonial political and religious policies. I recognize that harmony can come in many forms, that it may be part of a local tradition or part of a system of pacification that has diffused across the world along with Western colonialism, Christian missions, and other macro-scale systems of cultural control. Apparently, the basic components of harmony ideology are the same everywhere: an emphasis on conciliation, recognition that resolution of conflict is inherently good and that its reverse—continued conflict or controversy—is bad or dysfunctional, a view of harmonious behavior as more civilized than disputing behavior, the belief that consensus is of greater survival value than controversy. Harmony ideology can be powerful even when it contradicts the common realities of disputing.

This book's central thesis is that harmony ideology in Talea today is both a product of nearly 500 years of colonial encounter and a strategy for resisting the state's political and cultural hegemony. The contemporary relationship of harmony ideology, local solidarity, and resistance is embedded in the social organization of the local community and reflected in the workings of its courts. Talean social organization promotes order by preventing fragmentation or cleavages in individual and group relations. Talean harmony ideology promotes local solidarity.

The ideology of harmonious relationships can be explained as a consequence of a type of village social organization and as a result of contact that the Zapotec have had since the arrival of the Spaniards. Talea has been geographically isolated for long periods and, during my first stay, was connected by telegraph. Phone lines disrupted during the Mexican revolution had not been replaced, and there were no radios. Perhaps as a result Talea differs from many places studied by anthropologists. It is a place where the sense of community is strong despite unequal encounters with colonial or state regimes. Legal involution is effective because local third parties share norms and values with their constituents, who are full participants in the court system. Local courts offer both courtroom and bargaining models and handle substantial proportions of disputes in a manner not at odds with the state. In Talea, political elites compete successfully against agents of the state, preserving local solidarity and cultural identity, partly because of their harmony ideology. The Taleans work together to create and maintain an effective local identity against the state. With admirable effectiveness local legal actors monopolize institutionalized social control.

Spanish Colonial Policy

The contemporary dimension is part of a process that began in the sixteenth century. The colonial policy of the Spanish Crown in the sixteenth century resulted from maneuvering among the Crown, the colonists, and the Indians over issues of relative power. To guard against combinations of power that could rival the authority of the Crown, the Indians were declared direct vassals of the Crown, like the colonists themselves (Wolf 1959: 190).

After the first half of the sixteenth century, the Indians were made royal wards responsible to royal officials and supervised by the Crown. The seventeenth century brought an economic depression and a decline in mining and food production resulting from depopulation (Borah 1951). The century was, as Eric Wolf (1959: 202) observed, a "retreat from utopia," a phrase that reminds us that as in previous times of social and economic difficulties, Middle America retreated into its countryside. Wolf speaks of two patterns that emerged in the course of this retreat: the *hacienda* (a landed estate privately owned by the colonist), and the close-knit community of the Indian peasantry, the *república de indios* (ibid.: 202). The hacienda was to become an instrument of domination; the Indian community was to become an avenue toward autonomy. The Crown underwrote the legal identity of each Indian community:

A self-contained economic unit, holding a guaranteed 6.5 square miles of agricultural land, land which its members could sell only after special review by the viceroy. . . . Communal officials were to administer the law through the instrumentality of their traditional custom, wherever that custom did not conflict with the demands of church and state. The officers of the crown retained the privilege of judging major crimes and legal cases involving more than one community; but the Indian authorities received sufficient power to guarantee peace and order in the new communes. The autonomy which the crown denied to the Indian sector of society as a whole, it willingly granted to the local social unit. [Ibid.: 214]

The core of the Indian community was its political and religious *cargo* (office) systems. Responsibilities associated with the religious organization and the operation of the *municipio* (town hall), where the town courts were located, rotated among adult males. By means of this political and religious system, power and responsibility were allocated and reallocated at intervals to the men in the community, and ritual life was organized. The Indian community has been described as one in which the group is more important than the individual, where people are suspicious of conflict, where conflicts are adjusted, where economic imbalances are periodically corrected, and where status is linked to the number and quality of offices a man has held. The community defends its holdings against outsiders by prohibiting the sale of land to nonmembers and by endogamy.

Differences between Indian communities are commonly characterized by certain adjectives—open versus closed villages, traditional versus progressive villages, homogeneous versus heterogeneous villages, peaceful versus divided villages, belligerent versus passive villages. Such pairs reflect the transformative elements in these communities. As others have observed, the transformations are never independent of the wider world. The colonial policy that led to semiautonomous village communities left room for a range of political maneuvers, which is why we find diverse strategies within the same regions.

The story of ideological formation is more nebulous. There is little doubt that missionary activities in Oaxaca and the zeal of the missionary orders affected the basic ideological structures of the na-

tive populations, whether promoting submission, rebellion, adjustment, or autonomy. The "missions of penetration" spread in advance of Spanish political control. Indeed, the missionaries were
sometimes the advance guard of the Spanish soldiers (Wolf 1959:
174). There was an attempt at spiritual conquest. Robert Ricard,
in his work (1966) on the evangelizing methods of the mendicant
orders in New Spain from 1523 to 1572, emphasized the holistic nature of this penetration, which had to imbue the native peoples with
Christianity. Over 400 years later, we can only examine the result of
this Christianity, whose purpose "was . . . to create a new environment, in which to allow a new spirit to unfold" (ibid.: 290).

Ricard (1966: 290) refers to the missionary policy of protecting
the Indians from contact with Europeans. Indeed, Europeans were
excluded from native villages, and the priests had formidable power,
a situation that created difficulties with the civil administration.
Missionaries maintained the barrier between the Christian Indians
and the Europeans by not teaching the Indians Castilian despite the
formal orders of the Crown. Ignorance of Castilian created a gulf
that "kept the Indian mass outside the general evolution of the
country. The religious served as guides for the administration and as
intermediaries between it and the Indians, but when . . . their zeal
was extinguished the bridge was broken. . . . The Indians were once
more isolated . . . and retreated within themselves" (ibid.: 290).
Ricard also notes that some Indians avoided the churches and con-
vents altogether and escaped to remote corners where they could be
free of Spanish influence (ibid.: 142).

The organizational forms given the Indian communities of Middle
America by the Spanish Crown were designed to keep them isolated
and self-maintaining, with their own legal identity, with their own
local administrative council, and with their own local chapel or
church dedicated to a patron saint with rights over village lands and
resources. With special Indian courts, Indian villages were further
able to observe the intention of the Crown to separate Indians and
Spaniards (Wolf 1959: 146). In sixteenth-century Castile, compromise was the ideal and preferred means of ending disputes. Lawsuits
were thought to be at odds with Christian belief (Kagan 1981: 18)
not only in Castile but in the New World as well.

The idea of the separateness of the local community and courts
from the outside served Indian autonomy and helped ensure the
physical continuance of the community, whatever the original intention. The heart of this book examines the manner in which this
separateness has survived into the twentieth century. The Talean

Zapotec have clung to the idea of a bounded community, which is both a fiction and a large part of their reality. Colonial policy still influences Mexican Indian village courts.

Disputing, Ideology, and Autonomy

If it is true that the imperialists study their colonial charges, it is equally true that the charges study their masters—with great care and cunning. Who shall say which understands the other more? [Borah 1983: 226]

The struggle to restrict the impingement of superordinate power is carried out . . . consciously. Aside from outright resistance, those involved in the struggle have two principal means at their disposal: an appeal to tradition and rigorous attention to legality. [Colson 1974: 76]

An examination of village social organization and the workings of village law courts among the mountain Zapotec of Talea reveals the heritage of penetration. The processes of internal and external forces appear in the interconnectedness of social organization and in the styles of disputing processes. The Rincón Zapotec villages have been organized as politically independent, self-reliant, endogamous places that remain free to determine their lives only to the extent to which they manage themselves successfully. Villages with divisive feuds or problems that escalate to the district seat in Villa Alta, to the state government, or beyond are vulnerable to state interference. For the Taleans, the ability to manage the wider world depends on their ability to manage their internal world. The illusion of peace is crucial to the maintenance of autonomy, or the ability to decide one's own destiny.

The state of Oaxaca is divided into districts. Each district is divided into a number of *municipios* (townships), which vary in area and population size. These townships administer their own affairs through elected town members and are also responsible for smaller villages and dispersed settlements (*rancherías*) located nearby and referred to collectively as *agencias*. In a political sense, several agencies lie within each township, several townships lie within each district, and all districts combine to form the state of Oaxaca. Geographically, however, these subdivisions do not lie within one another because agencies and townships have their own territories with established boundaries, which in some cases date from before the Spanish conquest. In regard to the case at hand, Talea lies in the district of Villa Alta and has jurisdiction over three agencies. In over a decade of fieldwork reported on here (1957–68), these communities had a combined population of approximately 2,400 people. The municipal building in Talea is the largest in the Rincón. In this building are located the three village courts of Talea.

Taleans have been hearing their own cases in village courts at least since the founding of the village in the sixteenth century. The local court hears all cases—family, land, slander, debt, and so forth. With the exception of cases where blood has been drawn, the village has the right under state law to conclude the case if the litigants so wish. The court deals mainly with cases involving individuals, but it also handles disputes between both intra- and inter-village groups if brought before the court by the litigants. In these small courts traditional ideas are formulated and expressed, and legal ideas introduced by the state are applied or challenged. It is a place where conformity is taught and rewarded, where local values are expressed, where images of the external world are built, and where village autonomy is declared. Like endogamy and the prohibition of the sale of land to nonvillagers, dispute-handling processes contribute to village self-determination.

The Talean court is both administrative (it manages the physical plant of the town, deals with life-cycle events such as birth, marriage, sickness, and death, and manages relations with the outside—*relaciones exteriores*), and judicial (it hears and handles disputes). I studied the users of this court—the litigants and the court officials—who they are and what they expect from a hearing in court and the degree to which they reflect the dispersal of power in the village. But studying what people do to resolve conflicts and what officials do about them is only a small fraction of the study of disputing. The disputing process is neither merely a process of solving problems nor merely a study of the manner in which problems are addressed. It is a political process whereby divisions are created or overcome, whereby ideologies are formed (Nader and Todd 1978; Nader 1984b). A study of disputing asks why resolution of village conflicts has been left to the people born in these mountain villages and how it is that harmony styles are used as internal accommodations to superordinate powers, sometimes quite consciously.

In their presentation of self, Talean leaders are intent on believing and having outsiders believe that internal relations are harmonious and in equilibrium. Even when one becomes more of an insider and hears of many instances of discord and division from individual users of the court, Taleans still prefer to describe themselves as peaceful and harmonious. Harmony, they argue, is what differentiates them from others—the peoples of the Sierra, the Valley, or the Cajones—who are not peaceful. We are thus more in the domain of ideological thinking than in that of real-life circumstance. Taleans operate on the premise that if they were not living peaceful, harmonious lives, the state would interfere in their business. The image of harmony thus dominates their description of self to outsiders, or what they like to refer to as relaciones exteriores. It is their theory about how their society related first to the Crown and later to the Mexican state. As they note, "We are peaceful in this village, and by being peaceful and minding our own business we keep control of our village. We keep it in local hands, and by so doing we can maintain a relative autonomy." This attempt to present a united front in response to external contact is not an uncommon reaction to colonization and is part of what Eric Wolf (1959: 148) calls "the tug of war between conquerors and conquered."

The political effectiveness of the Talean court depends on local participation, whereby it disperses power and reinforces community solidarity. In the name of harmony, the court can hold private power accountable for the general good of the village. In the name of autonomy, the court encourages decision-making that is accountable to the townspeople. In the name of solidarity, it makes decisions reflecting concerns about long-term consequences in order to avoid factionalism. It is through its legal processes that the court expresses and ranks social values important to the village and to its relationship with the outside world. The village court can compete effectively with the district court, for villagers generally opt for local dispute-handling processes (Parnell 1989). The courts are the vehicle through which political interest is pursued, using legal procedures grounded in the concepts of harmony and balance that permit conflicting interests to be accommodated. In terms of actual case handling, the harmony model pays attention less to the facts of a specific case than to the language of disputing in the village court as opposed to the state courts. Villagers fend off the outside world by consciously differentiating their courts from those of the state.

The aesthetic and emotional value placed on balance and on equality, the particular social facts of this small society that urge cooperation, the requirements of a social organization that is directed toward village independence and autonomy and away from dependence on the state, the types of cases brought to the courts, whether they deal with human conduct or with the distribution of scarce resources—all these facets are aspects of the particular Talean situation that have resulted in a strong focus on harmony. If we look at harmony as a permeating component of a political ideology, housed in the mind, we come close to understanding the wider meaning of compromise for court users. Village court officials propagate harmony ideologies to validate village autonomy in the face of outsiders. For the officials harmony rhetoric acts as leverage; it also promotes their own legitimacy since it relates to the social good. Villagers cite disputes as validation for harmony ideology because from a court user's view harmony is reached by means of litigation.

In order to account for this particular ideology and social organization in a straightforward Simmelian fashion, one might argue that external threat brings internal order. But in the Sierra Juárez, and in the district of Villa Alta, not all villages respond to external threat as the Taleans do. The people of Yalalag, a large town also located within the jurisdiction of Villa Alta, are a divided, fragmented group, with a high incidence of violence (de la Fuente 1949). The village of Ixtepeji, located in the district of Ixtlán in the Sierra Juárez, is historically characterized neither by order or disorder, and its unification derived from belligerence and from raiding other communities (Kearney 1972). Resistance and collaboration are diverse and inconsistent in these mountains, but members of all these communities agree that danger comes from outside, and they all say they are united (*unidos*). Lack of an integrated policy has left people with open options for response, differently adopted over the years. The terms "closed" and "open" communities reflect two such responses (Wolf 1959); the terms "traditional" and "progressive" are sometimes synonymous with "closed" and "open." However, these four terms do not address the crucial issue of autonomy, which relates directly to harmony ideology.

It is generally accepted that a divided village is more susceptible to external domination, and thus villagers wishing to maintain some degree of autonomy develop avenues to internal cohesion. Taleans are explicit on this point. In divided villages, other values override the value of autonomy or, as happened in Talea in the 1980's, fighting is seen as a way to resolve division. Yet in communities like Talea, the usual strategy is twofold: managing the internal world of the village through systems of social and cultural control; and developing through the court and more broadly through town meetings ways to maintain village loyalty and instill a unifying ideology. Jane Collier (1973) vividly describes this strategy in Zinacanteco Chiapas, where villagers and the state struggle for control over domains of relative power. She concludes: "Zinacanteco law will survive as a system apart from Mexican law only so long as Indians continue to use native ideas of cosmic order to justify procedures and outcomes" (ibid.: 264). I would argue that Talean Zapotec law will survive as a system separate from Mexican law only as long as village law rather than Mexican law is perceived as meeting village needs *and* only as long as the Mexican state (like the Spanish Crown previously) continues to regard local rule as in its best interests. As long as the Mexican state can continue to regulate the economy (labor, resources, consumption) and as long as local disorder does not threaten the state, local village law will continue in its present manner, fluctuating around changing issues but ever mindful of the connection between harmony and autonomy.

Anthropologists, Their Informants, and Anthropological Theory

Although this book deals with the relationship of disputing processes, social organization, the political conduct of governments and religious institutions, and the people over whom they exercise power, it raises the more general questions of where anthropologists get their ideas and why anthropologists have sometimes insisted that disputing among non-Western peoples aims to restore harmony to social relations, that harmony is either functional in face-to-face societies or the product of their specific social organization.

One effect of anthropologists' deep involvement in empirical analyses is that they are heavily influenced by what their informants tell them. And in good empirical tradition, the telling that is part of their data becomes part of their analysis as well. In the case of Talea, harmony is a part of the people's ideology—their theory of how they can maintain some autonomy from the state. The ideology of harmony thus becomes transformed into the image of themselves that Taleans present to outsiders and may reflect to some extent what missionaries have preached to them for over 400 years—that harmony is the Christian way. This ideology and this image of Talean social life not only have been approved by outsiders, but also have helped maintain village solidarity.

Anthropological theory is shaped not only by the Western world and by such social philosophers as Emile Durkheim, but also by the ideologies presented by informants. That this ideology may have had Western origins makes even more interesting the attempt to trace the sources of anthropological ideas and to answer the question of why Taleans employ the principles of harmony and balance in dispute settlement and in dealings with outsiders. Although earlier (Nader 1969b) I focused on how the "natives" use harmony, this particular issue has now brought me closer to understanding how anthropologists use the natives' harmony model and how anthropological theory has been shaped by both colonial policies and Christianity as preached to indigenous peoples. In the history of anthropological theory, structural-functionalism becomes more understandable when we realize how colonial policies have been used by our informants and how these people and their ideologies have been reflected in our analyses. Ideology and anthropological theory thus become part of a common circle.

Part I ❧ Social Organization and Control

Chapter Two

The Experience of Place

Early reports by Spanish friars describe the southern part of Mexico that is now the state of Oaxaca as a land of many different tribes, languages, and cultures. Maps made by these friars plot the distribution of at least fifteen language groups. The largest of these groups in area and in sheer number of speakers is the Zapotec, a people often described as intelligent, industrious, acquisitive, and progressive (Nader 1969c).

Zapotec, which today numbers approximately 425,000 speakers, is listed in the 1980 census as a single language, although the Zapotec dialects are in fact languages as distinct from one another as the Romance languages (Swadesh 1949). Several language groups surround the Zapotec (Mixtec, Chatino, Chuchones, Chinanteco, Méxicano, and Popoluca), but right in the midst of the Zapotec area are Mixe-, Zoque-, Huave-, and Chontal-speaking groups. In addition, Spanish is to be found everywhere, often serving as a lingua franca—a tool especially useful in trade between Zapotec and Mixe, Zapotec and Mixtec, and Zapotec and Zapotec.

The Zapotec have lived for more than 2,000 years in what is now the state of Oaxaca. The legacy of ancient Zapotec civilization remains in the ruins of Mitla and Monte Albán; the legacy of conquest remains in the language, which today is being replaced by Spanish, and in the social and political organization of the Zapotec peoples. According to the 1980 census, 338,276 Zapotec speakers are bilingual.

Colonization brought dramatic changes: the reorganization of labor, the heavy use of taxation, the use of Indian slaves in the mines and fields, which changed the traditional division of labor between men and women, and the concentration of Indians in larger compact settlements. It was only much later when new crops were brought in from Europe (wheat, sugarcane, and fruits of various kinds) and new tools (such as the wooden plow and the horizontal loom) and arms (the steel machete, axes) that economic changes benefited the Indian and the developing mestizo and creole classes.*

The process of contact between Spaniard and Zapotec that began in the sixteenth century is still going on. The least acculturated Zapotec are still to be found in the southern and northern mountains of Oaxaca despite early entrance by the Spaniards into the latter area. In the north, the Zapotec contacted the Spaniards for aid in their war against the Mixe of Totontepec, and the Spaniards gladly exploited the opportunity to seize local riches. Since the sixteenth century, the valley and isthmus Zapotec have been the most intensively open to Spanish and later Mexican contact, and now foreign missionary contact.

The physical habitat of these Zapotec is as diverse as their linguistic environment—a series of mountain chains, isolated peaks, deep canyons, and a few valleys scattered throughout the area. Crude boundary lines may be drawn between mountain, valley, and isthmus peoples, but within these different terrains we find variety based on economic organization. Although the Zapotec are frequently referred to as commercially minded folk interested in trade, most of them farm for subsistence, sell excess produce themselves, supplement their agricultural base with small regional industries, and produce cash crops for national and international markets. Even in urban Zapotec areas, commerce and agriculture go hand in hand.

The Rincón Zapotec

The Zapotec people I write about in this book are mountain people, who until recently did not call themselves Zapotec. The area they live in, the Rincón (see Fig. 1), lies approximately 200 kilometers by road northeast of Oaxaca City. Rincón villages are sheltered in the folds of a grand mountain system that rises from the south around the district of Tlacolula. A series of mountain chains leads into the Rincón area from the highest mountain triangle in the northern Mixe area, known as Zempoatepetl (Veinte Picos), nourishing heavy-flowing rivers that move east toward the state of Veracruz, where they form part of the great Papaloapan drainage system. Both geographically and culturally, these waterways serve to link the Oaxaca mountains with the Veracruz plains, referred to as Los Bajos.

*The word *mestizo* is used here to refer to an individual who is no longer a monolingual Zapotec speaker. Often he or she is of mixed cultural and genetic heritage (European and Zapotec) as well.

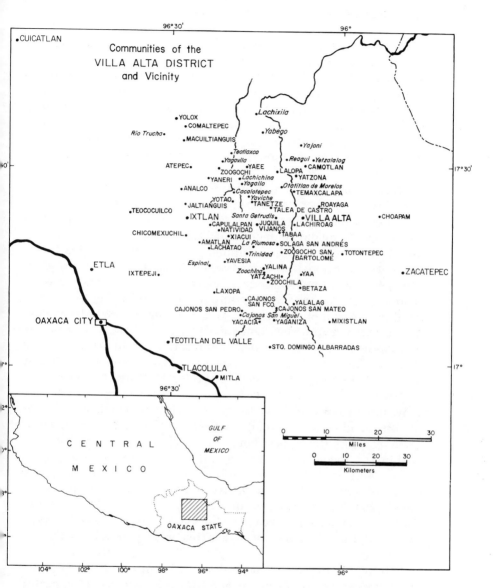

Fig. 1. Communities of the Villa Alta district and vicinity. The importance of a settlement as an administrative and commercial center is reflected in the type size. The least important settlements are identified by italic type. The size and style of type do not indicate population.

The Rincón (literally corner) is the home for these northern rivers and mountains, and as the name suggests, the people live between the peaks. The formidable Zempoatepetl, which stands over 10,000 feet high, the threatening, massive Maceta (la Montana de Siete Picachos), and El Machín all surround the pueblos of the Rincón. It is no wonder that the inhabitants refer to themselves as Rinconeros; they are virtually cornered by mountains on three sides. The one free opening bends with the rivers toward Los Bajos of Veracruz (see Fig. 2).

The climatic feature that distinguishes the region is excessive humidity. November, December, and January are the coldest months. Cold west winds during this season may cause the temperature to drop to 30° F (midday temperature). Usually, however, the temperature during these months is around 50° F, but the combination of humidity, occasional rains, and winds often serves to make even this temperature uncomfortably cold for the inhabitants. Between February and May, the temperature may rise to 110° F; this is also the driest season of the year. In May, the summer rains begin, and the natives refer to May, June, and July as the rainy season. The rains let up somewhat in August but return again in September and October. Sometimes the rains are torrential downpours that last for weeks, but usually they take the form of drizzles lasting for several days.

Within this seasonal variation, local climatic conditions are diversified, and so is the cropping. There is often a drop of 2,000 or 3,000 feet from the highest house in a pueblo to the lowest section. Within the towns these differing altitudes influence climate and affect conditions for land cultivation, resulting in a diversification of crops, some of which may be cultivated only in hot zones, some only in cold zones, and some best in the temperate zone. Those indigenous to the area readily recognize the various zones, the diversity of soils, and the crops usually associated with particular soils and temperatures (Fig. 3).

This mountain region is often described as one of the most fertile in the state. Trees are abundant, and although there is a recognizable amount of soil erosion due to slash-and-burn agriculture, charcoal burning, and seasonally heavy-flowing rivers, it is light in comparison with that of the lands to the south of Talea around Yalalag or with that of the very badly eroded lands of the neighboring Oaxacan Mixteca.

The traveler, walking along the mountain paths from one town to another, is always dimly aware of the settlements enfolded by the mountains. The villages seem to remain in the distance until one

Fig. 2. Topographical map of the Rincón area. The *zócalo* (plinth) of Talea sits at 1,580 meters above sea level.

suddenly arrives at the destination point, wandering down a well-worn path to the center of the town. In a moment there are houses everywhere—houses made of forest and of earth baked in the sun, terraced into the hills. There is a vivid green that contrasts with the brown houses, and the eye is immediately caught by orchids clambering down trees, coffee plants in bloom, and, some distance below, sugarcane ready for harvest.

The land provides a livelihood for the inhabitants in the form of

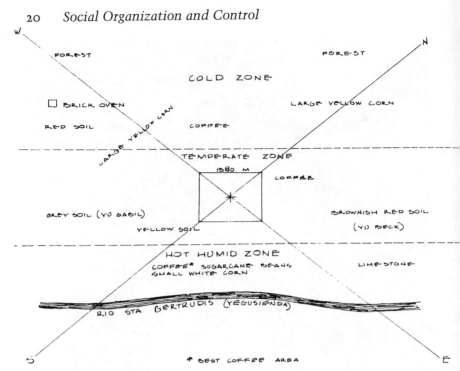

Fig. 3. Climatic zones, Talea de Castro

the staples—corn, beans, and sugarcane—and of the principal cash crop, coffee, a turn-of-the-century introduction. As a category, land and place in general are seen as animate. The yields of vegetables and fruits (squash, yucca, onion, prickly pear, pineapple, citrus fruits, mango, bananas, and others) are not animate. A wide variety of wild plants is gathered and used for food and decorative and medicinal purposes. Between December and February, the rivers are full of *bovos*, a fish special to the area, and trout. Sweetwater shrimp are best in June. Pueblos with good grazing specialize in cattle. The larvae of a wasp called *panal de tierra* (*villaj* in Zapotec) occasionally supplement a family's diet. Among the fauna are some hunted by the Rincón Zapotec: wild boar, armadillo, tapir, badger, rabbit, racoon, fox, and an occasional wild turkey. Deer, once hunted regularly, are now scarce.

Variety results in a lively trade within the area and between the Rincón and other areas (See Fig. 1). Talea, for historical and geographical reasons, is the main market center for the Rincón area, and there are minor markets in San Juan Yaee, Lalopa, and Villa Alta. Until October 1959 there was no vehicular road into the Rincón. Traders had to walk into the region from the Sierra Juárez by way of

Calpulalpan and Maravillas, and this path was often cut for weeks during the summer rainy season. The oldest route from the Rincón to Oaxaca runs south to Solaga, Tlacolula, and Mitla and then northwest to Oaxaca. Until October 1959 this was still the route by which coffee, loaded on donkeys, was shipped out of the region. Now, however, the impassable mountains that previously "cornered" the Rinconeros have been opened to connect the Rincón with the Valley of Oaxaca.

Most Rinconeros live in clustered mountain villages that are in many ways similar. They speak the same language, grow the same subsistence crops, and share a similar political and religious organization. They call themselves *buIni* (people) *rshidza'*. When, however, one studies the representatives of these pueblos, their similarities are less striking than their diversity. Differences are present as subtle variations in speech, in dress, in body language, and in social organization. Although the meaning of the variations was the central focus of my first monograph on the Zapotec (Nader 1964a), in this book the idea of variation is used to explain the contradictions resulting from harmony and disputing behavior within the village of Talea.

The Town of Talea de Castro

San Miguel Talea de Castro* was founded in 1525, when Fray Bartolomé de Olmedo and his party came from Mexico City to baptize and preach Christianity among the Zapotecs of the Rincón. It is said that in the previous year the respected elders (*ancianos*) from various pueblos of the Rincón (Calpulalpan, Tepanzacualco, Tanetze, Yaee, Yagallo, Juquila, Yatoni, Yoxobe, and the ancestors of the Taleans and Villa Altecanas) had gone to Mexico City to request that the new king, Cortes, send ambassadors of the new religion. When they came, they founded Talea. The population of Talea in the sixteenth century was probably smaller than that of the surrounding towns of Yatoni and Juquila, for the maps in the town archives show only a handful of houses for that period.

Since its founding, however, Talea has changed in size and composition more than any other Rincón pueblo. Older informants remember Talea at the turn of the twentieth century as a small, compact, largely agricultural community with a population of perhaps a thousand. It was important only because it was an incipient commercial center on the route to the Hacienda de Santa Gertrudis,

*In other writings I have used Ralu'a, the Zapotec name for Talea de Castro.

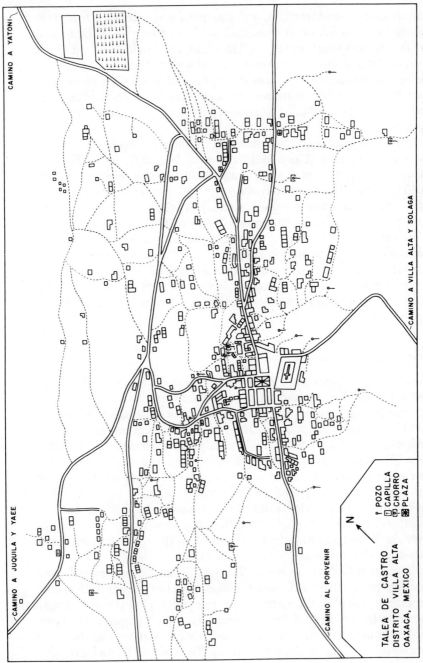

Fig. 4. Settlement map of Talea de Castro, showing roads and paths, ca. 1960. *Pozo* means "well"; *capilla,* "chapel"; and *chorro,* "waterspout, spring."

a mining settlement some 2,000 feet below Talea on the Rio de la Cantera. During the nineteenth and early twentieth centuries, Santa Gertrudis was the scene of an active gold and silver mine, which attracted nonagricultural workers from the surrounding pueblos and from the Sierra Juárez. At that time Talea had no market, and the largest market in the region was situated in Santa Gertrudis.

About 1905 the mines closed permanently. Many of the miners, originally from a number of pueblos, settled in Talea, where they began to farm for a living. Some were mestizos from outside the region and from the Sierra Juárez who spoke Spanish and Sierra Zapotec, some of them were monolingual Zapotec speakers from Rincón pueblos such as Reagui and Cacalotepec. The mine administrators spoke Spanish. Among the miners Rincón Zapotec predominated. Even the Sierra Juárez miners had to become conversant in it.

Following the miners' move to Talea, the market also gradually moved there. Because of the closing of the mines, Talea became the most important commercial center in the Rincón region and today boasts many well-stocked stores. It was probably no historical accident that Talea became a center of commerce, for the gradual accretion of lands from neighboring pueblos had not been rapid enough to provide all the newcomers with land. Many turned to commerce as an adjunct to farming; they began to buy and sell and to make products that people from other villages would purchase. Talea, however, remained a compact town; its citizens live in the town, and those who are farmers walk daily to their fields.

In the early 1900's coffee cultivation was introduced. Talea was the first Rincón town to grow the new crop, and in all probability its acceptance was related to the advantages that coffee production had for a town suffering from a land shortage. An acre of coffee land could provide enough cash (if the price of coffee was high enough) to buy several acres of corn harvest. Thus the cultivation of coffee relieved the land shortage for the time being.

Coffee provided Taleans with cash, which made it possible for them to buy land from other towns. It increased the commercial possibilities of the town because traders and coffee buyers came from Zapotec regions to the south around Solaga, Yalalag, and the Cajones. But more than this, coffee changed the relationship that Talea had with the surrounding pueblos. Apart from the prestige accruing from wealth in cash that coffee afforded, Talea became more dependent on the surrounding villages. The more time Taleans spent on coffee production and commerce, the less time they spent on cultivating corn and beans, the subsistence crops. Until contact with the Valley of Oaxaca was made easier in the late 1950's, the town of Juquila was the main supplier of corn and beans to Talea. In selling a surplus of corn and beans to Talea, Juquilans turned their subsistence crops into cash crops.

Another important factor in the evolution of the town occurred some forty years after the closing of the mines and the introduction of coffee. In 1946, approximately thirty Talean men left to work for one or two years in the United States as part of a migratory labor team imported from Mexico. The Taleans themselves state that before this time all men in the town wore the traditional dress of hand-woven shirts, white *calzones* (cotton trousers), and huaraches. Many changes came with the return of these workers, and many more workers followed their example and looked for work in the United States. These Taleans returned wearing shoes and colored trousers and shirts, and gradually, by conscious persuasion, they convinced other citizens of the town to change to this new dress. They encouraged women to abandon the traditional peasant blouse and skirt for the dress of the city and made an active effort to have people learn Spanish. When I arrived in 1957, the town could be described as being 80 to 90 percent bilingual Spanish-Zapotec.

When I began my work in 1957 among the Rinconeros, the villages of the area fell into three categories of population size. Talea was the largest, with a population of approximately 2,000, and Juquila Vijanos was second, with about 1,700. Tanetze, Yaee, and Lalopa each had about 1,000 inhabitants. The rest of the villages, Yobego, Lachichina, Yagallo, Yaviche, El Porvenir, Yatoni, and Otatitlan, had fewer than 500 people each. The population remained stable for about a decade after my 1957 fieldwork and then emigration accelerated. Some of the villagers moved to the largest town, Talea, but the greatest exodus was from Talea to Oaxaca and Mexico City. This book basically covers the time period 1957–68, unless specifically noted otherwise.

Unfortunately, information on the development of Talea from 1525 until the turn of the nineteenth century is scant, but every Indian village in Mexico has in one way or another been affected by the arrival of the Spaniards and the ensuing growth of Mexico as a country separate from Spain. Albeit sometimes heavily disguised, symbols of Old World culture are found in the most isolated regions of Oaxaca, and the Rincón is no exception. Spanish and Mexican influences are reflected in religious and political organization, in the use of Old World plants, and in all that results from modern communication. Change may have come swiftly and directly by choice or by cultural conquest as a result of contact, or it may have come slowly and gradually. In the more remote and inaccessible corners of this great territory of Oaxaca, contact for the most part was linked to economic exploitation. The Rincón was such a place.

The district of Villa Alta, which includes the Rincón, was linked to the outside despite its remote location. During the colonial period, the district of Villa Alta was famous for its riches, particularly its cotton production and its gold and silver mines. Spanish administrators vied to be sent there (Hamnett 1971: 16–17, 36). Political control of the area was a major result of Spanish colonial organization; each village was to be a self-contained autonomous unit (Gerhard 1972: 14). Mining and cotton production, which declined after independence from Spain, were revived in the middle of the nineteenth century when Don Miguel Castro, lawyer and politician, came to the vicinity of Talea to build up the mining industry again (Pérez-García 1956: 2.129). Talea flourished and became a town of importance in provisioning the miners. There was enough division of labor so that some 200 people could engage in nonagricultural jobs: miners, blacksmiths, carpenters, charcoal makers, brickmakers, butchers, bakers, candlemakers, weavers, tortilla producers.

When the mines closed at the turn of the century, people returned to subsistence agriculture, which strained the capacity of land that was already scarce. By the 1930's, most of the occupational diversity had disappeared, and the townsmen had turned increasingly to cash cropping. At this point, the Mexican government introduced the Papaloapan plan, fashioned after the U.S. Tennessee Valley Authority, to integrate the Sierra with the rest of Mexico. Again there was an economic boom, followed by a temporary setback because of the drop in coffee prices in the late 1950's and early 1960's and the completion of the road, which allowed imports to compete with regionally produced goods (Berg 1974: 109–10). Economic fluctuations have left their mark on the development of Talea.

As mentioned previously, Talea owes its existence to the Spanish friars who founded the village. As a new settlement that lacked the residential continuity of surrounding towns, Talea has, throughout the past 400 years, been considered by its neighbors as an intrusive element in the region (even though the ancestors of most Taleans were from the region). Being considered neither fish nor fowl, Talea, not surprisingly, has apparently always been hospitable toward strangers and even accepts people from neighboring villages as citizens.

Minority groups often use recruitment as an avenue to greater strength and power, and Talea is no exception. Talea became a place of refuge, a village that attracted Zapotecs who had left their own villages for various reasons, Mexican nationals escaping the series of revolutions that shook the country, or unemployed miners seeking a new means of subsistence. These same people probably would not have been accepted as residents in Juquila or any other Rincón village. In the continuum of change, these facts about Talean recruitment may be traced back to its founding by the Spanish and to the economic benefits derived from nonagricultural miners who came to the area, as well as to Talea's initial and continued partial rejection by other Rincón villagers. These elements are an integral part of the history of Talean contact with Spanish and Mexican cultures. Villagers relatively accustomed to dealing with strangers and incorporating them into their organization are also likely to venture beyond the Rincón. Since the 1940's, Taleans have left to work in Oaxaca, Mexico City, and the United States—a movement that encouraged others to follow.

Apart from such attitudes about the non-Zapotec world, the economic and ecological considerations I have mentioned figure in the kinds of outside contacts initiated by Taleans. I speculated earlier that their interest in coffee was probably related to the land shortage and the waning of occupational specialization. When Talea began to grow and depend on a cash crop such as coffee, it necessarily could not ignore the Mexican national scene because national and international fluctuations in coffee prices seriously affected the Talean economy. Furthermore, when Taleans began producing large quantities of a crop that had to be shipped to the Valley of Oaxaca to be sold and distributed, they committed themselves to improving transportation and lowering shipping costs. Hence, Taleans have been very active in promoting the various road projects sponsored by government agencies. Taleans desire modern facilities, whatever they may be, including modern Western medicine, and many Taleans value, per se, social intercourse with non-Rinconeros. Some Taleans may not be in sympathy with this trend, but for the most part they have not been politically powerful.

If we look at the story of contact with the outside, various themes prevail: religious, economic, and governmental. Shortly after the Conquest, the Spanish, motivated by religious as well as by colonial fervor, made contacts in the Rincón that were renewed at various intervals thereafter. For centuries, the local religious center of the Catholic church was located in the village of Tanetze, and it was not until 1958 that the central location of the Catholic church's organization in the Rincón officially moved to Talea. The success of Catholic activity in the area is reflected in the elegant church buildings found in Tanetze, Talea, and Yagallo. However, for the most part, the population has participated in Catholic ceremonies and other duties independently of any direction from the Mexican Catholic hierarchy and, indeed, at times has done so in opposition to it.

Mexican government contact with Talea has been sporadic. Taxes are collected with varying degrees of efficiency. The public schools are administered by the state through the district capital of Villa Alta. Traditionally, Taleans try to obtain all they can in the form of government aid and were particularly active during the 1950's, the peak years of the Papaloapan Commission. Under the auspices of the commission, road engineers, agronomists, medical specialists, and educators were sent to all the Rincón villages as part of an all-out integrated program to develop this Oaxacan zone.

It is difficult to evaluate the meaning of this program. In addition to material accomplishments, such as finally connecting the Rincón by road to the Valley of Oaxaca, initiating coffee nurseries, and improving and sanitizing the water supply, the commission was an important catalyst for Westernization, particularly in Talea, as we shall see. Besides the Papaloapan employees, medical students have, at one time or another, spent their six months of required social service in Talea, either because of personal contacts with Taleans or because of Talean requests to the authorities at the government health center in Oaxaca.

As a village, Talea has some choice features: land flat enough for buildings and free from *barrancas* (ravines), water (but not so much as to undermine the buildings), and good soil for agriculture close to the town center. Although compact, the town is not laid out in a grid, but follows the local topography. In keeping with the style of the Rincón, Talea is divided into a number of sections for census and taxation purposes. An individual may live in one of four sections: north, east, south, or west. The village boasts a large central space for its market, an impressive church, a large town hall, and several schools. The town paths are wide and well maintained, and the section *capillas* (chapels) are neat and well cared for. There are several stores and a number of bars and small restaurants catering to visitors and participants in the Monday markets. Even before the road came, Talea was well stocked with almost all the necessities and a good number of amenities.

The houses of any community, in their design and organization and use of space, are important for understanding social organization since a great deal of social life goes on in and around them. House size and design vary with wealth; a man who can afford to build a house with two or more rooms will do so, and most families have such houses. The house is the place where food is prepared and eaten and where shelter for sleep is provided. It is where the saints on the family altar watch over the family's welfare. It is where members of the family are born and die. It is where the harvest is stored and where social gatherings are held. It is the place where little children and their mothers spend most of their time, but it is not a site for discussion and gossip among friends or neighbors. The wells and mills, the cantinas and marketplace, all provide a better environment for this sort of activity.

The church in Talea took decades to complete. The organization that supports it reflects a church managed by its users rather than its priest, or at least this was so until the late 1970's. The president of the temple, as the church is known, is the key administrator. He is the communicating link between the priest and the town and sees to it that the secretary, treasurer, and the religious aides (*fiscales* and *sacristanes*) fulfill their duties. The building itself is always open, a place where Taleans and visitors to Talea may enter to worship, to meditate, or to rest. The houses, the church, and the town hall (which I will discuss later) are all organizational keys to understanding the operation of social control in Talea, as are the many groupings that may not be located in architectural spaces.

Talea as Part of the Nation

The Rincón Zapotec in no sense form a politically organized unit. Each village is primarily an endogamous organization that is largely self-sufficient economically. The people of each village own the land they cultivate. In this sense Zapotec villages are autonomous units, but since the political structure of these communities follows a pattern set by the nation and state, we must also look at each pueblo as part of the national political scene.

As I move the analysis into questions of law and social organization, it is useful to remember several facts about the place. The Talea area is rich in land, water, and minerals. The agricultural base of the area has at different times absorbed nonagricultural workers. The area has been linked to the outside by its products—cotton and minerals during the period of Spanish colonization, minerals during the post-independence period, coffee during the post-revolutionary period—and is now linked by those of its people who have moved into urban centers.

The municipio of Talea has jurisdiction over three agencias: Yatoni, Otatitlan, and the Hacienda of Santa Gertrudis (see Fig. 2). In 1964 these communities had a combined population of 2,400. The pattern of civil organization found in the municipio of Talea is a combination of aboriginal, colonial, and recent Mexican influences. Positions in the town government are referred to as *cargos*, which in Spanish means posts, duties, obligations, or burdens. All male citizens of a town are expected to serve in various municipal cargos in their lifetime. These positions in the town government are ranked in a hierarchy. As one works through this hierarchy to the top positions, one gains experience in government. Responsibility and respect accrue with experience. There are a fixed number of positions for each town, thus the number of times a citizen serves depends on town size and the candidate's characteristics—his financial position, the amount of schooling he has had, his general reputation in the town. Positions in the town government afford the most important kinds of both temporary and lasting prestige.

The municipal building in Talea is the largest structure of its kind in the Rincón area. It has two rooms used by the elected town officials and a jail to hold difficult defendants. The first is a large room, the *presidencia*, where four of the town officials—the *presidente*, the *sindico* (responsible for the police and investigations), the town *secretario*, and the *tesorero* (treasurer)—conduct their official business. The presidente has a large desk, as does the sindico; litigants sit facing these officials. The *regidores* (aldermen) sit in the presidencia or in the corridor outside. The police sit and sleep in the corridors of the building. In the second room, called the *juzgado*, the *alcalde* (town judge) and his secretary carry out their responsibilities. The building itself was built over many years by *tequio* (communal work) and by the labor of defendants in lawsuits who could not pay their fines in cash and were required to contribute work instead. The municipio is the place of law and government; it is where citizens learn by performing the various offices of government and where citizens come for redress.

The most influential leaders in Talea, referred to as *principales*, are the only officials without space in the municipal building. These men are considered, and consider themselves, best qualified to advise elected officials in the municipal government. In actuality the principales decide town policies and are often successful in carrying them out. When they overstep their role, defined by the town as merely advisory, they are open to public criticism.

The principales are said to be chosen by the presidente every year. In actual practice they are a self-perpetuating body of local power-holders. It is they who nominate the three candidates for the position of presidente, who upon election names these same principales as his advisors. During the period under study, there were 13 principales serving at any one time. These men were recognized for qualities deemed important in Talean leaders: formal education, financial success, wisdom based on traditional experience in the town, and knowledge based on experience outside the immediate cultural area.

Old age is not a necessary prerequisite for political leadership in Talea. In 1957 the principales ranged in age from 35 to 75. Nor is it necessary to have passed through the hierarchy in the civil organization, although more than half of the 13 principales had occupied all the cargos open to a Talean citizen. These men advise on administrative, legislative, and judicial matters whenever needed.

The municipal presidente (chosen from one of three candidates nominated by the principales) is elected at a town meeting. Only males can vote. Ideally, candidates for presidente are selected from town citizens known for their leadership abilities, for justness, and for the economic ability to serve without pay. Once elected, the presidente chooses the secretary and treasurer, who work in the same office with him. He has the authority and duty to call town meetings, to make town rulings, to resolve complaints and administer justice, to consider petitions, to perform marriages, and to take an active part in the nomination of other town government officials. The presidente is expected to represent his townsmen and to watch out for their welfare. A shirker may be reprimanded by the principales and by the citizens at the town meetings. Indirect control through public opinion is also powerful; only in rare cases may a presidente be asked to resign.

The sindico (also chosen from one of three candidates nominated by the principales) works in the presidente's office, and since much of the sindico's work involves close cooperation with the presidente, it is desirable that these two men be able to work as a team. The sindico manages the police force, investigates serious crimes, and administers the communal work program. He is the official legal representative of the village in its dealings with the state government. Both the sindico and the alcalde appeal cases to the *ministerio publico* (prosecutor) and the district judge in Villa Alta. Any case appealed beyond Villa Alta goes to the Tribunal Superior of Oaxaca.

Three regidores are nominated and elected directly at a town meeting; they serve full-time for a year. In the past, regidores were chosen as representatives of the three *barrios*, or nonlocalized cooperative groups in the town, but since the members of one of these barrios now constitute an overwhelming majority of the population, the idea of equal barrio representation in town government has been abandoned. Regidores are now elected from the town at large, with only slight consideration for barrio affiliation. These men alternate in helping the presidente by running errands, pouring *mezcal* at fiestas, and attending visiting government officials.

Each regidor has as his responsibility one of three domains: the town treasury, the municipal hygiene department, and the police department. In these departments they act more as observers of the presidente's and sindico's actions than anything else, and as subordinates they are often allowed to sit in on court cases and observe municipio business in order to learn the ways of government.

The alcalde's duties entail the adjudication of all cases not resolved in the office of the presidente or the sindico. The alcalde is a man who may have an interest in and knowledge of legal affairs, a man whose abilities to arbitrate and reconcile conflicting interests among his fellow townsmen have already gained him renown. He is elected not as an organizer of men or as an administrator. He is not a legislator of rules. With the help of his secretary and two court witnesses, he is prepared to exercise his talents as a small-town philosopher capable of "making the balance" between town inhabitants and between his office and the district court in Villa Alta.

The *policía* are recruited by the outgoing police force at the close of their year's service. These policía may be men who are regarded as lacking special qualities of leadership or intelligence, but they are usually literate. Most generally, they are the village's principal troublemakers of the previous year and are recruited by the outgoing policía as a form of punishment for having delighted in annoying them. There are 12 ordinary policía, two lieutenants, and one head of police. The roughest, toughest man is usually chosen as head. They all report to the sindico.

The duties of the policía vary. They have common duties—to police the village by a vigilant 24-hour watch in order to maintain peace, to bring disturbers of the peace to justice, and to interfere in and break up all fights and noisy public quarrels. They also provide the brawn for maintaining all public buildings and pathways. When male citizens are called out for communal labor projects, the policía help administer the work and take roll call. They work together and alternate in sleeping in the corridors of the municipio when serving on the night watch. As a group, the policía form a well-knit unit. They measure the success of their day by the number of citizens they haul into the courtroom.

The cargo organization has been changing from a more perfectly age-graded system, which was also more egalitarian (everybody had to start up the ladder as a policía), toward a more hierarchical system, which now has elements of class built into the selection procedures. To age and experience, we can now add schooling and the ability to serve without compensation. If an individual enters the cargo ladder as a policía, he may ascend to the positions of regidor, sindico, alcalde, or presidente. Educated men who enter the town service as secretaries never serve as policía or regidores, for these positions rank below that of secretario. As a group the policía express direct opposition and hostility toward those who did not work their way up from the office of policía.

What qualifies a person for leadership in one society may be grounds for rebellion and strife in another. In Talea, leadership may be gained by economic achievement as well as by appointment. If a man proves he can lead his fellow citizens—that is, if he can show that he has ability as well as the power and knowledge—it may be possible for him to do so. The principales in Talea are citizens who have consciously and fairly aggressively achieved their quite powerful social positions. Taleans are willing to delegate authority to such men to a much greater extent than are the citizens of surrounding towns. The Taleans consciously emphasize social ranking and special personality qualities when choosing members of the civil organization. Consequently, a greater proportion of men qualify for leadership positions in surrounding towns than in Talea, where social ranking is developed to a point that outsiders can predict who will become presidentes in coming years and who will never progress up the traditional ladder beyond service as policía or regidores.

Official actors may be functioning under various constraints when we see them participating in court cases. Expectations and responsibility are one kind of constraint; service without pay generates another; contact with the district court another. Beyond such constraints on the way the actors play their roles are structural considerations. A basically egalitarian hierarchical system is operating within a changing pattern of stratification and is becoming more hierarchical and semi-exclusionary. At times, this situation confuses people's expectations about the behavior of officials, and may even confuse the officials themselves. The overall organization of municipal government is set within the bounds of national law, but, as with the operation of courts, there is leeway to accommodate local variations. The integration between state and village is at this moment loosely structured.

Chapter Three

Order Through Social Organization:
Stratifying, Leveling, and Linking

Much of the research on conflict since the nineteenth century, especially since anthropologists began to do field research on the subject, has resulted in findings that challenged Western assumptions about law and order. For example, when anthropologists discovered that courts, police, and the like were not necessary for the presence of order in many societies, the question became how societies without centralized authority, without enforcement agents such as police, maintained order. We were forced to reevaluate our notions about order, what it is and how it is maintained, and we were forced to reevaluate the often weaker control of enforcement agencies even in state societies with courts.

Malinowski forced the crucial question when in 1926 he asked why people obey law, why there is any order in society:

The rules of law . . . are sanctioned not by a mere psychological motive, but by a definite social machinery of binding force, based, as we know, upon mutual dependence, and realized in the equivalent arrangement of reciprocal services, as well as in the combination of such claims into strands of multiple relationships. The ceremonial manner in which most transactions are carried out, which entails public control and criticism, adds still more to their binding force. [1926: 55]

Talean social organization works as control in many subtle ways. An understanding of the rules of social life is the first step to understanding order, but the real understanding of order comes with a recognition of how rules are contextualized in life transactions.

The idea that social and cultural organization is one and the same as social control organization is not a new one. Patterns of organization are primary elements in creating and maintaining order and control—or disorder and the absence of control, for that matter. When anthropologists describe social life as ordered by means of arrangements that coordinate social activities and organize social relations, disorder becomes a problem arising from the sabotage of the idea of community through factionalism or immigration. Today, it is also recognized that social systems are power systems that not only resolve but also exacerbate differences of social and individual interests, rights, and obligations as well as produce conflict.

In describing the controlling aspects of Talean social organization, I define social organization as the rules of the game and the playing of the game. Since adherence to rules varies from player to player, legal and other specialized control measures and institutions develop to handle disputes that may result from unusual plays—a recognition that direct social interaction between individuals may not be controlled by social systems. This chapter serves as an introduction to later chapters that deal with the organization of Talean law.

Hierarchy, Symmetry, and Linkage

In the social organization of Zapotec villages, many ties link citizens—ties of kinship, locale, common work interests, friendships, and shared obligations and values. Individuals and families maintain relations with other groups, possibly also containing family members. The intensity of interaction with those outside the family circle inevitably affects intra-family relations. Various economic, religious, civil, and recreational organizations also play important roles in integrating or voicing competing interests.

Three dimensions of Talean social organizations best demonstrate how principles of social control operate outside of the governmental framework. They are found embedded in Talean life but, as I noted earlier, are not coterminous with any one sphere of social activity. All three dimensions—hierarchy, symmetry, and cross-linkage—carry different weight and are found at all levels of social organization.

Talean kin, governmental, and religious groups are organized along hierarchical lines with rank based on sex, age, wealth, or experience. As we will see in the rules for the family, hierarchy is based mainly on sex, generation, and age. Wives are obedient to their husbands, or should be, unless they are wealthier than their husbands; sons and daughters are obedient to their parents, as are younger siblings to older siblings. In the male civil and religious organizations a ladder system prevails, as it usually does in indigenous Mesoamerican communities. As one moves up the ladder, one assumes a greater amount of responsibility and authority and achieves a greater amount of respect. How far a man climbs and the number of positions in which he serves before retirement vary with the size of the town and the qualifications of the candidate. In work relations, depending on the task at hand and the availability of land, one is either a boss or a worker, and again an individual's situation can vary through time with changing circumstances.

Because hierarchy refers to rank relationships where each role is defined as subordinate to the one above, the leveling dimension, the value placed on symmetry, may be seen as either contradictory or complementary. The concept of leveling, of balanced proportions, operates in many of the same contexts in which hierarchy is found, as well as in additional situations. Leveling mechanisms serve to mediate the harsher aspects of hierarchy, but at the same time they do not function to sabotage superordinate/subordinate relationships. In the family, although older brothers have authority over sisters, all children are supposed to inherit equally. In the celebration of fiestas, the task of providing food and drink is expected to be borne by those who can afford the financial burden—a leveling device. The highest officials in the town are chosen for similar reasons. Symmetry is also part of the aesthetic and harmonious sense of these mountain Zapotec. It is unappealing to be too rich or too poor, too fat or too skinny, too pretty or too ugly. Asymmetry is often the underlying cause of envy, witchcraft accusations, or disputes in courts.

The dimension of cross-linkage is found at the level of village organization and structure, unlike the dimensions of hierarchy and leveling, which permeate the daily round of activities. Cross-linkage brings a number of groups or individuals together, while dividing them by linking certain members with different groups. The degree to which inter-group relations cross-link affects the development of balanced oppositions or factions in the town. People who are members of the same barrio may not be members of the same musical organization. Neighbors may share barrio membership with people from other parts of town.

The manner in which authority, symmetry, and cross-linkage operate as ordering and controlling processes is affected by internal and external changes and also by individual relations. Stresses, strains, and fissures usually end up in court or in functionally equivalent settings, either because these controlling processes are not sufficient to channel behavior or because behavior slips between the fields where such processes operate or because standards are not homogeneous or universally shared. For the moment, however, let me turn to selected aspects of the social organization of the family, of work, and of a variety of other forms of relationships. In all these contexts, as in the legal context specifically, the dimensions of hierarchy and symmetry operate to buttress traditional or contemporary values (which may conflict). Cross-linkages ensure the presence of third parties for mediating disputes both inside and outside the courtroom, because without a social organization characterized by links and cross-links third-party mechanisms do not develop.

Kinship Relations and Inheritance

The Talean household is ideally a nuclear family, usually located at no great distance from other family members. At different stages in the life cycle, it houses family members other than mother, father, and children. At transition times, such as early in marriage or old age, children's marriage partners or parents may join a nuclear family. The ideal, however, is nuclear. Like any ideal, it is subject to change and contradiction. Between 1957 and 1967 matrilocal residence and mother-child households began to emerge—a phenomenon rarely found in any of the surrounding villages and associated with land scarcity in Talea.

The ideal or preferred residence pattern among the Rincón Zapotec is patrilocal or patrisponsored neolocal residence. That is, the father of a newly married son either makes arrangements for his son to continue living at the parental home with his new bride or provides the couple a separate house, usually next door to the parental home. Even though Taleans consider patrilocal (extended family) or patrisponsored (neolocal) residence as the cultural rule of residence, the actual patterns of residence are much more varied. A couple may start out living with the wife's parents because her parents are sick or old and in need of help. Later they may find it more convenient to live by themselves, and the wife's father may allot to his daughter and son-in-law a nearby plot of ground. The father of the husband may then offer to help build the house. Each set of parents should contribute equally. If the preferred patrilocal residence rule is followed, parents keep their sons but not their daughters close after marriage. However, predicting who gets to share the same neighborhood with related people is impossible without reference to the patterns of property transmission.

Inheritance is bilateral and lineal in Talea. Individuals rarely inherit lands from their siblings or their parents' siblings. Parents are supposed to divide their property equally among their children or their grandchildren, but in actuality daughters inherit from their mothers and sons from their fathers. Even this pattern varies considerably and often is closely related to the amount of wealth either parent has accumulated. In Talea, where land is scarce, parents might give their farmland to their son and their house to their daughter—an arrangement that has served to increase matrilocality in Talea. This is insurance in case the daughter's marriage does not work out, and indeed marriages here are brittle.

A child may be apportioned the greater part of inheritance at the time of marriage. What is left when all the children are married goes to the child or children who take care of the parents during sickness and old age. Usually, but not always, the youngest child remains to care for the parents. The division of property often incites arguments over the amount to which each child is entitled, but the right of children to inherit is not questioned.

When a childless man dies, are his wife's inheritance rights greater than those of his siblings? Does a stepchild have the right to inherit from a stepparent? Do children by a second marriage have equal rights to inherit with their older half-siblings? Can godchildren inherit from godparents? What rights do illegitimate children have? These and other issues are regularly contested in court.

There is one common theme in regard to property: property (houses and land) is individually owned. A piece of property may be inherited jointly by a pair of siblings, but this joint ownership is usually temporary. One sibling may buy out the other, or both may sell the property and divide the payment equally. This action is often taken to avoid conflict, for joint ownership of property foreshadows conflict.

The individual-ownership pattern, which is partly determined by inheritance rules, does not imply that the use of property is individual. On the contrary, individual ownership is accompanied by joint use of property with the nuclear family. Property and the disposition of money from the sale of it may be jointly controlled by a married couple, but in the last analysis, it is the individual owner of a property who decides to sell or lend it.

Consistent with ideals of patrilocality are ideals of patriarchal authority; generally the older males are considered by men and women to be the undisputed authority figures in the family. Which spouse actually exercises the greater amount of authority in the family may depend on such factors as residence location, personality, and relative wealth, as well as on whether the marriage was an arranged one.

If a man is sponsored in residence by his wife's parents and if his wife has more property than he, it may be difficult for the husband to exercise his authority, although Talean men like to think that they have ideal male-dominated households. If a woman agrees to an arranged marriage, then her parents, particularly her father, will take her side in marital conflicts. Husbands are supposed to decide whether their wives should make a pilgrimage; fathers are supposed to decide whether their sons should leave home to find work in the city; older siblings have a right to exercise authority over younger siblings. But actual decision-making is not so clear-cut as some informants would have us believe. What is clear is that the patriarchal ideal is not shared by wives, particularly wives who do not presume to describe themselves as members of the Talean elite, if I may use that term. Among families who engage primarily in subsistence farming, women expect husband-wife relations to be more egalitarian. .

Beyond the nuclear and extended family, unrelated families are able to connect by means of marriage and ritual kinship. Marriage creates kinship relations between a man and a woman and between their respective families. Since village endogamy is the rule among the peoples of the Rincón, marriage tends to cross-link those in the same village. Apart from the affinal relations necessarily created by marriage, the whole complex of marriage initiates a series of ritual kinship relations.

Throughout the region marriage is monogamous. Most marriages take place in a series of ceremonies conducted over a period of months. They begin with the first formal negotiations that the family of the boy initiates with the girl's family and ends with the groom's family presenting the brideprice (usually in turkeys) to the bride's family in the presence of kinsmen and friends. In return, the family of the girl gives the daughter in marriage. Marriage is for the most part considered legal without the performance of the civil and church ceremonies, although traditionally in Talea couples do not live together until the completion of an exchange ceremony between the families.

If a girl marries a man her parents have recommended and approved, obedience means future security for her. Taleans usually marry their daughters between the ages of 15 and 18 and their sons between the ages of 18 and 22. Individuals who marry outside the ideal age range are gossiped about. Girls who marry earlier are compared derogatorily with the girls of neighboring monolingual Zapotec villages, who may be married as early as age 9. In fact, only a few decades ago Taleans also married at an earlier age. Talean marriage

customs are undergoing changes that have increased tensions between husbands and wives and between affines as well. These transformations are related to a changing division of productive labor, a
changing distribution of authority, and the possibility of new life-
pattern choices such as migration.

In addition to consanguineal and affinal family relations, the
Taleans have ritual kinship—*compadrazgo*. Ritual kinship refers to
the relation established between godparent and godchild (*padrino-
ahijado*) and between godparents and the child's parents (*compadres*). These relations weave a network throughout the community
and well beyond it. When compadres are not related, and they usually are not, the compadrazgo works to extend solidarity and reciprocity beyond the lines of the immediate family and to integrate
society on horizontal (between same classes) and vertical (between
different classes) planes.

Among the Rincón Zapotec no one rule determines how godparents are chosen; prestige, sentiment, and expedience are all factors. To a degree, however, godparents are sought among those of superior social and economic status. Compadrazgo thus tends to be
asymmetrical; that is, it often occurs between people of unequal
power and wealth. Taleans have made elaborate use of compadrazgo,
and it has served them in a variety of ways: to supplement the de-
creasing economic self-sufficiency of nuclear families by operating
as a kind of social security; to strengthen family or intra-family relations, whatever the need may be; to increase the dependence of one
class of people on another (the have-nots on the haves, the monolingual Zapotecs on the bilingual); and to extend the influence of
Talea beyond the village into the region.

The Division of Labor

The division of labor in Talea is in many ways an extension of
family organization and the dimensions mentioned earlier: there are
vertical ties reflecting authority and hierarchy, and there are horizontal ties reflecting a concern with symmetry or egalitarian values.
The Rincón Zapotec nuclear family can perform all the labor necessary to maintain itself at a subsistence level. In general, men focus
on the preparation and cultivation of the land for agriculture, and
women on childcare, food preparation, and the care of clothing. All
kinds of work are equally valued. Both men and women take care of
animals, gather wood, harvest crops, and market any surplus they
may have. Some work is separate—women care for children and

they derive income from pigs, men from cattle. The work the nuclear family cannot do is performed by three other kinds of work groups: *gozona* (mutual aid), *compañía* (partnership), and *mozos* (hired labor). The growing importance of these work groups within the town accounts for increasing degrees of stratification.

Two tasks are of importance to all Talean families: the working of the land by the men for subsistence (preparing the soil, planting, weeding, and harvesting) and the making of tortillas by the women (grinding, shaping, and cooking the corn patties). In Talea two classes of male kinsmen work the land together: unmarried sons and their fathers. For married sons to work with their fathers is as rare as it would be for married brothers or uncles and nephews to do so. Once married, a Talean male, no matter what his residence situation, no longer works as part of his nuclear family of origin unless he is working with them in a compañía, gozona, or mozo relationship. A son usually receives his share of land legally at the time of marriage, and from that time on he is responsible for working his own land, apart from his father's household. If he does not inherit at marriage, he usually continues working with his father.

Whether a son receives his lands at marriage or at the death of his parents seems to have important implications for the division of labor within the nuclear family and for the continued integration of the family after its members begin to form their own families. In Talea, a father may shed all economic responsibility for a son after giving him his share of land at marriage. The son works this land alone or in compañía or gozona, or he manages by hiring a mozo aide or by being hired as a mozo. However he chooses to work, he seeks work aid predominantly from nonkin sources. Thus, at marriage, a Talean son ceases farming with his father and unmarried brothers and is forced to ally himself with other members of his town, on whom he now must depend for help to work his lands.

Women's work also requires cooperation between members of the family group. Only unmarried daughters are expected to help in preparing and cooking the tortillas or other family chores. A married daughter or a daughter-in-law who daily performs these tasks for the family is usually one who shares the same hearth and house with her mother or her mother-in-law. By 1960 many unmarried daughters with children continued to live in the parental household, and these daughters, of course, helped in the home. A new daughter-in-law may live for six to eight months with her mother-in-law and help her before she and her husband separate from the parental household. But often a couple spends only a few weeks with the husband's parents before they set up their own household. Thus, a Talean mother may lose a daughter when the daughter marries, and she does not gain a daughter-in-law to aid her in her household chores when her son marries. Similarly, when a son marries in Talea, his father loses him as a member of the family work group, and when a daughter marries, her father does not gain a son-in-law to replace the son.

The previous description is an abstract of observed regularities, something interpretivist anthropologists call a construction. It is such, but it is also part of the Zapotec presentation of self. Circumstances and individual preference, however, dictate modifications. Certainly, it is important that the Talean division of labor in the nuclear family has changed with changing economic circumstances and presently contrasts with that of surrounding villages. If in earlier years the family work group had included married children and their partners, then the partners' silent expectations might have caused problems between affines.

The first type of work group—gozona or *gozún* in Zapotec—is a form of mutual aid among kinfolk, friends, and neighbors. It is a presentation of services, of short duration, with implied reciprocity. The settings in which people exercise gozona are unique to each town, and each community is aware of the kinds of gozona that the next pueblo practices. An informant in neighboring Juquila described the situation in Talea by saying, "Allá en Talea todos hacen gozona para cualquier cosa, aquí no" (There in Talea everyone uses gozona for anything; here it is not so). And, indeed, the observation seems accurate. Taleans may call on kinsmen, friends, and neighbors to build or repair houses and to help in preparing land and in plowing, planting, and harvesting. Taleans volunteer gozona during weddings, funerals, and fiestas. They even carry on gozona between communities; for example, the band and orchestra from Talea have played in fiestas in Villa Alta, Yatzona, Solaga, Yalina, and Yaee, a service that is appreciated and for which the musicians are fed well. These communities reciprocate in kind.

The gozona in Talea often has work for its excuse, but it is much more than the most expedient way to handle tasks that cannot be handled by the nuclear family or individuals alone. Some Taleans have pointed out that the gozona is not the most efficient or economical way to build a house. They can vouch that it is more costly to run a gozona for housebuilding purposes, for example, than it would be to use hired labor. A man may invite some 15–25 men to participate in a gozona for two days of housebuilding. This means he must feed them and their wives, who come to help prepare the food, and also provide alcohol. Soon the gathering becomes a merry work party—the gozona becomes a festivity.

In Talea the gozona is primarily a neighborhood affair, but in some of the smaller Zapotec villages in the Rincón—Yobego, for example—the whole population of some 300 people would be invited to a gozona for housebuilding. In such a town there is much more festivity, drinking, eating, and cost than in Talea.

When gozona is used for agricultural chores, fewer people participate, but the same principles of organization apply. People are invited to help in the harvest. They are fed and given mezcal to drink. The following week these same people may ask their host of the past week to do gozona with them, and then they provide the food and drink. Elsewhere in the world with the coming of cash crops and wage work, reciprocal work parties have practically disappeared, but in the Rincón they are still used.

Mutual aid of this type is something more than economic cooperation: it is an expression of equality, of mutual respect and courtesy. Everyone who is invited to do gozona participates in the work. It is considered inappropriate to pay a man for gozona, for gozona is an expression of the social ties that bind men in an unwritten contract to aid one another, what in another setting Vélez-Ibañez (1983) called the bonds of trust.

The neighboring Juquilans also practice gozona, but principally in agricultural tasks such as slashing and burning, plowing, planting, and harvesting. They do not have gozona for funerals, weddings, fiestas, or housebuilding. They believe that the family should be responsible for weddings, housebuildings, and funerals. In Juquila, in contrast to Talea, extended families often operate as a work group.

At Talean funerals not only do friends, neighbors, and kinfolk lend a hand, but each person who attends also contributes a candle plus money, beans, corn, coffee, or cigarettes. In this fashion, the cost of the funeral is shared by the group rather than borne by the small nuclear family. And the Talean nuclear family reciprocates by returning this aid through participating in gozona for twenty or thirty years afterward.

The use of gozona works against the isolation that results from the division of labor and inheritance in the family. In Talea, because a man usually inherits his land at marriage, he cuts his lineal or vertical dependence and thus seeks aid when necessary among members of horizontal and nonkin groups. Here, where a smaller proportion of an individual's total interaction takes place within the extended family, we find extensive use of gozona.

An alternative possibility for mobilizing labor is referred to as work *en compañía*. When two people form a partnership, they are working en compañía. Two actual cases can serve as examples. A Talean widow who has good lands for sugarcane works en compañía with a man whose lands are inadequate for planting sugarcane: they have a verbal contract whereby she provides the land and the plants and he provides the labor. The produce is divided equally at the time of harvest. In the second case, an unmarried boy who supports his mother, a widow, works en compañía with his brother. Both contribute lands and seeds and labor, and the harvest is divided equally. Work en compañía lasts from the time the land is prepared for a crop until harvesttime. For sugarcane this would be two years, enough time for tensions to accumulate. En compañía is also used during harvest periods, particularly for coffee.

Finally, hired labor may be preferred to gozona and work en compañía. A *jefe* (boss) hires *mozos* (laborers) and pays them wages. The mozo-jefe work relationship is found throughout the Rincón, but there are differences in pattern and performance. In Talea and the neighboring town of Juquila, certain men are always jefes and never mozos, but the proportion of such men is greater in Talea than in Juquila, where most of the male population may be mozos one week and jefes the next week. In Juquila the mozo-jefe relationship is symmetrical. In Talea the relationship is increasingly asymmetrical, tending toward the formation of well-defined classes: those who hire laborers and those who work as laborers. Asymmetrical relations most often end up in court. This tendency toward class formation is fostered in Talea by the predominance of a cash crop, coffee. Cash enables an individual to hire and pay laborers, a situation similar to that occurring at the turn of the century when occupational diversity also encouraged craft workers to hire and pay laborers.

Tequio, communal work by all able-bodied men for the benefit of the community, exists throughout the region and is a work grouping (unlike the others) in which only men interact. When village officials in Talea call for a tequio, they usually recruit staggered groups of about ten men. Tequio is used to repair public buildings (the municipal buildings, the church, the school, and the priest's house), to reconstruct the public water supply and drainage system, and to keep the roads and pathways in good condition. The largest amount of tequio duty is carried out just after new municipal officers are installed in January.

Unlike the reciprocal labor groups and tequio, which are predominantly male, both men and women participate in informal interactions that result from daily activities: prayer, ceremonies, agricultural production, food preparation, commercial activity, and clothes washing. The daily round is particularly important in understanding patterns of female interaction, which are more varied than those of male interaction.

Perhaps the most important and most frequent social contacts of Talean women are the informal groupings resulting from the daily round. The women get up about 5:00 in the morning to take their corn to be ground at nearby mills. Since they usually have to wait their turn, this is a good time to visit with other women. They then return home to fix the family breakfast and to prepare lunch for their husband, who will work in fields that may be a one- or two-hour walk away.

During the day, the town is occupied largely by women, children, merchants, and old people who no longer work. When the older children go to school, a woman may put her little one on her back and go to church for an hour or two, usually with her mother or mother-in-law. Women carry out certain religious duties: daily prayer, decorating the church with flowers, and sponsoring shrines to particular saints or statues of various virgins. After church, still carrying her youngest child, she will usually gather up the family wash and leave for the well. There she is in physical and social contact with women of her general neighborhood. The visiting and gossiping makes this one of her most pleasant tasks. It is also a prime setting for disputes. In the afternoon, if her work at home is done, she may accompany a sister, a daughter, her mother, or in-laws to gather firewood. In the late afternoon, she returns home in time to go to the mill again and then prepares supper for her children and returning husband.

This description of how a woman may spend her days emphasizes the distinct spatial and contextual division between the usual activities of men and women. The daily round associates women with other women. Men must necessarily spend their days in the fields alone or sometimes in the company of other men. At night when the men come home from the fields, they may spend the evening in the cantinas or stores or just standing around the plaza talking in doorways. If they live far from the center of town, they chat with neighbors or retire soon after supper. Sunday and the market day on Monday break the solitude of work on the land. On these days, men spend time working around the house or go out drinking. Since these activities often set off quarrels between husband and wife, Monday is likely to be a busy day for the courts. The weekly round is also broken by the celebration of saint's days and other religious holidays, when men, women, and children gather for several days of celebration.

Other Associations Based on Common Needs and Shared Values

The economic necessities of religious celebrations are the basis for additional associations. In Talea there are three barrios: San Pedro, La Trinidad, and El Rosario. The barrio is a nonlocalized group that functions as a cooperative bank or savings-and-loan association. Little is known about the origin or historical development of the barrio system in the Rincón area, but there is some evidence that these groups evolved just before the turn of the century with the decline of the traditional *mayordomo* system, in which a few men took turns underwriting religious fiestas. The barrio system is one way in which the cost of a fiesta has been shifted from an individual to a group. What used to be primarily an individual venture is now a cooperative one. The traditional mayordomo system changed from a mechanism that distributed wealth to one that kept the poor man poor and made the rich man poorer. For years, the state government has disapproved of the mayordomo system. Barrios allow for the accumulation of funds through an organization that bears the burden of the costly fiestas. These are no longer, to any great degree, a prestige-gaining mechanism for the mayordomos, who are now simply those in charge of the saint's day celebration.

Most Taleans belong to one of the three barrios, whose declared functions are to lend money, to use the interest to conduct their respective saint's fiesta, and to pay their members' taxes to the town government. Until one barrio came to overwhelmingly outnumber the other two, each had supplied representatives to the town government. Since the groups are not localized, the membership is distributed all over town, linking people from various families, occupations, and sections. Talean adult males are free to join any barrio. They may change membership from one barrio to another or not join any at all, in which case they pay their taxes directly to the municipal treasury. Usually, however, a son joins the barrio of his father, and a wife belongs to the barrio of her husband.

Each barrio has a patron saint. On the day dedicated to this saint, the barrio collects taxes from all its members and the interest on loans made during the past year. The interest is used to celebrate the saint's fiesta and to pay taxes to the town government. Apart from collecting and lending money, the barrio is also a landowning unit, lending its land each year to the mayordomos, who plant corn and beans that are subsequently used for the fiesta.

Taleans are rather detached and perfunctory with regard to their barrio; their feelings about them are much the same as those of Americans about their bank. This attitude contrasts with that of the neighboring Juquilans, who feel strongly loyal to their barrio. Juquilans emphasize lineality in barrio recruitment (membership is prescribed by birth for a man and by marriage for a woman), and strong loyalties and attachments result. These associations may be significant, since the numbers of barrios found in each town may reflect alliances broader than the family.

Social linkages are not wrought solely on the basis of biological and economic interests in Talea or elsewhere in the Rincón. In addition to family organization, work groups, and barrio organizations, common values as well as the perceived village-wide need for government and church organization also cause grouping.

Music plays a special role in developing alliances. In most of the towns of this region, musicians are generally organized in groups referred to as bands (*bandas*). The number of bands, like the number of barrios, varies in each town; some towns of 300 people have two or three bands, whereas a town of 2,000 people may have only one. These organizations of musicians reflect more than an interest in music per se. The musicians usually represent opposing factions in the town.

Talea had only one band until about 1930. At that time, a native Talean priest, seeking to further "civilize" his hometown, organized a second group of musicians, which is referred to as "the orchestra." There are about thirty men in each organization. Membership reflects differences in occupation and values. Traditionally the band is made up of farmers of the "conservative" element in the town. The orchestra, on the other hand, is composed for the most part of "progressive" farmers, merchants, and coffee producers. Each organization has its own house in which the instruments are kept and where the men rehearse and enjoy each other's company. At times, the members use these buildings for sleeping. Musicians are expected to perform at religious celebrations, funerals, and weddings, and to entertain visiting government officials. These men are exempt from communal labor and also from municipal offices.

As stated earlier, musical organizations often represent the differing factions in the villages, in particular the enmity and struggle between progressives and conservatives, and between young and old. In 1957, for the first time since the formation of the orchestra, both musical organizations played together for an evening. During this period Taleans were nervous and feeling especially insecure about the expected arrival of the road and with it more frequent contact with the "outside" world. Harmony was a theme of every public discussion. And what better way to express harmonious relations than by consolidating the band and the orchestra? On the following day, however, when people were more sober, they no longer considered such a consolidation possible. The Taleans could not figure out how to combine the band and the orchestra and still maintain the now important uniqueness of the two types of musical expression. They could not resolve what to do with the two leaders, nor was the outside threat enough to overcome the very different attitudes of each group toward social change.

The Taleans, whose love for association and civil participation is exhibited in the ever-increasing committees, associations, and organizations dealing with neighborhood and village-wide issues, use associations mainly for specific tasks. For example, all the men whose wives wash at a particular well have an association whose purpose is to maintain that well and the water supply and to protect their rights should anyone cut off or threaten this supply. The leader, secretary-treasurer, and two aides are elected by the neighborhood group for one-year terms. Taleans also use associations to maintain the local chapels, but the chapel leaders, secretary-treasurers, and aides are appointed by the town hall (the municipio).

The church organization is more complex and in some ways parallels that of the town government, although its officials are named by the town government. The president, secretary, treasurer, fiscal, and sacristanes are all designated to run the church for the townspeople. There has never been a resident priest. The president of the church, usually an older man, is the administrator and sees to it that the secretary, treasurer, fiscal, and sacristanes fulfill their duties. The treasurer collects money for the church and is responsible for keeping the church's money box. The secretary records all financial statements. These two men are usually about 40 years old. The sacristanes open the church, clean it, and perform any tasks the priest may request. They also make and sell candles and submit a financial report of their sales to the treasurer. The two sacristanes, who may be either young or old, alternate their days of service. The fiscal rings in each day and helps organize town fiestas. He is an older man of about 45, who is about to retire from all obligations to serve the town. Like the barrio, various associations, and the town itself, the church owns property in the form of agricultural land and religious goods. The organization of church offices follows the pervasive ladder organization of cargo systems found in both civil and religious organizations throughout Mesoamerica.

The governmental structure and function of all Rincón communities follow a pattern set by the nation and the state and are part of the national Mexican political scene. (A discussion of governmental organizations will be interspersed in later chapters. Here the focus is aspects of social organization that relate to social control.) Every structure, by virtue of its intrinsic nature, prevents or causes dispute and conflict, and certain structures in the extrajudicial arena influence and, indeed, sometimes determine how people choose to manage dispute and conflict.

In thinking about the evolution of Talean social organization, one cannot deny that the changing economic and political history of this town determined the pluralistic origins of the villagers. Over time people came from outside the region and from other villages in the region to settle in Talea for a variety of motives. But whether their motives were generally economic, political, or personal, the people who came had a will to physically leave traditional situations. They probably moved as individuals, or at most in nuclear family groups, and this movement in turn probably encouraged the proliferation of secondary nonkin groups such as barrios, associations, and fraternal societies (*palomillas*) as backup support in the absence of extended families.

The secondary groups have been characterized by recruitment patterns that stimulate the development of personal networks. An individual may be related to some people through barrio membership, work settings, or required town obligations and to a very different range of people through fictive kin relations. When we consider groups in their entirety, their memberships crosscut, and the result is what Kroeber (1917: 86–87) in another context called a "marvelous complexity guaranteed to guard against segmentation, rift, or fission." Although this type of social integration has been observed in a number of settings, Kroeber's comments on the Zuni apply to Talea as well.

Four or five different planes of systemization cross cut each other and thus preserve for the whole society an integrity that would speedily be lost if the planes merged and thereby inclined to encourage segregation and fission. The clans, the fraternities, the priesthoods, the kivas, in a measure the gaming parties, are all dividing agencies. If they coincided, the rifts in the social structure would be deep; by countering each other they cause segmentations which produce an almost marvelous complexity, but can never break the national entity apart. [Ibid.: 86–87]

In Talea, the barrios, the musicians' groups, and the jefes would all be dividing agencies if they coincided. There are ties that link a number of men together in a group or as individuals, but other ties divide them by linking some of them with different groups. Thus the organized groups are penetrated by other relationships that cross-link their members. In Gluckman's (1959) use of the term, "linkage" should make for cohesion. This kind of crisscrossing would seem to have a harmonizing function in a town as densely populated as Talea, where varied residence patterns and greater density force people to live close to nonkin. Although cross-linkage may strengthen relations between social groups and thus produce harmony, this cohesive crisscrossing may result at the expense of other ties, such as those within the family. If this is true, one might expect to find a proportionately higher volume of court cases involving kin rather than nonkin. We might also expect to find that most disputes taken to court are between individuals rather than groups, or that disputes between groups are between ones like the musicians' organizations, or between members of different classes, such as jefes and mozos.

Earlier I noted that hierarchical and command model dimensions of the social organization function to stratify Talean society. Stratification has occurred in a variety of contexts. In the family, the increasing absence of egalitarian relations is most striking between husband and wife, a situation now generally accepted as a concomitant of Westernization. It is particularly noticeable in Talea, first because this change was initially found among those who had more contact with the external world and second because it strongly contrasts with the more equal sharing of authority between husbands and wives in neighboring villages such as Juquila.

In the context of town service, the pre-Hispanic pattern of stratification by age and experience has been modified to include other variables such as wealth and education. If a certain level of education guarantees that a man will not start his official duties as a police officer or, by contrast, that he will not make it all the way up the ladder, then we have the beginning of a class system. The process was not yet complete in Talea, but the lines were being drawn even in the 1950's. Again, the contrast with surrounding villages made a blurred picture look clearer.

Taleans are more willing than neighboring villagers to define clearly the rights and obligations of officials and are more willing to delegate authority. In the monolingual Zapotec towns, there is suspicion of delegated authority. But witchcraft is also practiced more regularly in such towns and acts as a deterrent to the delegation of power to town authorities and the acceptance of them.

The most profound changes in Talea have taken place in the economic arena. Traditional leveling devices, such as loading the heaviest religious cargos on the richest men, no longer exist. Instead, the economic burden has been shifted from wealthy individuals to the group by the creation of the savings-and-loan organizations known as barrios. In the domain of ritual kinship, the poorer people of the town depend increasingly on the rich to fulfill compadrazgo obligations to their children. As an institution, the compadrazgo has begun to decline in importance. If we look at the changing division of labor, we still find the equivalent exchanges such as those between mozo and jefe and between people working en companía, but the trend is toward fewer people hiring more people (Hirabayashi 1980).

As Talea has moved into the contemporary world, leveling devices have given way to stratifying devices. Social order has been maintained by ensuring that citizens are members of a variety of organizations and that they share the idea of *ciudadano*, or citizen participation in the functioning of the town, the idea of *rinconero*—a people psychologically isolated from the outside—and the idea of harmony as expressed in organizations that prevent escalation of disputes.

Chapter Four

Grievances and Remedy Agents: Comparisons in Social Organization

Implicit in the presentation of materials on the social organization of grievance settlement is a model that emanates from the concept of multiple systems. To put the idea simply, within a single society several legal systems may complement or conflict with each other, or one may dominate over the others. This concept has a long history in anthropology. Marcel Mauss and M. H. Beuchat (1906) described the presence of two legal systems among the Eskimos, which they used alternately during the summer and winter seasons, and Richardson found similar patterning among the Kiowa (1940). In 1926 Malinowski discussed a number of more or less independent systems in Trobriand Island law. Nadel in 1942 discussed the tripartite division of legal labor among the British colonial, the Moslem, and the customary law courts of the Nupe in Nigeria. Schneider (1957) similarly explored the different agencies of punishment on the Micronesian island of Yap. In his work on the Kapauku of New Guinea, Pospisil argued that "every functioning subgroup of the society has its own legal system which is necessarily different in some respects from those of other subgroups" (1958: 272). What is at issue in this ethnography is competition in the task of social regulation and cultural control, not pluralism per se.

The interaction of processes of social and cultural control, of which legal control is but one facet, is the relationship between what law professionals call law and other agencies that people see as functional equivalents of law. These equivalents are sometimes referred to as extrajudicial equivalents of law. Here I subsume them under the idea of remedy agents in order to shift the center of gravity from law to control. In addition to serving as forums in which grievances can be aired, remedy agents also act as controls or deterrents, and each agency is characterized by ideas or even ideology reflecting values such as social harmony or individual punishment.

The strength of the court, the family, and supernatural powers as controls on social behavior, either in resolving grievances or in preventing them, varies with the amount and expression of power by these systems and their situation in social structures. For example, as physical mobility increases, family authority decreases. As family authority decreases, court authority increases. The strength of these agents also varies with the initiative of remedy agents in molding patterns of use, as, for example, when courts or the police initiate cases (Nader 1966b; Black 1973).

Gathering Data on Remedy Agents

It has proved impossible to collect uniform data on the activities of remedy agents in the Rincón. That Taleans, contrary to evidence, deny that conflict or strife occurs in their town indicates an ideology of harmony. They hasten to assure the visitor that Talea compares favorably in this regard with surrounding towns (but as I was to discover, such assurances do not seem to interfere with the strategy of pursuing rather than avoiding a grievance). Certainly, some Rincón villages have a reputation for being especially discordant, and even in Talea civic-minded citizens cite individuals as exceptions to the Talean rule of peace and harmony. In retrospect, I find that my data were in part collected by chance encounters with disputes and greatly enhanced by access to court records.

The first court materials I obtained were gathered for me by a Talean citizen who wrote down a brief description of the cases that entered the presidente's office during one month's time. Later a secretario collected cases from the presidente's office that included verbatim records. This material was supplemented by case documents copied intermittently from the sindico's and the alcalde's offices between 1957 and 1965. Apart from this court material, I elicited further information on grievances from reports of situations resolved outside the court. The fullest accounts were those related while the heat and indignation of the case were still alive. Interviews of a more formal nature turned out to be less productive of disputing materials than informal daily conversations because formal interviews elicited talk of harmony ideals that were contradicted by everyday realities.

Disputes develop from a variety of events seen as personal affronts, including adultery, drunkenness, debts, the moving of bound-

TABLE I

"Trouble Spot" Settings for Disputes, by Sex and Marital Status

		Conflicting parties		
Setting	F vs. F	M vs. M	M(m) vs. F(um) F(m) vs. M(m)	M(um) vs. F(um) F(um) vs. M(um)
Well	X	0	0	0
Mill	X	0	0	0
Coffee harvest	X	0	0	0
Neighborhood	X	X	0	0
Market	X	X	0	X
Home	0	0	X	0
Cantina	0	X	0	0

NOTE: F = female; M = male; (m) = married; (um) = unmarried; X = present; 0 = absent.

ary markers, inheritance, gossip, and robbery. The settings in which such grievances reach a point where one or all parties seek a remedy in or out of court are to a great extent patterned and therefore predictable. In fact, informants often describe such settings as being "trouble spots." These trouble spots may be charted to show the sex and marital status of persons likely to collide in a particular setting (Table 1). A woman arguing with another woman over a debt is likely to do so at the well, in the market, on the street, outside the mill, or while working on the same lands during the coffee harvest. It is in the cantina or the marketplace that men with conflicting interests argue to a pitch that makes remedy-seeking imperative. Talean women, on the other hand, never fight in cantinas (they criticize their neighbors, the Juquilans, for doing so). Conflicting interests or strife between husband and wife usually develops in the home. This is to say that the Taleans hold strong ideas as to the suitability of particular social settings for conflict display and remedy seeking, although of course displays sometimes erupt between points.

Remedy Agents in Talea

Remedies in Talea include the supernatural, the family, and the court. They range from self-help to the court, from the family to the priest, from the saints to ritual kinsmen. The role of supernatural powers as remedy agents is ambiguous and multifaceted, in appeals not only to witches but also to the Catholic god and the saints. Besides being called on for redress, both God and the saints are asked to inflict harm. God and the saints, witches, *duendes* (little gremlin-like men), the Man of the Mountain (el Señor del Cerro), and "bad lands" (*terrenos malos*) are all endowed with supernatural powers that are called on to explain otherwise inexplicable actions and to punish what is considered improper behavior. For example, the Señor del Cerro is a supernatural one asks money and favors from, but the supplicant always has to promise something in return. Thus, when the first accident occurred on the new road, the Señor del Cerro was charged with having taken his first victim because certain town citizens had promised that if he allowed the road to come in, he could take a hundred lives. If someone falls on a piece of ground and suffers fright and soul loss, it is because the ground where he fell was terrenos malos. It is then necessary to "feed wealth" in the form of coffee beans, corn, or money in order to regain one's soul and become well. If a rich man suffers from a leg infection, it may be explained that someone is getting back at him through witchcraft. If a woman dies of cancer, it is because God was punishing her for depriving a step-relative of a rightful inheritance.

The data indicate that Taleans believe that supernatural powers may control as well as provide remedy. The stories that continually circulate make certain social norms explicit—that greed is bad, that land should be treated with special reverence, that riches are frowned on, that kin must be given their due—and all of them contain the reminder that various supernatural powers punish those who ignore these norms. Another strong and clear message is to have recourse to the supernatural in hopeless situations. For instance, a woman who was not able to collect a debt before her debtor died might go to church to *poner velas*, that is, to light candles and make a request for payment. Such an appeal to a supernatural is now a last resort. Regardless of sex or economic status, powerless Taleans still have access to the supernatural powers. Should even this appeal fail to bear fruit, the powerless console themselves with the knowledge that everything comes out even in the end—*todo se paga*. Symmetry is a consoling thought, and alternative remedy agents function as safety valves for hostilities.

Taleans have the notion that stewing about a wrong is bad for one's health. Generally they do not allow their grievances to go unremedied for long, although, at the time of this research, they could afford to wait for the right time since most people remained in the village throughout their lives.

Several informants stated that the attractiveness of using a witch (male or female) as a remedy agent lay in the fact that one could commit a retaliative, aggressive act without being punished or scorned for doing so. For example, if María is aware that Juana is stealing the love of her husband and María wishes to retaliate, she will probably choose to consign retribution to a witch because she will have little fear of being found out. Moreover, even if the witchcraft is discovered, there will be no proof, and without evidence she can hardly be punished. A bewitched individual may go to another witch to be cured. This other witch, of course, is able to find out who arranged for the witching, but she never tells her client "because this would cause the conflict to continue."

Witchcraft is used to counteract previous acts of witchcraft. Those who fall sick and believe they have been witched may go to a witch to retaliate by harming the other individual through counter-witchcraft. The plaintiff in these cases is initiating personal action against an unknown defendant in order to obtain a remedy for injury. The witch does not divulge who the responsible person is, but one may find out by other means. For example, if a third party finds out who is responsible some time after a plaintiff hires a witch, then the plaintiff's witch is deemed successful. If the defendant then dies, the witch is given credit. Witchcraft is in direct contrast to the Talean court style of using third-party intervention in "making the balance" or trying to minimize the sense of injustice; witchcraft is "getting even."

Taleans do not rely on witchcraft as a remedy as frequently as do other Rincón villagers. Talean witches do not boast about being witches (*oudzao* in Zapotec), as witches in other towns do; rather, they lead secluded lives in order to avoid public attention (Nader 1964a: 218–82). Taleans say that the only people who are susceptible to being witched are those who believe in witchcraft, or that the best witches are to be found in other towns. But they relate with relish how witches come to know and aid one another during night meetings at crossroads. Their attitude toward witches, then, is highly ambivalent. Witches are often hired by women involved in love intrigues or social asymmetries. Witches are not supposed to judge the case. The plaintiff has already decided on the guilt of the defendant and asks the witch to use his or her special supernatural powers to injure the defendant.

The Catholic god and saints are more visible than witchcraft in Talea as remedies. Talean women, especially, appeal to these supernatural beings by prayer and ask them to cure or to harm other people. The theme that runs through all such appeals to supernatural agents is that trouble is always caused by another human being. Consequently, by discovering who the offender is, some remedy can affect placation, retaliation, or adjustment.

The family plays a restricted role as a remedy agent. In the case of conflicts between two relatives, older family members often act as mediators, arbitrators, and adjudicators, depending on their relationship with those involved. The following case illustrates procedures used when the family is involved as a remedy agent.

Case 1. Pedro's son was married. Since the son's wife was an only child, the son went to live with her family. Very soon after the marriage, Pedro's daughter-in-law came to him with the complaint that her husband was always drunk, that he did not work, and that he did not treat her well. The father warned his son to behave better. Soon the daughter-in-law complained again. This time the father whipped his son, but all this was to no avail, so the *padrinos de pano* (godparents of the marriage) and later the town priest stepped in to try to remedy the now very serious situation. One night the son came home very drunk and beat his wife. The conflict gained momentum. The wife had tried various remedy agents with no success. What was left? She referred her case to the town court officials.

A woman usually seeks her father-in-law as a remedy agent if she does not live in a patrilocal or patrisponsored household, but she appeals to her own parents if she lives with her in-laws or in a house sponsored by them. Thus in conflicts between kinfolk there are various remedy agents: parents, parents-in-law, ritual kinsmen, the town priest, and the town court. We might expect, since there are a goodly number of possible alternative third parties for kin cases, that fewer kin cases would get to court. On the other hand, perhaps the penalties for disputes among kin are so great that the sheer availability of alternatives is not a good predictor of what kinds of cases predominate in court. The greater number of remedy agents might be matched by a greater amount of interaction in troubling areas. In Talea the usual causes of kin conflict have to do with living up to behavioral expectations in husband-wife or sibling roles, or in the fulfillment of adult child–parent obligations. Family cases revolve around marital conflict, frequently affected by the incidence and consequences of alcoholism, and the inequitable distribution of inherited property.

When a conflict occurs between nonkin, participants in the dispute may seek remedy through self-help or by appeal to the court. There are no formally designated persons outside the court to whom a person can go for arbitration or mediation, although a witch may be resorted to secretly and ritual kinsmen might give advice. In the case of kin there is also the village priest. For example, if two unrelated men begin to argue over the division of a harvest resulting from work en companía, they either resolve their conflict through direct negotiation, or if the conflict escalates, one or both takes the case to court. However, if the conflict is serious enough to threaten community welfare, a third party, usually a group, may step in and mediate the situation without being asked, as in the following case.

Case 2. One of the neighborhood wells in Talea is called Los Remedios. As is the custom, each woman in the neighborhood had her special slab of stone on which to wash her clothes. Sometimes when a woman arrived to use her stone, she would find it in use by another. If she asked the trespasser to move, the latter might insult her for her lack of generosity and then words might begin to fly. Or one woman might "accidentally" splash water on another woman's dress, and old grievances would be remembered and more fuel added to the fire. Sometimes these quarrels became serious conflicts and were referred by one of the parties to the municipio. Sometimes they would simply simmer down on the spot. One year it was noticed that the water had begun to dry up at Los Remedios. This misfortune was blamed on the great amount of bickering and fighting that had gone on at this well. The men's well association, whose duty it was to protect and maintain the well, had a meeting and decided to renovate the well. They removed all the washing slabs, previously considered private property and inheritable, and built two dozen cement tublike affairs for washing. It was then stated that no one could own or reserve a space for washing. The priest was asked to bless the new well, and from then on there was water.

Thus, apart from self-help in nonkin conflicts, remedy is brought about through third-party intervention either in or outside the town court.

As I stated in Chapter 2, the court is located in two separate rooms in the municipio of Talea, a building that citizens began to construct during the second decade of this century. It is situated to one side of the marketplace, among the multitude of houses crowded into the town center. The presidencia (which also houses the presidente and the sindico) is open from 8:00 A.M. until about 5:00 P.M. On market days, when there is an unusual amount of activity, the presidencia does not close until 8:00 P.M. The juzgado (alcalde's court) is open all day Monday and during the week whenever the alcalde is either hearing a case or awaiting a referral from the presidente's office. An outsider might describe these courts as examples of informality.

The dispute duties of the officials that constitute the town court of justice are commonly described as follows. The presidente, who is responsible to the town, deals with the lighter problems—disputes that may be resolved easily, such as conflicts between spouses, between creditor and debtor, and between drunken individuals. The presidente also handles cases of "rebellion in the ranks," that is, when individuals refuse to comply with their obligations as citizens. Cases of family conflict, debt, and assault and battery due to drunkenness that remain unresolved by the presidente are passed to the alcalde. Cases unresolved by the alcalde are, as I said earlier, passed on to the district court in Villa Alta.

The kinds of conflict treated by the presidente and the alcalde overlap. It is the seriousness of the conflict or the intransigence of the litigants rather than the class of grievance that determines whether a case is passed into the hands of the alcalde. The sindico, however, is responsible for processing a special class of problems, those classed as crimes (*delitos*). It is the duty of the sindico to investigate all crimes such as murder and theft. The sindico gives judgment in the settlement of property disputes as well. If he is unable to resolve property and theft disputes, he refers such cases to the alcalde. All murder cases are supposed to be referred directly to Villa Alta.

This division of labor is not strictly adhered to. A powerful or wise presidente may succeed in resolving many cases that an incompetent one would pass to the alcalde. However, the administrative or personal duties of a presidente may make it impossible for him to be present to deal with all cases as they arise. In such situations the sindico substitutes for him. Both presidente and alcalde are averse to making decisions for fear of retaliation and may pass a case back and forth until the parties either withdraw the case or seek aid outside the village court system. There are other situations that are ambiguous enough to warrant handling at an open town meeting, with discussion and decision by a vote of townsmen, a last-resort remedy I do not consider here.

The duty of town officials in handling cases is to *hacer el balance*, to make things balance out. The Spanish word *justicia* is most generally used when speaking Zapotec, but the concept of justice is expressed when a plaintiff tells a defendant, "Vamos a hacer el balance." The way the members of the court attempt to make the balance, the power they exert, and the kinds of action they take to affect this power are peculiar to each town in this area.

Three Comparisons

Anthropologists often find comparison useful to illuminate the particular properties of whatever it is they are looking at and to keep themselves uncomfortable about what might be taken for granted. For example, it may seem "natural" that (like people everywhere) the Taleans have developed third-party mediators or adjudicators, but from a cross-cultural perspective it is hardly natural at all. Some societies, such as the Jalé of New Guinea (Koch 1967), have never developed third-party intervenors, and many nations that do have them, such as the United States, prefer direct negotiation instead (Best and Andreason 1977). The conditions for the development and use of third-party arrangements, as we will see, are to be found in the type of social organization at hand or, as indicated later, in the prevalent belief system.

In 1961 I spent a summer studying dispute processes in the Shia Moslem village of Libaya in southern Lebanon (Nader 1965a, b). The towns of Talea and Libaya shared certain common features: both were rather isolated, mountain peasant villages, both had general village endogamy, both had cash cropping, both had populations of about the same size. However, the public mechanics of settling conflicts were entirely different. A comparison between the two organizations clarified for me the relation between social organization and the development of dispute mechanisms and suggested the necessary preconditions for the development of third-party handlers.

The village of Libaya was divided into two endogamous factions. Loyalties were unidirectional and directed to the half to which an individual belonged. Conflicts within a faction were generally resolved by go-betweens; conflicts between factions, or between a member of one faction and an outsider, were settled ultimately at appeals courts in larger towns by means of intermediaries who pleaded for the villagers before the judge. At the village level, conflict divided people by accentuating the hostility that members of each faction had toward those of the other faction. Division into two competing groups does not encourage the development of third-party handlers of disputes. In Talea, as we have noted, many groups cross-link town citizens, and a belief in harmony matches the social structures. Loyalties are multidirectional, with none being directly antithetical to the village as a whole. There is a proliferation of secondary groups not based on kinship. Conflicts between individuals and between groups are publicly solved by a court system that succeeds in putting a period on most cases without referring them to courts outside the village. In Libaya villagers are forced out of the village to make use of third-party dispute handlers in resolving disputes between factions, and the prevalent belief system is built on opposition.

The comparison suggests that villages divided into two groups are probably incompatible with village court or council systems of conflict resolution or with harmony ideologies. It also suggests the corollary that wherever village court systems do develop (in contrast to where they are imposed), secondary groupings that cross-link citizens can be found. If, as in Libaya, loyalties within the village are attached only to a large kin group or to the intermarrying half of the village, this loyalty competes with any system of adjudication that may pretend to be impartial. Villages that have a proliferation of secondary groupings cross-linking citizens, like Talea, provide a good setting for the *presence* of councils or courts of conciliation and adjudication.

One characteristic of the Talean dispute resolution system is the range of remedy agents to whom people can appeal for help. In my earlier description, I indicated that availability did not necessarily indicate *use pattern*. A second comparison, this time between Talea and a town in Chiapas, the state to the southeast of Oaxaca (Nader and Metzger 1963), refined our understanding of the use of available remedy agents. In both communities a range of remedy agents was present: family, supernatural powers, and community officials.

The use pattern of remedy agents in Talea can be correlated with several factors—the sex of the parties, their roles and ranks, the subgroups to which the plaintiff and defendant belong, and the class of conflict. Females usually take slander complaints to the community court, whereas male plaintiffs ordinarily take similar complaints to a local witch. Conflicts between nonkin can be settled only at the community level, but kin conflicts can be settled by several remedy agencies. High-ranking families usually settle their squabbles out of court; low-ranking families are more likely to utilize the town court. Husbands only reluctantly take a complaint against their spouse to the town court, whereas wives almost invariably do.

In the comparison with Chiapas, we explored the hunch that the distribution of power to settle conflicts is directly related to the distribution and specialization of authority in a society and that the different levels of legal control act on each other and are interdependent. In Donald Black's phrasing, "law varies inversely with other social control" (1976: 107). We focused on cases involving husbands and wives. Although both communities had inherited similar town courts from their Spanish and Indian pasts and although both communities provided alternative strategies to the court, the use pattern of the courts was in complementary distribution. Very few husband-wife conflict cases reached the Chiapas court in com-

TABLE 2

Settlement of Husband-Wife Conflicts in Two Mexican Communities

| | Conflict outcome | | | | | |
| | (1) Reconciled | | (2a) Severed | | (2b) Severed and penalized | |
Adjudication level	Oaxaca*	Chiapas	Oaxaca	Chiapas	Oaxaca	Chiapas
Family	X	X	—	X	—	—
Community court	X	—	X	—	—	X

*Talea

parison with the great many such cases in the Talean court. When we looked at why people went to court, it became clear that the Chiapanecans went to court to sever a relationship, to separate, whereas the Taleans went to court in hopes of reconciliation (Table 2). The extended family is a more significant group in Chiapas than in Talea as measured by its ability, in effect, to sever as well as reconcile marital relations. We have already seen how Talea was populated by immigrant wage-earning families, and their separation from their extended families encouraged the development of alternative support systems. In the Chiapas community the extended family is the only significant social group. In Talea, there are many important social groups beyond the family. Both demographic and historical factors are responsible for the distribution of authority in the towns.

Patterns of authority are central to an understanding of the distribution of conflict resolution. In both communities, husbands and wives in conflict recognize the authority of older family males as well as the authority of the community court. However, Metzger and I (1963) theorized that the authority of older family males is greater in the Chiapas town than in Talea, for the reasons developed below, and that this contrast is mirrored in the use spouses make of the courts in the two towns. The crucial fact is that in the Chiapas town the family heads assume exclusive rights to judge marital conflicts and their judgments may not be appealed, whereas in Talea spouses make further attempts to settle their conflict by appealing to the community court or even to the district court. One might argue that a father can maintain this kind of authority over his son only if the latter sees some payoffs as a result. Conversely, a father is interested in maintaining such strict authority only if he benefits in terms of economics, power, status, or personal satisfaction.

One indicator of the strength of paternal authority over sons is the existence of different modes of inheritance. In the Chiapas town, inheritance begins at marriage for both spouses and continues inter-mittently until the senior lineals die. The aim is to equalize the eco-nomic status of each child by adjusting his or her share of the inheri-tance and compensating those relatively less well off. In Talea, the custom of transferring the bulk of a child's inheritance at the time of marriage weakens a father's ability to command or influence a mar-ried son or daughter.

Residence is another variable that may be associated with the na-ture of parental authority. A father would seem to have greater con-trol over his married children when they live near him, especially if he provides the home. In Chiapas, most couples live near, if not within, the house of the husband's father. Within the household, the father controls all scarce goods and resources and exercises consider-able authority over his son's behavior, both private and public. When the son lives in a separate but nearby household, the father con-tinues to offer advice and impose sanctions, and he is regarded as the spokesman for the son in community decisions that involve heads of families. As I noted earlier, in Talea a shortage of land has led to the practice of parents dividing their land among their sons and leav-ing their house to their daughters. Hence only about a third of the married men of the community live with or near their father. If a son lives with the wife's family or separately, his father's influence is weakened by infrequency of interaction and the father's lack of con-trol over the son's economic activities.

Another factor in the different legal strategies of men and women in Talea is the growth of small restaurants. During a one-month pe-riod, 12 women brought charges against their husband to the town court officials; during the same month only one man brought charges against his wife. It is possible that women take marital con-flicts to the courts much more often than men do largely because they can find no other authority to which their husband is account-able. The husband is no longer responsible to his father and often lives far from him; the wife's father, even when coresident, has no claims on him. In contrast, a wife's behavior seems subject to sev-eral constraints. First, she is relatively more likely to submit to the authority of her husband and his family, for if he abandons her, it is easier for him to get along economically than for her. A man can now buy his meals in town—and thus subsist without a wife—but a woman finds it relatively difficult, although not impossible, to sup-port herself without a husband. In the Chiapas town, neither men nor women can conveniently live alone without spouses, nor can they in many of the towns neighboring Talea, where it is rare to find either a man or woman living alone.

Some families in Talea not only refuse shelter to their married children in case of a separation, but decline to use any influence at all toward resolving the conflict. As I noted earlier, this attitude frequently prevails when a couple has married without the consent or against the advice of the parents. Traditionally marriages were arranged between families, but independent choice of spouses is becoming more common as the age of marriage is now postponed to comply more with the limits set by Mexican law. In the Chiapas community, in contrast, families assume responsibility for marriages even though independent choice of spouses is the rule.

In Talea, then, the limited authority of senior family males is associated with early inheritance, separate residence, the availability of substitutes for both parents and spouses with respect to subsistence and sex, and the deliberate refusal of families to accept responsibility for marriages they have not arranged. The court, which has become increasingly powerful as Talea has developed as a commercial center, has gradually assumed the responsibility lost or abandoned by the family, and it exercises authority over marriage vested in it as a representative of the state. The term *el padre del pueblo*, which the villagers frequently use to describe the role of the presidente, symbolizes a continuation of tradition, an extension of the paterfamilias's role to the court official. In the Chiapas community, delayed inheritance, patrisponsored residence, and the absence of substitutes for parents or spouses tend to support the authority of senior male lineals in the resolution of conflict between spouses. The role of the court there is residual, particularly since institutionalized political organization in general is much less concerned with the legal aspects of marriage than is the Talean organization (Nader and Metzger 1963: 589).

Above, I have sought to explain the conditions necessary for the development *de novo* of third-party dispute resolution mechanisms such as courts and to understand why such an institution, once it is present, may be used or avoided. Below, in a third comparison, I attempt to describe the context in which institutionalized political organization concerns itself with increasingly broader aspects of social life. The three comparisons together support the evolution of law as governmental social control (Black 1976). In combination, they suggest a sequential relationship: first the development of public third-party mechanisms, then their increasing use by litigants and the abandonment of private mechanisms, and finally increasing initiative in dispute settlement by officials of the third-party mechanisms themselves.

The third comparison concentrates on two opposing principles that seem to operate in the courts of neighboring Talea and Juquila and that stem from patterns of law "mobilization" (Black 1973) and economic interests of the courts. The Talean court is characterized by initiative in dispute handling and by an entrepreneurial philosophy of doing business, particularly when dealing with outsiders on market days. The Juquilan court, by contrast, does not take the initiative in acting. By increasing mobilization patterns—by going after the defendant—the Talean court may be said to be biased against the defendant; by insisting on court costs in the form of "respect," the Juquilan court may be said to be biased against the plaintiff. Let me elaborate.

In Talea, the court is supposed to be conducted in a serious, well-ordered fashion, without alcohol, which is considered shameful in this setting. In 1957 the presidente of Talea was a happy-go-lucky man who enjoyed drinking. When there was nothing to do in the municipio, he would spend his time at a nearby cantina. People began complaining. The father of the presidente's secretary went to the presidente and threatened to withdraw his son from secretarial service, saying that he had not sent his son to serve the town from a cantina. The Talean court is supposed to be, and generally is, a place where citizens may present their grievances and expect the full and sober attention of the court.

In Juquila, the plaintiff enters the court with "respect" in the form of a bottle of mezcal. The drinking in the court contrasts strikingly with the formality of the Talean court. In Talea a successful litigant may buy a bottle of mezcal for the court, but it is never drunk during the trial. The fact that the Juquilan court allows court officials, plaintiff, and defendant to drink encourages the use of the courtroom as a place where an individual may not only voice grievances but also mellow the participants. The presidente of Juquila told me about a woman who accused her husband of having beaten her. The husband was brought to court, and as the discussion wore on and more mezcal was consumed, the plaintiff began to mellow. When the presidente announced his decision to fine the husband, she rose in his defense, saying that he was not really responsible because he'd been drunk when he struck her. Such a response would be unlikely in the sober setting of the Talean court, where, comparatively, the setting tends to strengthen the individual's belief that wrong has been done.

The citizen's view of the function of the courts may be summarized by quoting two statements. The first was made to me by a Talean woman, the second by a Juquilan woman. The Talean said, "It's shameful for the court officials to accept bribes, for aren't they the fathers of the townspeople? It is their duty to carry out justice as a father would do for his children." When I asked the Juquilan woman whether husbands and wives use the courts to settle marital difficulties, she exclaimed, "Why should I? Are they my parents that I should take my troubles to them?"

In comparison with Juquila, the Talean court may be described as particularly paternalistic. Its overt purpose is to keep control and harmony. The court may readily impose redress in a situation where no one has complained. Any drunken individual is likely to be picked up off the street, thrown into jail, and later fined. On market day, if the policía notice the least bit of argument and pushing, they, under orders from the presidente, jail the offenders. Neither party to an argument need register a complaint. Any man who, in intoxicated glory, gives forth with the famed Mexican *grito* (shout) is hauled into court in Talea and fined.

In addition to considerations of control and harmony, the Talean court has modeled this sort of initiative with practical purposes in mind. My field notes contain a blatant expression of this consideration: "Carlos's padrino told us with glee that when he was presidente in 1929, when the municipio was still being built, he would send a regidor out on Mondays with money especially destined to be used to get visiting Juquilans drunk. The court would jail them for drunkenness, and the following day would fine them a day's labor or two on the municipal buildings." In January 1960, when the treasury needed replenishing for the big fiesta of the year, the presidente ruled that any individual *echando un grito* (coming out with a loud cry) would be fined five pesos for each grito.

In Talea, laws governing personal behavior are unofficially being redefined. The effect of this redefinition is to bring money, from fines, into the town coffers. Talean citizens hesitate to admit that economic gain is a motive for reworking the laws, and court officials stalwartly insist that such laws are being created to impress citizens of neighboring towns as well as Taleans with the importance of peace and orderliness. Reform, then, is at least an ideal concern of the paternalistic Talean court.

In Juquila, most crimes and offenses become actionable only when there is a plaintiff. The rare cases of court interference in private quarrels in which no party has complained are those involving actions that occur in front of the municipal building. The Juquilan court does not bring a drunken man lying in the street into the courtroom and charge him with drunkenness; court officials do not interfere in quarrels between individuals until one party asks for help. Similarly, unless a wife complains that her husband is beating her, they let her resolve her own marital problems. Usually the court takes initiative only when protecting specific town interests, for example, when an individual refuses to pay town taxes or when a man does not appear for communal labor projects. The Juquilan court exists to protect the interests of the town and its citizens, but it takes neither the responsibility for reforming citizens nor the initiative in defining new laws for this or any other purpose.

The cost of obtaining justice in a Juquilan court is a common complaint, but for different reasons than in Talea. The "respect" that the Juquilan plaintiff must present to the court is often prohibitive. Ten pesos' worth of mezcal represents from two to three days' work, and as many citizens comment, it does not pay in most cases to take a grievance to court because they may lose more financially than they gain. (The cost of obtaining justice, it may be noted, is one of the oldest and most common grievances throughout the history of the English common law system.) Increasingly, Juquilans take advantage of market day in Talea to bring their disputes into the Talean court, where bringing the "respect" mezcal into the courtroom is not a custom.

Both techniques—court initiative and pretrial payments—are used to gain scarce resources. That law courts should be used for purposes other than maintenance of peace and order is not unique to the Zapotec. Throughout the development of the British common law, the king's court was well known for defining property laws with economic gain in mind. What is of special interest here is the particular bias that seems to result: to keep plaintiffs out of court or to bring defendants into court.

The idea of using the courts as a source of village income is ingenious. Talean citizens allow this because those who benefit are Taleans and those that suffer are either visitors to the Talean market or newcomers to Talea. Whether it does indeed encourage a bias against the defendant is discussed in Chapter 8. When court costs are high to begin with, as in Juquila, there is little doubt that the bias against the plaintiff lowers the court's work load. The fines that are accumulated in the Juquilan court are usually "burned" (drunk) on the spot as part of the court ritual in order to avoid suspicion of pocketing the money. The reins of government are still in the hands of the Juquilan town meeting, and should the court initiate changes in legal procedure at the expense of Juquilans, woe be to the innovator!

There is another contrast between the two towns. In Talea a case may be appealed to the alcalde's court before being appealed to the district court. In Juquila, no such town appeals court ever developed. A Juquilan plaintiff presents his or her case to any official who is there to listen. A case need not proceed in any particular order. It often simply passes from one official to another. The alcalde is not separated from the presidente for appeal purposes. A defendant who does not agree with a judgment of the town court may appeal to an external court—the district court in Villa Alta—and such appeals are frequent in Juquila, although the Villa Alta court often does not accept these appeals. Alternatively, a court official may himself appeal to the district court for advice and protection, especially if external factors such as witchcraft enter into the case. The only appeal the court can make within the town is to a town meeting.

The Taleans, by contrast, have developed an appeals court within the town: a case, if not settled, proceeds from the presidente to the sindico or the alcalde. The use of these internal appeals has increased Talean independence. Many more appeal cases go to Villa Alta from Juquila than from Talea. The Juquilans do not seem to mind, even though they are frequently turned back in Villa Alta. The Taleans, on the other hand, ask, "Why not settle the case here rather than give the money to Villa Alta?" Why, indeed, give money and importance to your competitors, especially when the alternative is greater village autonomy? For Talea village autonomy by means of increasingly self-reliant village courts has increased with the development of a heterogeneous and stratified town population and the general rise in social intercourse that accompanied market and commercial developments even before opening of the road. For Juquila belief in witchcraft weakened the possibilities for strong municipal control and for a division of labor in the local court. Nobody wished the total responsibility for fear of retaliation. As the Juquilans themselves say, "Para no cargar la viga lo pasa al sindico, o al presidente" (In order not to carry the responsibility, it is passed to the sindico or the presidente). A game of musical chairs encourages appeals to the outside.

One possible historical reconstruction of the sequence of changes is as follows. (1) Subsistence farming does not yield enough surplus to allow a farmer to make himself continuously available for daily municipal duty, and the judges in such a situation are substitutable. (2) The increase in surplus production with cash cropping and the ability to hire laborers to pick the harvest make it possible for court officials to present themselves at the municipio on a daily basis. (3) Community development projects initiated through political officials mean a reordering of the division of labor, and officials re-allocate the time spent on work projects and the time invested in dispute handling. As officials become more involved in town con-struction projects—schools, roads, airstrips, health clinics—they will be away from the hearing table with greater frequency, and once again cases are heard by whichever official is around rather than in sequential progression.

Decisions as to which judge hears a particular case also result from special circumstances, as we shall see. We can perceive the hearing as the result of dominant ideologies or as the sum of a series of choices made by all the participants—litigants as well as court officials. There are choices as to who should hear the case, choices concerning procedures to be followed by court personnel, and choices concerning strategies. The range of substitutability in the court-room represents the sum of choices made by the participants, and knowledge of the dominant patterns is central to understanding the different models of law and the process and direction inherent in such models (Nader 1966b, 1978; Black 1973). Donald Black (1973) differentiates between two models of legal intervention. In one, the state sets the legal process in motion, and this he refers to as the social welfare model of law in which legal ideology might well pre-dominate. In the second, the citizen sets the legal process in motion, in which case the model is entrepreneurial, more strategic than ideological. After initiation of the case, the hearing may be directed by the state or by the encounter between participants. In the first instance social harmony predominates; in the second, personal jus-tice. As we shall see in later chapters, the hearing in Talea has a situational structure, reflecting an interest in justice, control, and harmony, but first I present data about the actors as participants in a case.

Part II ✍ Court Users

Chapter Five

Setting the Law into Motion

Although anthropologists often concentrate on social organization, they cannot ignore individual actors, who initiate decisions that are both caused by and result in patterns of organization and belief systems. In describing the litigants and the court personnel in Talea, I am at pains to portray something about what motivates and constrains them as actors. The analysis moves away from social organization seen as interacting social roles and into the arena of the courts viewed as a locale for the competing values of participants. It is the participants who set the law into motion. It is the actors' sense of place in the organization that provides them with guidelines for making choices. As we shall see in this and in the next chapter, variations in roles are relevant to understanding the individual and social functions of this system of conflict management, which is intent on achieving harmony by designing *convenios* (agreements). In the previous chapter I related patterns of social control to aspects of social organization; in this chapter I stress how the performative aspects of order and harmony are related to the participants' definition of the situation and to the changing structural constraints on the judicial encounter.

Court Officials: Constraints on the Job

The life style of a Talean citizen changes drastically when he is asked to serve his pueblo in some political or administrative post. Perhaps all the difficulties inherent in the shifts in life style during the year of service are exaggerated in particular because the men who serve, without pay, sometimes suffer serious economic hardship. Most officials we interviewed long after they had given their year of service agreed that in addition to receiving no salary, they had had to greatly neglect their crops and other activities and often required more than a year to recoup their losses.

Talean men are agricultural workers, accustomed to long and hard hours in the field. Even those who are artisans or merchants lead physically active lives. When they find themselves in public service, one of the most difficult adjustments is to *estar sentado no más*—to just sit. Not all of them have to "just sit," however. The job of the presidente is considered to be principally administrative, and his functions are described in terms of public works (roads, schools, building an airport), as well as in terms of settling disputes. The rewards are greatest for accomplishments in public works and least for dispute settlements. This involvement in public works also allows these men to be active physically, and presidentes have turned more to public works in recent years, as more and more ambitious projects have become possible. More than one presidente interviewed answered the question "What did you like best in your job as presidente?" with something like "The school, the school. There stands my work." This concrete work also allows one to avoid the dilemmas of decision-making, as we shall see in the next section.

Most officials we spoke to mentioned asking for God's help before beginning their year of office. In particular they had one type of problem in mind. They asked for help from God in order that they might not be touched by *esa de mala*—a reference to killings—and that they might leave office as they entered it, with town governance intact. Serving one's town involves heavy responsibilities, a burden that may become oppressive and drive officials to drink. Killings are a threat because they always involve Talean officials with the state and the unpredictable behavior characteristic of dealings with the district court. State law provides a constraint on town authority, and there is strong motivation to settle cases within the town, within a framework of harmony. This means a high value on compromise solutions that satisfy both parties, as well as the officials, who do not then have to tangle with Villa Alta.

Involvement with other villages also precipitates involvement with the district court, and again the strategy is to settle such disputes in such a way that Talea is not entangled in state law procedures. Cases that involve other villages or villagers are often thought to be serious and delicate. In one incident where two Talean youngsters had stolen two goats from the town of Solaga, the sindico exclaimed, "Lo serio de estos es que estos niños están manchando el nombre de esta población" (The seriousness of this is that these boys are soiling the name of the community). For that reason decisions on such matters may be reached in town meetings. As we shall see, this fear of the results of outside contact is well grounded in experience. Summons from the district court are especially dreaded, because of the hardships of the trip to Villa Alta and of dealing with the Villaltecan authorities, who are regarded as abusive of their power and greedy in their fines.

Another burden of public office is criticism from dissatisfied citizens. All authorities are publicly accused by their fellow citizens: "Cualquier autoridad por más buena que sea, por más experto sea en diligencias, no dejan de ir a acusarlo en la cabecera o alguna cosa. Que por abrir un camino, o por falta de conocimiento" (Every government, no matter how good or how expert in deciding cases, is accused to the district court for some reason, whether because of opening a new road, or because of something they don't know). Such criticisms may lead to serious legal cases and jeopardize one's reputation. What bothered Talean officials most in another case that involved the stealing of goats was not so much that there was a robbery but that Taleans went to rob elsewhere. As one former presidente and sindico said, "They could have treated this case as a simple robbery, but what most bothered people was that a telegram was sent from Solaga saying that the thieves were Taleans. Why had they gone to give a bad name to Talea? This was given much attention, in order that the reputation of this pueblo not be harmed again."

Then, as we shall see repeatedly, there are other pressures—from the policía, the principales, the schoolteachers—and the fear of witchcraft. In the view of the sindico, who has to lead them, the police present a problem to the authorities. We interviewed one sindico who was extremely successful in his handling of the police. His plan was to ensure that the officials of his year were never drunk in public so that the police couldn't march them off to jail. His recipe: "they [the police] have to respect us from the first." Social distance was part of his strategy: not to join too much with the policía, not to go drinking with them, not to sit on the bench and visit with them, not to use them as "go-betweens with the women of the town," or put more positively:

Sometimes you have to invite them to take a drink of mezcal in order that they are happy, or invite them to smoke a cigarette. Sometimes you have to say to them, "Hijos de la . . . , van a trabajar, o a vienen?" [Sons of ——, get to work, or what are you here for?], or to call their attention—"There are only six more months, boys, then you can rest for six years." But I can't ask them to do something and myself sit on my behind. You have to be an example; otherwise they will say, "Why doesn't he work?" Not everybody knows how to handle the policía as well, and as a result others say, "With the policía there are always problems." They fight, they threaten to leave, that they are not going to give service, especially when they are drunk. And when they are sober, then they don't say anything—only that they were unaware of the disorder they had caused the night before. "We didn't know," they say. "Here we are now."

Managing the policía is one of the major problems of office for the presidente and the sindico. In addition, there is interference from those who feel they *know*—the schoolteachers. Schoolteachers are always there with their opinions based on their knowledge of the outside, and there is always the implicit threat, especially to the less sophisticated officials, that they should be listened to or else outside officials might hear about what is going on. In some respects the principales of the town also play this role, and indeed most of the long-term schoolteachers are principales.

The fear of witchcraft appears to be minimal in Talea. In the decade under study, no official would admit that he had done something because of fear of witchcraft, as officials of the surrounding villages might admit. But there is fear of envy—and anything that obviously differentiates one person from another in this town is liable to leave one open to envy. The fear of envy, however, decreases as the reference group widens from the town to include people in and well beyond the region to the state and national capitals.

In addition to the personal stresses mentioned above, officials often experience frustrations resulting from the contradictions inherent in having both administrative and judicial responsibilities. Contradictory messages stem from outside regulation and pressures from the state and from citizen discontent that may be voiced either through town meetings or gossip. Let me elaborate on the duties of the three officials. The presidente and the sindico have administrative as well as judicial duties; the alcalde has only judicial decision-making powers. The presidente represents the village to outsiders, including the federal government, calls town meetings, is responsible for village improvement projects, and issues municipal rulings. The sindico is the chief of police and notary for property deeds. The police watch over the town, and they are responsible for law and order when the officials are sleeping. The greatest contradictions arise where there is a multiplicity of duties, such as in the position of presidente.

The dual roles of judge and administrator affect the kinds of decisions the presidente can make. For example, it is the presidente's responsibility to see that the treasury has sufficient funds to cover the expenses of the municipio. These include office supplies, the upkeep of municipal offices, community building projects, and other costs incurred by the village. A major source of income for the municipio is the fines levied in court; presidentes have on occasion made administrative and judicial rulings for the primary purpose of exacting revenue.

Taleans have built and maintain schools, roads, paths, the main town buildings—the municipio, the church, and the market—and more recently an airstrip and a clinic. The labor for these stems from the communal work called *tequio*, or *cuota* (the traditional labor service donated by all adult males in lieu of individual town taxes) and from the efforts of the police. All these projects require materials, which have to be brought from Oaxaca City, and specialists, who also have to be imported and paid. The Mexican government has on occasion initiated projects for the region contingent upon contributions from each community. It is the presidente's duty to meet these financial obligations once the village has agreed to support the project. The amount of money spent on community building projects is considerable, and much (though not all) of it comes from fining violators of town law. The alcalde has none of these financial responsibilities, nor does the sindico.

In his capacity as judicial decision-maker, the presidente is subject to the least outside control among the three judges. If the contestants are dissatisfied with the presidente's solution to a conflict, they may appeal to the alcalde for a retrial at no inconvenience or expense. An appeal from the alcalde's office to the district court at Villa Alta, however, at times necessitates economic sacrifices much greater than the cost of appearing in a Talean court. The contestants have to pay lawyers to plead their cases, and, it is said, they may have to bribe the judge to assure a favorable decision. In addition, the parties must undertake the arduous and time-consuming trip to Villa Alta to present their grievances, and they must forfeit income on days they do not work. On the other hand, the alcalde is not under only community pressure to resolve cases satisfactorily; he is also motivated to protect himself because in dealings with the district, one false step on his part may mean fines or even a jail sentence for himself. He has to keep records of his cases, and his files may be perused by the state authorities. He may have to account for his decisions to the district court, and in fact alcaldes have on occasion been convicted for abuse of office by Villa Alta authorities. Accordingly, the alcalde is constrained in a way the presidente is not;

the district court has minimal direct control over the presidente as a dispute handler.

In addition to state-imposed safeguards or controls or constraints on the making of decisions, there are also safeguards that originate within Talea and ensure against judicial idiosyncrasy and keep decisions in line with precedent and the Talean sense of harmony and justice. One safeguard is embedded in the yearly rotation of village officials; the man serving as alcalde one year may well appear as a contestant in another year before a judge who was a litigant in his court. "Do unto others as you would have others do unto you" becomes an important guiding principle. Officials also monitor themselves on occasion; for example, if they are not fluent in Zapotec and the case requires fluency, they will pass it to another official who has the necessary fluency.

Another control originating within the village is community pressure exerted through gossip and boycott either of the courts or of a community project such as the building of a new clinic. In meetings of the elders and at town meetings, villagers, although they do not have the power to overrule judicial decisions in Talea, can and do voice their opinions, including dissent directed toward the municipal officers. The appellate system, which allows dissatisfied contestants to appeal to the alcalde and to the district court, also serves as a control over extravagant sanctions, in theory at least.

More directly, the people of Talea will not take their cases to an incompetent judge, and since, as we shall see, most cases originate with citizen complaints, the role of the active citizen is a crucial safeguard. In trying to understand the discrepancy in number of cases, by season and by year, I once asked why such and such a presidente had so few cases. The answer usually was that word gets around quickly as to whether the authorities "arreglan bien los casos, o no" (settle cases well, or not). Comments on one official ranged around observations that the presidente simply did not know how to do anything well, except to chase skirts and to boast. Another characteristic of officials that was disliked was a lack of independence. Some presidentes ask the advice of more "educated" people in town or those who act as if they know the law better than the authorities themselves. These are the presidentes "que se dejan ser apantallados"; that is, they allow people other than the authorities to wear the pants, the implication being that the people from whom they ask advice are motivated by self-interest or arrogance. Other observations were that the authorities were drunkards, that they ignored everything discussed in the court, that they did not have the intelligence necessary for the job. On the other hand, Taleans approved of a presidente who was well prepared, a nonalcoholic, not easily influenced or easily intimidated by *tinterillos* (lay lawyers). A presidente might also be praised because of his understanding of the litigant's particular situation. Only one presidente, however, has ever been elected to serve more than one term.

In general any complaint brought to the courts is usually heard. During the late 1960's, however, a group of entrepreneurial and commercially minded Talean citizens came into office. These men thought that the town should not waste its time on certain kinds of cases. They made it clear from the very beginning of their term that "no vamos a tratar as unitos que no tienen nada de importancia" (we are not going to handle small matters that are not important), "unimportant" cases such as chickens eating a neighbor's corn, or husbands complaining about their wife's cooking, or family cases in general. The tactic they used to discourage such cases was to levy higher fines. They were personally too busy and there were too many important projects, such as the work on electrification, for them to be spending time on chickens in the neighbors' gardens. And in spite of pressure from the district capital, they avoided forwarding cases. Their intention was to augment local judicial autonomy and to increase the powers of officials to decide what was important; their priorities were increasingly determined by values relating to economic development.

This administration was not interested in wasting time on problems that did not add money to the treasury. "In the past the authority has been so much more permissive, so that when people are brought in for walking around town drunk and for firing bullets, they take the arrest in a personal way, rather than as an act of responsible and impartial authority." One woman went to the municipio to complain that a stray dog had come into her home and eaten all her meat. Although she returned three times, the presidente refused to hear the case. For officials in the late 1960's, progress meant increasing the treasury so as to build bigger and better projects; it also meant that they were too busy to deal with problems like losing the week's meat due to a trespassing dog. Their perspective had no lasting impact.

The Litigants and Their Allies

Over the years and with only some success, I have discussed with several hundred Talean citizens the troubles that they or their neighbors have had and what they did about them. Like people elsewhere, Taleans talk best about troubles that they are in the midst of, or about somebody else's trouble. They rarely speak about philosophy. The recall problem is accentuated by the fact that Taleans do not like formal interviews and, in fact, think it rude to ask questions. I tried formal means and pushed informal questions only after they had known me and had come to accept the fact that American anthropologists were *preguntones*—big question askers. I supplemented talking and interviewing with observations and examined court records. Research assistants from Berkeley and Mexico followed up initial work with litigants (after the fact), and three town secretaries went beyond a legal-style reporting of cases and at my urging wrote down verbatim portions of cases. The stylistic variety of the cases I have chosen to publish reflects the manner in which they have been collected. From this, knowledge of the litigants' perspective, as well as their strategies, emerges.

Taleans in trouble follow whatever path seems likely to result in a desirable outcome. The choice of path depends on a host of variables, ranging from the personal morality of the aggrieved to the physical presence of the opponent. For example, a case involving a mother who was slandering her daughter was first heard by the sindico, then was referred to the brother of the slandered girl, and finally was heard by the town priest. Some people are patient and wait years to resolve a case; others wait for the right informal moment to discuss a problem with an official. The following are cases in point.

Case 3. I loaned ten pesos to a man from another pueblo. His name was Jaime. He had come to buy avocados. He said that he would come to buy again in eight days and that he would pay at this time. He never paid. That was four years ago. I didn't do anything about it because he never came back. I did go to talk to Tiburcio [a principal and his compadre] to seek advice. He asked me why I had loaned him money in the first place. . . .

Rarely are litigants interested in the social impact of their grievance, although caution about consequence to self is often implicit.

Case 4. Felipe Pascual started talking to a lot of people saying that Lorenzo had no reason to pay his civic dues. He wasn't a citizen of Talea. Lorenzo likes to live here. He wants to cooperate as a citizen. What Felipe said was an insult to him, for he is also a Mexican. I told the sindico. The sindico said he would take care of it, but Lorenzo doesn't know if he did. The sindico did talk with Felipe, but Felipe doesn't know if there was a fine. I talked to the sindico when we were both working on the road three years previous. . . .

Case 5. I loaned six cans of sand to a fellow. He went to sell it in the market to get money. He told me that he would pay me back in about eight days. After two years his wife paid me back. She gave me tortillas made of corn.

I had talked to his wife and told her that if she wanted to pay me back, little by little, in this fashion she could. . . .

Indications of social conscience are often present, as in the pre-ceeding and the following case.

Case 6. A man went to cut coffee in my field. A neighbor told us that he had been there at night to steal the coffee. I didn't want to file a complaint against them. They were poor. I pardoned them. I told Tomás [father-in-law] because he had given me this piece of land. He told us to pardon them for this time, but that if they did it another time to file a complaint with the authorities. He [the thief] knows I know, but we have never talked about it in order that as friends we should not have any misunderstandings among friends. . . .

People avoid escalation in order to protect friendships.

Case 7. Adelberto, a man known to be addicted to alcohol, went to steal six large tables from the house of Fidel Ricardo. He sold the tables to Atagracia Gómez to get money to buy mezcal. Fidel went to investigate when he found that his tables were missing. Another person, a witness, told Fidel that he had seen Adelberto take the tables to Atagracia's house. Fidel's wife went to see if the tables were theirs. The wife of Fidel and Atagracia solved this case between themselves because they were good friends. They didn't seek outside help.

People also avoid the courts when they know they don't have the proper witnesses.

Case 8. I fought with a woman over my children. The woman said that my two kids stole her loom. She said that it was my kids' fault. My nine-year-old daughter was involved. We are neighbors. I thought about going to com-plain at the municipio, but I decided that it was better not to. I didn't have any witnesses. The woman did say she went to place candles because God knows about this case. . . .

This same woman informant was apparently often involved in fights at the washing stones. She told of another instance.

Case 9. A woman hit the nine-year-old daughter of another. She went to ask why the woman did it, and the woman denied it. Another woman at the well told her that this woman really had hit her daughter. The mother went to see her and they fought in the road by her house. "I didn't make a com-plaint. It was Holy Thursday. We didn't go to the municipio. I told my hus-band and the women at the well. I said she was a terrible woman. . . ."

Some people simply settle a dispute on the spot. One man told about donkeys on their way to market eating the corn and sugarcane in his field. The owner of the animals, who was from Zoogocho, paid for the damages. "I went to tell him about what had happened. He told me, 'I'll pay you.' Then he paid me 40 pesos. The case was settled amicably."

Under certain conditions, even serious cases are solved outside of court; as we have seen, friendship or the absence of a strong case are factors. The seriousness of a case does not guarantee that it will be taken to court, but drunkenness may be a factor impelling people to outside settlement. A villager recounted:

Case 10. Three years ago one friend of mine fought with another friend. The one fellow told the other that he wanted some money which he had loaned him. The other was drinking and didn't have the money at the time. The fellow was disgusted. They began to fight. I broke it up to avoid difficulties because they were both friends of mine. I took the one who had picked the fight home. They settled the matter between themselves the next day.

People do not hesitate to bring a case against a court official. For example, in one case the sindico propositioned a citizen's wife; the husband, who told us about the case, filed a complaint with the presidente.

Case 11. The presidente talked to him [the sindico] and asked him if it was true. The man denied it. The presidente talked to him when they were both at the municipio. He asked him why he had committed this abuse. The sindico denied the charge. We had told the presidente all sorts of facts: time, date, place, what the woman was doing at the time, and so on. The presidente fined him 40 pesos. The sindico said that he would pay another day. The presidente told him that he had to pay within one-quarter of an hour. He said that he wanted to pay later in the day when he sold his corn. The presidente told him that if he didn't pay in fifteen minutes, the case would go to Villa Alta. The presidente also upped the fine to 50 pesos. He paid, and I wanted to see him pay. Since then there have been very bad relations between us. He hates me.

Sometimes litigants see court officials as biased.

Case 12. My father owned all the land in the field below this house. When he died, we were growing coffee there. He had told his sister that she could have one-third of the property to cut coffee or to get money for living expenses. At that time his sister was living here in this house with us. She lived here for three years. Then she went to live with her sister Paula. When my father died, there was a problem of inheritance because he had not written a will and he couldn't speak distinctly on his deathbed. Because of this

Paula went to the authorities to claim [for herself] the land which had been given to her sister. Paula didn't have the right, but she was good friends with the authorities and her sister was not, so she won the case. When the sister died, we brought the case up again. My mother talked to her [the deceased sister's] oldest son, and he went to the authorities with Paula. The case was first heard by the sindico and then by the alcalde. Paula won again. We signed the *acta*. We didn't seek any other help. We told the whole family about this.

Sometimes, as I have said, and for a variety of reasons officials refuse to take cases.

Case 13. This dispute was over the ownership of a little piece of *cafetal* [land planted with coffee], which is right below this house. Crisanta López came up while Lina was washing and started to insult her. Then she tried to fight with her. Afterward Crisanta told other people that Lina had started the fight with her. Crisanta said that Lina was a thief, that she had moved the boundary stones on the piece of land and thus had stolen some of her property. Lina's brother [Felipe] went to file a complaint against his sister. He went three or four times to the sindico Miguel Moreno, but Miguel said that he didn't have the authority to settle this. He said they should go to see the *juez* [judge] in Villa Alta. Felipe never went to Villa Alta. (Lina herself told us that they went to see the presidente after Crisanta assaulted her, but "nobody was in the office when Felipe arrived, so we dropped the matter.")

At times the presidente is lax about being in the office, and his absence is discouraging to people who may have walked from the far end of the village to see him. These people value their time and would rather not bother to press charges for lack of progress in a case.

Case 14. A fellow named Arastro Gómez came and said he wanted to sell us some plants. We gave him 90 pesos. He was supposed to bring the plants, but he never came with them and he didn't return the money. This was over six years ago. José went to the presidente several times, but Arastro never appeared. The presidente said that he would summon Arastro, but he never did. We never got the money or the boards. Arastro left to work in Yatoni three months ago. He usually lives right below our house here. José said he didn't want to bother pressing further because he didn't want to lose his time.

Self-help characterizes the Taleans, whether in the strict sense of helping themselves without resort to a third party or in the more specific sense of activating the third party, in court or elsewhere. The following is an example of more traditional self-help techniques that failed.

Case 15. When there weren't trucks, we used to send coffee out by donkey. At night in the mountains thieves came and stole my uncle's coffee. All of his relatives went to look for the robbers. We did not find them. I don't know who they might have been. Well, he just lost the coffee. The animals were not taken; just the coffee was stolen. They took it during the night while the teamsters slept.

Theft is one of the most serious crimes in this part of Mexico. One informant told of former ways of handling thieves in the nearby town of Ixtlán, when the local authorities were still willing to overtly violate state law.

Case 16. In my pueblo there was a band of robbers. The leader of the band was a man named Miguel Juárez. These men robbed everything. Especially they stole bulls, killed them, ate the meat, and sold the hides. One time they went to rob money from a church. The *presidente municipal* ordered Miguel put in jail. The pueblo wanted to kill him. The presidente told them they couldn't. The presidente went to the *jefe politico* (in those days we didn't have an *agente del ministerio publico*) of Ixtlán. The presidente told him the situation, and the jefe said that we didn't have the legal authority to kill a robber. The presidente came back and told the pueblo this.

The jefe said he would come to the pueblo the next day to resolve the affair. He came with five soldiers. The jefe explained that you can't kill a robber. The people answered him that you can't kill a thief with your laws, but we can kill him. The bandit chief was in jail, and the people killed him with rocks, poles, knives, and so on. They killed him in the presence of the jefe. The jefe didn't do anything because the pueblo was a large one and there were a lot of people present.

Fifteen days later an order from the governor came. It said, "The jefe tells me that you have violated the law and killed a robber chief. Here are two sentences for your presidente. You can take your choice: two years in jail or 500 pesos fine." That was a lot of money in 1912. The presidente asked the people what to do. They laughed and told him to accept the 500-peso fine. They said they could all chip in 25 centavos to raise the money, and it wouldn't put anyone out much. "We are the guilty ones, not you."

When the thief is from out of town, sometimes not much can be done, but other times the situation calls for an open town meeting. Cases such as the following are hopeless unless the victimizer appears again.

Case 17. Sometime ago we bought corn. We had coffee to sell, and a merchant from Solaga came, selling corn. He told us that he had all kinds. We told him to bring us 600 pesos worth. After fifteen days he brought 200 pesos worth. We traded corn for coffee. Then he told us to give him 240 pesos worth of coffee, and he would bring more corn. Then he went, and he hasn't come with the corn. We don't even know if he is still alive. We just waited for him to arrive and he never did. We told friends and relatives of this, but not the authorities.

Both stealing and borrowing cause mobility, and sometimes the mobility is forced. The following cases illustrate how decisions about thieves are made in open town meeting sessions. In these situations all the townsmen take a part in judging.

Case 18. The priest had a servant. He said that the servant was his brother. Another man was presidente in the *templo*. He [the servant] robbed money from the church. He is still living. The *presidente vecinal* [church president] went to see the presidente municipal. He told him that the man had stolen some money. The presidente told him to file a complaint if he robbed another time. This occurred in an open *junta* [town meeting].

Case 19. A man went to steal coffee. The thief's name was Tereso. He came from Lalopa. He went to Teo's coffee field and stole some coffee plants. Teo filed a complaint with the presidente. The man admitted his fault. He said that he had gone to sell the coffee plants in Solaga.

We had a junta. The presidente asked the pueblo what punishment they should give the culprit. The pueblo said that it was best not to send the case to Villa Alta. We sent the man home. The policía from Talea took him to Yatoni. The policía from Yatoni took him to Otatitlan, and from there to Lalopa. He never came back here. What was the punishment? Nothing, we just kicked him out of the pueblo. We didn't want him here. . . .

Case 20. There were two women from Tabaa. They [the people of Talea] put a sign on them which read: "We robbed coffee from Mr. X's house." They walked around the streets for half a day wearing the sign. This is the only time they have made women wear such a sign. The owner of the coffee went to file a complaint with the presidente and took them to the sindico. (In answer to the question whether the women could come back to Talea if they wanted to, the informants said, yes, but they would be ashamed.) . . .

The whole village may become involved in decision-making in certain types of cases other than theft.

Case 21. A man came from Betaza. He owned a store in Talea. At first when he came, he grew coffee. Later he opened a store for clothes. He had married a girl from here. We kicked him out because he fought with people here a lot. . . .

Outsiders are fair game. The most successful and generous entrepreneur who ever came to Talea was poisoned, and the reasons given all related to envy. The following is another case of murder because of envy.

Case 22. A girl from Santa Gertrudis went to Mexico City to work. She lived with a man there. Then she returned here with her fellow. He went to work on the church; he was a builder and was employed to repair the church in Talea. At night he always went to Santa Gertrudis. He was used to getting drunk on Mondays. He met some other fellows from Santa Gertrudis in a bar, and they fought. Later these fellows waited for him in the road outside of town. They killed him with a machete; they cut off his head. They threw away the machete and ran off. He was found in the morning, and people went to advise the authorities. The authorities found the culprits, and they were sent for trial in Villa Alta.

Serious disagreements or fights often die, but arguments over debts can go on for at least two generations.

Case 23. We loaned some money to a man who is now dead. This happened four to five years ago. He said that he would pay us with coffee, but he never paid. The debt was 50 pesos; my sister loaned him 50 pesos also. We didn't file a complaint with the authorities; we thought that his son would pay us, but he died too. The man's wife also died. (Throughout the story the informants kept saying that they expected God to take charge of the affair, and they expected to be paid in some form. They felt as if they had been cheated and that God had to arrange things.)

Dividing up the harvest is sometimes a cause for grievance.

Case 24. I was partners with a woman in growing milpa [corn]. She went to harvest some of the new corn. I was sick, but I sent my sister to see what she was doing. The woman harvested the corn and sold it without giving me my share. There were about two *almudes* of corn [an almud is equivalent to a sixth of a *robo*, which is 1.76 liters]. My sister said that we should go to get my share from the field without telling her. She went and got it for me. And there the matter ended. This happened two years ago.

Debts are often related to mobility much as drunkenness is elsewhere (Spradley 1970): each causes and is caused by mobility patterns.

Case 25. I loaned 100 pesos to a man. He went to Natividad. His wife had died in Natividad one year before, and he was living there then. He again lives there. But he originally came from Talea. This loan happened one year ago. I just wait now. I am not sure if he will come or not. I sent him two letters, and he didn't respond. I only told my relatives about this. When he comes back here again, I will place a complaint.

Sometimes there are mitigating circumstances.

Case 26. We loaned beans and corn—1.5 almudes of beans and 2 almudes of corn. The woman we loaned it to died two years ago [eight years after the loans]. We had been to talk to her about it. She said that she would give it back but at the present she didn't have it to give. I asked God to pardon the woman because she was poor and couldn't have paid us back. I went to do this when she died.

Such a case also indicates the power that people think they have of reducing the sentences of opponents after death if they are poor.

There is also a value placed on "not hurting other people."

Case 27. There was a fellow from here who stole a married woman and took her to Loma Bonita. Later they returned to live here. What did the husband do? Nothing. He didn't do anything because he was a good person [*buena gente*] and didn't want to hurt other people. . . .

Other cases of wife stealing do not end this way.

Case 28. First the woman went to live with another man. Then her husband went to the authorities to file a complaint. He wanted to be repaid for the expenses he had incurred in marrying the girl. The other man paid so that he could live with the woman. . . .

The variability of factors that might explain why a person actively seeks to do something about an unjust situation is great: personality, the type of case, the state of the opponent (his wealth, shared membership in a village, envy, recurrence of action, intention), the complainant's own state of wealth and his relationship with possible third parties, or a great desire for justice. However, a few basic guidelines determine if citizens decide to mobilize to do something or to leave well enough alone. First, citizens see themselves as empowered, active agents of law. They can take steps to right a wrong, or they can take steps to give clemency should the situation warrant. They not only are able to activate remedies for their own cases but are used as consultants by town officials for cases dealing with sensitive matters, such as contact with other villages, that have the potential to involve the district court. Second, relations that are by nature potentially long-term, such as loan-debt relationships, usually become part of a well-thought-out long-term strategy for recouping the debt. *Pleitos* (fights) die, but debts do not. However, there is never any loss here in the ultimate sense, since God punishes people who do not pay their debts. Third, group responsibility for decision-making is stressed in all decisions that might trigger or initiate relations with the state.

For litigants, it is what people do about a particular situation that is important. "A bad agreement is better than a good fight." Being a good person (*buena gente*) is more important than winning. Compensation is valued over vengeance. Cases that need immediate attention, such as slander, are acted on quickly even by the mildest people since they deal with personal reputation. Property cases are pursued tenaciously. All this is especially true if you are speaking about somebody else's case.

Defendant Strategies and Case Outcomes

The previous section presented data gathered from interviews of one sort or another. The next few pages contain data from an analysis of court cases and/or observations in the courtroom. The emphasis is on what an outsider sees defendants doing in specific cases and encounters in the courtroom. What, in particular, do defendants look like to others—to the anthropologist or the court officials?

The defendants' *declaraciones* allow us to relate particular patterns to certain elements of social structure and values in this community. The role of litigants in legal proceedings is important because the settlement of cases is frequently based on an agreement signed by those involved. One of the essential characteristics of the defendant's role in Zapotec courts is that testimony is not restricted to a guilty or not-guilty plea. Nor is it limited to a simple positive or negative response. The *demandado* (person against whom the complaint is directed) responds to the accusation by giving his or her version of the matter, including whatever information is felt to be pertinent.

An analysis of approximately a hundred Talean court cases that occurred between 1964 and 1965 revealed that defendants' strategies varied from acknowledgment of guilt to complete denial of the charges. Taleans seldom go to court unless they are sure they have a case. For this reason, relatively few defendants totally denied the charges, although numerous strategies were adopted to defend or explain their behavior. Without reference to guilt or innocence, the defendant's declaration included additional information either about the specific incident or about aspects of relations with the plaintiff that were not readily apparent or about previous incidents between the two that might affect the case.

In other instances the defendant discussed the plaintiff's role, making reference to provocative acts or to ulterior motives. When the defendant accepted responsibility for the charges, he or she almost always added the qualification that there was no *intent* to commit the violation by claiming drunkenness or ignorance of the possible effects of the action. Other postures included the assertion that the defendant was basically a good citizen whose motives were without malice. In some cases the defendant accepted the charges, but indicated an intention to initiate countercharges against the plaintiff.

Typically, a defendant summoned before the presidente or one of the other officials appears before the court to hear the complaint and then is asked to respond to the question "What do you say about that?" (Usted qué dice de eso?) Very rarely does the presidente ask, "Did you do that?" or "Are you guilty of . . . ?" At this time the defendant has the floor and can usually spend a good deal of time presenting an alibi or, more commonly, a version of what happened.

Defendants who admitted fault said very little or offered minimal justification for their actions. In these cases fault was easily discernible, either because of the nature of the incident or the presence of witnesses; perhaps in some cases the defendant was reluctant to argue the case in the hope of a lenient decision. A church sacristan accused of failing to perform his duties admitted his fault by stating that he did not have enough time. Another man attributed his failure to complete his assigned work on the highway to financial problems. One defendant responded to his wife's charge of misbehavior by promising to behave better in the future.

The additional testimony given by the defendant does have an effect on the verdict and on the sanctions imposed by the authorities. When the defendant in a case of a fight between two women described the provocations given by the plaintiff, the presidente fined both of them. In another case, the defendant denied the accusation of stealing wood and brought a complaint against the plaintiff's wife for insulting his wife. A woman appeared before the alcalde charging a man with refusing to marry her after being responsible for her pregnancy. He was fined 90 pesos, but she was fined 180 pesos for fighting with the defendant's wife (whom he had only recently married). Countercharges were initiated against the plaintiff in about 8 of 100 cases; several resulted in fines for the plaintiff.

If the defendant completely denied any responsibility for the charge, the authority assumed a more active role, requesting the litigants to provide further evidence, data on antecedents, facts, or witnesses, and even conducting visual inspections. In a 1964 arson case heard by the alcalde in which the defendant emphatically denied any guilt, an official inspection resulted in concrete evidence against the defendant. In such cases it is not uncommon for the official to ask for the litigants' cooperation by reminding them that it is their obligation to help. Although the authorities usually avoided directly questioning the defendants by asking, "Was the gun yours?" or "Were you drunk?" they would ask, "Why did you do it?" when the evidence was very clear. Another common strategy was to remind the litigants that an unsolved case had to be passed on to the district court—a procedure most Taleans try to avoid. In most cases the defendant offered no alibi, but implicitly accepted responsibility.

Other Participants

The emphasis and importance placed upon the role and declarations of all the litigants can be seen in the *actas*, or records of the proceedings, made by the secretario, who quotes verbatim the statements made by the litigants as often as or more often than he does those made by the presidente. The active participation of all litigating parties in the procedure reinforces the emphasis on harmony or "making the balance" between parties. Their participation ensures against their being coerced to accept the sentencing of a legal authority.

Outcomes of courtroom encounters are based partially on how litigants plead their cases, on whether they use persuasive and appropriate language in the courtroom. In one case a husband, although drunk at the time he assaulted his wife, did not plead drunkenness as an excuse, nor did he follow the custom of apologizing to his wife and promising to reform. The judge sanctioned the husband with an exceptionally heavy fine for his offense and granted the wife a separation. The severity of the fine and the reason for awarding the wife a separation were attributed in the court records to the husband's deliberate refusal to respond "appropriately" in the courtroom. Had he protested "that he was drunk and did not know what he was doing," had he apologized and promised never to assault his wife again, he probably would have received a lighter fine and would not have given his wife grounds for separation.

In a small community the judges know the contestants, and the litigant's character and reputation enter into judicial outcomes. In one case, the secretary reported the court's evaluation of the litigant. The transcript noted that the contestant's word was "unreliable" because she was known as "habitually irresponsible," a "liar," and a "slanderer." Since the judge did not trust her, he put her in jail. She would have assuredly lost her case, since she was treated like a criminal, had she not appealed to the district court. In another case, the defendant, a married man, was charged with rape of another woman. During the trial the municipio initiated a second complaint against him based on hearsay, for being remiss in his financial obligations to his family. Character and reputation do affect outcome.

Hypothetical situations put to informants indicate that contestants' age and socioeconomic status also influence outcome. Real cases support this generalization. The alcalde in 1960 varied awards given mothers in paternity cases from 50 pesos to 365 pesos plus food, clothing, and medical expenses for the child. In the case of the highest award, the young girl's lover came from a relatively wealthy family who could afford to pay more in child support. Where 50-peso and 100-peso compensations were assessed, the fathers owned no land and worked as mozos. In these cases, also, the lovers were in their thirties and "should have known better."

Relatives or friends of contestants have the greatest range of possible roles in court. They may appear as witnesses, possibly representing an aggrieved party who is a minor, is ill, or is pregnant. In an inheritance dispute, the legal guardian may press charges in the child's name against the executor of the will. In a bloody assault case (see Case 70), while the adult male victim lay wounded in bed, his father and cousin brought charges against the attacker. It is the unwed girl's mother (see Case 47) or father (see Case 45) who sues the lover in paternity cases. Sometimes the head of a household acts as the litigant's representative in court, even when the contestant is a healthy, adult male (see Case 44). In an instance in which a young couple lived with the wife's parents, the father-in-law appeared in court in his son-in-law's stead, pleaded his case, and paid the fine. Kinfolk also enter into cases when they are charged with fault in a complaint (see Case 58). Twice wives filed for divorce on account of ill-treatment by their children, and these children were summoned by the court. In another marital conflict, an aggrieved husband brought his wife to court on charges of desertion and his mother-in-law on the supplementary charge of giving shelter to her runaway daughter (see Case 57). In sum, parties other than the chief contestants and the judge enter into judicial proceedings and decision-making.

Chapter Six

Deciding Cases
"They Make Your Head Hot"

In a Talean court, decision-making in a single case consists of a series of successive choices influenced by the overall pull toward harmony or "agreement." A sociology of the case recognizes different segments such as initiation, allocation ("passing" or picking a judge), a hearing (the total participant encounter), and final outcome. An analysis of decisions uttered by judges is a study of only one decision-making segment. In a relatively homogeneous community court operated by lay people, however, judicial thinking is bound to reflect community priorities and values as indicated in expressions of social harmony, as well as a conscious recognition of social utility as the basis for the decision of a case that, if not settled, would move into the arena of state courts. Although litigants play an important role in deciding cases, it is primarily the town officials to whom the authority to decide has been delegated.

In previous pages I raised questions about decision-making: What is it that motivates a litigant to bypass the court and use alternative dispute systems, to take a case to court, to appeal an outcome, to do nothing, or to wait to resolve a pending controversy? What is it that encourages a court to accept a case, to keep it once it is accepted, or to pass it on? But the flavor of deciding is embedded in culture more generally, not only in the specific case. This must be kept in mind as we proceed along the way through a case in order to understand the process by which decisions are reached by Taleans participating in *justicia*. Various incidents illustrate this point, which in this chapter is a prelude to an interview with a former presidente that reflects a good deal about the general rules underlying decision-making in Talea. The interview provides information of a structural nature and segments the courtroom encounter by its procedural and substantive components.

The Court Encounter

The empirical data on allocation (the step of passing or picking a judge) reveal repeat patterns as well as unique or at least unusual behavior. Buck-passing, for example, ranged from little discretion in deciding who should hear a case to a good deal of discretion resulting from choices made by litigants and court officials as well from the type of case involved. Often, however, it is difficult to see patterned behavior because of flux in the composition of the court as well as changes in issues before the court over time. Decisions about allocation are commonly situational, cultural rather than social, and not always deliberate or conscious. They are also forced by the behavior of another individual. For example, during one year when the presidente and the sindico did not approve of the alcalde's handling of complaints, they made a special effort to solve as many cases as possible between themselves. During the year, they passed to the alcalde only four cases, and of these, two were reported to have subsequently been passed to Villa Alta.

The plaintiff's options in choosing a judge may be limited by administrative responsibilities of the judges. If the sindico is working on the airstrip and the presidente is the only one present, the litigants have little choice. Or one official may decide to pass a case to another if he feels he does not have sufficient authority or skill to effect a resolution. During one case the sindico accused the defendant of mocking him, meaning that she was not paying adequate respect to the office, and declared he would send her case to the alcalde, who he claimed had sufficient authority to put her in jail if she did not pay her debt.

One could argue that the high value placed on harmony leads the participants to try to reach a settlement (convenio) by any means. Officials and litigants would take the steps necessary to have the best person deal with the case. A case would enter the court system and gradually gravitate to its proper place of resolution. Court personnel would be shuffled and would assume roles and attitudes designed to facilitate the making of a convenio. Whether they be officials or litigants, Taleans are impatient with dead ends. When it becomes apparent that something is stopping a case from moving, a different approach is tried that facilitates the settlement or completion of a case.

In one case the plaintiff, seeking justice for assault and battery, bypassed the presidente, going directly to the alcalde and demanding that he consign her case to the judge in Villa Alta. The alcalde urged that the case be heard neither by the Villaltecan juez nor by himself, but by the Talean sindico. After an afternoon of discussion in the alcalde's office, the plaintiff yielded and agreed that it would be better to have the sindico hear the case. Although it was within the sindico's jurisdiction, the presidente also attended the court sessions and participated in most of the discussions. The two officials cooperated in jointly handling the single case perhaps because the presidente and his administration owed an important debt to the defendant, whose brother was in charge of one of the most important public work projects. The presidente participated in the case personally along with the sindico in order to ensure that it would be settled as quickly and quietly as possible.

The litigants themselves play an active part in the choice of court personnel and, accordingly, may influence the nature of their hearings. Litigants may ask relatives or friends to accompany them, or they may appear in court alone. It is also possible for them to arrange to be represented or not to come to court at all. The most interesting variation in personnel occurs in cases where the litigants themselves do not appear or where they take an insignificant part in the proceedings.

In one case the plaintiff and the defendant (both female) initially appeared in court and gave their statements to the presidente. The next day the defendant reappeared in court, but the plaintiff's husband, who came to plead in her place, reported that she was ill and could not appear. At this point the presidente decided that the case should be consigned to the alcalde, and the court was adjourned. When the alcalde convened his court, an aunt of the plaintiff, rather than the husband, appeared to take her part. After the defendant and the representative of the plaintiff had discussed the case for several hours, the alcalde summoned the husband of the defendant into his chambers and, ignoring the defendant herself, arranged for an agreement between the defendant's husband and the plaintiff's aunt; not one person present at the beginning of the case participated in the signing of the written settlement. The hearing official was different, and both litigants had representatives acting in their stead.

In sum, there is usually a clear division of responsibility between judges, and most litigants represent themselves, but alternative arrangements are made to accommodate people, rather than having people accommodate themselves to preordained procedures. That procedures can be redesigned to accommodate needs attests to the explicit problem-solving function of the courts and tells us something about the role of kinfolk in facilitating agreements.

The litigants and officials involved in a case determine, by the type of interaction, what kinds of events take place during a trial. Two cases demonstrate the varied roles that may be adopted by litigants trying to resolve similar conflicts.

Case 29. A young man was brought to court by the woman with whom he had been living. He had allegedly beaten her while he was drunk the previous night and threatened their three children. The woman complained that her partner neglected to give her enough money to provide for the family's needs, and asked the court for permission to live apart from him.

The woman took the most active role in court. Initially the presidente asked one of his assistants, a regidor, to hear the case. The plaintiff talked to this regidor for about half an hour, while the regidor and her lover sat silently listening. Then, apparently unsatisfied with the hearing she was getting, the plaintiff moved her chair over to the presidente's desk, interrupting his work, and began to address herself to him. The presidente listened to her in a polite fashion, asking questions from time to time.

After asking the defendant whether he would attempt to behave better in the future and asking the plaintiff whether she would consider continuing with her partner, the presidente began to discuss the subject of a fine with the plaintiff. Later he instructed the regidor to remove the defendant's wallet from his pocket, which the regidor did. The money was counted, and the presidente decided on a fine of 25 pesos. He also announced that he would keep the rest of the money (70 pesos) in security for the plaintiff. If the defendant failed to provide her money to buy necessary household stores, the presidente would give her some of the 70 pesos.

Case 30 was heard by the same presidente.

An unmarried couple living together got into a fight when the man discovered that some of his property (some corn) was missing. The woman summoned the policía and had them put her lover in jail. The next morning, when their case was heard by the presidente, a more typical courtroom procedure was followed. The presidente asked each party for a statement. Each responded with a lengthy story, and after the statements were concluded, the litigants argued with each other forcefully in the presence of the presidente. A good deal of time was devoted to displays of their respective bruises by the litigants. After the presidente had talked to them for about an hour, he announced that both parties were guilty, since each had injured the other, and then proceeded to fine each ten pesos. He also suggested that they get legally married to make their relationship less ambiguous and to provide a better basis for future relations.

In both cases, the presidente took an unambiguous stance toward the litigants, in the first place by assuming control of the defendant's money and in the second by fining both parties and suggesting that they get married. However, the roles assumed by the male defendants differed markedly in the two cases. In the first case, the defendant remained passive and allowed himself to be controlled by the court and his partner. In the second case, the defendant took the role of an active participant and managed to convince the presidente that his partner, as well as himself, was guilty, and both parties were fined.

Two cases heard by the sindico demonstrate that court officials vary in the role they project from case to case.

Case 31. A policía had assaulted another policía while on duty; the sindico guided the hearing. He stood while the litigants sat and pressed them for information in harsh tones. Immediately after hearing their statements, he said that he did not feel he could resolve the case and thought that it should be consigned to the alcalde, who had more power and authority. The litigants begged him to terminate their case within his jurisdiction, and he finally agreed that the case could be settled if the defendant paid a 50-peso fine

In another case, discussed above, the sindico played a passive role. As mentioned earlier, the sindico and the presidente heard the case together. Feeling that their administration owed a debt to the defendant's brother, they both tried to settle the matter as quickly as possible. They, accordingly, remained in the background and allowed the litigants' representatives to adjudicate the issue more or less by themselves. The action in court was limited to bartering between the defendant's brother and the plaintiff's brother-in-law, the two trying to arrive at a suitable figure for compensation to the injured plaintiff.

One might think that, with so much variability in the Talean court, from case to case, from official to official, from year to year, it would be sheer chaos from the point of view of users of the court. If one considers a wider sample, however, in addition to the shared culture, each of the three judges tends toward consistency from case to case because of distinctive personality traits. Litigants considered the personality characteristics of court officials in deciding which official they wanted to hear their case. Data from the summer of 1965 indicate that the then presidente was an easygoing man who rendered mild decisions, whereas the sindico had a reputation for being autocratic and drastic in his performance in court. In contrast, the alcalde usually assumed the role of a friend and tried to get the litigants to make their own decisions.

The interview that follows suggests there is also an ordering that reflects a shared culture; value patterns make decisions fairly predictable. The avoidance of extended conflict and an emphasis on harmony and agreement are themes that run through all Talean cases. There are restraints and constraints that affect officials and litigants. Both groups know what "correct" behavior is for a litigant as well as for the court officials. The concept of "correct" behavior is a sum of the principles governing court structure or court culture.

Interview with a Presidente

The presidente bridges and combines both the administrative and the judicial functions of town government. He symbolizes the past and the future and, depending on how he carries out his job, is considered a representative of his people. I have over the years met and talked with many presidentes in many different situations. I have watched them in action, filmed them, participated in their festivities, and in a number of ways have recorded their behavior. The data collected have been used to try to understand the position and functions of the presidente rather than the orientation of any particular presidente. I present selections from an interview with one former presidente that lasted approximately two and one-half hours. His responses illustrate the social and cultural dimensions of decision-making and the possibilities and constraints.

This particular presidente was interviewed by happenstance. He had been presidente the previous year, but I had never known him in office. During one of my summer visits to Talea, I wanted to introduce a graduate student to a former presidente and to one way of conversing with or interviewing such a man. We went to his home in the early evening and found that he had already retired. He graciously got up, dressed, and offered to come with us to a quiet room where we could talk. The interview was explorative and open-ended, and yet a number of themes appeared throughout in relation to a presidente's options.

Q. What did you like best about this job?
A. Work . . . because one is only sitting. . . .
Q. What work did you do?
A. We opened a pathway. . . . We opened this path last year . . . along with Tino the miller, who was acting as sindico. He left because of a fight. . . . He stopped being sindico, . . . but we continued making the paths here. I worked alone until we named another sindico. We began with the work on the school in July. I enjoyed this work very much. . . . We were working every day with construction workers from Oaxaca. . . . All the material was from Oaxaca . . . cement.
Q. You had other works in the municipality, didn't you?
A. We had to cut the bushes at the side of the road all the way to Maravillas. We fixed the road up to Yatoni. . . .
Q. How about the work that you have as an administrator in the municipio?

A. Administration? You mean of not violating the law . . . when you fine or order someone when they don't work it out well. . . .

Q. Did you have many cases?

A. No.

Q. Why are there many cases some years and not so many others?

A. Who knows why that happens? They denounce authority. . . . Don't you remember how it happened to Pedro? Remember there was a fight between this person from Yaviche. I believe it cost him 5,000 pesos . . . because the women here tell lies. Let anything happen to you, and they pass it to the authorities. They tell it to the authority in Oaxaca. The authorities believed her since she is a woman and they punished [us] by fine.

Q. Is that the way it happened?

A. Yes.

Q. They fined Pedro?

A. No, they fined the authority, not everybody, just the presidente.

Q. And when the presidente is fined, does he have to pay from his own pocket?

A. No, from the presidente's pocket.

Q. And that was a woman's case?

A. The authorities, I believe, sent the policía to remove the lady's things from the house, because the owner of the house had ordered her out [see Case 108]. So they removed the things. The lady . . . became angry. In Oaxaca, she accused the authorities here of removing her by force, and of stealing money and things. Orders came from Oaxaca that our authorities explain. It was they who fined him. . . . That's where it went bad for the previous presidente. The year before it didn't happen, and not to me. I didn't have [bad] "things."

Q. How is it that the presidente should make justice when people go to him with the problems and fights?

A. There are people who get drunk at night. They hit others and fight in the street. Then the owner of the place or bartender will demand to be paid. The policía are sent to bring them and lock them in jail. The next day they [the plaintiffs] will tell the authorities these people did so and so. The authorities then fine them 25, 30, or even 50 pesos. If the fight was serious, then the fine goes to the treasurer who enters it in the book of *ingresos* [record of money that comes in]. . . . When it is serious, they fine him according to the cause.

Q. But you have to say something to the defendant or the plaintiff?

A. Yes, the presidente has to say something so they can feel . . . and then he enters this in the files.

Q. But don't you talk to them, give them advice?

A. Oh yes, I tell them not to do it again. The fine will serve as advice because they know what will happen now. . . . If they do it again, the fine is doubled. If they do it again the next week, then they will come back and pay.

Q. Do they always pay the fines?

A. They pay; if not, they go back to jail. If they don't pay the presidente, the matter is referred to the sindico, and from the sindico to the alcalde, and if things are not settled with the chief of public administration in Villa Alta, . . . then the judge of Oaxaca [will handle it].

Q. What is meant by *ergjoonz* . . . balance?

A. That is called a convenio, an agreement.

Q. . . . Sometimes the presidente will fine both the plaintiff and the defendant. Why is that?

A. Because he doesn't know what to do. He doesn't know which of them is telling the truth. One or the other could be lying. The authority fines the two lies. For example, if someone tells you, you owe him, . . . how can you prove otherwise? . . . You can't. Therefore both are fined.

Q. Why is it that when a man fights, sometimes he will be fined 20 pesos and other times 50 pesos? Why is the fine variable?

A. It is because some fine more and others fine less. It depends on the authority why the fines vary.

Q. But it is the same presidente.

A. Yes, but he has so many matters to attend to that they confuse him. . . . As Octavio knows, . . . they pile up. On Mondays this happens. They come from Otatitlan, . . . Yatoni, . . . from the ranchos. . . . They pile up. . . . It doesn't matter who is fined more or who is fined less. . . .

Q. When they fine like that, is that an agreement?

A. There is no agreement, unless the authority makes it. They tire you [these cases]. One's head is not fresh and not ready to say what someone deserves. They are fined so they will leave the town promptly.

Q. But is this justice or not?

A. They aren't reaching an agreement, . . . only trying to get cases out.

Q. But sometimes the presidente has to reason things out, no?

A. Sometimes . . . when the case is serious, . . . but not when people fight because they are drunk.

Q. Can you tell me of a serious case you had?

A. Like the Federico affair? As you know, it dealt with robbery of a water drum. . . . The owner of the drum did not know what happened to it until he learned that there was a stolen drum in Federico's house. The owner came to me saying that he had lost a drum. We circulated an official notice throughout the town stating that whoever had stolen or taken the drum should hand it over. Federico did not. If he heard the announcement, he ignored it.

It was then we learned that the drum was in Federico's house. We had to think of a way to get it out. We brought Federico before the court. A regidor was sent to Federico's house, and there he found the drum and brought it back with him to the court. When he arrived with it, the owner identified it as his. Then I asked Federico, "Whose drum is this?" "It's mine," he said. "Who did you buy it from?" I asked. "From someone named Antonio," he replied. "I didn't catch his last name." "Well then, if you aren't sure, you must have stolen it." "No, I didn't steal anything. It's mine." "Well, friend, how can you have bought it if the owner is standing here and says it belongs to José?" . . . He gave no reply; he knew the drum belonged to José. I sent him to jail. I decided later that he would be fined 250 pesos and that he should return the drum to José. . . .

Q. What happened to Federico?

A. He had to pay the fine. After he paid, I let him out of jail, and he returned home. But he had to buy the drum so as not to stay embarrassed.

Q. And there the matter ended?

A. Yes.

Q. But why did Federico leave Talea?

A. Because he went to look for work in Oaxaca.

Q. And did you give Federico advice such as not to do it again?

A. Yes, I told him. . . . I told him he is not an ignorant person, not a farm-hand, not a poor person without money. That since he knew what he was doing he was not ignorant, . . . someone else perhaps, but for him it would only bring shame, . . . since he was a man of wealth. He had means at home, and being a man of understanding he should not have done this thing. If the drum had really been his, he should have gone to José and told him so, then all right, but not to go at night and steal. This was very bad; he stayed in jail one night as punishment.

Q. Suppose he was a poor man, without education, with nothing. Then how would you have resolved this matter?

A. I would still have to arrest him in order to correct him. He could commit worse crimes, . . . steal money or a bull, . . . things that are worth more money. I would have done the same if he were poor. One person stole a radio, and since he didn't have any money I had him work one month at the school . . . as punishment so he would not do that crime again. He had no money; he was poor, so he worked.

Q. Did you have other serious cases besides theft?

A. Apart from theft? Some policemen once told me to levy heavy fines against those committing crimes in the street. I saw that the offenses were not very serious, so I paid little attention to them. I fined the defendants according to what they had done, . . . from 15 to 20 pesos. The policía wanted me to fine them 50 to 100 pesos, . . . a heavy fine. They were angry with me for not fining heavy.

Q. What was it they had done?

A. Those who fought, yelled, drank beer, . . . or did nothing more than make noise . . . the policía wanted me to put them in jail and fine them 100 pesos. But I didn't, so the policía got angry. Then one night the head policía and others sent in a sealed envelope their resignation. They turned in their sticks and whistles and said, . . . "Here are our things. We are no longer going to serve." . . . And they left. They shouted quite a bit before leaving.

I didn't know what to do. I asked the aid of some private citizens that were not police, to help out that night. Then I asked Augustín [a previous presidente] what I should do in this case because I was thinking of going out and arresting, one by one, all the policía. I was thinking of punishing them. Augustín said that was not a good idea . . . because they were probably together and would hit anyone who went to get them. They would all resist. So there would be no further escalation, leave them alone, he said. Tomorrow they would settle the matter.

The next day they went to Villa Alta, to accuse me of not attending to their complaints. The agent there gave them a document saying I should give the policía guarantees. But that was not enough for them, so they left shouting and making a scene. When they returned here, the following day, I asked them why they went to Villa Alta. To tell Señor Juez to give them guarantees, they replied. They had said before that they were not in agreement with what I was imposing. I told them they should have told me this, not leave shouting. I then put them in jail. . . . There were six of them. I did not give them dinner or covers or anything. The next day I fined the chief of police 100 pesos, the lieutenant 50 pesos, the policía 25 pesos each. I fired the chief and the lieutenant. That is how I solved the policía case.

Q. Why did it interest them if you fined heavier?

A. Because they are foolish, . . . bad. They wanted me to jail these men because they were drinking beer. They wanted me to follow them, to show me, but I did not want to do so. . . . They became angry. We had a fight with the teacher over them also.

Q. How was that?

A. I believe they saw the teacher drinking over there, so they grabbed him and put him in jail. They [the two teachers] were angry, so they wrote to the higher authority, and said that the authorities were doing this and that, when it was not true. It was really the policía and the teachers. After that the policía no longer arrested them. They [the teachers] were drinking but without making noise. Enrique [the secretary] knows this. It was he who brought peace between the policía and the teachers. The policía no longer bother them.

Q. Aren't there always problems between the policía and the presidente?

A. It's that some people want to order. . . . They want to make the authority. When the authority allows it, you can; when it doesn't, you cannot order. It is better to remove these men or fine them or put them in jail. Better to remove them and put in new ones that are obedient.

Q. There are those who say that the presidente makes good justice and others that he is making bad justice. When do they say he is making bad justice?

A. Sometimes they [the presidentes] drink and do bad things.

Q. What kind of bad things?

A. For example, he could be drunk and a case come up and he would ignore it. Or he could fine the defendant and the plaintiff without thinking. Or he could take money and not give it to the treasurer but put it in his pocket—all this is bad justice.

Q. Have you ever heard the people say, "This presidente only fines"?

A. Without saying what was done, without judging . . .

Q. What is judging?

A. Say you did something, or you're not certain that you hit so and so. . . .
Nothing more is said, but you are going to pay a fine. They fine without
knowing anything, whether you're guilty or not guilty. That is bad justice. Not to ask, not knowing what is true, yet putting you in jail. . . . For
example, someone owes money that is due in a month. He does not pay
and must get an extension. If he does not get an extension, then we have
a case.

Q. At times the presidente has to be very patient?

A. Yes, if he is not, he will get very hotheaded. What is done more is to go
drink mezcal, and not do anything. Many people leave the municipio
drunk . . . like Pascual. He could not drink. . . . They didn't want to make
him a hothead.

Q. What do you mean when you say you do not want to make his head hot?

A. They do not want to attend to justice of the people, so instead they start
to gossip. Certainly when the people come and see a drunk, they would
rather leave.

Q. What do you do when you have a marriage case?

A. You mean a fight between married people? It depends. There are some
cases where one hit another, or where they do not give one the market
money or clothes, or where he has something else in the street. Then I
tell him to leave his street women and return to his wife. But if the problem is money for market or what the woman needs—clothes, medicine—then I make him sign that he will conform, and we send them
home. There are some husbands who do not wish to go home. These I put
in jail; then I fine him so he can be corrected.

Q. And do they learn this way?

A. They hesitate, but they learn with the fine. We have to give them advice
so that they will treat their women well, and not to do it again. We tell
them that the law is not bad; they are the ones who are bad, and for that
reason we punish them. We give them advice so they will not do it
again. . . .

Q. In our country the judge is more interested in finding out who is guilty.
The judge does not know one or the other litigant. It is another type of
justice.

A. They do this in Villa Alta because they do not know us. Here, yes, we
know each other. We are all neighbors, and we can do that. In Villa Alta,
in Oaxaca, you cannot.

Q. How do you view the justice in Villa Alta?

A. I don't know how it's done there.

Q. You've never been there?

A. Yes, one time. They accused me of falsifying documents. They put me in
jail. I told them this was not true because my uncle made the document.
They did not fine me; they let me go.

Q. Were you presidente then?

A. No, this was way before.

Q. Is the justice the same from presidente to presidente?

A. It follows.

Q. Why? How does it follow? Is it exactly the same?

A. No, each judge has his own style. If one knows more, he will fix it better. If he does not, then as well as he can. We are only *campesinos* [farmers], so I do not think we have much knowledge. The one that knows more Spanish knows more about law. One goes by the laws; if not, by the conscience. If there are people who do not know much Spanish or much law, but if he has a good head, then a good head does things.

Q. What do you mean, a good head to do things?

A. How can I explain? A person that does not go to school seems stupid, but can resolve things. He can apply his head to things like that; he has a common sense that can help him say that this is good and this is not.

Q. Was Don Augustín like that?

A. Yes. Augustín Mateo, Augustín García—that fellow had a good head and not much education.

Q. I notice that it is usually the same people who come to the presidente. Are there others who do not come?

A. Yes.

Q. Where do they go to fix their problems?

A. In their own home. They do not go to the authority. This is called a private affair—only between us in the family. But if it is serious, I will say, so then we go to the authority. Certainly it is more formal, tactful, better—but there are those who would rather not go. They would rather fix it [at home].

Q. When you were presidente, were you sometimes afraid?

A. No.

Q. But much trouble?

A. Yes.

. . . . .

Q. The authorities here in Talea do many things on their own. For example, if they see a drunk, not doing anything, they will grab him and put him in jail. Why is that?

A. That is the custom here. But it also depends on the presidente. Some presidentes don't like drunks to be on the streets, and nothing is done. But not here. We put them in jail so there won't be drunks, because sometimes they die. They get drunk and drown.

Q. What if the policía do something wrong? [Do they go] to jail?

A. To jail. Police, regidores, even the presidente; if he commits a wrong, then the sindico fines the presidente, and if the sindico commits a wrong, the presidente fines him or puts him in jail.

Q. Is there any difference between the justice of an alcalde and that of a presidente?

A. A little. The alcalde's penalty is usually heavier, the presidente's lighter. The alcalde judges more than the presidente. The alcalde has to be a better judge of things, whether they are true or not [he has to find out]. If the matter is large, then the affair will go to the capital with the testimony. There everything is said—where, when, how much, at what hour. Yes, the difference between the alcalde and the presidente is that the alcalde must judge everything—witnesses and who viewed what.

Q. Since Federico's case was serious, why didn't it go to the alcalde?

A. He didn't want to because he was ashamed to tell his story. That's why he wanted to pay the fine.

Q. How did the town react to Federico's case?

A. They were surprised because, as I said, Federico was not ignorant or poor. Only a poor person or ignorant person would do such a thing. . . . Federico had too much ambition. He would even rob to get rich. A person should work, work to have so you will not have to rob. Better to work much than not work, but there are those who do not want to work. They would rather steal. That was the case with Federico.

Q. What is the most serious crime? Robbery?

A. Yes.

Q. Is it more serious than killing?

A. About the same because if you would steal millions of pesos, it is like killing the people. You leave them without clothes.

Q. Do you think Talea has more or less disputes today?

A. I think . . . less . . . because there were many fights before.

Q. Over what matters?

A. Questions of land. Say you have some land and I wish to take some. So I move the marker and take some. Then you will demand that I return your land, and we will argue at Villa Alta.

Q. Today they do not fight as much?

A. Very little.

Q. Why?

A. Because now they know that this is bad. It is better to give up the small bit of land than to waste money going back and forth to Villa Alta. It is said, *"A bad agreement is better than a good fight"* [my emphasis].

Q. That is a good saying.

A. One tires of making trips to Villa Alta.

Q. But why is it that they realize this now?

A. There were more ignorants before, but they see that the argument does not benefit either side; usually it turns out bad for both. So it is better not to be stubborn and not fight. It is better to make an agreement than to go to Villa Alta and give money to the judge. Before there were many fights like this, now not so many.

Q. Nowadays what are most fights about?

A. There aren't many fights nowadays. People know this is bad. Better not to fight and save time and money.

This interview was rich in contrasts that allow us to summarize significant dimensions for the presidente in his role as judge and decision-maker. These dimensions may be checked against actual case materials. When making decisions, this presidente was attentive to certain dimensions in relation to types of complaints, types of relations between litigants or parties to a case, types of justice, qualities of presidentes, and types of advice. He viewed his options as the following six, alone or in combination:

O1. Fine without judging
O2. Fine with judging
O3. Advise only
O4. Pass case along to another court
O5. Make an agreement
O6. Send to jail

The complaints were cut along the following lines:

C1. More serious, almost criminal
C2. Light
C3. Long
C4. Short
C5. With witnesses
C6. Without witnesses (e.g., not able to know facts of case)

The litigants were described according to their personality characteristics or to their state as:

L1. Good people
L2. Stubborn people
L3. Drunken people
L4. Thinking people
L5. Fighting people
L6. Street defendants
L7. Acquainted
L8. Unacquainted
L9. From the same village
L10. From different towns
L11. Rich
L12. Poor
L13. Ignorant

Types of justice were distinguished as:

J1. Presidente's justice, administrative justice
J2. Alcalde's (and sindico's) justice
J3. Judging well
J4. Not judging or fining

J5. Good justice

J6. Bad justice

J7. Agreement or resolution

J8. Finding guilt

The qualities of the presidente serving at any one time were related to the types of justice:

P1. Patient

P2. To have a head that is hot (rather than cool)

P3. To have a good head

P4. To not have a good head

P5. To be there just gossiping

P6. To not attend to justice, to not receive cases

P7. To go and drink mezcal

P8. To be overly influenced by others

P9. To pocket the fines

Fines and advice are directed toward:

A1. Correction

A2. Shame

A3. Punishment

As we begin to compare statements to the actual handling of cases, we will see which of these pieces of information are the most important in the evolution of a case. The interview did not produce guidelines implicitly held by the native actors regarding implicit behavior in the courtroom; it did, however, indicate some of the dimensions. Interviews with other presidentes and sindicos and alcaldes supplemented the near-verbatim interview recorded above, with little contradiction, and underscored a number of observations made in it.

A set of political oppositions that must affect the decisions on cases is important: the elected authorities in opposition to the police, to the schoolteachers, to the officials in the district court and beyond. The police were described as a problem for each new set of authorities. Some officials used distancing mechanisms to gain the respect of the police, and others used the buddy system, but all those interviewed agreed that the police were difficult to control, that they interfered in many cases and indeed were the cause of numerous disputes—particularly disputes involving drinking—that they were generally disgruntled because they could little afford to serve without pay. The schoolteachers are a worry because they have a direct line to the outside and to outside power in particular. Officials often consult the teachers when deciding serious cases, but such consultation is viewed by the citizens as compromising independent decision-making by the officials elected to do the job. Among the many threats seen to emanate from the district court are conflicts over jurisdiction, over the right of the Talean court to handle certain kinds of problems. It is with good reason that Talean court officials feel a deep concern about these three groups because the result of interaction with any of them often ends with a direct threat to the authority of the village court.

The interviews also clarified questions of procedural decision-making—who will hear a case? Although certain types of cases do seem to be heard according to personal preference, officials stress that in specific instances the procedures do not vary: the sindico and the alcalde are the only officials designated to hear cases involving property issues and, in particular, cases relating to wills. The venue for involving assault and battery cases varies, as it does for any case involving alcohol. There is contradictory information as to which of the officials fines the heaviest. Some presidentes feel that sanctions decrease as a case is appealed to the sindico and alcalde. Some sindicos and alcaldes feel that the sanctions increase with each appeal, culminating in the district court. In fact the sanctions vary depending on the policy of the presidente's office vis-à-vis the needs of the local treasury. The consequences for case flow are important. High fining in the presidente's office would discourage people from coming to the presidente's office or entering the court process at all, or it might encourage people to bypass the presidente and go to the sindico or alcalde.

Although the officials cooperated in answering questions, they most enjoyed discussing the work done during their tenure, and work always meant public works, such as electrification, road building, and work on the airstrip, and never referred to dispute management. When pushed to discuss their role in dispute management, they often focused on a case that was particularly difficult to settle peacefully, that posed many difficult decisions. Usually these were cases that involved more than two people and threatened village harmony.

All the officials interviewed underscored situational factors that influenced their decisions about cases, such as economic factors. As one sindico expressed it:

It depends on what kind of an economic situation the person is in. When a person appears who has money, we make him feel a little by a large fine. But if a guilty person is poor, that has to be taken into consideration. Fining him a lot might exacerbate the controversy, so we put him to work for one or two days. Or if someone has money but is lazy, you make him work to make him feel.

Another official stressed the behavior of litigants in court—particularly their ability to state their case clearly and correctly. Others spoke about whether litigants were outsiders or insiders and whether as outsiders they had conduits to Oaxaca City.

Deciding cases in Talea is an interactional process framed by cultural experience. Gulliver (1979: 49) contends that in adjudication the disputants surrender to a third party their ability to decide an outcome. In negotiations, however, "the disputants are interdependent in the absence of authority. The outcome results from an interactional process of information exchange and learning which leads to joint decision-making by the parties themselves, so that both must accept the outcome as adequate enough in the perceived circumstances at the time."

In the succeeding chapters, I explore the degree to which these two modes are combined within the same court or even, as Gulliver has suggested, within the same case in the process of seeking resolution of a dispute. It is the combination of social and cultural factors that make up the style of a court, and it is to the styles of court procedures that I now turn.

Chapter Seven

Court Styles

"A Bad Agreement Is Better than a Good Fight"

In this chapter I analyze the courtroom encounter in terms of style (Kroeber 1957). Some aspects of a courtroom encounter are determined principally by the type of case and the characteristics of the participants. These inconstant aspects are discussed in Chapter 8. However, the continuous features that permeate court activities and constitute the form and manner of the court give it its style. It is these features that concern me here.

One constant that runs through case materials from the Talean court may, for present purposes, briefly be described as the value placed on harmony and on achieving balance or agreement between the principals in a case. It is compromise arrived at by adjudication or, in some cases, adjudication arrived at by compromise. The *settlement* to a dispute may be designed to fine, jail, ridicule, or acquit the principals in a case, but the *outcome* desired is rectification. It is outcome rather than decision that is important to style. The outcome is the effect the decision has on the litigants and their dispute; outcome centers attention on desired results.

With the exception of cases initiated by the town itself (as in charges of public drunkenness), court officials *aim* to rectify by achieving or reinstating a balance between the parties involved in a dispute, a word synonymous with imbalance among Taleans. Balance is an ideal of many systems of law, including our own, but the definition of balance differs among cultures. The Talean balance is focused not on an "eye for an eye," as reported for the Arab Bedouin (Kennett 1968), for example, but rather on that which restores personal relations to equilibrium. This is not to say that the judgments in cases always do so.

In his work on the Mexican town of Tzintzuntzan, George Foster notes that "traditional behavior in Tzintzuntzan is pointed toward maintaining an equilibrium, a state of balance or a status quo in which people must at least feel they are neither threats to, nor threatened by, others" (1967: 12). He goes on to say that "a direct confrontation in which two candidates are in direct opposition—and hence one must lose . . . is disturbing to all . . . and every effort is made to avoid such situations" (ibid.: 172). Although the Talean court encounter is exactly that—litigants seemingly in direct opposition—the cultural values of mutual aid, balance, harmony, and equality result in a style of court proceedings that aims for agreement, or adjustment, or that says that it does.

My interest in court style was inspired by an earlier analysis of footage that resulted in the film *To Make the Balance* (Nader 1966a). The overall flavor of the courtroom encounter, rather than the segments that make up such encounters, was made obvious through filming. I was motivated to film the Talean presidente's court because I thought that film would be better than the written word for communicating courtroom processes. Here I am faced with describing in words what was so vividly recorded by the camera, and I attempt the task through the use of field notes and official court records, much of which came from the translated tapes used in the film. What follows is an analysis of the elements of dispute settlement that determine the style of settlement processes, a summary of the five cases appearing in the film, a comparison (again with the help of recorded cases) of the style found in the presidente's court, the sindico's court, and the alcalde's court, and finally an analysis of the conditions that appear to generate a particular disputing style.

What Constitutes the Style?

The value that Taleans place on equality or balance is critical for understanding the motives for disputing as well as the motives for finding outcomes that support the ideal of village harmony. I was once present at a fiesta in Talea, listening to the orchestra play some well-known Spanish *pasodobles* and keeping company with the people present. The trumpet player was a talented musician whose performance moved me to praise him publicly and ask if I could record his solo. Not long after, a drunken fellow came up and hit the trumpet player, breaking his front tooth—a serious loss to a trumpet player. The case went to court the next day.

In one sense the balance had been made when the player was hit and had lost his front tooth. His excellent musicianship had itself

created an imbalance, but the court was now concerned with another, though related, kind of balance. The settlement was in favor
of the plaintiff, but the damages paid were less than minimal—
20 pesos. The tooth certainly could not be replaced for that price,
and yet the plaintiff did not ask for more in damages, perhaps because he did not know the cost of replacing his tooth. The trumpeter
indicated to me that the score would have to be settled by less public
means, where retaliation would not be so likely. The case was more
complex than I have indicated here: the Taleans chose sides, and
many people would have been implicated if the dispute had not been
at least publicly sealed by a court decision. The point here is to indicate that the value placed on balance both promotes disputing as
well as settlement once such cases find their way into the courtroom.

Another important Talean value is mutual aid, as contrasted to
partisanship. The role of a third party is not to apply "the law" as
codified elsewhere, but to help the parties to a case find adjustments, to ease a problem. There are undoubtedly selfish motives,
such as replenishing the treasury. But a feeling of mutual aid is related to the way in which Oaxacan villages have been organized as
politically independent, self-reliant, endogamous places that remain
free to determine their lives only to the extent to which they can
manage themselves successfully. Villages with feuds or problems
that escalate to the district courts or beyond are more vulnerable to
state interference—or so the Taleans perceive the situation.

The cases presented below were originally recorded with the help
of a camera, a tape recorder, and pen and paper for the production of
To Make the Balance. My purpose is to separate the common features that permeate these cases from those substantive aspects that
vary from case to case. The next several chapters are concerned with
variation in the substance of the cases.

Case 32. Case of the damaged chiles. Señor Ignacio Andrés Zoalaga, a merchant, 55 years of age, appeared before the court. He stated: "I am coming to
make a complaint about the driver of the cream-colored truck that is on the
platform, in the midst of which is a damaged basket of chiles weighing 47.5
kilograms." The driver of the cream-colored truck was called. He arrived fifteen minutes later and said that his name was Mario Valdéz Herrero. The
presidente asked him whether it was true that he had damaged the basket of
chiles, and he answered, "Actually, I damaged it, but this happened because
I don't have anyone to direct me. It is the truck owner's fault because he
ought to let me have a helper. Also, I could not see because the driver's com-
partment is high. Besides, it is the señor's fault—they put the things they
have for sale on the ground, knowing that there is truck traffic."

The presidente asked Señor Ignacio Andrés, "Why did you put your merchandise down, knowing that the truck would go by?" Señor Ignacio answered that there was room for the truck to pass. The driver then said that this was not true, since the space there was at an angle. Señor Ignacio said, "Look, Señor Presidente, the truck came this way, then this way and that way." The presidente said that it would be most convenient in this case if the driver paid for the damage he had caused, and that the basket of chiles should be brought in so that an estimate could be made of how much of it had been ruined.

The plaintiff left, and the presidente ordered the regidor to have the merchandise brought in. The regidor returned with Señor Ignacio, carrying a basket of chiles between them, which they emptied on the floor. The regidor sorted out the chiles on the floor and put aside the damaged ones; he then told the presidente that the quantity ruined was about 1.5 kilograms. The presidente asked the owner of the basket how much he wanted to be paid for the damage. Señor Ignacio answered that it was not much—3 pesos. The presidente told the chauffeur that he had to pay 3 pesos for the damage. Upon this the chauffeur said, "All right, I will go right now for the 3 pesos." Meanwhile the court presidente reminded the plaintiff to be more careful the next time and to watch where he put his booth—not to put it just anywhere and especially not in front of a truck. . . .

Case 33. Case of the frightened little boy. Señora Juana of Juquila filed a complaint. She stated that she was living in the adjacent hills between Juquila and Talea. She made the following complaint against young Teodoro García: "The son of Teodora assaulted my little son. We were cutting coffee in the field of Señora Quiroz, grandmother of Teodoro, and I asked him why he had hit him [my son]. He told me to complain wherever I wished, because he went to school, and he could defend himself. My little boy got frightened and yells during the night and now has diarrhea because of the fright. Therefore I am asking the presidente to help me make my little son well again. I asked Señora Quiroz, Teodoro's grandmother, why he [her grandson] had been attacking my little boy. He is older, and he started the fight with my little boy, who is only six years old. She answered, 'Fight, fight, and continue to fight; there is enough room in this field.' I am making this claim because Teodoro does not have any right to beat my son, and he hit him."

Young Teodoro was summoned to respond to the incidents of which he was accused. When he arrived before the presidente, he was informed of what Señora Juana had reported. . . . "It is not true, Señor Presidente," Teodoro replied. "He is a mischief maker and he takes advantage of us because we are working. I will not tolerate his calling me miserable names; he said very ugly things."

The presidente now said to Señora Juana, "If you know how the young man [Teodoro] acts, why don't you leave or not go there any more for work?" "It is his grandmother who is always asking me to work for her in the field," said Señora Juana, "but that Teodoro treated us that way." Teodoro said, "I did not ask you to come to work," and the señora replied, "Your grandmother is the one who did, not you." Teodoro responded, "You have to work, that's why you came!" Señora Juana answered, "I want the presidente to know that I have always worked, but nobody treats me badly." The presidente, in order to finish this matter, asked how much Señora Juana wanted Teodoro to pay for a treatment. She answered that she wanted 30 pesos for her little son to be cured. Teodoro said that the boy didn't have anything wrong with him, but Señora Juana told him to take her son home and then he would see how he yelled at night. Teodoro said he wouldn't do that even if the boy were his own son. "Look, Señor Presidente," Teodoro said, "I am not willing to pay 30 pesos, but I would pay 20 pesos." The presidente asked the señora whether she would agree to accept the 20 pesos that Teodoro had offered to pay. She accepted, and the accused paid cash, which was given to the señora in his presence. The present session was finished at 4 o'clock in the afternoon of the same day.

Case 34. Case of the assertive wife. Señor Jaime Ruiz, a married man, 40 years of age, appeared to present a complaint against his wife, Carmen Ibarra, native and inhabitant of the same town. He said, "I come to present my complaint about my wife because she cut the coffee without my consent." The presidente answered: "All right, let's arrange [settle] this matter, but we have to call Señora Carmen Ibarra so that she can explain what she did and why she did it." Señora Carmen Ibarra was called, and she appeared at 11:30 o'clock on the same day.

The presidente spoke. He said to the defendant, "I had you called so that you could clarify the matter of the claim made by your husband, who is here present. Why did you have the coffee cut without his permission?" Here the plaintiff interrupted, saying, "Señor Presidente, I am here to complain with the help of your authority that this woman, who is my wife, had my coffee cut from a piece of land that belongs to me. I know that my wife's helper did the cutting on her order, but without my consent or permission, and this is why I am here to claim that this coffee should be delivered to me." Señora Carmen Ibarra, wife of the plaintiff, said excitedly, "Señor Presidente, this man really does not think at all. Why shouldn't I cut the coffee, since it belongs to both of us, and besides we have children to support and feed? I am a woman. I do everything to look after our children, and he has left us, left the house, with nobody saying anything to him. He left because he wanted to and he went to the house of his sister so that he could pick up some tales [gossip]—he always had this habit."

"I am in the right, Señor Presidente," exclaimed the plaintiff, "I can't stay with her in the house because she says she is the valuable one, she does nothing but work, and I am the weak one and this is thanks to my mother and father, who left me the house and some money." The wife interrupted: "He just does it that way! He goes to his [our] house, where we are hiding a few things of value. He takes the key or he hides it, and when we need something, there we are looking for it everywhere, but he has to have this habit of taking the key! Now he is complaining about the coffee. It is true, I ordered the coffee to be cut. What can I do? I have to take care of his children, so I think I have my rights. After all, we are legally married, and nobody hindered him in carrying out his own wish to get out. The presidente of last year knows this because I informed him first of it so that no one could say that I left my husband. Now all I have and what we both have is neither for me nor for him. It is for our children, it is their lives, and we shouldn't be quarreling anymore, but this man does not think so, he does not think of our children. Look, Señor Presidente, my little girl is at this moment in Mexico [City] for a treatment because she is sick, and he does not even think that his daughter needs some money for treatment. He hasn't even asked. He knows very well how sick she is."

"I don't agree with that, either," said the plaintiff, "because she [the daughter] left without my permission and did not come to tell me, and I didn't even know that she had gone." "That's how he does things, Señor Presidente," interrupted Carmen. "Why should his daughter go to him and tell him that she is leaving if he doesn't even help her with the things he could do for her? Now he says that I didn't say anything about her going. If she were dying, would you want me first to ask your permission so that she could die? When there is urgency for treatment, one has to look for a way. That you should have thought about before leaving us, having a sick daughter."

Señor Jaime responded, "Señor Presidente, you heard now how it is. I had fully thought I would not return to her anymore for many reasons. First, we have come here to the municipio several times already, and always she promises she will behave well and it won't be the same, but after a while she returns to the same thing. Now, for instance, she has a little liquor store, and I don't know anything about it, how it goes, whether there are any money entries, or how she manages it. Clearly, she makes a nobody out of me. Now too, she goes out on her errands and comes back late and I ask where she has gone and she answers angrily, 'Why do you want to know? I had to do my errands because you don't know anything.' But I say," continued the plaintiff, "'It is my right to know where you are going and what kind of business you are attending'—and there are more things she has been doing, but now I don't want this case to drag on longer. I only want her to return the coffee to me." Whereupon Señora Carmen Ibarra said, "Yes, I will deliver the coffee, which you said I took, but you have to pay in front of the presidente the bills for the treatment that our daughter had to have—poor little girl, who wants so much to be cured, as she says in her postcard, 'Mama, do sell some part of my interests for the treatment.' And I am doing everything to get hold of some money so that she can have the treatment, and this man, for a little bit of coffee which I went and cut off, he is making such a terrible fuss."

"Look, Señor Presidente," explained the plaintiff, "I planted the coffee seeds for my wife and she has enough, and now she tries to take mine and wants to have more, but the only thing I want is for her not to cut my coffee without my permission."

The presidente, now having heard what the parties in the lawsuit had to say, pronounced: "You should now think like mature people about what you are doing, and the only thing you should do is to get together again, forget the troubles of the past, think of your sick child, and don't think about yourselves. You should both be home worrying about how your daughter can be cured." And directing himself to Señor Jaime Ruiz, he continued, "Nobody has thrown you out of your house, but you walked out without any motive. Therefore, return to your home and think about how to resolve the problems of the home. The man as the boss of the house is responsible for the expenditures and necessities of the house, and the chores that have to be done should be the duties of the wife, with the wife letting him know what is being done. Well, the husband should give the orders with regard to what should be done, but in the event the husband abuses his authority in the home, then the wife has every right to protest, and has a reason to do so. As to the woman, the obligation of the wife is to be there where the husband orders, as long as it is in agreement and to the benefit of the home; and the woman is also the only one responsible for the food and like necessities, that is, for the kitchen."

Having listened to what the presidente had to say and after a long silence and reflection, the couple became reasonable and said that they would unite again and that they would follow the advice of the presidente. But Señor Jaime Ruiz added, "I am willing to go home if in all ways my wife behaves to me as she should and we are in agreement in everything, as you said. But only if you allow me to go home when my daughter returns from her treatment in Mexico [City], then I would go back to my house, but as long as she is not there I will not go." His wife was asked if she would agree to what her husband, Señor Jaime Ruiz, had just finished saying, whereupon she answered, "Yes, whatever he wishes. He could return now or when our daughter arrives."

The presidente then said to Señor Jaime, "All right, when your daughter returns, then your case will be finished and you may go to your house," and turning to Señora Carmen, "and you may then advise this municipal authority when your daughter arrives in order to settle the case." With these words he finished the proceedings, leaving the case open until further notice from the señora.

Case 35. Case of the delinquent son. Señor Benjamín Mendoza Cruz, appeared to make a complaint against his son Clemente Mendoza, unmarried, 25 years of age, native and inhabitant of the same town. The complaint concerned a violation the son had committed on the plaintiff's property and for which he, as the father, demanded recompense for the loss he had sustained. Taking note of all this, the municipal presidente ordered the accused to be summoned. Having already been cited earlier, the son was present, and now informed of the context of the complaint.

The accused, being allowed to speak, said the following: "Without a witness I can declare that I went to my father's field in order to cut some coffee. I admit I was at fault, and now he can say how to punish me. A year ago my boss [my father] allowed me to cut some coffee on his property called Suyagtuluc. But now I wish my father would forgive me for the fault I have committed. He is in the right and he has his rights, but he might consider how to view this matter. I was confident that he would give the coffee to me. I ask for forgiveness and would like to have Professor Raymundo Vásquez to be my legal advisor."

The presidente ordered the teacher to be called, and he arrived at 10:15 of the same day. The teacher asked why he had been called, and the presidente explained that young Clemente Mendoza, present in the courtroom, had asked that he should be called in order to represent him. The nature of the case was explained to the teacher, and he advised young Clemente, in the presence of the municipal presidente, that if he admitted his fault and if he had been harvesting the coffee in question, and being the son, he should ask forgiveness and pardon from his father. "Apologize to him, because what you did was an abuse," he said. After giving his advice, he asked permission to leave, since that was all he had to say.

Now Señor Benjamín Mendoza said the following: "I am, as his father, very sad that my son Clemente should have done this wickedness to me. I did not believe that it was he who had done it until the Juquileña, with whom we have adjacent land, informed me. She was the one who told me that it was my son who had cut the coffee, and it hurt me that my son should have done this because on earlier occasions I had noted that coffee was disappearing. I came here earlier to inform the presidente and to let it be precisely known to the authorities of the villages of San Juan Juquila that there is a path which is always used, and if there was someone on the ranches in this municipality who had done this crime, he should be punished so that he would not go on doing it. However, I now know the truth and I know who has been doing this crime, and now my son even admits his wrongdoing, so I leave it to the judgment of this authority to decide what is suitable, because for my part I can tell my son to do this or that when I know he has made a mistake. As his father, I have to help him and look after him, but he should not act this way, disposing of the fruit of my harvest, without my consent."

The presidente intervened here, saying to Clemente, "Now you have heard what your father has said, and I will tell you that your father does not have an obligation to give you, his son, anything, nor is he obliged to give you what is his. If a father loves his son very much, he may give him something, but nobody can force him to do so. Now you have abused him, and, as you have admitted, there is no reason why your father should help you because you have committed this wrong."

Young Clemente Mendoza said again, "I am not asking anything of my papa. He is the one free to decide. I admit having taken the coffee without his consent, and you will have to say how you would like this matter to be settled. I don't want this to go on any longer, but I repeat I am guilty." The presidente, having taken note of all that father and son had declared, and wanting this case to be resolved administratively, asked both parties if they would come to an agreement. They accepted.

The presidente now dictated the following order: "The lost coffee should be restored to the plaintiff, and he should calculate the approximate quantity in kilograms that was lost."

Señor Benjamín Mendoza said, after making a calculation, that there were approximately 25 pounds of dry coffee. "I don't want to say more, because it would not be correct. Many people would do this and sometimes say even much more, but I, for my part, say what I think is suitable; and what I think should be replaced and delivered to me is 25 pounds of dried coffee. With regard to the fine, you are authorized to set it in accordance with the form by which you judge the case." The presidente said the following to young Clemente: "Without delay you have to deliver the coffee, and the deadline is Friday the 21st of this month, and for the wrong you have committed, I impose on you a 200 peso fine, which you have to pay today." When defendant Clemente Mendoza heard of the fine and of the coffee that he had to deliver to his father, he assented and paid the fine. After that he said, "In case I cannot keep my promise regarding the coffee, my father has the right to claim it from me again."

Since both parties had been informed about the agreement and of the fine imposed by the presidente, the document between father and son was formalized. The presidente then cautioned the litigants, especially young Clemente Mendoza, that he should not inflict reprisals on his father or stepmother and should realize that the plaintiff had the right, as a father, to correct any of his faults, and that he, as a son, should ask his father for full permission to harvest some coffee or to dispose of some of his father's interests, in order to avoid being offensive to his father and stepmother in his father's house, and to behave as a good son is supposed to behave.

With regard to the part of the agreement relating to the father, the presidente said: "Whenever he wanted to, he could dispose of something and give it to his son, help him in mutual agreement, guide him in all work he might undertake, but in fact the father does not have any obligation to give his son anything; and on the other hand, the son cannot demand from his father to be given any interests. It is entirely in the hands of the father whether he wants to give or not."

After this disposition was repeated by the presidente and both parties again agreed, the present act of investigation and consent was cleared. It then being 11:35 of the same day, the participants signed.

Case 36. Case of the policía. The police of this town were assembled to testify before the public about a quarrel in the bar called La Frontera. One of the policemen had been bitten on the arm by Victoriano Bautista, and another policeman said that Victoriano had hit him a great blow. Victoriano had come to the bar with Horacio Domínguez.

The presidente asked why Victoriano had hit and bitten the policemen.

All [the police] said that the night before they had taken Victoriano's brother Miguel from the bar because he had insulted the police. "When we went out of the bar with Miguel Bautista because of the disorder he had started, we met Benigno León, who said that he would vouch for Miguel. Benigno started to impose himself on us; we saw it was useless and that he [Benigno] wanted to free him [Miguel] by force, so we took him, too, into prison, and he did not care what was happening to him, and he started an argument."

But a few minutes later the chief of the section came into the courtroom and declared: "Last night I went to the bar in order to see that they closed it, as it was already very late; there came out Miguel Bautista completely drunk, 'You all go to hell, go away—all of you—and your presidente.' He tried to kick me but did not touch me; then I called my companions with a whistle in order to get help, and once the other policemen came, we took Miguel Bautista, and near the house of Martín Elías we met Benigno, who said he would be responsible for his friend and why were we taking him away? After a while Miguel's friends and his brother Victoriano came [to the municipio] and they raised hell so that we should be forced to let Miguel and Benigno go, and they were vouching for Miguel. Victoriano did not talk like decent people do, he started to insult us, and he bit my companion and delivered a blow in the face to another. All the policemen said the same thing; if Victoriano and Miguel's friends had come with good words, as had Horacio Domínguez and Miguel's papa, it would have been different because we police are also decent people, but the way they did it, they hit and insulted us—and we would not accept this. Then there came Pepe [another friend of Miguel's], and he said that he had enough money to put down as a guarantee and we should let Miguel go. But we did not let him go free, and they were disgusted and told us they would make a note of this and would take revenge."

The presidente now had been informed of the complaint the policemen had against Señor Miguel Bautista, who had been arrested and in prison since the night before, together with Señor Benigno León.

At 10:30 of the same day, the presidente asked Miguel Bautista why there had been a scandal the night before and why he and his friends had insulted the policemen and the municipal authority, as the policemen had testified was their behavior. Señor Miguel Bautista answered, "We did not insult them. All were drunk, and I want the policemen to come here and say it." Then the policemen entered, and the chief of police said that Señor Celedonio [the section chief] had told him to go to the bar to see that it was closed, when Miguel Bautista came out and insulted and kicked him. Miguel Bautista then said, "It is not true. The bar was already closed and as soon as the policeman arrived he started to whistle, . . . and a policeman said Miguel was talking with us." Miguel said that as soon as the police arrived they whistled and one policeman said that the bar was not closed. The chief of police said, "Look, Señor Presidente, what these men did last night and see how they bit the arm of this policeman." (The policeman showed his left arm, which had a big mark on it.) Miguel retorted, "Look, Señor Presidente,

A Talean woman selling panela at the large Monday market, which brings merchants from surrounding areas to Talea. Some women are regulars in the market; others sell their produce seasonally or occasionally when they are in need of cash.

Juquilans celebrating a fiesta, an opportunity for reunion in the town center for inhabitants, who spend most of their time on homesteads scattered in the mountains.

Mother and daughter in Talea; the sharing of time and space while carrying out daily chores creates an atmosphere of confidence between mothers and daughters, who rarely end up in court on opposite sides.

The church in Talea, said to have been copied by Taleans from a picture. Buildings from the pre-Hispanic remains at Mitla to contemporary structures testify to Zapotec architectural skill and ingenuity.

The processing of sugarcane to make panela brings family groups from the town center to an area several hundred feet below. Tepache, an alcoholic beverage made of panela and pulque, contributes to the spirit of festivity.

Oxen are used to crush the canes. Usually the animals are borrowed or rented during the springtime harvest and processing period.

Preparing timber for house building usually requires the work of two men—one an employer (*jefe*) and the other an employee (*mozo*). Wood is scarce in Talea, although neighboring Juquila is rich in timber. Courtesy of Odyssey.

Making and selling posonke in Talea's Monday market is woman's work and one way to raise cash. Posonke is a refreshing drink made of boiled corn water and *pinole* (cereal meal), *cacao*, and *cocolmecatl*.

In the 1950's and 1960's, the orchestra in Talea was directed by a talented musician, who was also a composer. The group has received special recognition from the governor of the state for its excellence on several occasions. The orchestra members are occupationally diverse; many of them are craftsmen and store owners. They think of themselves as progressive in their acceptance of state-organized development plans.
Courtesy of Odessey.

The band in Talea is composed principally of campesinos who are prone to caution in dealings with the outside and conservative about plans for development. Every village in the Rincón area has at least one band and quite often two, representing different political factions. Only Talea has an orchestra. Courtesy of Odyssey.

Musicians are role models for young Talean men, and both the band and the orchestra are male peer groups. The comraderie within each group is very powerful. Courtesy of Odyssey.

Food, clothing, tools, and animals are sold in the marketplace. The market is also an occasion for social exchange: people from different villages of the region beyond the Rincón meet, become involved in trading relations, create bonds of ritual kinship, and sometimes fight. Courtesy of Odyssey.

The municipio in Talea is an imposing building, which, like the church, was built over a span of many years and by many people earlier in this century. The first floor houses the offices of the presidente, the sindico, and the alcalde, as well as the jail. The second floor was at one time used for classrooms. The municipio is primarily a hall of justice at the center of Talean life. Courtesy of Odyssey.

The space in front of the municipio is used for festivities and evening town meetings. It also serves as a volleyball court and on Mondays as the marketplace.

This view from Talea toward Matahombres and the Villa Alta district center fails to evoke the difficulty of the six- to eight-hour walk that faces litigants wishing to appeal a case to the district court.

The work of the anthropologist has to be a cooperative endeavor with the people she has come to live with. The question of who is constructing anthropological theory is still a problematic one.

A passing exchange between a man and a Juquilan woman on her way to market can be an opportunity for flirtation. Courtesy of Odyssey.

Four generations of Talean women wearing different clothing styles indicate the successive periods of contact with the outside world. It is not uncommon for Talean women to wear the various styles one on top of another, with the aboriginal wrap-around skirt covered by a fuller European-style skirt or contemporary European-style dress. Courtesy of Odyssey.

A Talean husband and wife in front of their house. Spouses remain at a distance from one another in public. It was not uncommon in 1957, when this picture was taken, for a woman to go barefoot and for a man to wear huaraches, which were necessary for walks to distant fields. Men were fast exchanging the traditional *calzón* for trousers, and women were beginning to favor dresses over skirts and blouses. Courtesy of Odyssey.

last night when they brought me here they stole from me 50 pesos which I had in my pocket. I don't know which one of them took it out of my pocket." The presidente said, "Listen, Miguel, last night after the meeting I passed by the house of Luis Huachic, and I myself heard how you insulted me and my secretary. I don't want to oppose you because it is not correct, but I, personally, heard it and you cannot deny it."

The presidente asked the policemen how they wanted the case arranged. The police said it was in his hands how to resolve it. Then the presidente continued to Miguel: "You admit your mistake, so I authorize you to pay 50 pesos, so that you will be careful next time." Miguel asked to pay only 20. The presidente would not accept this and repeated what the policemen had said. Miguel answered, "The policemen are to blame, too; they were drunk." The presidente replied, "It is not possible that they were drunk because at the meeting all were all right; not one of them was drunk."

Then Benigno repeated that Maurilio should come and testify. Maurilio, the policeman, arrived and said that Benigno had vouched for his companion, and he found out enough—Benigno was also drunk. Maurilio continued to Benigno: "You started with threats. Had you been reasonable, nobody would have said anything to you, Benigno." "I made threats because they hit me," said Benigno. Miguel said, "They tore my shirt, and the policemen hit me with a stick." Presidente to Benigno: "Listen, son, for the mistake you made I fine you 15 pesos—." Benigno: "I won't pay anything because they first did damage to me." Presidente to Benigno: "Why did you get mixed up with this? It was none of your business. When one is doing a favor like this, it always comes out against us." Benigno: "Yes, that is true, but I could not leave my companion." Presidente: "With reason, yes, but not with menaces. Horacio came and spoke decently and they intervened, speaking reasonably as friends do." Benigno: "They grabbed me and hit me, tell me why? So that it hinders me at work because the hand hurts me. I am delicate, and it is quite painful. It is not swollen, but the hand hurts." Presidente: "In any case, you will have to pay a fine of 15 pesos."

At that point Miguel interrupted and asked that the matter be arranged, and he said he would give 40 pesos and asked that they not bother his companion. Benigno: "I won't pay for anything because they already have seized me and beaten me." Presidente: "It is the sanction which I impose on you so that another time when there is a dispute among drunks, you should [know] not to take part and get involved or so engaged." Benigno: "Now I know for the next time. But the policemen already have beaten me and put me into jail; they already have made justice twice." Presidente: "To arrange this matter, I will give you another fine, 10 pesos, so that you don't insist [argue] any more; Miguel must pay 40 pesos, and you must pay 10 pesos." They agreed and said they would come back and pay. The presidente said that was impossible, but they said, "Yes, we will come back and pay. We will do that and not go somewhere else with the 40 pesos." They begged and said they would bring the money the next day. The presidente gave them permission to pay the next day, and they left.

Then the policemen came again and said that Victoriano should be called because it was he who had bitten one policeman's arm and struck another. They threatened, "If you don't arrange this matter, we all could quit being policemen." The presidente then cited Victoriano Bautista to respond to the charges of the policemen and ordered that Victoriano be called. He answered that he would appear in the afternoon because he was selling meat [he was a butcher] and nobody could replace him.

When the defendant Victoriano appeared, he said: "It is true. I came Sunday night to see what had happened and not knowing that it was my brother who was arrested. I came with Horacio, and when I arrived, one of the policemen said, 'Now comes the other one.' I thought I would complain to you, for all were drunk. They did any amount of bad things to me and hit me with the stick. I have the marks on my shoulder where Marcelino had hit me and one of Zoloaga's. Zoloaga was very drunk. I had my provocation, but I didn't bite; besides, I know I cannot bite. I was not doing anything. I did not get angry. Etziquio was the worst; he used his stick, and no matter how troubled one becomes, one has to be able to realize what one is doing. I know I have not beaten anyone. When somebody does a certain thing, naturally one has to admit it. They [police] were pleased when we arrived, but they did not expect us to speak up."

Marcelino, the policeman, answered, "When you hit me, I was not drunk." Victoriano said to the presidente: "If you want to continue the investigation, we can go on, but it is not likely that they will tell the truth. I repeat that when I arrived with Horacio I was fine. I repeat, I won't compromise myself for anything. If you want this to be settled here, we will arrange it. If we cannot, continue until later; I can go on until they realize this and don't come back later with the same things. All the police have done the same—they never wait until one explains to them." Horacio said, in effect, "I arrived with Victoriano. The policemen whistled, but we didn't know they were going to bring us out of the bar, and later we knew it, and his brother Miguel and I spoke to them reasonably and wanted them in turn to be reasonable, but they did not want to be. I even promised to vouch for Miguel if they would agree not to present the case." The presidente then said, "If you, Victoriano, recognize your culpability, we can settle this matter here." "All right," said Victoriano, "so be it. Tomorrow I shall come and pay." "It can't be," said the presidente. "You have to sign a promissory note first, and then you can come to pay when I so order." After signing a promissory note in favor of the authority, Victoriano Bautista and Horacio Domínguez were given permission to leave. The matter was hereby closed, 12 hours after the case began. The amount of the fine was not recorded.

The Presidente's Court

The presidente's court has but few formalities: men take their hats off upon entering the court; the plaintiff sits to the right of the presidente, who is sitting, and the defendant is placed in front of the presidente; when a new case interrupts one that is being heard, the presidente stands up behind his desk to receive the case. In fact the proceedings are often interrupted by people who have administrative business. The presidente, upon being presented with a complaint, attempts to settle it immediately. The litigants may present their case quietly or vociferously. To Western eyes, the time spent in court seems interminably long and disproportionate to the amount of action that takes place there, but that is because the untutored eye sees very little of the "action." Many of these cases are linked to previous conflicts known to the presidente. Part of the "action" is giving the parties time to think, time for different points of view to take shape.

The presidente is a citizen, not a professional, giving his year of service to his fellow Taleans. Whether he spends most of his time hearing cases or doing other work depends on his reputation and his personal style. He decides cases without using written law, resolving conflict by minimizing the sense of injustice and outrage felt by the parties to a case. Ideally, his investigation of the facts is nondirective and flexible; there are no rigid rules of evidence. The presidente's stance, when patient, encourages litigants to decide what issues should be discussed and to present both real and abstract evidence to support their claims; there is no concept of objective truth. In family cases he is more likely to be directive and paternalistic and seeks to remind kinfolk of their responsibilities to the community. He is expected to use what he knows of town affairs and is theoretically selected for such knowledge. The presidente is expected to render a verbal and written agreement for each case—an agreement that town consensus would consider equitable. He is not expected to explain the basis of his decision. Legal documents do include the litigants' statements, the agreement, and/or a statement mentioning the fine, if any. It is what happens to the litigants that is central to the legal documents, not the reasoning of the judge in the case.

Although both parties have to agree on the decision, the "compromise" is not always a result of mutual concessions because it is the presidente who, after listening to the case, decides where the middle ground is or encourages the litigants to make their own agreement. And the decision is often the presidente's understanding of what is best for "making the balance"—which often means the restoration of relations to a former condition of harmony where conflict was absent.

However, it is sometimes difficult to perceive that any decision-making process is going on. There are often long periods of waiting during a hearing; then suddenly a decision is made, and the discussion turns to implementation. The best way to "make the balance" in the policía case was to fine rather than ask for damages, which the defendants would have interpreted as adding insult to injury, and which surely would have caused them to appeal the case. The punitive fines go to the third party—the presidente's office. In this same case, the presidente sought to reestablish a condition of relative peace between the litigants and at the same time to prevent escalation of the conflict to feud proportions. In the case of the bruised chiles (no. 32) and in the case of the little boy with fright (no. 33), damages paid to the plaintiff were considered the best way to restore the earlier conditions of peace and harmony, and advice was given to prevent conflict from breaking out again. In both these cases, the litigants did not share a common residence in Talea. In the domestic dispute (no. 34), the presidente thought that neither damages nor punitive fines would aid in restoration of peace, but conflict over the division of property would be eliminated if both husband and wife returned to a normal marital state presumably devoid of dispute.

In the father-son case (no. 35), the presidente was least successful in finding a harmonious solution. The decision was punitive—both restitution and a fine, an attempt to encourage the son to act like one. The immediate dispute that gave rise to the theft was the unwillingness of the father to pay the brideprice for his son. The presidente could not handle such a dispute because, as he himself said, "This is not a legal question." Had the father not already given the son the equivalent of brideprice several times over, he would certainly have enjoined the father as to his moral obligations, as he did in the husband-wife case. Settlement and prevention of recurrent conflict are the tasks of the court, and even punishment is meted out with this in mind. The principle of vengeance cannot dominate even when, as in the policía case (no. 36), the presidente personally feels strongly disinclined to accept the defendant's arguments.

The presidente's role is that of mediator, adjudicator, and group therapist, depending on case requirements. His principal function seems to be to listen, often asking questions to clear up contradictions and pointing the way to a more harmonious condition. He usually does not cross-examine, but rather allows the litigants to spell out their arguments. In this way he brings out the nature of the conflict, the basis of the points at issue. The contenders talk about anything they consider relevant, without the presidente attempting to confine the discussion to the original charges. Points of fact are not definitely settled; matters of fault are not pursued to a conclusion. Implicitly at least, all parties realize that what is important in settling disputes is not what is "objectively so" but rather what the two sides perceive as being so. So fault-finding and fact-finding are considerably played down, unlike the property cases brought before the sindico, as we shall see. One has the feeling that what is going on in the presidente's court is more expressive and less game-like.

In each case the presidente offers the litigants advice about avoiding recurrences—to watch where the truck passes through the marketplace; to reconcile family differences and to respect the traditional family roles of husband and wife or father and son; to consider working at a different place if the present one is uncomfortable; to be cautious about helping drunken friends when they get themselves in trouble; to make peace.

Time brings changes in the Talean presidente's court. Over nine years I noticed a change in types of cases, a change in direction toward more family cases, more assault and battery cases, and fewer property cases. Over this same period some things do not change. Settlements during any one week vary from adjudication to mediation, and the decisions may be punitive or restrictive, compromising or adjudicative, but certain features do not vary.

1. A legally constituted official who recognizes norms and interests hears the case.

2. The procedure is seen as a way of finding out the real basis for the trouble.

3. The principals may exchange positions as rulings are made on other than original claims.

4. It is not necessary to establish past facts or to establish guilt. Reasoning is prospectively oriented, that is, directed toward future harmony rather than past misconduct.

5. The goal of the court officials is to have parties compose their differences; the principle of give-a-little-get-a-little rather than winner-take-all prevails.

6. Compromise may prevail even if the decision is winner-take-all and either/or.

7. Utilitarian thinking is valued. The decisions of the court emanate from the characteristics of the village network of relations. Greater social relevance is considered in solving a particular dispute.

8. The decision is agreed upon by the litigants and backed by the force of the municipio if necessary.

What Relationships Generate Style?

Theories explaining court style have accumulated over time, and each theory usually puts forth a favorite variable. Analyses based on interaction theories are insightful and complement approaches that examine courts using culture theory to delineate style as emanating from ideologies far more pervasive and interpenetrating than social relationships. Indeed ideologies may mold social relationships.

Beginning with the work of Maine (1861) and later Gluckman (1955), the forms of dispute resolution have been explained by the characteristics of the relations between the litigants—simplex or multiplex, broad or narrow, continuing or noncontinuing—all seem to be causally associated with different models of dispute management. It seems obvious that those in continuing relationships will seek negotiated or mediated settlements with compromise outcomes (Nader and Todd 1978; Gulliver 1979). Although such an explanation is insufficient, family relationships may give rise to disputes over inheritance or equally they may act as a constraint on escalation. In situations in which scarce resources form the basis of a dispute (Pound 1959: 70; Starr and Yngvesson 1975), the types of claims may override relationships to directly affect the development of a style. In the context of dual systems of law, issues relating to social integration may outweigh individual interests.

The motives for using dispute mechanisms also affect style, depending on the disputant's degree of dominance, of course. Litigants who use the court as an area in which they can engage in behavior with different meanings may complicate the problem-solving and peacemaking functions of a presidente. Litigants may be willing to lose a skirmish if, in the end, they win the war; a judge may be willing to compromise in a difficult case if the peace of the village is at issue. A decision-maker may be a local-level authority whose loyalties are tied into neither the national system nor the local system of relations, but into personal ambition.

In addition to social and individual variables are cultural variables. Because social scientists disagree over what factors determine the manner of dispute management, it may be useful to ask if all three Talean courts exhibit the same style to see whether considerations are different enough to generate particular components in each court or whether the ideal of harmony permeates all three courts. The fact that cases entering the sindico's court regularly involve scarce resources and represent the interests of the state (since the sindico is the representative of the ministerio publico) may alert us to the role of scarcity or the role of the state in generating disputing styles. The fact that a dispute is brought to the alcalde may be an indication that the parties want to fight it out and are therefore less interested in reconciliation, negotiation, mediation, or any other bargain model (see Van Velson 1969: 149, on the absence of compromise in appeal courts), which would lead one to expect more adjudication in the alcalde's office. By contrast, the purpose of the presidente's court seems to be to encourage the litigants to come to agreement without visual inspection of evidence or the extensive use of witnesses.

The Sindico's Court

In the sindico's court, an air of privacy pervades the initial stages of the hearings. Many of the sindico's cases begin with *se presentaron;* that is, the disputants present themselves, singly, before the sindico for legal advice, much as they would go to a lawyer in the United States for advice on a will. The sindico usually speaks to the plaintiff first and alone and tries to see his or her degree of intransigency, and then does the same with the defendant. If necessary, he then uses *careo* (confrontation) as a fact-finding device, in order to find out what the truth or the lies are, as one sindico put it, and not in order to have the litigants mutually agree. I would not say that reconciliation is unimportant to the sindico, but it is not the only tool he has at his disposal; he can also investigate and establish facts. Certainly this would seem to create a different tone from that in the presidente's court, but it is a matter of degree. The sindico may make references to the *código penal*, and a reading of the cases provides instances in which a sindico has used coercive power. Still, he gives the litigants a chance to "make the balance," but if they do not wish to do so, he has at his disposal techniques that allow him to adjudicate a decision and force a compromise based on his fact-finding, and he is more likely to do so than the presidente.

In the following case a woman from the nearby dependence of Yatoni made a formal complaint against a man from Talea to the ministerio publico in Villa Alta. Since the Talean sindico, like other sindicos, is the representative of the ministerio publico, he was asked to investigate the case and decide whether the complaint had merit.

Case 37. The complaint was made by a 45-year-old spinster from Yatoni against a 55-year-old married man from Talea. The woman accused the man of having stolen her coffee on land that lay between the boundaries of Talea and the municipal agency of Yatoni. Upon being informed of the complaint, the defendant said that it was a false accusation because he had never even stood on the piece of land in question. He also noted that he had previously owned a large coffee parcel in that area, but that he had sold the land during the previous year to a man from Talea. All parties were called to the municipio for a confrontation.

The plaintiff was asked to identify the defendant as the person she was accusing, and she did so. She was asked whether she personally saw the defendant picking coffee, and if he was alone or accompanied, or whether she had obtained this information from another person or persons as eyewitnesses. She answered that she did not see the defendant commit the crime, nor did she have witnesses, but that she supposed that it could not have been anyone else, since she had been disputing with him for years over her piece of land. She was asked on what she based her calculations to determine that she had lost six *arrobas* [150 pounds] of coffee, and she answered that she took as a base what she had gathered from another coffee plot of the same size.

The defendant was then asked, "Is it true or not that you went to steal the coffee from this woman on the 23rd and 24th of January?" The defendant replied that the accusation was totally false, and he requested that the woman be sanctioned for the crime of defamation of honor because he had not gone to said property, and because he had sold the land in question. The new owner, who was in the courtroom, presented the deed to the land he had bought. The new owner was asked whether he had gone to pick coffee during the past month and answered that he had gone on the 21st and 22nd of January with his son to pick coffee. He was asked how much coffee he had cut, and he answered three-quarters of 1 arroba of dry coffee. He was asked if he went again to cut coffee, and answered no, but that on the 5th of February it had been reported to him that two women were in his cafetal. When he went to inspect, he found that someone had indeed been there and that he had suffered a loss of stolen coffee, about a medium-sized basket worth.

Two expert witnesses were present who had inspected the site. They reported that the coffee was in normal state, but affected by an excess of shade, and that the coffee had been picked, an amount equivalent in value to 42 pesos and 75 centavos.

Based upon his investigations, the sindico decided that the theft of which the plaintiff complained was nonexistent and that the said owner of the land was no longer the owner of the land. It was also discovered that the plaintiff had seriously exaggerated the amount of coffee that she indicated had been picked in her coffee site, and that the entire crop her land could produce that year was 3.5 or 4 arrobas. In regard to the land litigation between the plaintiff and the new owner, the sindico recommended that the case should be determined by a competent authority. In conformity with the order from the ministerio publico of Villa Alta, the sindico informed Villa Alta of these preliminary investigations.

Another case handled by the sindico ended in friendly agreement after listening and problem solving with the litigants.

Case 38. The plaintiff appeared before the sindico to complain that the defendant had destroyed some of his property by fire. The plaintiff wanted the defendant held responsible for the fire that had ruined his land and for the theft of two piles of cordwood. The plaintiff also complained that he had not been able to make any friendly agreement with the defendant and in fact found the defendant cutting up some of the burned wood and taking it to repair his neighboring ranch house, which had been ruined by the same fire. The defendant did not appear when summoned, and so the case was postponed.

When the defendant appeared, he admitted that he was the cause of the fire, but he begged the plaintiff as a humanitarian to be lenient with him, because he was known to have no money. The sindico granted the two men an opportunity to arrive at a friendly agreement and at a legal agreement with the owner of the destroyed oak trees. After a quick discussion they arrived at the following agreement. The plaintiff pardoned the defendant from paying for the burned oak trees, but imposed upon him the obligation of giving one day of work, to fell and chop the trees and bushes which had died or were not developing properly because of the fire, and to stack the firewood where the plaintiff could make use of it. He also requested that the defendant pay 60 pesos each for the two cords of wood that had been burned, and to return the wood he had taken to rebuild his ranch house.

They agreed that the defendant should have ten months to pay the 120 pesos he owed. The sindico advised the defendant not to fail to comply, or he would take measures to punish him for *burla de autoridad,* or contempt of court.

The Alcalde's Court

Of the three court officials, the alcalde is the only one whose job is dedicated solely to judicial matters. For reasons I still do not fully understand, the man chosen for the post of alcalde often speaks only Zapotec or is weak in Spanish. A knowledge of Spanish is considered an important qualification for the offices of presidente and sindico, since these men in their administrative capacities so often need to communicate with the "outside." The alcalde does not have these "outside" responsibilities, but the style of his court is remarkably similar to the presidente's court even though the cases often take longer to hear, are often more complicated, and involve a greater number of witnesses and more lengthy testimony. The alcalde would also agree with the saying "A bad agreement is better than a good fight." The following examples illustrate the value placed in the alcalde's court on some kind of agreement, preferably voluntary agreement.

Case 39. A 74-year-old father (with a Zapotec interpreter) presented a complaint against a man whom he accused of physical aggression against his 27-year-old son one evening on a public street of the village. The sindico first heard the complaint and elicited the testimony from the wounded man, the defendant, and a 16-year-old girl who was called as a character witness. Then the sindico passed the case to the alcalde "so that the alcalde might proceed through legal channels as necessary." The crime had been identified as assault with an unknown weapon that left the victim wounded and bloody. The defendant had been apprehended and jailed until two men appeared and requested that he be freed under bond. Upon presenting the case to the alcalde, the sindico stated his opinion of the probable guilt of the defendant. When the alcalde began hearings, the sindico was present, and he participated in the hearing with the alcalde and his respective aides.

Motives for the dispute revolved around an incident between the plaintiff's son and the defendant's wife. The plaintiff's son was accused of breaking into the defendant's home and attempting to abuse his wife, which left her in a state of *susto*, or fright. That incident had led the defendant to attack the plaintiff with a deadly weapon, a broken Coke bottle, and according to him, justified his aggression. The 16-year-old girl presented testimony relating to the wandering eyes of both defendant and plaintiff.

After several days of testimony, the disputants came to an agreement. Both agreed that for mutual convenience they would pardon each other for the offenses they had committed, and asked the authorities to cancel all complaints registered. They also decided that the cost of medical attention should be paid by the wounded one, and concluded by saying: "We beg you, with all due respect, to take note of this agreement, which we have arrived at on the basis of Article no. 106 of the penal code, thus extinguishing the penal action."

Accompanying this agreement was a letter from the leader of the local orchestra, in which he stated that he knew of the quarrel between the parties, that both disputants were members of the Recreation and Labor Orchestra, and as director of the orchestra, he wished to petition the court for a unanimous transaction, an agreement between both parties, that they would not permit the furthering of this quarrel, which could have the effect of disorganizing the orchestra. He added that the orchestra practiced in a house belonging to the defendant, and because of this, he did not want displeasure on the part of the owner of the house or difficulties among the members because of positions taken for or against this particular quarrel.

The alcalde ratified the document of agreement. Because of the petitions the quarrel between the litigants was declared "passed over." Each litigant, however, was required to pay a fine of 30 pesos, to be paid in cash to the municipal treasury for public works.

The father of the victim might not have been so eager to report the assault had he had prior knowledge of the motives at play. Once the case was in the hands of the authorities, however, they had to investigate. As it turned out, the defendant was settling a debt that the victim in part recognized in the agreement. The court in part ratified the defendant's behavior; the law allowed a man to defend his honor (the defendant had balanced the "injustice" committed by his opponent). It may also have been important that the defendant was both well known and relatively wealthy, but the arguments of the orchestra director most certainly carried weight: "Don't escalate. It could polarize the musicians' group. Don't be too harsh on the defendant; we're depending on him for space. Peace."

A second example illustrates a situation in which the disputants are provided with an amicable agreement by the alcalde after a long hearing.

Case 40. The plaintiff complained that the defendant has used his land for planting sugarcane. The defendant claimed that he had used the land with the consent of the son of the owner, although he had no written contract to that effect. An agreement was made whereby the defendant was to deliver a portion of the harvest (3 *pantles* of unrefined brown sugar) to the landowner. The sugarcane and banana plants that had been planted on the property by the defendant were to be left to the owner of the land to do with as he saw fit. This agreement was described as a voluntary arrangement, and the defendant was instructed to discontinue planting on this land.

Cases involving drunkenness are handled in much the same way as in the presidente's court. When the police and a cantina owner accused a man of knifing a customer during a bar brawl, the defendant was found guilty, fined 30 pesos, told not to offend by word or action, and pushed roughly out of the courtroom into the street. If there had been a prior history of hostility, there would have been a more extensive exploration in this case. In a case that involved a drunken man "invading" the home of a woman to whom he had previously been married, the woman's present husband requested (and was granted) reimbursement for the money he had spent at the time of the death of the defendant's son. In paternity cases the alcalde tries to work out equitable agreements. In other words, as with the presidente's court, the requirements of the case as viewed by the participants influence its development. The requirements of the community give preference to agreements that are geared toward harmony.

Talean court style resembles a type of procedure that is situationally determined. Although in the West this type of justice system has usually been described in derogatory terms and wide discretion may be seen as unfair because of the absence of universal standards, many societies hold another view. The Taleans use a fluid rather than a fixed frame for solving social problems, and disputing is seen as just that: a social problem. The evolution of any dispute is a result of its cultural history and the relations over time among a number of participants, only some of whom may be in the courtroom. Remember that for a number of cases, particularly among those heard by the alcalde, the victim is never present in the hearing; family members may initiate cases on behalf of relatives.

Whereas in Western law legal procedure ideally lends itself to a narrowing of the focus for judicial dispute resolution, the Talean process is broadening, encouraging agreement or decision by a back-and-forth hearing of different accounts of the problem. In the case of the orchestra leader, the outsider to the case linked it to wider issues of sociopolitical order, a factor to be weighed. Many times wider issues dominate over individual considerations of justice. However, fact-finding procedures now imposed on the sindico make it less possible for that official to carry out a Talean style of justice, which on occasion is more concerned with wider questions of order and group interest.

Law and Contextual Styles

As I said in the introduction to this chapter, the features of Talean court style have something in common with models presented by anthropologists and sociologists for some other societies (Cohn 1959; Hahm 1967, 1968; Aubert 1969; Gulliver 1969; and Yngvesson as quoted in Nader 1969a). These similarities appear despite great differences in social organization and levels of economic and political development. Why? I was particularly struck by the conclusions to Gulliver's (1969) essay on the Ndendeuli, a society characterized by the absence of third-party decision-makers or courts. Gulliver's conclusions could equally apply to the presidente's court in Talea. He describes the settlement as "typically some kind of negotiated compromise between conflicting claims . . . dependent not only on ideas of norms, rights, and expectations and on the respective bargaining strengths of both principals and their supporters, but also on considerations of its effect on other men's interests and the continuance of neighborly cooperation and concord . . . an agreed settlement accepted by both principals . . . put into effect immediately, if at all possible" (ibid.: 67–68). In Gulliver's book on negotiations

(1979), he contrasts negotiation and adjudication and notes that "a fundamental characteristic of negotiation is the absence of a third-party decision-maker" and that the "paramount distinction between the two modes . . . comes from the fact" (ibid.: 3). In negotiations, he argues, the decision is made jointly by the disputing parties themselves.

For Aubert (quoted in Nader 1969a), the difference in style of dispute settlement is linked to the two kinds of institutions: the court and the administrative agency. Their respective features, listed in Table 3, indicate the similarities in models that have appeared in the social science literature.

To my manner of thinking, it has not been productive to link the mode of dispute management, whether it be adjudication or negotiation, or what Aubert (in Nader 1969b) in a 1966 memo calls "the court model" and the "bargain model," with different kinds of institutions, as does Aubert, or with the presence or absence of third parties, as does Gulliver in his book on negotiations (1979). The style of dispute settlement needs to be viewed independently of formal expression by a court or agency. The examples of a study of the Berkeley and Oakland, California, small claims courts, which, respectively, had a bargain model and a court model, that I cite in my original paper on styles of court procedure (Nader 1969b) made that point. Looking at cases in the Talean presidente's court from an internalist perspective suggests that situational factors determine

TABLE 3

Two Styles of Dispute Settlement

Court model	Bargain model (linked to administrative agency)
Triad	Dyad
Coercive power	No coercive power
Application of norms highly valued	Pursuit of interests (values)
Establishment of past facts	Establishment of past facts not necessary
Retroactively oriented reasoning	Prospectively oriented reasoning
Legal experts participate	No legal experts participate
Conclusion is a verdict	Conclusion is an agreement
Purely distributive decisions	Distributive/generative decisions
Either/or decision	Compromise
Reaffirmation of legal cases	No necessary implication concerning validity
Affinity to legal scholarship	Affinity to science or utilitarian thinking

whether the third party decides the case or whether there is a joint decision by the litigants in spite of the presence or absence of a third party. Talean *ideas* about order and disorder appear to be critical elements. As we see later, a focus on the case is too narrow to reveal the full complexity of style. Court styles are an internal accommodation to European conquest that has grown out of, and that has constructed, Talean values of harmony, mutual aid, social order, equity, prevention of escalation, and village growth and solidarity. An analysis of social relations may explain the case but not the overall style.

This chapter should have informed the reader of the operation of three courts that share the objective of defusing, problem-solving, and sometimes forcing harmony. Scholars working in regions where two or more legal traditions come into contact often describe the situation as one of conflicting systems resulting in disintegrated and disorganized societies. The Talean system is neither disintegrated nor disorganized. Over a period of some 400 years, its people have evolved a court style that supports village autonomy. The ties of village law to the larger district and state system is an indicator of one part of the network of communication between federal, state, and local governments. Contrary to my experience in Lebanon (Nader 1965a), the remote Oaxacan situation has allowed local rural peoples to operate in a semiautonomous situation that discourages dependency on the state.

Chapter Eight

Dissecting Cases to Understand Court Users

Legal historians have noticed that the litigation process in Western courts may be either marginal or central to society. In discussing U.S. legal history, Willard Hurst (1981) observed that nineteenth-century state court business involved only limited sectors of American society. He also observed that the array of litigating parties changed little from the nineteenth to the twentieth century: in both centuries people of small means were seldom plaintiffs except in tort or family matters (ibid.: 421).

Comparison with other times and places helps in assessing the significance of court use patterns. Sixteenth-century Castilian society was a setting in which courts were used by a wide array of people with an equally wide array of problems, and the courts reflected a diverse population and their needs (Kagan 1981). Kagan uses this example to explain the evolution and devolution of litigation patterns. The primary-court records of several African nations show a declining rate of civil litigation over a 25-year period (Abel 1979). Abel argues that as the courts became more Westernized, they became less accessible—a fact he finds predictable, given the change from precapitalist to capitalist modes of production. Westermark (1986), on the other hand, provides an example from Papua New Guinea where village courts have mixed formal and informal processes that are widely used.

Information on the users of courts or their functional equivalents in non-Western societies has been sporadic. The bias toward the belief that non-Western societies are homogeneous has in the past led researchers to focus on commonalities rather than variety. In addition, the Western bias that courts are top-down institutions where decisions are determined by judges formally trained in law has not always granted non-Western litigants (and indeed Western litigants) their sociological significance in determining what the law is to be. An understanding of the users of Talean courts and of the court as a place of interaction is central to any understanding of the basis and direction of village law. In this and the following chapter, I profile the users and leave to later chapters analysis of the social life of the people as reflected in case materials.

Who are the users of Talean courts? I should begin by explaining what I mean by "use" and "user." The concept of use is related to ideas of social function and individual need. Dictionary definitions that include both the idea of "availing oneself of" and "converting to one's service" are helpful because they indicate that the concept of use need not be static. In this chapter, facts about court use and users are stated numerically. I draw on these samples to reveal the regular and irregular patterns of action by court users, identifying them by sex, age, relationship, and class, and indicating what they use the courts for and how sanction is applied. A profile of change or continuity in the status of court users over a ten-year period may provide an empirical base indicator of change and drift in a legal system, or of nonchange and continuity.

In looking at cases, I intend to find out who uses the Talean courts and for what, and in the process to determine whether the court system can be described as an institution central or marginal to Talean society. The concepts "marginal" and "central" refer not to whether the actors in the court are present in proportion to their numbers in the population (although in some cases, as in the numbers of males and females, they are), but rather to the degree to which the categories in the population are represented in court use. Implicit is a hypothesis about how law grows and changes. If all the users of Talean courts participate in making law, and if the users reflect the diversity of the population, then the law can maintain a generality of function close to the daily round of life. In addition, legitimacy will be ensured. If the array of users and use is a narrow one, then conditions of social stress, such as the divergence between cultural values and practice, or a conflict between cultural values, may lead to a crisis of legitimacy in the law.

The Talean court is a place where resources are gathered and competed for. The spirit in the court is tenacious, if anything. Town government officials as users see both plaintiff and defendant as potential sources of funds and labor for town projects, and by virtue of their mandate to protect citizens from violence and predation, they see the court as a source of legitimation for their authority, which maintains the peace. Plaintiffs use the court to make people do what they want (to empower and legitimize their requests for appropriate behavior by relations or friends), to gain compensation, and to dispense another resource of the court, punishment. Defendants, although often unwilling participants, use the court as an asylum, a safe place in which to vent their anger, a place to rebuild their damaged reputations by fair and accommodating behavior, and as a means by which they may reduce the potential resources of the local court by appealing to the district court, thereby undermining local authority. All these uses are manifestly expressed, and of course there are more.

In the discussion on social organization in Chapter 3, hierarchy, symmetry, and cross-linkage were found to be important dimensions of a Talean Zapotec's worldview. All three dimensions are used and recognized in courtroom encounters. The presence of a respected third-party authority indicates hierarchy. The function of the court as a leveling institution ideally contributes to the reduction of asymmetry, or situations of inappropriate inequality (as in relationships defined in terms of reciprocal rights and responsibilities). Linkage, of course, is provided in the courtroom style, which contributes to community building by strategies that cool hostilities and emphasize a middle ground. But what is the role of court user in defining this kind of court? Is the model an impositional or an interactive one? Are court decisions judicial decisions or something more? In a word, are the users of law in Talea making the law?

A Note About Cases

All ethnographic fieldworkers collect cases, no matter what their focus of interest. The basic approach is simply to examine particulars prior to, or as part of, forming generalized conclusions. To date, the most systematic and conscious use of the case method has been by ethnographers working in the fields of law and medicine. Case materials are used, for example, to ascertain dominant patterns (as in the analysis of statistically large samples), to discover the configurations of cases, or to illustrate particular points relevant to broader analyses (as with the analysis of single cases). Thus far in my analysis, numbers have only rarely been mentioned, and in this sense my work has followed the tradition of ethnographers of law who have worked in areas where it is difficult to collect large and consecutive samples of law cases.

This chapter makes use of 409 cases, all collected from the presidente, sindico, and alcalde courts during the period 1957–68 (see Table 4). Preliminary analysis indicated that these cases could be used as a set without differentiating according to year. Some of these materials were copied from the records by myself or my assistants, and these are part of the formal record; others were recorded during firsthand observation over long periods of time and are more extended and conversational, and occasionally downright confusing. In cases taken from the record, unexplained names may appear, and kin terms shift with the speaker. To the extent that the cases are "cleaned up," we lose an aspect of law in Talea in order to gain "clarity." In two places in this chapter, I use subsets of the larger set of 409 cases. The analysis of class relies solely on the 80 cases from the alcalde court in 1959 because I had supplemental social and economic data on the disputants from this period. I also use a subset of 216 cases for an analysis of repeat offenders. I selected these cases because they have been translated into English. These 216 cases represent certain years' actions and courts (Table 5).

TABLE 4

Number of Cases by Type of Court, 1957–1968

Year	Presidente	Alcalde	Sindico	Total by year
1957	62	—	—	62
1959	—	80	—	80
1960	39	39	34	112
1961	—	23	10	33
1962	—	—	20	20
1964	40	—	—	40
1965	9	24	19	52
1968	10	—	—	10
TOTAL	160	166	83	409

TABLE 5

Translated Cases by Type of Court, 1957–1965

Year	Presidente	Alcalde	Sindico	Total by year
1957	62	—	—	62
1960	—	34	39	73
1961	—	2	23	25
1964	6	—	—	6
1965	20	20	10	50
TOTAL	88	56	72	216

Although we all might agree that a corpus of cases is a useful means of checking on observation and intuition, use of case materials runs into problems and raises questions that make our findings, at best, provisional. The cases recorded in Talea follow a protocol dictated by the district court; this sometimes results in separating the various parts of a case into hearings (*diligencias*), decisions (*actas*), and agreements (*convenios*). When we copied court records, we sometimes could not find all the parts to a single case; for example, we might have access to the records of hearings but not to actas and convenios for a particular year. This means that for some cases we have no information on the outcome of a case, or we may not know the age of the plaintiff or defendant. In presenting this material, we simply treat such lacunae as missing data.

Furthermore, it is clear that not all case activity was recorded. Whether cases were or were not recorded may have depended on the energy of the secretaries whose job it was to type up the cases. It may also have depended on whether the town officials wanted anybody to know about the cases or whether the town's involvement in building a road or the airport left officials no time for paperwork. Another example of complication at the district court level was the Villa Alta judge who excluded intergenerational kin cases from the docket and from settlement when the plaintiff was younger than the defendant, as happened when a daughter took her mother to court. Fieldwork and participant observation, in particular, are important for discovering these types of systematic recording biases. I alert the reader where I think such a bias was operating in recording cases. In spite of such complications, it is astonishing that the record-keeping was as good as it was. In comparison with such activities almost anywhere, the Taleans are responsible recordkeepers.

Those of us who recorded or transcribed the over 400 cases tried to be consistent and complete, but we included some information and excluded other data from the case, no matter how conscientious we were. This is not particularly worrisome if one is aware that what is included or excluded follows a pattern; we must know something about the pattern of selection. In Talea, my first recorded case materials fairly consistently missed any extended record of outcome or consequence that resulted after a case was concluded in court, the metalanguage such as gestures used by court participants, any mention of the amount of time the case took, or the social consequences of a court decision. Film was later added as a recording medium. When I first viewed the footage of the cases we filmed for *To Make the Balance* (Nader 1966a), I was surprised to realize that somehow sitting in the courtroom and attempting to write down whatever I could about what was going on was not conducive to seeing the case proceedings as a whole. Students in the classroom also mentioned that the film gave them a view of what the proceedings were "really like" that was different from my earlier written summaries of case materials. With these limitations in mind, I will proceed by noting the problems we encountered in coding the cases.

The process of resolving conflict in Talea affords room for maneuverability at every point. Individuals may enter a case in the role of witness, but as the case proceeds, they may begin to add their own complaints to the record and in this way become plaintiffs. A person may take a case to court and be greeted by a countercomplaint and end up the defendant. Even the decision reached at the end of the case is not necessarily the one implemented. This maneuverability often works to the advantage of court users, and it is an essential characteristic of courtroom practice in Talea. In recording cases, however, I recorded the positions and complaints to reflect the Talean view of the litigants as defendants or plaintiffs. All complaints presented in the case at any point were recorded; a person who moved from the position of witness to that of plaintiff by the end of the case was recorded as a plaintiff in the code. Thus, coding the data unfortunately smoothes out ambiguities.

Other aspects of the case material lost in coding are the references to morals and values that accompany so many arguments and decisions. Court officials use the courtroom as a forum to instruct people in the community in their duties and obligations toward one another. There is no way to analyze these cultural elements of the court proceedings quantitatively, although they are crucial to understanding courtroom dynamics. These qualitative dimensions of law in Talea integrate the courts into the cultural system, and an aberrant case, a case that does not fit the code, may be the event that triggers change. Despite wide margins of error, what can we find out about users from our count?

Who Uses the Courts

In analyzing case samples I looked at sex, age, class, and relationship, since these characteristics are thought important by theorists of Western criminal law. I wished to find out whether men or women are more likely to avail themselves of the court's remedies, to discover the ages of court users, to test hypotheses about court remedies among the land-rich and land-poor citizens of Talea, and to examine the degree to which recidivism is a pattern and an issue in deciding cases. The case samples furnish us with some sense of the status of citizen users of governmental law and as such enable us to picture more clearly the place of the courts in the lives of these people.

Sex of Users

Although men and women have different status and rank in Talea, they both use the courts, and as we shall see, patterns of court use are fairly consistent and clear-cut by sex. Table 6 illustrates the sex of plaintiffs in the three courts. I was interested in the number of women plaintiffs because there is widespread agreement that urban Zapotec women claim and exercise their rights with ease (Chinas 1973; Royce 1974), and because the number of women who contest cases in Talean courts appears to be high from a cross-cultural perspective, suggesting that Talean women are not totally subordinated by men.

The overall proportion of males and females who use the courts as plaintiffs is relatively equal. Those who appear as plaintiffs are often those without recourse to family members who would be their first resort. In the presidente court, 32 percent of the plaintiffs were male and 45 percent were female. The distribution for the alcalde court is the same for both sexes—46 percent. The sindico court is almost the

TABLE 6

Plaintiffs by Type of Court, 1957–1968

	Presidente		Alcalde		Sindico		
Category of user	No. of cases	Percent of total	No. of cases	Percent of total	No. of cases	Percent of total	Total cases
Male	49	32%	84	46%	38	45%	171
Female	69	45	85	46	29	34	183
State	23	15	5	3	8	10	36
Couple	1	1	3	2	2	2	6
Nonadversarial female	7	4	2	1	1	1	10
Nonadversarial male	2	1	2	1	5	6	9
Nonadversarial group	1	1	—	—	—	—	1
Adversarial group	1	1	2	1	2	2	5
TOTAL	153	100%	183	100%	85	100%	421

TABLE 7
Defendants by Type of Court, 1957–1968

Category of user	Presidente		Alcalde		Sindico		Total cases
	No. of cases	Percent of total	No. of cases	Percent of total	No. of cases	Percent of total	
Male	124	73%	133	73%	62	64%	319
Female	36	21	43	23	23	24	102
State	2	1	—	—	3	3	5
Couple	—	—	—	—	1	1	1
Nonadversarial female	2	1	1	1	1	1	4
Nonadversarial male	6	4	4	2	5	5	15
Nonadversarial group	—	—	—	—	—	—	—
Adversarial group	—	—	2	1	2	2	4
TOTAL	170	100%	183	100%	97	100%	450

exact opposite of the presidente court, with 45 percent of the plaintiffs being male and 34 percent female. The state brings few cases to any of the three courts, and in all three courts an even smaller percentage of cases are nonadversarial, by which I mean the court is involved in routine tasks such as recording a transfer of land or legitimizing an agreement already reached by the disputing parties. The rare cases listed as being brought by an adversarial group reflect actions taken by a group of neighbors or townspeople against an individual or another group. These cases may develop around conflicts over land or water rights or may reflect conflicts involving physical violence between groups. Most of the cases brought to the village courts, however, are brought by males and females as individuals.

If we look at defendants who "use the courts" (Table 7), the pattern is also clear: men use the courts as defendants in greater proportion than do women. Individual and adversarial males account for 73 percent of the defendants in both the presidente and alcalde court and 64 percent of the defendants in the sindico court. The numbers are in one sense skewed because Talean males drink in public whereas Talean women do not, but both males and females visiting from neighboring villages drink in public. This drinking pattern means that men in general are more vulnerable to being charged with drunkenness in public, but only women from neighboring Zapotec villages are vulnerable to the charge.

Age of Users

Age is a second characteristic of the user regarded as important by students of Western criminal law. In the United States in recent years, the delinquency age has moved down the age line to include pre-teenage children. This is not true in Talea. There, people seem to get into trouble with their fellow citizens and with town officials primarily between the ages of 31 and 50 (see Tables 8 and 9), and pre-teens are rarely users of the court as plaintiffs or defendants.

In the presidente court, for example, 63 percent of the plaintiffs

TABLE 8

Age of Plaintiff by Type of Court, Selected Years, 1957–1965

Age	Presidente		Alcalde		Sindico		Total
	No. of plaintiffs	Percent of total	No. of plaintiffs	Percent of total	No. of plaintiffs	Percent of total	
11–20	2	2%	2	2%	—	—	4
21–30	9	11	22	19	8	19%	39
31–40	31	37	27	23	10	24	68
41–50	22	26	28	24	14	33	64
51–60	9	11	14	12	4	10	27
61–70	7	8	16	14	3	7	26
71–80	3	4	8	6	3	7	14
81–90	1	1	—	—	—	—	1
TOTAL	84	100%	117	100%	42	100%	243

NOTE: Data collected in 1957, 1959, 1960, 1964, 1965.

TABLE 9

Age of Defendant by Type of Court, Selected Years, 1957–1965

Age	Presidente		Alcalde		Sindico		Total
	No. of defendants	Percent of total	No. of defendants	Percent of total	No. of defendants	Percent of total	
11–20	2	8%	3	3%	2	3%	7
21–30	6	25	15	13	11	17	32
31–40	8	33	35	30	20	32	63
41–50	4	17	32	28	10	16	46
51–60	—	—	17	15	14	22	31
61–70	4	17	6	5	5	8	15
71–80	—	—	6	5	1	2	7
81–90	—	—	1	1	—	—	1
TOTAL	24	100%	115	100%	63	100%	202

NOTE: Data collected in 1957, 1959, 1960, 1964, 1965.

are between the ages of 31 and 50. This same age group accounts for 47 percent of the plaintiffs in the alcalde court and 57 percent of the plaintiffs in the sindico's court. A similar pattern holds for the defendants in all three courts. The 31–50 age group accounts for approximately half of all defendants.

There is no clear-cut explanation for this cluster, but there are some indications. During the years when adults lose their parents, and when their own family responsibilities are greatest, court use is high. Yet, the nonappearance in court of parties under 20 does not necessarily mean that young people have few serious problems. Families and teachers serve as efficient remedy agents for younger people. Furthermore, the sample does not disclose any pattern of friction between any two age groups.

To check the hypothesis that the profile of court users might be different in the Talean appeals court, I took a sample of 80 cases from the alcalde's office, comprising all the cases heard in the alcalde court for the entire year of 1959. In these, I was able to elicit further information to supplement that in the recorded cases; the age of the users, their occupation, the extent of their landholdings, and their relationship to the opposing parties are not mentioned in the official record.

Table 10 is a summary scaled for greatest activity in the alcalde court by age for 1959. Again, it seems that ages 30–39 and 40–49 deliver most of the defendants and plaintiffs, about half the totals for all six age groups of adults. This finding comes out clearly in Table 11, which gives information about the age of plaintiffs for person and property cases. We see that, in general, younger people are involved with the courts over person cases and older people are involved over property cases. It is in the 30–39 and 40–49 age brackets that both plaintiffs and defendants are plagued by both person and

TABLE 10

Greatest Court Activity by Age in Alcalde's Court, 1959

Rank	Age	No. of plaintiffs	Age	No. of defendants
1	40–49	24	40–49	27
2	30–39	21	30–39	25
3	20–29	15	50–59	17
4	50–59	13	20–29	8
5	60–69	12	60–69	5
6	70–79	5	70–79	6
TOTAL		90		88

TABLE II

Type of Complaint by Age for 80 Cases,
Alcalde's Court, 1959

Age	Person complaints	Property complaints	Total complaints
20–29	16	5	21
30–39	24	22	46
40–49	22	30	52
50–59	17	12	29
60–69	6	11	17
70–79	2	10	12
TOTAL	87	90	177

property matters; ages 20–29 are concerned mainly with persons and ages 60–79 mainly with property. Those in their twenties use the courts primarily to settle conflicts with spouses (see below). At any rate, if there is a delinquency age in Talea, it cannot be said to be young.

Social Class of Users

Along with sex and age, class is popularly assumed to affect court use. In Western industrialized societies, the rich have often used the law to promote their own interests and to control the activities of the poorer classes. Although Talea is a culturally homogeneous town, it has both rich and poor. Because Taleans usually measure the degree of wealth or poverty by the amount of land, I decided to use landedness and landlessness as central indicators of socioeconomic class. Taleans usually speak of others as having a lot of land or a little land without specifying the actual amounts.

People with little or no land do not seem shy about appealing cases to the alcalde court. Again I used the 1959 sample of 80 cases from this court, for which I had additional data. In this sample, 35 individuals who had little or no land appeared in the court, 21 of them as plaintiffs and 14 as defendants. The distribution of landed vs. landlessness during 1959 in terms of Talean categories suggests that the Talean poor probably use the courts in proportion to their actual numbers. The poor were involved in 17 cases dealing with person problems and 12 with property complaints. The property cases involved debt, robbery, inheritance, theft, boundaries, and one case of purchase of property. The person cases involved family cases ranging from paternity, desertion, and adultery to assault and battery of a wife or mother-in-law. The poor were involved in only five assault and battery cases—four cases of male lovers assaulting the women they lived with, and one case of a woman hitting another woman's children.

It would be hard to argue that the poor are any more or less violent than the wealthy in Talea. There is also little evidence that the rich use the courts as plaintiffs more than as defendants or that poor plaintiffs are harassed in the Talean courts in any direct way, although they were exploited for their labor if alcoholics. Indeed, landowners often mediate for day laborers in court cases. Nevertheless, the more landed one is, the more likely he or she is to bring property rather than person cases to the alcalde as plaintiff. Such a pattern, however, does not preclude the possibility that the landed are brought to the courts as defendants in person cases.

Relationships Between Plaintiffs and Defendants

Because Talea is a face-to-face community, the cases that come before the courts usually include a high proportion of disputants who know one another. In Table 12 I categorize five different types of possible relationships between disputants in the courts and examine the distribution of relationships across the total sample of 409 cases (excluding those cases that involved either the town government or groups as plaintiff or defendant).

As indicated in Table 12, there is a tendency for individuals to

TABLE 12

Relationship Between Plaintiffs and Defendants by Type of Court,
1957–1968

Type of relationship	Presidente		Alcalde		Sindico		Total
	No. of cases	Percent of total	No. of cases	Percent of total	No. of cases	Percent of total	
Consanguineal kin[a]	11	10%	10	8%	6	17%	27
Affinal kin[b]	26	24	49	40	12	32	87
Lovers	10	9	14	11	2	6	26
Neighbors	5	5	6	5	5	14	16
Other	58	53	43	35	11	31	112
TOTAL	110	100%	122	100%	36	100%	268

NOTE: Not included here are 141 cases that involved either the town government or groups as plaintiffs or defendants.
[a] In Talea, this category comprises close blood relatives.
[b] In Talea, usually the spouse's parents and sibs.

TABLE 13
Categories of Family Relationship by Type of Court, 1957–1968

Plaintiff vs. defendant	Presidente		Alcalde		Sindico		Total cases
	No. of cases	Percent of total	No. of cases	Percent of total	No. of cases	Percent of total	
Husband vs. wife	1	4%	6	17%	1	9%	8
Wife vs. husband	17	63	22	61	5	45	44
Parent vs. child	3	11	3	8	4	37	10
Child vs. parent	3	11	4	11	1	9	8
Sibling vs. sibling	3	11	1	3	—	—	4
TOTAL	27	100%	36	100%	11	100%	74

avoid bringing nuclear-family consanguineal relatives to court. Affinal relatives, however, appear in court quite frequently; usually this category comprises the spouse's parents and sibs only. Relations between both types of kin account for approximately half of the cases brought to the alcalde and sindico courts and a third of the cases in the presidente court. This pattern does not surprise me; it is common in towns like Talea that are not factionalized. The remaining cases are between lovers, neighbors, or others; the large numbers of cases listed under "other" reflect missing data.

When we focus on family cases alone (Table 13), we see that the bulk of disputes occurs between spouses; if we included here the cases of women and men who live together as lovers (Table 12), the category would be even larger. These tables contextualize the pattern of high female court use noted earlier. Husbands rarely bring their wives to court, and children seldom bring their parents. According to Table 13, 37 percent of the cases in the sindico court involved parents' complaints against children; in the presidente and alcalde courts such cases accounted for 11 percent and 8 percent, respectively, of the total cases in each court. The high percentage of parent vs. child cases in the sindico court may reflect the small sample of family cases from that court, the fact that the sindico deals with property cases, which often involve family inheritance, and the fact that the case is serious. Such cases in the sindico court frequently deal with property settlement and more rarely with physical abuse. Cases between siblings are rare in all three courts.

TABLE 14

Residence Patterns of Plaintiffs and Defendants by Type of Court,
1957–1968

Plaintiff vs. defendant	Presidente		Alcalde		Sindico		Total cases
	No. of cases	Percent of total	No. of cases	Percent of total	No. of cases	Percent of total	
Together	27	27%	8	30%	3	43%	38
Separate	71	71	17	63	3	43	91
Transitory	2	2	2	7	1	14	5
TOTAL	100	100%	27	100%	7	100%	134

Despite the large number of family cases brought to the courts, Table 14 shows that few cases are between family members who live in the same household as compared with those who live in separate households. About two-thirds of cases in the presidente and alcalde courts involving family members fall into the latter category. The exception seems to be in the sindico court, where the percentages are equivalent (43 percent). Again this figure may be distorted because of the small sample size, or it may reflect a specialization of the sindico court.

At any rate, most people who appear together in Talean courts know each other, and most of them are related by marriage because in the absence of strong extended families the courts are heavily used by women embroiled in marital conflict. If women in Talea make extensive use of the courts to defend their domestic rights, they are exceptional in comparison with women in other parts of Mexico. Although data are scarce, in the Chiapan village studied by Duane Metzger (Nader and Metzger 1963), women there rarely if ever take their husbands to court. From other Talean data I know that ties between husband and wife, as between all affines, are conflict ridden, but we cannot generalize from this to consanguineal relations. For example, it would be highly unusual for a Talean mother to take her son to court.

Chief Causes of Complaint

The broad range of complaints in Talea indicates that the courts are not specialized but generalized institutions that handle the daily problems of a rural, mountain, agricultural community largely isolated from urban problems. Even though the ideal division of labor between the courts makes the sindico court the most specialized of the three, the users of the courts push to make them nonspecific. Villagers believe that courts should take care of the problems that come to them and should disregard central government attempts to give them specialized jurisdictions. The range of complaints and the overlap of complaints among the different users of the court indicate the range of rights and duties that citizens share, have serious conflicts about, and insist town officials address.

In this section, using the 409-case sample, I examine the kinds of complaints presented in the three courts, and then, focusing on property cases and matters of violence—the most common complaints—I examine the relationship between males and females in this context. Using a subset of 216 cases, I look at repeat users in relation to the types of complaints they bring to the courts, to the ties between plaintiff and defendant, and to the incidence of drinking.

In the total sample of 409 cases, 531 formal complaints were presented to the Talean courts (see Table 15). In all three courts, complaints involving property form the largest category. Other common problems involve contracts, physical and verbal aggression, conjugal and family duties, and drunkenness. If we lump property and contract complaints together under the rubric of complaints dealing

TABLE 15

Categories of Complaints by Type of Court, 1957–1968

Type of complaint	Presidente		Alcalde		Sindico		
	No. of complaints	Percent of total	No. of complaints	Percent of total	No. of complaints	Percent of total	Total complaints
Property (movable and immovable)	55	25%	66	32%	37	35%	158
Contract	18	8	17	8	15	14	50
Physical aggression	39	18	47	23	14	13	100
Verbal aggression	27	12	25	12	15	14	67
Conjugal or family duties	37	17	34	17	9	8	80
Drunk and disorderly	31	14	9	4	10	9	50
Administrative	5	2	1	1	5	5	11
Other	9	4	5	2	1	1	15
TOTAL	221	100%	204	100%	106	100%	531

NOTE: "Administrative" complaints include the making of wills and the payment or non-payment of taxes. "Other" complaints include contempt of court, perjury, and cases of health emergencies; the court sometimes figures in decision-making in life and death situations.

with movable and immovable property, and physical and verbal aggression together under the rubric of complaints dealing with persons, we do see some evidence of specialization. The case load of the presidente court was divided almost evenly between property complaints (33 percent) and person complaints (30 percent), as was that of the alcalde court (40 percent property and 35 percent person). The sindico court, on the other hand, heard almost twice as many property complaints (49 percent) as person complaints (27 percent). The sindico court dealt with fewer complaints having to do with conjugal or family duties (8 percent) compared with the presidente and alcalde courts (17 percent for each).

Table 16 focuses on property cases in relation to the sex of plaintiff and defendant. Although the highest percentages of property cases were between males (presidente court 38 percent, alcalde court 37 percent, sindico court 33 percent), in both the presidente and alcalde courts the percentages of such cases involving males vs. females were not significantly different (31 percent in the presidente court and 29 percent in the alcalde court). In the sindico court the percentage of property cases that involved males vs. females was considerably lower (5 percent). No female vs. male cases involving property were brought to the presidente court. This type of case accounted for 17 percent of all property cases in the alcalde court and 24 percent in the sindico court. Women sued other women over property in 11 percent of cases in the presidente court, 6 percent in the alcalde court, and 14 percent in the sindico court.

TABLE 16

Property Cases by Sex of Plaintiff and Defendant and by Type of Court,
1957–1968

Plaintiff vs. defendant	Presidente		Alcalde		Sindico		Total cases
	No. of cases	Percent of total	No. of cases	Percent of total	No. of cases	Percent of total	
Male vs. male	10	38%	13	37%	7	33%	30
Male vs. female	8	31	10	29	1	5	19
Female vs. male	—	—	6	17	5	24	11
Female vs. female	3	11	2	6	3	14	8
Other[a]	5	20	4	11	5	24	14
TOTAL	26	100%	35	100%	21	100%	82

[a] Cases in which a male and a female, not married, were the plaintiffs.

TABLE 17

*Violence Cases by Sex of Plaintiff and Defendant and by Type of Court,
1957–1968*

Plaintiff vs. defendant	Presidente		Alcalde		Sindico		Total cases
	No. of cases	Percent of total	No. of cases	Percent of total	No. of cases	Percent of total	
Male vs. male	6	20%	14	41%	7	59%	27
Male vs. female	—	—	1	3	—	—	1
Female vs. male	12	40	15	44	4	33	31
Female vs. female	2	7	1	3	1	8	4
Other[a]	10	33	3	9	—	—	13
TOTAL	30	100%	34	100%	12	100%	76

[a] Cases in which a male and a female, not married, were the plaintiffs.

Cases of physical aggression were preponderantly female vs. male
and were usually heard in the presidente and alcalde courts (see
Table 17). Male vs. male cases of violence accounted for 20 percent
of all such cases in the presidente court, 41 percent in the alcalde
court, and 59 percent in the sindico court. If the sindico and alcalde
courts are seen as lying in a more direct line of authority with the
state district court compared with the presidente court, then one
might hypothesize that as Taleans move toward the use of external
law more males are involved as court users. More is said about involvement in the district court in the next chapter.

Complaint Patterns and Repeat Court Users

When I asked Taleans about court users, some of them complained about people who were always in court, and so I decided to
look at the recidivism pattern to see if indeed the same people do
continuously use the courts. I took the sample of 216 cases from
1957–65 (Table 5) in which there were 329 people. Of these, 71 were
repeat participants, 57 of them appearing twice in court and 14 others
appearing from three to five times (Table 18). The frequencies with
which male and female repeaters appeared as plaintiffs and defendants are shown in Table 19.

The principal issues in cases involving repeat users were the same
as those in the complete sample. Table 20 compares participation by
repeat users and nonrepeat users. Repeat users are more likely to be

TABLE 18
Number of Court Appearances by Repeat Users, 1957–1965

No. of appearances	Male	Female	Total repeat users	Total no. of appearances
5	2	—	2	10
4	3	2	5	20
3	6	1	7	21
2	42	15	57	114
TOTAL	53	18	71	165

TABLE 19
Repeat Court Use by Sex, 1957–1965
(N = 165)

	Male	Percent	Female	Percent
Plaintiffs	42	34%	29	71%
Defendants	82	66	12	29
TOTAL	124	100%	41	100%

TABLE 20
Number of Complaints Registered by Repeat Court Users Compared with Nonrepeat Users, 1957–1965
(N = 216)

Complaints	Repeat users	Nonrepeat users
Property	17	16
Civil disturbance	15 (15)	15 (1)
Wife beating	18 (17)	3 (2)
Assault/battery	15 (3)	5 (0)
Debt	12	8
Theft	10	6
Slander	6	6
Paternity/child support	7	7
Desertion	6	4
Failure to fulfill obligation because of drinking	3	1
Miscellaneous[a]	25	11
TOTAL	134	82

NOTE: The numbers in parentheses indicate the number of cases in the category that involved drinking.

[a]This category includes insults, contempt of court, perjury, the breaking of agreements with employees, marital quarrels, and adultery.

involved in violent behavior (civil disturbance, wife beating, assault and battery) than are nonrepeat users. Out of a total of 71 repeaters, 48 of them, or two-thirds, involved violent behavior, usually of one person against another; of these 48, 35 involved drunkenness. Alcoholics appear to generate a "hard core." Court appearances of repeaters in cases of property complaints (17), debt (12), and theft (10) also reflected high percentages of the total. Many of the 71 repeat court users out of the total of 329 were implicated in cases dealing with both civil disturbance and wife beating; one repeater was sued four times by town officials for civil disturbance.

Co-occurrence of complaints is common in Talea. Cases of assault and battery are nearly always found in conjunction with drunkenness. Adultery rarely stands by itself as a cause of complaint; it is usually associated with assault and battery or lack of support or drunkenness, or a combination of these complaints. In other words, as long as a man supports his wife, as long as he does not verbally or physically abuse her, she does not complain to the courts about his adultery or drunkenness. Such complaint complexes, which may be seen as escalatory, are as relevant to an understanding of how the plaintiff or defendant presents and pleads a case as they are to descriptions of the judicial decision-making process or to repeat cases.

A more detailed breakdown of repeat court users' cases by the sex of the litigants is presented in Table 21 in order to show the rubric under which these parties brought suit against one another. As this material shows, there was a tendency for men to sue one another primarily for property damage and assault and, less commonly, for them to sue women for slander and debt. Suits by the town against men involved drinking in all but 7 of the 22 cases in Table 21; the town brought no repeat suits against women. Court officials believe that by having the police arrest men who are drunk, disorderly, and violent, they are preventing such behavior from escalating. They believe that this form of social control benefits the entire community by preserving the peace through the removal of potentially disruptive individuals from public settings.

Women primarily sue those men with whom they have intimate relationships—spouses or lovers—because of beating, failure to acknowledge paternity or to pay child support, and desertion. Men who beat women are fined or imprisoned; that may deter repetition of such behavior. In cases of child support, the court makes sure that the woman receives money or other goods for her offspring. In cases of desertion, the court may fulfill a cathartic function for the aban-

TABLE 21
Cases per Repeat Litigant and by Type of Complaint, 1957–1965

Sex of litigants (plaintiff vs. defendant)	Complaint	No. of times	Total
Male vs. male	Property	12	
	Assault	11	
	Debt	4	
	Insult	4	
	Theft	3	
	Slander	2	
	Failure to perform job	2	
	Miscellaneous[a]	5	43
Male vs. female	Slander	3	
	Debt	3	
	Theft	2	
	Assault	2	
	Desertion	1	
	Miscellaneous[a]	6	17
Talea vs. male	Civil disturbance	15	
	Failure to perform job	5	
	Theft	1	
	False testimony	1	22
Female vs. male	Beating	18	
	Paternity	7	
	Desertion	5	
	Theft	3	
	Debt	2	
	Property	2	
	Assault	2	39
Female vs. female	Property	3	
	Debt	3	
	Fighting	2	
	Theft/slander (1 each)	2	
	Miscellaneous[a]	1	11
Missing data			1
TOTAL			133

[a] See note *a* to Table 20.

doned party, while ensuring that the children of the broken union are temporarily provided for by forcing the father to be financially responsible for his offspring. In this manner, the court compels men to fulfill their social obligations toward the women with whom they are living. Women sue one another primarily over property or for unpaid debts; fewer cases deal with fighting, slander, and theft.

As this sample shows, men were the more frequent repeat users of the courts. The numerical disparity in participation between males and females would, however, be reduced if cases involving drunkenness were removed from the sample.

Out of the total of 134 cases brought by repeat users, 29 were suits brought by one repeat user against another. Within this small sample, suits involving assault and beating were most numerous (12), with debt and property cases being the next most frequent (5 each). In some of these cases, the parties filed suits and countersuits against one another. For example, a woman sued by her sister for debt in turn sued the sister for adultery with her husband. On two occasions women brought suits against each other for beating. Litigants in close personal relationships (spouses, relatives) filed 54 out of the total of 134 complaints. Three cases involved neighbors, and three were against employers.

To summarize, cases involving repeat users divide rather evenly between movable and immovable property complaints on the one hand (land, debt, theft), and person cases involving violence or physical attack (wife beating, assault and battery, civil disturbance) on the other. Well over half the cases of physical violence are associated with some form of alcoholic consumption. When the repeat users are compared with nonrepeaters in this sample of 216 cases, the findings indicate that inebriation plays an important part in acts of repeated male physical violence, whereas verbal violence seems to be a way in which sober women aggress repeatedly. Both drinking and gossiping may be addictive behaviors. The data on repeat users indicate that although the number of chronic repeaters is small, their transgressions divide almost equally between person and property cases. Some hostilities die hard, and debt and other property cases have a chronic nature.

The villagers themselves have noticed an increasing number of cases of physical violence involving repeaters and attribute such cases to the growing use of alcohol by men and to what they call the "discontrol" that accompanies modernization and the intrusion of foreign cultural elements into their lives. Modernization may be affecting men and women differently, at least in their disputing patterns, but as far as I can tell, Taleans who think sociologically ascribe men's drinking behavior to the influence of outside elements but ignore the fact that the increasing stresses on women might be of the same origin. The slant of decisions in these cases usually indicates that Taleans often see and understand specific behaviors in relation to the wider context.

The Slant of Decisions

To return to general patterns of court use, the distribution of case verdicts between the plaintiff, the defendant, and the court, and the distribution of sentences are also central to the profile. In an early paper on this subject, Metzger (1960) isolated the community membership of plaintiff, defendant, and court as a variable crucial to the slant of decisions in a village in Chiapas, Mexico. He pointed out that plaintiffs, defendants, and courts have different conceptions of the "ideal legal product"; the "plaintiff seeks to maximize payments of damages awarded to himself; the court seeks to maximize payments of fines; and the defendant seeks to minimize payments of either kind" (ibid.: 36). For the town of Chulsanto in Chiapas, Metzger went on to say that in local cases, the balance of power among plaintiff, defendant, and the court is approximately equal, but he suggested that when court participants come either from other Indian communities or from Latino communities, the balance of power shifts in favor of the party that may have easier access to courts of appeal. For purposes of analysis, I separate verdict from sanction or sentence, which may be different from the social outcome that results from the court action or in spite of court action. In addition, I explore the value of community residence as a determinant of decision.

It was in the 1957 set of 62 cases from the presidente court that I first noticed that the plaintiff usually won in verdicts of a win-or-lose nature (Nader 1964b). This observation also applied in the total sample of 409 cases from 1957 to 1968. In the majority of cases, most rulings were against the defendant (see Table 22). In the presidente court 57 percent of all decisions were against the defendant, compared with 42 percent in the alcalde court and 38 percent in the sindico court.

The next most frequent decision was reconciliation or agreement (presidente court 16 percent, alcalde court 39 percent, sindico court 28 percent). There were differences among the three courts. The presidente court was least likely to reconcile a case, and the alcalde court was least likely to appeal a case (4 percent of all decisions versus 15 percent for the presidente court and 19 percent for the sindico court). In all three courts, decisions against the plaintiff were rare (presidente court 2 percent, alcalde court 3 percent, and sindico court 3 percent).

Why does the plaintiff prevail so often in Talea? In formal courts in the United States (with juvenile and small-claims courts as pos-

TABLE 22

Decisions by Type of Court, 1957–1968

Decisions	Presidente		Alcalde		Sindico		Total cases
	No. of cases	Percent of total	No. of cases	Percent of total	No. of cases	Percent of total	
Against plaintiff	3	2%	3	3%	2	3%	8
Against defendant	82	57	50	42	24	38	156
Against both	10	7	5	4	2	3	17
In favor of both	2	1	3	3	—	—	5
Dropped by plaintiff or court	2	1	6	5	4	6	12
Court refused to hear case	1	1	—	—	2	3	3
Agreement/re-conciliation	24	16	47	39	18	28	89
Sent to a higher court	22	15	5	4	12	19	39
TOTAL	146	100%	119	100%	64	100%	329

sible exceptions), judges may consider only the evidence presented by the two parties. No evidence may enter into a decision unless it is presented and judged admissible at the trial. Gossip, personal history, and hearsay evidence, for example, are excluded. In Talea, as we have seen, such informal evidence is not disregarded. The defendant is fully aware that the men rendering the decision know him or her well, as does the plaintiff. They know if he has been "playing around," if he is addicted to drink, if he has assaulted his wife, or if he is in general a problem citizen. They have a fairly good pre-hearing knowledge of her personal history and may use it in her favor or to her disadvantage. Realizing that the judges know the full history of the case, the defendant pleads guilty in nine out of ten cases, and the plaintiff only brings a case that is winnable in these terms.

Most cases lost by a plaintiff involve ambiguity of marital status. Analysis of appeals suggests that if a defendant who lost in the presidente court appealed the verdict to the office of the alcalde, he or she had a better chance of winning. However, the decision in favor of the plaintiff remained a dominant pattern throughout the larger case sample and was undoubtedly related to the plea of guilty by the defendant in nine out of ten cases.

The next question is whether local residents were favored in court verdicts. In contrast to the Metzger findings in Chulsanto (1960), the data from Talea revealed no obvious bias in favor of local residents. In my 1959 alcalde sample, 24 cases involved outsiders. There were 11 cases of Taleans vs. outsiders, 8 cases of outsiders vs. Taleans, and 5 cases of outsiders vs. outsiders. In all 24 cases the decision was biased toward the plaintiff, whether insider or outsider. The slant is independent of community residence and seems more closely correlated with ideas that Rincón Zapotec have about court use. They use the court only if they have an airtight case; they know that otherwise the decision may be made against them and their reputations may be impaired. Exceptions are women who use the courts to vent their spleen; when this goal is obvious, they lose their cases.

However, there is another way to consider the question of slant in decision. The court may award the verdict to the plaintiff but apply a sanction in its own favor. What happens when one is declared guilty and what penalizing sanctions follow the rendering of a verdict of guilty? Radcliffe-Brown (1952) and others have conceived of the broader category of legal sanctions in physical terms, but as Pospisil (1958) points out, legal sanctions are of many varieties. In fact, anthropologists have developed little in the way of a theory of sanctions because they have excluded the ethnographic context for sanctions and penalties. In Talea, legal penalties take the form of fines paid in pesos, of fines paid by labor on public works, of public reprimand, or all three, along with jail sentences. In addition, of course, there are damages awarded the plaintiff.

The most prevalent sanction was a fine (Table 23). Fines were gen-

TABLE 23

Sanctions by Type of Court, 1957–1965

Sanction	Presidente		Alcalde		Sindico		Total cases
	No. of cases	Percent of total	No. of cases	Percent of total	No. of cases	Percent of total	
Imprisonment	16	14%	7	11%	—	—	23
Public works	5	4	1	2	—	—	6
Fine	75	67	39	62	23	96%	137
Compensation	13	12	13	21	1	4	27
Banishment or expulsion	1	1	1	2	—	—	2
Escaped before decision	1	1	1	2	—	—	2
Fine changed to public works	1	1	—	—	—	—	1
TOTAL	112	100%	62	100%	24	100%	198

erally under 15 pesos and went to the town treasury. Whereas both the presidente and the alcalde court used a wide range of penalties (imprisonment, labor on public works, fines, compensation, banishment), the sindico court used only fines and in one case compensation.

Data on penalizing sanctions may be ordered in several ways, depending on the purpose of the inquiry. If, for example, the sanctions are ranked from the least to the most severe, we have for one thing an index of the seriousness of the cases. In an earlier study (Nader 1964b), I used the cases from the 1957 presidente court to rank penalizing sanctions. At the bottom of this ranking (fines of 10–40 pesos) were such offenses as street fighting, drunkenness, disturbing the peace, nuisance to the court, failure to complete municipal obligations, and flirting with unmarried females. Grievances requiring payment of 40 to 100 pesos included abandonment, abduction, assault and battery, attempted murder, slander, boundary trespass, and improper advances by a married man.

Such a ranking, besides its usefulness as an index of seriousness, also provides information on the range of possible sanctions for a similar set of offenses. An illustration is the case of the two flirts. In Case 41, a single woman complained to the court that Señor X had appeared beneath her window the previous night and made the equivalent of American "wolf calls." The defendant pleaded that he had done so only because the woman had flirted with him the previous week and had even invited him to collect firewood with her. The court fined her 30 pesos for flirting and the defendant 60 pesos for improper advances since he, as a married man, should have been at home with his wife. The distinguishing feature of this case, according to the judge, was marital status. The discrimination in fines was made primarily because the woman was single and the man married, and only secondarily because she was a woman and he a man.

An interesting feature of these courts is the lack of differences in the style of social control they exercised (penal vs. compensatory, for example). A classification of cases according to their common features reveals that the sanctions may differ in cases involving the same complaints. Examination of the distinctive features in such cases helps to unravel why. For example, three family cases that occurred in Talea during the same year shared the following elements: all the plaintiffs were women; all the defendants were men; and the complaints were drunkenness and assault. The cases illuminate the way sanctions are in fact decided.

In the first case the defendant threatened the plaintiff but did not actually strike her. His sanction was 25 pesos less than that in the second case, in which the defendant both threatened and struck his wife. In the third case, in which the defendant likewise both threatened and struck a woman, the woman was his mother. To the Taleans this was an important difference—a son should respect his mother—and they consequently fined the defendant 15 pesos more than in the second case, in which the victim was the wife and thus not in a position of authority or respect equal to that of a mother.

In many cases, however, the "logic" of the difference in sanctions is not so obvious, and the explanation may lie in facts not reported in court. These might include ability to pay, the degree of inebriation of the defendant (which would reduce his punishment in cases of assault and battery because he was not of right mind), the proximity of residence of the two litigants, or the relationship between the litigants and the judge.

Decisions of the court, whether in the form of sanctions of various sorts, agreements between the litigants, or the payment of compensation, are not *judicial* decisions, strictly speaking. They result from the interaction between the parties and the official in the context of wider societal values. This point is worth reiterating because behavioral scientists are accustomed to thinking about decision-making from a top-down vantage point—as if it were something judges do for court participants. In this context, the official may play a relatively passive role or an active role, a court may simultaneously appear democratic or authoritarian depending on one's perspective. From an individualistic vantage point, the courts appear authoritarian because of the intrusive and penal character of many outcomes and because of court regulation of personal conduct such as drunkenness. But if one's perspective is based in community autonomy and the court is seen as an agency responsible for maintaining community harmony, then the courts appear to fit a more democratic model. I deal further with this matter in Chapter 13 in discussing cases dealing with governance.

Discussion

In sum, the users of the Talean courts are a varied lot: they may be male or female, young adults or old, rich or poor. They come to the court with a wide range of complaints dealing with family matters, with property disputes, with conflicts usually between neighbors and acquaintances but sporadically between strangers, or relative strangers, over violence, debt, or slander.

In Talean courts the chief causes for complaint divide rather evenly between movable and immovable property disputes and person cases. In over half the cases of physical violence, including repeat users, alcohol is involved. Men predominate as defendants; women and men appear rather evenly as plaintiffs. Court decisions are biased in favor of the plaintiff. The main sanction of the court is the fine, which is used to build town revenues. For the most part the plaintiff does not ask for compensation because it would be perceived as tipping the balance. Although not indicated by official records of cases (but see Part III), decision-making is interactive rather than hierarchical or impositional. Life-cycle stresses that result in court complaints overwhelmingly involve older males between the ages of 30 and 50 as defendants. Most people who come to court know each other.

Court participants operate with the same set of norms as the general population, which may further explain the high rate of guilty pleas. Participants in Talean courts are a rights-conscious people who push for remedy, and this includes the remedy agents themselves. The users of these courts operate with a high degree of knowledge of and familiarity with court workings. During the period under study (1957–68), I would characterize the Talean court as central rather than marginal. Such a comfortable fit is probably but a moment in the evolution of Zapotec society.

The dynamics that produce changes in the law may center on the actions of individuals or groups and thus reveal the slope of a legal process, or they may be more historical, with accumulated institutional changes over time effecting a change in the processes of law. The intensive ethnographic approach looks for features that trigger a slope, whereas the extensive historical method outlines the waves of change that follow initial triggering.

This chapter is actor oriented and underlines the observation that not only does the law change people, but by their participation people make the law. The theory I have been examining stems from an assumption that the user, in particular the plaintiff—not an abstraction like the courts or judicial decision, or even variables like urbanization and industrialization—is the driving force in law. Isolating the direction of drift from a study of the slope of a legal process requires attention to the concepts of use and users and to patterns of access to the system (Nader 1978, 1986).

Anthropologists have observed that the plaintiff role is a relatively active one in non-Western societies. I argued above that in nation-states plaintiffs have shed their plaintiff role for that of victim and the state has assumed the role of plaintiff. Such an evolution changes the place of potential users of courts. In Western societies the individual plaintiff has gradually been removed from litigation, especially in criminal cases, and has moved from a position of relative power, which gave him or her procedural means to dispute, to a relatively powerless role (Nader 1984a, 1985). It is not surprising, therefore, that Western scholarship speaks about judicial decision-making. Loosening the grip of the judge-determined court and replacing it with an interactive model gives sociological significance to all court participants and becomes crucial to delineating the slope and direction of law.

Who is motivated to use the law and for what? In societies where user initiative is determined primarily by the court, the individual user recedes into a subordinate position, and at times the plaintiff hardly enters into theories about courts. Scholars speak instead of systems or courts. Lawrence Friedman (1983: 9) introduced a volume edited by Boyum and Mather (1983) with the statement: "Our concern is with the behavior of courts. We leave aside any primary focus on the litigants and their lawyers, though of course this comes up incidentally." In the same volume, Krislov (1983: 171) indicates (in a rejection of the notion that plaintiffs are major actors) that the major participants are the defendant, the lawyer, and the judge. According to such a view, the court, not the individual plaintiff, is the dominant user and major player moving the individual plaintiffs. By comparison Talean plaintiffs appear more powerful.

One theory of change removes the plaintiff from discussion, and the other rejects the popular notion that individual plaintiffs are the major actors. I have argued the need to analyze courtroom encounters as interactions since the early 1960's, and others (Kidder 1979; Westermark 1986) have noticed the need for an interactive model. In Talea, plaintiffs are major actors, and their attributes are significant. Since both men and women are users, their participation is reflected in court encounters. Courtroom encounters dominated by male judges, plaintiffs, and defendants exhibit male cultural behavior. Female discourse is not heard. In the Zapotec court, both female discourse and male discourse are part of the encounter, but such a pattern is not universal in the non-Western world and is uncommon in the Western world as well.

The question remains, What gives users of the Talean court their power? Parnell (1978b) has argued that the state system and the local system are competing with one another, each trying to gain jurisdiction over the dispute because solving a dispute is power. Because of the competition between the two systems, power shifts to the disputants. Parnell's argument is useful for attaching the user model to the peculiar situation of legal pluralism, a phenomenon that accompanies colonization and modernization as new systems are imposed on old systems. The old system does not crumble, however, but continues to exist along with the new system. For a period of time in the contemporary "modernization" process, people have a choice between two systems, a choice that confers power on one system or the other. The very possibility of choice increases the power of the litigants. Under the old system they may have had less power—they could choose only one forum for dispute settlement. And if centralization is complete, disputants lose power if there is only one forum for dispute settlement.

Chapter Nine

Over the Mountain to the District Court

The district court is located in San Idelfonso de Villa Alta, a mestizo village between six and eight hours' walking distance from Talea. In traveling to Villa Alta, one has to cross a mountain called Matahombres (killer of men). The name is apt, and I realized how motivated one would have to be to take a case to the district court after I had traveled the route myself. It is approximately an hour's downhill walk from Talea to the little hamlet of Santa Gertrudis, which is all that is left of a once active mining community. Then one has a steep climb up the mountain, followed by a descent to the only water between Santa Gertrudis and Villa Alta. From the river it is upward again for about an hour and a half to reach the small town of Villa Alta. In the 1960's the population of Villa Alta was 600 people. Twenty years later its size remains the same, and it is still necessary to walk the long mountain road to the district seat. Although a vehicular road has been open from Oaxaca to Villa Alta since the early 1980's, it would be roundabout to use it to travel from Talea to the district seat.

Villa Alta is a village with a Spanish- and an Indian-speaking population. It has been an administrative center since 1529 and to-day administers 25 municipios and their agencies (Chance 1978). Its population is characterized by a high degree of turnover—government officials and government workers come and go; the families of those imprisoned in its jail visit frequently to care for the prisoners or to plead for clemency; litigants come with their cases; and during its small Monday market commercial activity brings people together from the surrounding Mixe and Zapotec villages, and even from the more distant Chinantec communities. During the eighteenth and early nineteenth centuries, Villa Alta was a rich center for trade in

cotton and cochineal, an insect used to produce a red dye highly valued by Europeans. But Villa Alta's population never increased to
rival that of the large indigenous towns of the region (Lemoine 1966).

As the district seat, Villa Alta maintains an archive of law cases
from the sixteenth century to the present and houses the court
(Juzgado Mixto de Primera Instancia) and other state offices. In Villa
Alta one hears a mixture of unrelated languages and dialects of each
that are only partly mutually intelligible; Spanish is the lingua
franca. The permanent residents are farmers and small shop and cantina keepers, as well as teachers. Some of the teachers originate from
villages in the region and act as interpreters for the monolingual
peasant Indian peoples, who do not understand the state system of
law or the language of that system, Spanish. The district of Villa
Alta is thickly peopled by Indian-language speakers, people whose
experience with Hispanic culture since the Conquest has followed
an accordion-like pattern. In different times and with differing degrees of vigor, these people have been linked to the larger society
through taxation, law, a cash economy, disease, religion, and out-
migration/in-migration. In the 1960's the district could be described
as remote, populated mostly by indigenes, difficult to reach, an area
with a sparse historical record. The larger towns had a town tele-
phone, radios were scarce, and television absent. Transportation
in the form of bus, truck, or airplane was private and certainly
intermittent.

In 1953–62 the people of the Villa Alta district were about to
experience an onslaught of contact with Protestant evangelicals
and with the Mexican state, primarily through development that
concentrated on opening up the region by means of road and airstrip construction. But all that was yet to come, and the dockets
analyzed in this chapter reflect litigant concerns during a period
when community identity was still strong and out-migration minimal, a time when subsistence rather than cash cropping was the
economic mainstay of the villages. The state machinery was spread
thinly throughout the region, and local communities governed themselves as miniature village-state units. The unit in which these
Indian communities have endured was and is the free, landholding
corporate village, striving for autonomy.

In the last chapter I analyzed the use of the courts in one large
village, Talea. I now look at how the settlements of the Rincón used
the district-level court in Villa Alta by examining the dockets for a
ten-year period (1953–62). Along with Parnell (1989), who used the
extended case method to examine the escalation of cases in the re-

gion, I am interested in how scattered settlements and their residents decide to take cases out of their community to the state district court and how they use state legal categories as rubrics under which to enter cases. As we shall see, the reasons why people use the district court have influenced its development as well as the structure of social relations within the settlements themselves. The process of law is at least two-way. The same fundamental questions raised in the last chapter are raised here, even though dockets are not as rich as case materials: Which villages use the district court, for what reasons, and what are the possible consequences for local law? In addition, how are village goals modified by state officials?

A theme that I have stressed throughout my writings on law is that law is made by participating actors. In this chapter, individual actors represent more than themselves; the litigants represent collectively the interests of their village; district court officials represent the state. The fact that villagers use the courts to their own advantage and that the district court accepts cases through a process of selection means that district court statistics do not accurately reflect behavior. The villages of the Rincón are not without power to control the extent to which the district court intervenes in their disputes. Parnell (1978b) points out that although the right of district courts to intervene in village disputes is recognized, in practice their power to do so is limited by their need to rely on people at the local level for information and enforcement. The model between the state and local levels is competitive, and a discontented litigant may wield a good deal of power by playing the two levels against one another.

The basic unit in this and other parts of Oaxaca is the autonomous village. Rincón villages do not readily accept outsiders; they are for the most part endogamous and insist that landholdings pass within the village. In a word, they are bounded communities. In listening to Indian citizens speak about their villages, one has the sense of a village consciousness that is almost equivalent to national consciousness, and in fact, some local officials jokingly refer to relations with nonresidents as "exterior relations" as opposed to "interior relations." At any rate, part of understanding the appeals process is understanding it as a process that villagers use in portraying themselves to the outside as well as a way the state forms stereotypes of particular villages and of the region as a whole. All this is by way of saying that cases may be sent or taken to the district-level appeals court for a variety of reasons, but the end results are to identify relations between local level and state power and to sharpen the identity of individual villages as prone to homicide or robbery, or as divided or united. Indeed, villagers' reaction to internal disputes depends on whether their village is united or divided; in this region this is increasingly tied to penetration by Protestant religious sects.

Villages are also identified in terms of crime by the type of weapon used for deadly assaults. In some villages a machete is used; in others the knife or the gun or poison. Some villagers are known for biting, some for kicking. All these methods of assault are available, but the choice of weapon seems to ultimately reinforce local social identity. But whatever that identity is, both the state system and the local system compete with one another to gain jurisdiction over the dispute. To manage disputes is to have power. For the most part, Indian communities recognize the authority of the state but manage to keep it remote in its exercise of power by what Parnell (1978b) calls legal involution.

In Talea, local-level officials prefer to settle cases at home, but they may send a case to the district court if decision is difficult or if the presidente does not want to risk making an unpopular decision. Citizens themselves may take a case to the appeals court if they do not like local-level officials or if they feel that their chances of winning are better at the district level because state law can prevail in a conflict between Zapotec and state law. However, even after a case is appealed to Villa Alta, it may be rejected. Juquilans, for example, commonly appeal cases that are not accepted because district-level officials do not consider the act a crime, such as a mother taking something from her daughter or an accusation of witchcraft or comparable dealings with the supernatural. In order for local communities and their residents to use the district courts to advantage, they must have some knowledge of Mexican legal categories or, if not, the capability to use bribery (Hunt and Hunt 1967).

In addition to the decisions of villagers and local communities and district court officials' assessment of the viability of the cases presented, seasonality also enters the picture of district court use. The total case load tends to be heavier from August to December, then markedly slacken and gradually pick up again in April. In part, this pattern is related to weather conditions and farmers' cash flow. Talea is the one exception to this rule; the case load from Talea is heavy and evenly distributed throughout the year.

However, in cases of homicide or other violent acts in which blood is drawn, villagers usually turn to the district courts immediately because the state and state courts have made it clear since the colonial period that such cases are strictly their responsibility. I say usually because this rule, as we shall see, is not observed in

TABLE 24

Number of Cases in District Court by Village, 1953–1962

(N = 144)

Juquila	11	Talea	44
Lachichina	10	Tanetza	16
Lalopa	12	Yagallo	5
Otatitlan	7	Yatoni	10
Porvenir	1	Yaviche	8
San Juan Yaee	19	Yobego	1
Santa Gertrudis	0		

some cases, although villagers know that the district court will intervene and that the village may be heavily fined if such cases go unreported. Otherwise, the district level does not for the most part interfere in local cases, although now and then district officials visit the villages to review hearing procedures.

With this brief background, I now turn to the statistical data from the dockets compiled for ten years (1953–62) at the district-level court in Villa Alta, some of which I followed personally. These quantitative data highlight some patterns of appeals court use and raise questions for future investigation. As Table 24 shows, the 144 cases appealed from the Rincón over the ten-year period were unevenly distributed throughout 13 villages. Overall I would not consider this a high appeal rate.

Who Uses the District Court?

Parnell (1989) discusses why villagers prefer the social resources of the village to resolve their disputes rather than those of the state and illustrates how local conflicts develop into regional, political, and religious alliances as a response to changes sweeping through the area. Two decades earlier an analysis of state court dockets might have predicted which villages would respond to change through violence.

When I look at court use by village (Table 25), I am impressed by the overall diversity. Some villages use the district court for all possible types of claims; others for particular categories of crime. This variability in use pattern is independent of the overall appeal rate. Table 26 reveals the relationship between appeal rate and village size. Because the distribution of size of the villages is discontinuous (there are no villages with populations between 500 and 1,000), I have divided the pueblos into two groups: those with populations of

TABLE 25

Number of Offenses by Type and Village, in District Court, 1953–1962

Type of offense	Juquila	Lachi-china	Lalopa	Otatit-lan	Porvenir	San Juan Yaee	Talea	Tanetze	Yagallo	Yatoni	Yaviche	Yobego	Inter-village	Total
Personal														
Amenazas (threats)	0	2	2	0	0	2	6	0	0	1	1	0	1	15
Estupro (rape)	0	0	0	0	0	0	5	0	0	0	0	0	0	5
Golpes (assault)	1	2	2	0	0	3	4	1	0	2	1	0	1	17
Homicidio (homicide)	0	3	2	1	0	2	2	2	3	2	1	0	1	19
Injurias (insults)	0	1	0	0	0	1	1	0	0	0	0	0	0	3
Lesiones (blood drawn)	2	6	1	2	0	7	5	1	0	2	3	1	2	32
Rapto (abduction; rape)	0	0	0	0	0	0	1	0	0	0	0	0	0	1
Violación (violation)	0	0	0	0	0	0	3	0	0	0	0	0	0	3
SUBTOTAL	3	14	7	3	0	15	27	4	3	7	6	1	5	95
Property														
Daño en propiedad (property damage)	3	0	1	1	0	4	6	2	0	0	0	0	1	18
Despojo (vandalism)	3	0	2	2	0	2	7	4	1	2	1	0	1	25
Robo (robbery)	4	2	3	0	0	5	6	3	0	3	1	0	2	29
SUBTOTAL	10	2	6	3	0	11	19	9	1	5	2	0	4	72
Role-related														
Abuso de autoridad (abuse of authority)	2	0	2	0	1	3	4	2	0	2	0	1	0	17
Abuso de confianza (abuse of confidence)	0	0	0	0	0	1	1	0	0	1	0	0	0	3
Disobediencia (disobedience by a child of a parent)	0	0	1	0	0	0	1	0	0	0	0	0	0	2
Fraude (fraud)	0	1	0	1	0	0	1	0	0	3	0	0	0	6
Resistencia (resisting arrest)	0	0	1	0	0	0	0	0	0	0	0	0	0	1
SUBTOTAL	2	1	4	1	1	4	7	2	0	6	0	1	0	29
TOTAL	15	17	17	7	1	30	53	15	4	18	8	2	8	195

NOTE: A case may have more than one offense. Thus the number of offenses for a village is likely to exceed the number of cases for that village.

TABLE 26

Appeal Rates by Village per 1,000 Persons, 1953–1962

Small villages (Population under 500)			Large villages (Population 1,000 or over)		
Village	No. of cases appealed	Appeal rate	Village	No. of cases appealed	Appeal rate
Lachichina	10	22	Juquila	11	6
Otatitlan	7	20	Lalopa	12	12
Porvenir	1	7	San Juan Yaee	19	19
Santa Gertrudis	0	0	Talea	44	22
Yagallo	5	17	Tanetze	16	16
Yatoni	10	20			
Yaviche	8	20			
Yobego	1	3			

500 or under, and large pueblos with populations of 1,000 or over. The difference in appeal rates for the two groups is insignificant. Village size seems to have no effect on the willingness of people to turn to the appeals court.

If we control for population, Talea and Lachichina, with populations of 2,000 and 450, respectively, have the highest appeal rates. I had thought that local-level officials of large villages would use the district courts more frequently to reduce their larger work loads. Spreading cases across the various levels would be one way to reduce work loads, and it might indicate that the courts in larger villages were becoming bureaucratic in form with an emphasis on the rapid processing of cases. The data do not support the idea that large villages use the district court to relieve work loads resulting from population increases. Parnell's (1989) data are clear on this point— there was no change in case load between 1973 and 1984 in the district court. Parnell also notes that geographical proximity and ease of access have had no effect on willingness to turn to the district court.

Cases appealed by the villages to the district court are assigned immediately to the ministerio publico (prosecutor), who has no formal legal training and generally has learned his trade by working as a secretary to a ministerio publico. He is the state representative in the district seat for penal affairs. His is an arena that brings together village, regional, and state politics, and in his position he comes to know the people of the district. Basically he selects the cases from among those that come to him.

In this regional court, records are not synonymous with crime rates, and certainly an analysis of dockets does not permit a systematic study of the incidence of crime. Homicide is one act, however, that is systematically reported in criminal records (see Table 27). As such, it may be a more accurate reflection of levels of "order" and "disorder" in the communities in question (or at least more accurate than other indicators such as drunkenness) and the best source of information on intra-regional differences. I begin by looking at the number of all cases appealed by a village to see how this reflects the quality of the relationship between a village and the appeals court and differences between villages. At the time of this case sample, Talea was the only bilingual village; the rest of the villages were monolingual Zapotec-speaking.

Categories of Complaint Appealed

Over a ten-year period thirteen homicides were reported in the thirteen villages in the Rincón region. Table 27 lists homicide rates per 1,000 persons for the villages in the Rincón. Appeal rates range from a low of zero for Santa Gertrudis, the smallest village, to a high of 22 cases per 1,000 persons, which is shared by Talea (population 2,000) and Lachichina (450). Homicide rates range from a low of zero in four villages (Juquila, population 1,700; Yobego, 400; Porvenir, 150; and Santa Gertrudis, 100), to a high of 10 murders per 1,000 persons in Yagallo (300).

Again, although appeal rates cannot be taken as synonymous with actual crime rates for the reasons given earlier, homicide rates

TABLE 27

Appeal and Homicide Rates by Village per 1,000 Persons, 1953–1962

Village	Population	Appealed cases (N)	Appeal rate/1,000	Homicides per 1,000
Talea	2,000	44	22	1
Juquila	1,700	11	6	0
Lalopa	1,000	12	12	2
San Juan Yaee	1,000	19	19	2
Tanetze	1,000	16	16	2
Yatoni	500	10	20	4
Lachichina	450	10	22	6.7
Yaviche	400	8	20	2.5
Yobego	400	1	3	0
Otatitlan	350	7	20	4.9
Yagallo	300	5	17	10
Porvenir	150	1	7	0
Santa Gertrudis	100	0	0	0

may closely approximate the actual rates in this category. Although village population size does not correlate with appeal rate, it does appear that the factionalized villages are somewhat more likely than nonfactionalized ones to resort to homicide (see Table 28). Talea appeals a high proportion of cases (Table 27), but it is below the median in the number of cases of serious violence or deaths (Table 28).

If we look at Table 28, where villages are compared with reference to homicide rates, we see a difference in the homicide rates of the two groups of villages, with factionalized villages being more prone to homicide than nonfactionalized ones. Social organization is a better predictor of violence than population size: villages that are factionalized, regardless of population size, tend to produce the greatest number of acts of bloodshed. In this context, because Talean social structure is characterized not by deep rifts but by complex and cross-linking ties, we would not expect this town to have a high homicide rate. Yagallo, on the other hand, would be classed as a divided village; Taleans explain Yagallo's high homicide rate as due to evangelical Protestant activity. It may be, however, that factionalized villages attract evangelicals; cause and effect here is not simple to detect.

Table 29 lists the percentage of villages sending cases to the district under each of the categories listed. The most used categories under personal offenses are acts that result in wounds (*lesiones*), homicides (*homicidio*), assaults (*golpes*), and threats (*amenazas*). All categories under property cases show relatively high use, but under role-related offenses abuse of authority (*abuso de autoridad*) is the only category to appear regularly. The consistent reporting of the first three categories mentioned above corroborates the earlier observation that the appeals court in Villa Alta requires offenses in-

TABLE 28

Homicide Rates in Factionalized and Nonfactionalized Villages,
1953–1962

Factionalized village	Homicide rate per 1,000 persons	Nonfactionalized village	Homicide rate per 1,000 persons
Yagallo	10.0	Tanetze	2.0
Lachichina	6.7	Talea	1.0
Otatitlan	4.9	Juquila	0.0
Yatoni	4.0	Porvenir	0.0
Yaviche	2.5	Yobego	0.0
Lalopa	2.0	Santa Gertrudis	0.0
San Juan Yaee	2.0		

TABLE 29

Crime Category Use, 1953–1962

Category	Percentage of the 12 villages using category	Category	Percentage of the 12 villages using category
Personal		*Role-related*	
Amenazas (threats)	58	*Abuso de autoridad* (abuse of authority)	62
Estupro (rape)	8		
Golpes (assault)	61	*Abuso de confianza* (abuse of confidence)	23
Homicidio (homicide)	77		
Injurias (insults)	23	*Disobedencia* (disobedience by a child of a parent)	15
Lesiones (blood drawn)	85		
Rapto (abduction; rape)	8	*Fraude* (fraud)	31
Violación (violation)	8		
Property		*Resistencia* (resisting arrest)	8
Daño en propiedad (property damage)	50		
Despojo (vandalism)	77		
Robo (robbery)	69		

volving bloodshed to be sent to it, although if all such cases were reported the category would be even more swollen. Threats are a high-use category because these acts usually accompany bloodshed.

Fewer villages use the district courts for role-related offenses. The lower incidence of such cases in the district court indicates that such conflicts may not escalate into violence. The one category that frequently appears is abuse of authority, which often involves conflicts with persons in positions of elected power in the village. As we shall see when we look at who uses the district courts and for what, this category may reflect their use as a power equalizer, as when a person with less power attempts to balance the power differential, or as a mechanism that increases the power of those with money and knowledge of the state system.

Patterns of court use on a per-village basis indicate diversity in court use in this area. Tables 30 and 31 show that villages vary not only in the extent but also in the way they use the courts. Court usage may be either wide-ranging or specialized, and if specialized, the category of specialization may vary. Crimes that are more frequently appealed indicate something about the possible direction of the appeals courts. As I have said, the district court requires serious offenses involving bloodshed to be sent to it; and Porvenir sends role-related cases involving bloodshed but no other cases. The con-

TABLE 30

Crime Categories Used in Cases Sent to Appeals Court, by Village, 1953–1962

Category	Juquila	Lachi-china	Lalopa	Otatitlan	Porvenir	San Juan Yaee	Talea	Tanetze	Yagallo	Yatoni	Yaviche	Yobego
Personal												
Amenazas (threats)		12%	12%			7%	11%			6%	13%	
Estupro (rape)	7%						9					
Golpes (assault)		12	12			10	8	7%		11	13	
Homicidio (homicide)		18	12	14%		7	4	13	75%	11	13	
Injurias (insults)						3	2					
Lesiones (blood drawn)	13	35	6	29		22	9	7		11	38	50%
Rapto (abduction; rape)							2					
Violación (violation)							6					
TOTAL	20	83	42	43		49	51	27	75	39	77	50
Property												
Daño en propiedad (property damage)	20		6	14		13	11	13		11		
Despojo (vandalism)	20		12	15		7	13	27	25	17	12	
Robo (robbery)	27	11	18			17	11	20			13	
TOTAL	67	11	36	29		37	24	60	25	28	25	
Role-related												
Abuso de autoridad (abuse of authority)	13		11		100%	10	8	13		11		50
Abuso de confianza (abuse of confidence)							2			6		
Disobediencia (dis-obedience by a child of a parent)						3						
Fraude (fraud)		6	6	14			2			15		
Resistencia (resisting arrest)			6				2					
TOTAL	13	6	23	14	100	13	14	13		32		50

NOTE: Because of rounding, figures may not add to totals shown. The three totals do not equal 100 percent because offenses overlap.

TABLE 31

Percentage of Offenses Appealed in Four Categories by Village,
1953–1962

Village/appeal rate (1,000)	Personal offenses	Role-related offenses	Property-related offenses	Other offenses
Juquila/6	20%	13%	67%	—
Lachichina/22	83	6	11	11%
Lalopa/12	42	23	36	26
Otatitlan/20	43	14	29	30
Porvenir/7	—	100	—	—
San Juan Yaee/19	49	13	37	9
Santa Gertrudis/0	—	—	—	—
Talea/22	51	14	24	20
Tanetze/16	27	13	60	12
Yagallo/17	75	—	25	20
Yatoni/20	39	32	28	10
Yaviche/20	77	—	25	20
Yobego/3	50	50	—	—

NOTE: The figures do not add to 100 percent because cases may involve more than one offense.

sistently high rate of appeals of property case categories (except from Lachichina) may indicate that persons involved in disputes over land think they must turn to the district court to verify ownership because land sales are registered in district offices. If this is so, what is veiled as an administrative procedure has the latent function of increasing the power of the district courts. Another reason for property owners to take cases to the district is linked to social status: something in their position as property owners improves their chances in the district courts. If property ownership correlates with greater wealth, higher education, and personal connections with officials, then property owners are better "game players" at the district level than are the unpropertied.

Posing the questions who uses the courts and for what purpose may reveal whether courts are being used to balance inequities in power, to reinforce the status quo, or to support social change. In the process the investigator may discover which groups in the region systematically avoid the district courts, and how evolution of court use looks when it is examined from the viewpoint of plaintiffs, defendants, or a combination of both. The answers to these questions may indicate whose interests will be best served if the courts become more widely used.

However, it is important to realize that the types of crimes appealed may result in a distorted and erroneous perception of the villages at the district and state court level. Talea (Table 30), for example, uses the district court fully; that is, it sends cases that fit all possible categories. Lachichina, a village with the same appeal rate (22 percent), uses only half the available crime categories, and its use is concentrated mostly in crimes dealing with injuries to persons. Personal injury cases account for 74 percent of all cases Lachichina sends to the appeals court, but only 41 percent of the total sent by Talea. Yaviche, with an appeal rate (20 percent) similar to those of Talea and Lachichina and a population almost the same size as that of Lachichina, resembles Lachichina in terms of specialization. Yatoni follows the Talean pattern of sending a wide range of crimes to the appeals court. When communities in the Rincón are compared, bilingual ones tend to make full use and monolingual ones limited use of the district court (see Abel 1982).

The villages with overall low appeal rates show little diversity in use patterns, but more often, according to the public record at least, they tend to be limited users. Juquila, Porvenir, Tanetze, Yobego, and Yagallo are all limited court users. Lalopa is the exception because it is a full court user, as is Santa Gertrudis, although to a lesser degree. For example, the mainly monolingual Zapotec settlements of Juquila and Lachichina usually send property and personal injury cases, respectively. Among other such villages, Yobego submits an equal number of role-related and personal offenses, and Yagallo and Yaviche usually send cases of injuries and threats. This diversity indicates village differences in their relationships with the district court and in their perception of the flow of benefits. In general, the docket data suggest that large villages tend to full use and smaller villages tend to more limited use, but on the whole the district has a reputation for being peaceful.

Parnell's study (1989) found that a comparison of appeals in 13 villages indicated village schisms and weakened local leadership. More specifically, he indicates (chap. 5) that convergent villages with elected officials (such as Talea) tended not to appeal to the extent of divided villages with political bosses (*caciques*). Certainly the diversity in patterns of district court use underscores the point that we are not dealing with crime rates, and possibly not even with an approximation of crime rates. The reasons for diversity in court use could be explained by empirical data of a social-organizational sort collected within the villages themselves.

I suggested earlier that the district court records more closely approximate crime rates in those cases in which blood is drawn (see Table 32). Talea, whose overall appeal rate appears to be high, has a relatively low rate for crimes of bloodshed. This supports ethno-

TABLE 32

Appeal Rates for Crimes of Bloodshed, 1953–1962

(per 1,000)

Village	Homicidios (homicides)	Lesiones (blood-drawing wounds)	Golpes (assaults)
Juquila	0.0	1.2	0.0
Lachichina	6.7	13.3	4.4
Lalopa	2.0	1.0	2.0
Otatitlan	4.9	5.7	0.0
Porvenir	0.0	0.0	0.0
San Juan Yaee	2.0	7.0	3.0
Talea	1.0	2.5	2.0
Tanetze	2.0	1.0	1.0
Yagallo	10.0	0.0	0.0
Yatoni	4.0	4.0	4.0
Yaviche	2.5	7.5	2.5
Yobego	0.0	2.5	0.0

graphic data showing that Talea has a high overall rate of order. Its citizens' willingness to turn to the appeals courts in Villa Alta may contribute in part to this high rate of order. However, it may also leave the impression with state officials that Taleans are particularly litigious.

Sex Differences in Use of the District Court

The district court dockets for the years 1953–62 provide only the names of defendants, plaintiffs, descriptions of the complaints, and the place of origin of the participants; sex differences can be gleaned from the names given. No data on decisions are included. The data are too sketchy to help establish any relationship between social status and the use of the appeal court except for sex of users. Participation by sex can, however, be compared with earlier tables on the use of the Talean courts.

In 1959 I showed my Talean data to the eminent British anthropologist Meyer Fortes. I recall his surprise over the active role of Talean women plaintiffs and his comment that he thought this behavior rare cross-culturally. It is hard to know how unusual the large number of Talean women plaintiffs is. Ethnographers of law have not always dealt with gender in analyzing the disputing process or isolated sex as a variable except as members of different sexes appear in case materials.

Over the ten-year period, 22 female (52 percent) and 20 (48 per-

TABLE 33

Plaintiff Use of the District Court by Status and Type of Complaint, 1953–1962

(N = 124)

Type of complaint	Female		Male		Male & female		Official		Society	
	No.	Percent	No.	Percent	No.	Percent	No.	Percent	No.	Percent
Personal	22	45%	29	45%	2	67%	—	—	2	67%
Property	18	37	26	41	1	33	1	20%	1	33
Role-related	9	18	9	14	0	—	4	80	—	—
TOTAL	49	100%	64	100%	3	100%	5	100%	3	100%

TABLE 34

Defendant Use of the District Court by Status and Type of Complaint, 1953–1962

(N = 124)

Type of complaint	Female		Male		Male & female		Official		Society	
	No.	Percent	No.	Percent	No.	Percent	No.	Percent	No.	Percent
Personal	4	19%	46	55%	5	50%	—	—	—	—
Property	14	67	28	33	4	40	—	—	—	—
Role-related	3	14	10	12	1	10	9	100%	—	—
TOTAL	21	100%	84	100%	10	100%	9	100%		

cent) male plaintiffs from Talea used the district court, and 12 females (23 percent) and 40 males (77 percent) were defendants. The picture changes somewhat in the context of the total set of data for the same period covering the Rincón region as a whole (see Tables 33 and 34). Here females appeared as plaintiffs in 40 percent of the cases, and males in 52 percent. (Males and females complained as couples in only 2 percent of the cases, a reminder of the individualistic nature of disputing and the relative unimportance of the couple as such.) As defendants, females appeared in 17 percent of the cases, and males in 68 percent; males and females appeared as co-defendants in 8 percent of the cases, and officials appeared as defendants in 7 percent. It is men, not women, who come face-to-face with state punishment, and for some this is their first introduction to the non-Indian world. The symbolic importance of this sexual difference is a fundamental principle of order and disorder. In the region as a whole, there was a slightly higher use of the court by males as plaintiffs than by females and an overwhelmingly greater presence of males as defendants. Furthermore, as plaintiffs, females and males complained about similar problems and at nearly the same rate. Both females and males complained about personal violations in 45 percent of their respective total cases. Females complained about property violations in 37 percent and males in 41 percent of the cases in which they appeared as plaintiffs.

Thus, when a woman uses the district court, she is likely to be the plaintiff, and the majority of those cases involve physical aggression against her person in the form of assault and battery, abandonment, or rape. Charges of civil crimes such as falsification of documents, fraud, and abuse of authority are the next most common categories.

In the rare case in which a woman is the defendant, we can predict that the case involves violence to property or fraud, and almost never violence to a person. And, in these cases, the woman is rarely related to the other party in the case. If there are a multiple number of defendants, they are men and the crime is one of violence or physical aggression against a person, usually another male.

The major difference between male and female court use appears when they are defendants (Table 34). When women appeared as defendants, the offense was usually property related. Males usually appeared for offenses involving injuries to person. Women in this sample rarely killed. The conflict dyads (Table 35) were predominantly male vs. male (40 percent); thus, the majority of assault and homicide cases involved male assailants of male victims, the usual pattern across most societies. The second highest conflict dyad, but much lower, was female vs. male (24 percent). All other possible dyads were relatively evenly distributed. Some of these dyads are worth noting. Citizens took officials to court in only 6 percent of the cases. Citizens were inclined to oppose what they considered abuse

TABLE 35
Conflict Dyads in the District Court, 1953–1962

	No.	Percent of total
Female vs. female	6	5%
Female vs. male	31	24
Male vs. female	12	9
Male vs. male	51	40
Male vs. male & female	3	2
Female vs. male & female	6	5
Male & female vs. male	3	2
Official vs. citizen	5	4
Citizen vs. official	8	6
Society vs. official	1	1
Society vs. female	2	2
TOTAL	128	100%

of authority, whereas officials for their part (4 percent) accused citizens of nonfulfillment of their civic duties. Female defendants in the district court were there because of complaints by males (9 percent) and not by other females (5 percent). In fact, female vs. female cases accounted for a relatively low percentage of the total cases in the district court.

In the great majority of these cases, those in conflict were members of the same community; inter-village disputes were few, and in this sample most were initiated by Taleans. Crimes across village boundaries did occur; they were the result either of territorial disputes or of the activity of groups of road bandits, but they were rare occurrences. Or at least appeal of such cases was rare (in this sample 9 out of 147 cases were inter-village and involved both male and female plaintiffs and defendants).

Discussion

District court dockets reflect some dramatic events that take place in Indian communities. They are a manifestation of the stress, factionalism, and power plays of people who share, because of a common heritage, the need to express themselves publicly in the search for harmony or in prolonged controversy. The dockets appear to be limited to pathological behavior. In addition, they reveal a power struggle between two levels of law: local and state. District courts have been able to assert their authority in matters of homicide, and all villages are supposed to send cases where blood is drawn to the district courts. The reason property cases now regularly appear at the district level is more ambiguous; it may reflect the power over land cases that the administration of land sales at the district level gives Villaltecan officials, or it may reflect certain advantages that accrue to landowners as a result of their greater wealth. Also, the increasing value of land due to scarcity pushes for solutions that can be enforced. The state court is the major institution for deciding land title disputes.

Villagers do not turn to district courts for help in role-related cases involving daily life that reflect the villagers' autonomy in questions of personal values. Cases that involve abuse of authority are an exception. As I elaborate in Chapter 13, cases involving governance center on the obligations of both elected and appointed officials and the egalitarian nature of public authority, and they are often means for citizen harassment of officials. Villagers turn to the district to balance the power in a dispute with a local official. These officials turn to the district courts as well, though to a lesser degree, in their problems with citizens.

Overall, the relationship between Talea and the Rincón area in general and the district court is one in which Rinconeros use the district for extraordinary problems. Acts of violence, property disputes, and conflicts with local-level authorities push Rinconeros toward the district court. The ordinary problems of day-to-day life in the village remain under the jurisdiction of local officials. Whether this differentiation results from the desires of district officials or of local people, the effect is the same. District courts develop in response to the kinds of cases they receive. The district court in Villa Alta has a court apparatus to handle extraordinary problems. As long as local-level courts handle the ordinary problems, the two systems work together, albeit in an unplanned way; neither is the passive object of an overarching legal process. Should changes occur at the local level that leave villagers without a forum for their ordinary problems, we could expect either a marked increase in extraordinary acts, burdening the area with serious divisiveness, or the development of new forums. It is also possible that ordinary life problems will revert to family remedy agents, though this is less likely in the immediate future because change is bringing with it separation of loyalties in the family and a spatial fragmentation of family members due to migration.

The development of factionalism in a village divided over the desires of some for "progress" and of others for a more indigenous way of life, or over disagreements about the intrusion of Protestant missionaries and the resulting dissension over voluntary public service, is part of the testing of political alignment. Local-level courts may seem unattractive for one faction and may encourage the emergence of regional organization, a strategy for preventing or resolving controversy over the direction of change (Parnell 1989). Whatever the reason, a failure by local officials to deal with life problems that originate outside the community may be crucial in determining the patterns and transformations of forums for order and disorder.

As I move my focus from the Rincón area to particular villages in the area, I notice for each village a distinct pattern for managing its conflicts and for relating to the district court. Not surprisingly people contest different symbols. Informal rules have emerged: in one village only personal injury cases are frequent and taken to the district-level, and in another only property-related cases are common and presented in Villa Alta. Since the types of cases taken to the district courts are patterned, law not only controls, but is controlled. As I mentioned earlier, cases can come to the district court because of a decision either by local officials or by villagers. The patterns that characterize use of the district courts suggest a system of social control within the villages that affects officials and citizens alike. Both groups seem to share a view of the function of the district court. The view varies from village to village, but is consistent within each village. How the view is formed and how it continues to be effective or changes over time are subjects for another investigation. The existence of this patterning, however, suggests that we must look at law within the matrix of the social system and realize that it is both an agent of control and subject to control.

In the realm of cultural control, values about litigiousness are important. Earlier I pointed out that the degree of a village's litigiousness should not be considered an indicator of disorder. It may indicate the strength of the justice motive and the belief that individuals must rectify wrongs, that they must act in their own defense. Or it may indicate the need for harmony. Talea exemplifies this, but patterns of court use by sex raise other questions. As we have seen, females are not reluctant to take their problems to the district court. They go to the court as plaintiffs almost as frequently as do males, but they appear infrequently as defendants and almost never as defendants in personal injury cases. They are not hit by state power directly through penalty. When they do appear as defendants, they are more likely to have been taken to court by a male, not by another female. Female vs. female conflicts are rarely found in the district courts; district-level courts are places for male vs. male or cross-sex conflicts.

In many villages, the women's world has developed its preferred forums for handling female vs. female disputes, as is indicated in women's use of supernaturals. Females view the district court as primarily a place where problems with men are handled. Nation-state law, because it is a male-dominated system, could inadvertently strengthen preferred female dispute-settling forums. If nation-state law contributes to the demise of local-level legal systems by increasing its control over these systems and fails to recognize the existence of women's needs, the female-dispute handling forums may preserve the last vestiges of norms and values that distinguish one village from another and both from the national system.

Analysis of court users in Talea reveals an agenda fashioned by the needs of community. Taleans have a court process that officials equate with harmony and autonomy. Local law is created by citizen use and at the same time is being imposed upon a citizen body by citizen-officials. I described the process as interactive, although it is sometimes impositional. The Talean use of the Villaltecan district court is very much in the same mold: Taleans use the court for a wide array of legal complaints, and at least in terms of male-female use, the pattern follows in the same vein as the use of Talean courts by Taleans. In other words, it does not appear that Taleans change their posture in dealing with the district court. They view that court process, too, as interactional and at their disposal, although they know of its rigidities.

The court docket in Villa Alta reveals differences between state and village. On the one hand it is authoritative: the state determines what cases it accepts and what cases must be appealed to it. According to state law, village courts do not have jurisdiction over certain matters dealing with bodily injury and property. The court deals with the extraordinary, not the ordinary, and we should not be surprised to discover that there is no broad citizen participation. On the other hand, the district court means something different to each village in the district. In this sense, it can be seen as an institution with multiple meanings, one that can be used in a variety of ways by the villages. The Taleans, however, were consistent with use of their own courts: they used the district court for all categories of complaints, unlike other villages in the Rincón. All the users (the state and the litigating parties) shape the activity of the court. The underlying concept is still one of shared power, even though the distribution of that power is competitive and dynamic.

The single most important observation from this analysis of the district court docket, even correcting for nonrecording of cases, is how rarely that court is used. Taking a case to the district court is escalation, and Rinconeros do not escalate disputes both because escalation to an external system is linked to a loss of local autonomy and because village law is more elastic than the state system. The state system narrows disputes (Mather and Yngvesson 1980–81) in a way that does not permit participants the possibility for creative harmony.

Part III   The Substance of Legal Encounters

Chapter Ten

Rank, Intimacy, and Control
in Cross-sex Complaints

Numbers are useful indicators of broad patterns of court use, but they tell only a partial story about what using the court means. To say that women use the courts as plaintiffs about as frequently as men do and for roughly the same matters is too broad a generalization for understanding the roles of males and females in Talea and the way in which each sex is valued or devalued by the other and in the society at large. In other words, statements about the quantity of interaction are bound to leave out much of the substance of male-female jural relations. In this chapter, I use data from case materials to illustrate how men and women express themselves in court when under interpersonal stress and to point to the limits imposed on the courts by the broader sociopolitical realities in Talea and environs.

In Talea, no woman has ever sat as judge, and few women, as I have indicated, appear as defendants in male-female cases. Nevertheless, as we have seen, the most frequent complainants in cross-sex cases are the women, and for the most part, only women complain about physical abuse. The outcome of litigation is as stereotypic as the complaint itself; both are a result of the shape of women's lives in Talea. Women marry before they are 20, usually in the context of an arranged marriage or, more recently, as a result of choice free from parental persuasion or admonition. How a woman marries affects her complaint pattern. In an arranged marriage, the parents of the woman take part in ensuring that problems between the spouses are resolved, whereas free-choice marriage (or those entered with no ceremony at all) stimulates less parental responsibility and possibly more abuse from husbands or lovers. Relative rank (such as the personal wealth of a man or woman), the presence of extended family, and physical distance from family are also factors in the shape and outcome of disputes. And finally, the political and legal constraints on village law play a part in forcing a choice between compromise and agreement at the village level and confrontation under state law in Villa Alta, a choice that is often posed for the convenience of local officials.

In this chapter I present selected cases from the period under consideration (1957–68), all of which involve disputes between males and females. Four sets of cross-sex cases stand out. The first set deals with complaints surrounding paternity, which may be brought by women or by men in their natal family, and the second with complaints of physical abuse, brought primarily by women against their husband or lover. The third set involves men bringing women to court for abandonment or adultery. In the fourth set the court brings women to court who are accused of aborting a pregnancy, an act considered a crime (*delito*).

The styles of court procedure generally vary with each set: paternity cases are accusatory, and the plaintiffs demand compensation. In the physical abuse cases, the women often demand divorce or separation but instead usually receive conciliatory or remedial action. Participation by the woman's family in cross-sex cases of this sort increases the demand for action against the abusing male. And in the last two sets—cross-sex cases dealing with abandonment, adultery, and abortion—the style is largely penal, and the intent is to punish. Although I am comfortable with such overall generalizations about cross-sex cases, we will see that the particulars of each case do not always fit the overall pattern, dominant though it may be.

Paternity

Paternity cases deal primarily with three issues: determining paternity, recording it, and deciding the father's economic responsibilities. The issue may be brought to the attention of the court by the woman in question or by members of her family. For the most part, cases appear to be cut and dried and end with the writing of an agreement. In some instances the issues are argued all the way to the district court.

Case 42 deals with a paternity issue. María, a 27-year-old woman from neighboring Lalopa, presented her case to the president.

"Señor Presidente, with all respect I come to state my problem so that it will be resolved with your intervention. I am single. Before I arrived here in Talea, I was in Loma Bonita, Oaxaca, working as a maid, and it was there

that I met Donaldo from this village. We both agreed to set up house together. We were there together for a fair amount of time, and then we arrived
here. I am not with him now because he always leaves this village and goes
to work elsewhere. I thought it would be better to separate from him. Now I
am eight months pregnant, and soon I will give birth. And the reason I come
before you is for you to call him here so that we can make an arrangement
with him so that he will help me pay the expenses of the birth. I am poor,
and I cannot pay for all of my expenses. Furthermore, my parents are not
from this town."

Once María had presented her case to the presidente, Donaldo was summoned. Presenting himself a few moments later, Donaldo declared that he
was single and 28 years of age. The presidente said to him, "I had you called
in so that you would know that this woman says that you are responsible for
her state of pregnancy. She asked that you help her with the childbirth expenses because it will not be long before she completes her commitment."

Donaldo said, "Look, Señor Presidente, this woman perhaps is thinking
of damaging me because I am close to getting married. I did not follow her,
and I did not say anything to her. I left for Villa Alta to work as a mason in
that town. And when I returned to my house, she was no longer there. She
did not even say where she had gone. She did not say, 'Look, Donaldo I am
going, and I will tell you that I am pregnant and I ask you to help me when I
bear my commitment.' But she did not say anything. Seeing that she was
not in my house, I went to see her and begged her to return because she left
without motive. She did not want to return. I again went to Villa Alta to
work, and when I returned [to Talea] two months later, she told me that she
was pregnant. And I did not say anything to her. Maybe it was not even my
child. Think, Señor Presidente, that she did not say anything when I went to
ask her to return. And now she says that I am responsible. Maybe it is someone else."

The presidente said to the woman, "Is what Donaldo has just said true?
That you left your house without saying anything to him?" María answered,
"Yes, but he is the only one responsible for the state I find myself in, because I was with him for a long time. I did not say anything to him because I
was hardly pregnant. I know that he is going to marry, and I do not want to
hurt him. I only want him to help me with the expense for the birth and to
acknowledge his child, that is, that he come to register the child in the Book
of Civil Registry."

Donaldo answered that he was going to help her, but that he did not feel
he was responsible. . . .

The presidente asked María what she was asking for. She answered,
"That he pay for the midwife and that he buy some food for me while I am
in bed. And that he come to acknowledge his child at this presidencia as his
legitimate child." Donaldo answered that he was in agreement with what
she asked, but asked that she not continue to bother him because he was
getting married soon.

Both parties, in common agreement signed the act of agreement [convenio].

Agreements deal with the problems of immediate concern to women, such as covering the expenses of the birth, but when a woman also insists, as María did, that the father recognize the child to be his, she is orienting both parties to future needs that she may face while raising the child without a father. Although it may be relatively easy for both to sign an agreement, it may be more difficult to keep the father legally responsible while the child is growing up. Similarly, Donaldo was covering his tracks by arguing that María left him of her own free will and would not return, thereby mitigating his future responsibilities for her and their child.

In case 43, a woman brought her paternity complaint to the alcalde's office.

Adela told the court that she had had relations with Francisco since October. After he had been coming to her house, she informed him that she was pregnant and that he should take charge of the situation. He agreed to this.

In February Adela took her claim to court, and the defendant promised to arrange everything out of court. She again presented herself at the court, stating that Francisco had not fulfilled his part of the bargain because he claimed he was not Adela's only lover, that there were others including Pacho so-and-so.

An agreement was made by the court. Adela was satisfied with 100 pesos to cover expenses, and Francisco was freed from further responsibility.

A woman's reputation for fidelity or promiscuity affects the kind of settlement she is given. If a parent or grandparent takes an interest in a young woman's welfare, she may fare somewhat better. In Case 44, a great-grandmother accompanied her great-granddaughter to file a complaint against the unmarried father of the young woman's child, who came accompanied by his father.

Mica had an illegitimate child by Gil, and he recognized the child as his own and registered it in the annals. He had helped since the birth, but did not wish to marry Mica. The following agreement was drawn up. Gil and his father agreed to give Mica 200 pesos. If the child became ill, they promised to pay medical expenses. In case the child should die, the expenses would be shared by mother and father. They promised to help Mica with various crops, corn, beans, and *panela* [brown sugar], to help with the costs of his rearing. When he got to be six or seven years old, he would have to go to school, and the expenses would be paid by the father. Mica had received 125 pesos, which brought the total given to the mother to 325 pesos.

Sometimes, a parent will ask the court to formalize a relationship that involves pregnancy. In Case 45, a father appeared before the sindico to ask him to find out what verbal contract a young man had entered into with his daughter.

Señor Ramón appeared before the sindico in his duty as a father. He had come before the authority because his daughter Marta, who had been living under her parents' guardianship, had gone to live with Señor Camilo without asking the consent or the feelings of her parents. The young couple were summoned and notified.

The sindico told them of the error they were committing since they had not taken the obligation to advise both of Marta's parents of the union they had freely entered into. The father asked the presidente to find out what it was that Camilo proposed in relation to Marta and in relation to the state of pregnancy in which she found herself. He wanted to make sure the young man would assume the responsibilities when the time came that it was necessary.

Señor Camilo was asked about his responsibility, and he testified that he was willing to give to his "companion of home" all that was her due, that he would comply faithfully because they had entered freely and mutually into living together; also he promised before this authority to give all the attention due when the young woman gave birth. He would give her economic aid, and all that was necessary and would recognize the future child as a legitimate child, conceived during their free union. In view of all the foregoing, Señor Ramón, the father of the young lady, and his daughter and future mother were informed, and thus Camilo fulfilled his obligations and duties as a father to defend and protect his child, as is natural.

The conflict in Case 46 originated between two young people as a result of their having sexual relations during their courtship. The case was brought to the presidente for solution and then, three days later, was taken to the office of the alcalde.

In 1962 the complaint of breach of promise was brought to a close. The claim made by the plaintiff Margarita was as follows. The young man Jerónimo took advantage of his betrothal; he promised to marry Margarita and then seduced her. When she was two months pregnant, he no longer wished to fulfill his promise and, wishing to avoid responsibility, proposed that she have an abortion. The claimant did not agree to this and asked the court to convince the young man of the error of his ways and to make him make good his offer of marriage.

Upon hearing this claim, the young man tried to avoid the marriage commitment. He offered to give her some help, but did not want to marry her. At this point, the stepmother of the plaintiff was called, and she maintained she had just learned about her stepchild's predicament. The stepmother said that it was the wish of her husband that from this day on his daughter's welfare should be the responsibility of her boyfriend, since through her own will she had brought about her misfortune. With the father's decision in mind, the presidente brought the matter to a close. He proposed that the young man either take his fiancée to his house for a period of no less than two years and then see if they would marry or separate, or else appeal the case. After lengthy discussion, the young man decided to avoid conflict and agreed to take her home for that period of time and let the future decide the outcome for both.

The man who was presidente during this year was a schoolteacher, a man not highly thought of as a problem solver. Three days after the agreement in the presidente's office, the case appeared before the alcalde: the 76-year-old father of the young woman accompanied her to make a claim against the young man, stating that the defendant was responsible for the pregnancy of his daughter. At this meeting the father of the defendant was also present, and the judge concluded:

"The responsibility of the defendant has been duly shown, and a document drawn up before the presidente and signed by the plaintiff and the defendant. Along with this document and verbal petitions on both parts, both sides have reached an amicable settlement. The resolution contained in the original document, relating to the agreement to keep her at his side and at his house, has been modified. Instead, they have decided that she should be given monetary aid at the time she gives birth and that she should continue to live with her father." The judge asked both parties if it were true that they had reached an amicable settlement in this case, and they answered in the affirmative.

They were asked to tell what sum of money the young woman would receive. Both parties answered that they had arrived at the sum of 300 pesos and, as the only aid she would receive, that it would be delivered immediately. The plaintiffs were asked if they agreed on the sum of money mentioned, and they answered in the affirmative, as did the defendant and his father.

In this case it appears that the parties had come together outside the court and decided on an agreement they then had ratified by the court. It is unclear why there was a change of mind. It could be because the man was relatively young or because the sum agreed upon was attractive. It was described as an amicable settlement. Only time would tell how amicable the settlement would remain. The point is that the parties were aware of the preventive function of a formal settlement, as in Case 47.

A mother appeared before the presidente to claim that her daughter was pregnant and that she was not sure who was responsible. A month later she appeared before the court and named a young man, 22 years of age, and asked that he be held responsible. The mother asked that the progenitor of the expected baby be responsible for the pregnancy. She wished that when the child was born, the young man recognize the child by registering his name in the Civil Registry, and that he make clear the voluntary help he wished to give them for the expenses they would incur because of the birth, such as medicine and other necessities. The help could be monetary, and its amount and frequency would depend on the father and his sense of responsibility.

Both parties agreed to abide by the terms of each point dealt with and in this way avoid future quarrels that could be prejudicial to both parties.

There is something clear-cut about paternity cases when neither party is married. When paternity involves people who are married but not to each other, questions of adultery make the settlement more difficult and, as we shall see, complicate the determination of responsibility. Physical abuse cases, on the other hand, are not cut and dried unless alcohol is involved, and then the case reports sound formulaic.

Physical Abuse

Physical abuse in Talea is often found in conjunction with inebriation. Whether people drink alcohol in order to have a pretext to abuse others or whether they abuse because they are drunk is difficult to ascertain. What is general about abuse cases involving alcohol is that the state of drunkenness is usually offered as a reason or excuse. I do not know the incidence of home violence in Talea. I do know that it is not infrequent and that women, particularly mature women with children, feel they can bring this abuse to the attention of public authorities and receive a public hearing that is unequivocally anti-abuse, one that does not condone physical violence in the home. On the other hand, women do not always get what they request from the courts. In Case 48, a woman first presented a complaint against her husband in the presidente's office. When it was not solved to her liking there, it was passed to the alcalde's office for a hearing.

The woman was asked the reason for her claim, and she answered that it was due to the mistreatment she received from her husband when he was drunk. Also, she claimed he did not trust her and believed that she committed adultery. Because of this her life was upset, since she did not know what her husband expected, and she thought it might be a good idea to separate. She also said that she was an object of scorn to her husband's children. Viewing the state she was in and because of the attitude of the aforementioned persons, the woman did not accept a reconciliation with her husband.

The husband said that he did not offend his wife when he was sober, but perhaps he had done so when drunk. For this reason he requested that it be overlooked, since he didn't do it maliciously, and he promised not to repeat these disorders in order to reestablish peace and tranquility at home, and he guaranteed also that his wife could manage the household.

The wife requested that her husband manage the products and harvests he gathered, his own goods and legitimate property, and the expenses which might arise and that he should be in charge of collections and profits. The man accepted his wife's request.

The complainant in this case warned that any attempt that the husband might make against her in the form of threat or physical force would occasion her to ask the authorities to establish order and to sanction him. Her husband promised not to repeat his behavior in order to avoid the consequences. His wife accepted the reconciliation and would go on living in his house, he being a well-known person in this town.

The judicial authority requested the couple to help each other carry out the proposed tasks for their own good and for the good of the family. The couple promised to remain faithful and care for each other and do the same as regards any goods acquired during the union.

The case was closed, and the document of agreement drawn up and signed.

The following case, number 49, does not deal with abuse under conditions of drunkenness; rather, the motive appears to be jealousy. A 40-year-old woman appeared before the presidente with the following complaint.

Saturday night her husband pushed her and tore her dress, solely because he was jealous. "We were in the store where we sell liquor, when an unknown man who was slightly drunk appeared and placed a watch on the arm of my little daughter, who was also there. The stranger began to drink a few beers and again said to my little girl, 'I'm going to put this bracelet on you,' at which point I told him not to. He said, 'Okay, when I come to this town again, I will bring a smaller one for her.' While we were talking about this, my husband arrived, and the stranger invited him to have a beer. He accepted and drank it and left, and the stranger began to talk to us again. At this point my husband came and pushed me and tore my dress [she presents the torn dress]. And for this reason I have come so that he will be punished for doing what he did for no reason at all."

The presidente summoned the husband and ordered him to be detained in the public jail in order to deal with this matter on the next day. When the husband appeared before the presidente the following day, he was informed of the reason for the punishment he received. He answered with the following statement: "It was true that I pushed my wife, but I did not tear her dress. The reason for my doing so was within my rights. I am not a drunkard who just stands around. The reason was this. A man was in the bar, and he had his hand on my wife's shoulder and was talking with her. At this point, I came in and said to her, 'Why don't you go with him if you wish, once and for all, instead of doing those things with him in front of the children?' Then, the stranger grabbed me and wanted to hit me because I had pushed my wife, and I said I had the right to push her because she was my wife, not somebody else's. We began to argue when some friends separated us."

The presidente argued that a cantina was not a proper place for women and children, and that his wife should not continue working in his establishment because a place of drinking is not for women and children. He continued: "Any drunk or person in an alcoholic condition says many things unthinkingly and embraces and talks to anyone for any reason. An establishment where alcoholic beverages are served is not proper for the family and even less for married women. I believe that you two did not remember or did not consider the consequences of owning this kind of establishment. Your wife, sir, has to watch her children while serving, and you should know beforehand that it is a bar in which she works and not a chapel." The husband agreed with him.

The presidente continued: "If your establishment were a grocery and if upon your arrival you found someone embracing her, it would be one thing, but since you have a bar and you know how drunks are, the only thing you can do is advise them. Since there is no crime to pursue here, the only thing I can do is to advise you not to sell liquor and dedicate yourselves to something else, so that in the future you won't have this kind of difficulty. Besides, you know that you have small children and they also are exposed to words that will be bad for their vocabulary. I leave this up to your judgment so that you can think about it and decide."

The litigants answered that they were going to think about it and decide, and they said they would do whatever possible to settle this matter. The presidente said that they had a few months to resolve the matter and to advise him what agreement they had come to.

This ended the hearing. They returned home, the matter having been for the meantime settled, while they came to some agreement.

Not all acts of physical abuse are linked to single incidents. Some women are under constant threat from a drunken husband, but the pressures to settle and reconcile even under the most difficult circumstances are strong. Case 50 was brought by a woman threatened by her husband, who was carrying a knife. When she complained to the presidente's office, the case was heard and the husband sanctioned by fine. He, however, appealed the case to the alcalde's office, where it was heard two and a half days later. The woman was 25 years old and legally married to her man; both were natives of Talea. When the sindico asked her what she now thought about the matter, she responded, according to the court records:

. . . that she was thinking of never returning to her husband for this action and for the constant threats. He told her that it would be better to get a divorce because she was an Indian and stubborn. On the other hand, he was almost always drunk; it was difficult. For these reasons she was not disposed to return to her husband, and she wanted it recorded that because of the constant threats she received from her husband, she was leaving him.

Her husband was requested to appear at the same time and was asked to tell the truth to the officials, and he admitted all his faults in having threatened his wife with a sharp weapon . . . and [said] he would not mistreat his wife again and wished that she return home . . . , to which his wife answered that her husband was always drunk and constantly threatened her and told her that it would be better to get a divorce. . . . The husband then said that since his wife would not pardon his behavior toward her, despite his having humbled himself before her, he would not force her to return to his side. . . .

At this time the wife said that it would be better to return to her husband only for the sake of the son that they had and on condition that at no time should the husband harm her. The husband asked the court to settle the matter. The husband's offenses were again stated by the court as offenses made against his wife, and he replied that from this day forward he would not do her any bodily harm.

The wife requested that an agreement be drawn up to settle the affair, and the husband asked that the earlier sanction on his behavior be lifted. The petition was granted, and the document drawn up and signed.

Sometimes, because of expectations that develop—a husband habitually drinks, a wife becomes accustomed to his habit, and she develops the habit of complaining about her husband—reconciliation after apologies is more usual than not. In other cases, where drinking and assault and battery are not habitual, the wife may be even more angered and the relationship harder to reconcile. In Case 51, aggression with a deadly weapon was described as being of a penal character, having been committed by a husband against his wife. Both husband and wife were enmeshed in extended families, and the complaint reached the sindico's office two days after the event. The circumstances were narrated by Dolores, a 22-year-old wife and seamstress.

They were invited by her husband's brother-in-law (as were the rest of the family) to rethatch their house that Sunday. At daybreak her husband, José, arose and went to help with this job. Dolores went a few minutes later because she had to wait for her children to get up. After she arrived there, her sister-in-law sent her to the house of her husband's uncle on an errand. When Dolores arrived, she was not attended to immediately because her aunt was bathing her small child. At this moment a second person arrived, sent on the same errand. She was surprised, and didn't dare go back to the house she had come from. Her aunt said to sit and eat with her, and she did. After dinner she left there and went back to her own house.

It was now about 2:00 P.M. Shortly after Dolores arrived home, José arrived and without a word went into the living room and lay down on the bed, having already drunk liquor. He called the children to him to lie down with him. One of them began to cry. The father was offended and began to beat the children. The plaintiff's mother intervened to help and protect the defenseless children.

At the moment of her [the wife's] intervention, José grabbed Dolores by the hair and began to hit her on the head, part of her back, and the right side of the face. Her aggressor said that the reason for this was that she had not told him where the money was that her father had given her on the house which had been indicated to be her property. Dolores told her husband that he knew full well she had received no money from her father. The woman immediately advised her uncle (where she had had lunch) and her neighbor and, being fearful of some accident, sent someone to tell the brother-in-law.

Aware of the presence of the brother-in-law, the husband threw himself onto his machete with which he had menaced . . . his wife, pretending to be very drunk. Then between the brother-in-law and the neighbor and herself, they wrested the machete from her husband. Dolores tells that that night she suffered strong pains as a consequence of the blows, and the next day continued to have a nosebleed. As proof she presents her bloodied shawl to indicate the gravity of the aggressive action of her husband.

Then the 29-year-old husband, who was a tailor, was called in to testify and explain the motive for the aggression.

On Sunday, he left his house at an early hour to help his brother-in-law work on his house. His wife arrived later with the same purpose in mind, to help with the work of the house. The sister of the defendant sent his wife on an errand to his uncle's house, about 9 o'clock. After lunch, when the sister saw that she hadn't return with the necessary things, she then sent her little son to call her, but still his wife didn't return. Moments later she sent her niece to tell her to come back, but not even then did she come back.

After these children went to call her four times, she came back, not to the house of her brother-in-law, but to her own home, having thereby failed to do the work in the house of her sister-in-law. For this reason the husband says he was angry at the treatment his wife was giving to the work, both [of them] knowing full well that this brother-in-law is the person who is giving them help, a house in which to live, and all that is necessary. When he realized that the wife had gone home, he went home too, and being there he couldn't contain his nervousness because of the actions of his wife. But he confesses that he did commit an error in attacking his wife.

However, the wife was not satisfied to conclude her complaint by reconciliation, and she petitioned for the delivery of their minor children into the charge of her parents. The case was remitted to the alcalde so that it could proceed through legal channels. It was heard the very next day.

The wife repeated her complaint against her husband, while the alcalde told her that her case did not have the legal foundation necessary for dissolution of a marriage contract. She was questioned as to whether she willingly undertook this marriage, to which she answered in the affirmative. She swore she would not return to her husband's side. She was granted a period of time in which to reconsider and seek advice. The sindico was called in so he would be present at these hearings. The wife was asked whether her husband possessed wealth in cash or real estate at the time of their marriage. She answered yes and, in response to the next question, explained that the real estate was sold and that the whole family benefited from this money.

Her husband was informed as to the reasons for suit given by his wife and her decision. First, she firmly maintained a position of not wishing to return to her husband and said she would take charge of the children of her own volition, with the condition that she be free from her husband.

He answered that under no circumstances would he accept this, nor would he allow his marriage to be dissolved, since he was well disposed to find the solution to their problems and wished to be reconciled. She said that neither her parents nor any authority could force her to go back to him. He would not accept the separation.

The case was to be consigned to Villa Alta because it could not be settled here, since the alcalde could not dissolve a marriage. She was granted two more days in which to think over her decision. Her husband did not accept any separation and promised to be faithful and to dedicate himself to her and their life together, his goal being the return of peace and tranquility to their home.

This wife was not so easily reconciled, nor was she easily intimidated by the court. True, she was young, but she had a vocation and was able to earn a living by her work as a seamstress. In addition, she was from a leading family and probably had wealth of her own to which she could look forward. The man was less well established economically but was well liked and generally a mild-mannered person, prone neither to drinking nor to violence.

Women do not feel embarrassed to use the court, to appeal to it even during evening hours. In Case 52, a woman came to the presidente with an abuse complaint one evening, within minutes of being hit.

. . . the husband had come into their home in a state of intoxication, and . . . as one bereft of his senses, he had struck her with his hand, one of the blows landing on the left side of her face, and . . . rapidly she had begun to bleed from the nose, which could be seen at the time she was presenting her complaint. The presidente, upon hearing the complaint, ordered the apprehension of the defendant, who was jailed for the night.

At 9:00 A.M. the next morning, the husband was ordered released. He was informed by the sindico of the complaint against him, which was of a penal nature, and the reasons for his incarceration. The husband, being informed, recognized his fault and bad comportment and said that nothing would have happened if he had not been drunk. He asked his wife to forgive him. She would not pardon her aggressor and said she would not return to him. According to the investigations, the plaintiff did not wish her husband to return to her home because her husband had been deciding about their affairs and interests without consulting her, as is a duty within the state of marriage. . . . The sindico granted them a few hours in which to reconsider, and he advised them as parents to be prudent and make every possible effort. After prolonged discussion they effected a reconciliation under the following conditions:

1. The husband recognized the faults he had committed against his wife and promised not to repeat these offenses. The contrary being the case, the authority would take appropriate measures.

2. From now on the husband was obliged to submit to legal precepts of not proceeding in an absolute way of settling affairs, but would have a mutual agreement with his wife, in relation to things belonging to both, in order to avoid major difficulties, trying, within possible means, to have peace in the home.

3. The wife promised that as long as, and when, these conditions were met, she would return to the side of her husband, testifying that when another such incident should arise she would not be able to pardon her husband, and that then she would leave him forever because she had been taking care of domestic affairs and had been putting all necessary effort toward labor and material cooperation to help with the costs of the home. Within these conditions—the act of reconciliation of the pair and on petition of both—the legal procedures of the complaint were suspended. They were in agreement, and the case was resolved. The sindico fined the husband 30 pesos.

If the court official had not reconciled the pair, the case would have been treated as a penal case, for it is a crime (delito) to assault one's spouse. If the infraction is repeated, as it sometimes is, the fine is usually increased. Sometimes the husband, desperate to resolve his problems with alcoholism, will even suggest that all his property be placed in the hands of his wife and children to protect them from his vice.

In Case 53, a woman testified that her lover (or common-law husband) had used a knife to threaten her and her brother and that in order to avoid worse injuries she felt obliged to start proceedings.

The presidente ordered the police to put the man in jail. Later he was brought forward to hear the charge. The defendant acknowledged and requested that he be punished and the case be terminated. . . . The case was assigned to the alcalde, who fined the defendant 50 pesos. But the litigants decided to separate definitively. The woman only requested that she be paid for the eight months that she attended her lover while he was in bed. He promised to pay her 120 pesos for the eight months, 15 pesos a month.

Sometimes cases of physical abuse do not involve drinking. When both husband and wife assault each other, the presidente fines both parties and urges that an agreement be drawn up. Although rare, such cases are likely to be between a man and wife over the age of 60. In Case 54, a mother-in-law complained that her daughter-in-law had abandoned her home and small son. The story took a different turn with the testimony of the son and daughter-in-law.

The daughter-in-law testified, "It's not that I left, but that I was afraid. My mother-in-law was beating my husband, and it's not the first time; she does it regularly. Once she almost hit me, and it's for this reason that when I saw her hitting him, I ran out frightened. I went to my godfather's and told him what was going on."

The presidente asked her again why the mother-in-law had hit her husband, and she answered, "I don't know what my husband did for her to hit him. When he came home, I served him coffee and went to take it to where she was. She said to me, 'I haven't eaten either.' I answered her, 'I have no intention of serving you.' Once when my husband and I were eating, she took the plate of food away from us and we didn't eat. I have stood all these things. My husband and I are not fighting. It also happened when I had just given birth to my child. She said to me, 'Now that your pregnancy is over, you can go home. I can raise my grandchild. Don't think you're needed.' But I thought about my husband and didn't leave. Neither does she allow my mother or father to come and see me. Nor does she want me to go and visit them. She always says that I go there so they can give me bad advice and talk about her."

The presidente questioned her husband as to whether what she said was true. He answered, "It is true. My mother has a difficult personality. She doesn't think before she talks. My wife feels badly enough because she is somebody else's daughter. It would be different if I said to my mother what my wife says to her. I never complain about my wife in front of her. Besides, my mother gets angry if my in-laws come to visit, nor can I go visit them. The difficulties that have arisen are due to my mother. My wife and I don't fight; we live peacefully."

His mother interrupted, saying, "In any case, I have to correct you; you're not going to order me around."

Her son answered, "If I did anything wrong to you, I did not run away. You hit me and now you tell falsehoods when you say that my wife abandoned the house. That isn't so, but my wife was frightened by what you were doing to me. And now she [mother] is angry because I work with my father-in-law. What am I going to do? He is my father-in-law, not somebody else. Last week I went to work for three days, but our work was not completed and I went for five days. My mother is angry because I planted beans and I didn't tell her. I planted with my father-in-law. When I went out on my own, she gave me 1,560 pesos voluntarily, which I did not ask her for, and now she wants me to return them to her."

His mother answered, "I raised you, and you don't think anything about that. Now what I say doesn't count, and what your wife says is okay, of course, because she is your wife. Now since my son says that I am to blame and he is ungrateful, I don't want him to set foot in my house; let him figure out where he can go. He can go to his father-in-law's house, since that gentleman is a good man. I will not let him order me around. What I say goes. I have already made out the documents of the house in his name, but he probably did not imagine that we would come to this point. When my daughter-in-law's mother comes, they start to talk about me, and who knows what they say about me?"

At this point the parents of her daughter-in-law appeared and asked the presidente why their daughter was summoned to appear. The presidente answered that the mother-in-law said she had abandoned the house.

The father of the young woman answered that it was not true. "She didn't leave, but she was frightened because she says that Luis's mother was hitting him. And Señor Presidente, this is not the first time that she has done this; she does it all the time. I never thought that we'd have to come here to settle this. When I found out what was going on, I didn't know what to do. I went to the priest and asked his advice. I never thought it would come to this point. It is a shame for us to have this gossip and these fights before this authority. I am not in the habit of coming here for any little thing, but that is her way of doing things. She had done many things to my daughter. . . . I have had to intervene so that the trouble would not continue. My daughter is married legally, and I would not permit her to walk out just like that. Another time it was necessary to make a small kitchen for our children, and I willingly gave them some roof tiles for the little house. The situation reached such a point that once her mother-in-law went to the bathroom in their kitchen. I've never boasted that I gave them anything, but I'm just saying this now so that you know what kind of a woman she is. I have never offered what I don't have, but I have helped them within the realm of my own possibilities. You know very well that I am poor, and if I have helped them it is because I wish to, since they are my children. It is not right that she treats my daughter this way. I did not go to her and offer my daughter's hand in marriage; she came to ask for it. What I want is for them to live well and not like animals. She always criticizes the place where I live, and I feel that she talks about me because I am poor."

After hearing the statements of the litigants, the presidente said to the mother-in-law that she was the guilty party in this case. She was an adult, and instead of trying to work out arguments and avoid fights, she was provoking them: "I suggest that we come to some settlement. From the moment your son married, you as a mother lost all right to order him around; you must not interfere in his affairs. A man knows how to manage his own home. The only conclusion we can come to is that Luis and his wife do not live with you. You must not bother her, nor must her parents spread any gossip. Do not think that this means that you shouldn't talk to them; on the contrary, you must speak well to them, with words of affection, since they are your children. The work that they do should be their own; they got married for that reason. They themselves are not arguing. You are the one who is provoking the trouble. Now, in my judgment this is what should be done."

Then, he turned to the young couple: "You should go to live by yourselves. If your parents wish to help, accept it. Work and commitments should be to take care of yourselves, not anybody else, in order to avoid these fights." Then to everybody: "Are you ready to come to an amicable settlement and to put an end to this problem?" Everyone answered affirmatively. Luis's mother said she agreed that they live separately from her and that the sown land which she had with her son he could have entirely. This amounted to 5 almudes, in the land area called San Ramón; also other sown lands she had in Yugul with 3 almudes, one-half almud in Sach, and three-quarters almud she had in Biag Gechic—a total of 9.25 almudes were at his disposal. She willingly gave her son 50 *pancles de panela* [packages of sugarcane] and 3 packs of corn, and, as for the sown beans, she would like a part of them. She was prepared not to receive any but left that to the judgment of her son to perhaps give her some of the crop.

The young woman's parents, wishing that the children live by themselves, were ready to help them with 200 pesos and a pack of corn, and if they could help them further, they would do it willingly.

After the voluntary statements of aid were made, the young couple was questioned to see if they agreed, and they answered in the affirmative. The presidente spoke to them, saying that once things were arranged, they should not let parental aid be a reason for new difficulties to arise. If it came to the attention of the authorities that this agreement had been violated, the case would be transferred to a higher court. The meeting was adjourned, and the document was drawn up and signed by all parties.

There are times in the life cycle of Taleans that produce stress. In the preceding case a mother's psychological disabilities are exacerbated when her son marries and she has to deal with a daughter-in-law. In such cases the courtroom encounter provides therapy—harmony therapy. At other times stress is relieved by the creation of a dispute on thin grounds in order to vent or escape from pressure. In Case 55, a common triangle of husband, pregnant wife, and mother-in-law escalated into a court case. The mother-in-law in this case charged the son-in-law, Edmundo, with abuse.

"I come before this authority to let them know that my son-in-law hit my daughter, who came to my house, crying. I was not at home, since I had gone to my mother's house, and my young son came to tell me. I left for my house immediately, and when I arrived, my son-in-law was already there with my daughter, and he continued to hit her. I asked him what he thought he was doing, but he didn't answer me and began to hit me, too. And now, I want to know why he did this."

Upon hearing the complaint, the court immediately summoned the son-in-law to appear. He appeared a few minutes later . . . and the presidente advised him of the complaint against him. He replied, "My wife is calling my mother a thief. All this is because of the small amount of money that we had, amounting to ten pesos. She told me that she kept them in a trunk, and when she went to look for them, they weren't there. She is accusing my mother of stealing them and is calling her a thief. For this reason I have hit her. Besides, this isn't the only reason for the argument; there is another thing. When Señor [the defendant's father-in-law] died, several of us went to dig the grave, and we began to talk to Horacio, who said to me that he doesn't trust Anatol because he said he could fool around with my wife. He said this to me when we were coming back from the fields, and I thought that maybe this man is having relations with my wife, and perhaps in order to clarify things you ought to call upon Horacio to appear, to tell you what he told me."

Immediately Horacio was called to appear . . . and he appeared a few minutes later. The presidente advised him of the complaint and he answered the following: "Yes, when we went to dig the grave . . . it is true that I said this to Edmundo, for old time's sake. I told him not to trust Anatol, because when he and I were returning from the fields, he said to me that now you could fool around with Edmundo's wife. That's what he said, and he knows what he was thinking about. . . ."

Having heard the declarations of the plaintiff and the defendant, the daughter and common-law wife of Edmundo was called and asked about the fight between herself and her husband. She replied, "The reason we started fighting was because of the money. He asked me where the ten pesos were, because he needed them, and I told him that they were in the trunk and that I had closed it but had left the key inside the trunk. When I went for the money, I was surprised to find that the lock was open and the money was not there. I told him that it wasn't there and perhaps his mother had borrowed it. When I told him that, he got upset and began to hit me, and after, when my mother asked why he was doing this, he didn't even speak but began to hit her. What he did was very bad, since I am pregnant now, and the blows that he gave me are bothering me now. I feel terrible. He is responsible for what is happening to me. Besides he wants me to work like him. He wants me to work where he works and always says that I don't do anything, that I always stay in the house. I have said to him, 'If you want to know whether or not I do anything, let's go live in another house. Your mother comes to ask for something, I don't deny her her rights; she is head of the house, she has the right to say things to me, but I can't stand it. Your sister comes to say things to me that don't sit right with me, to order me around.'"

Interrupting, the presidente asked her: "Did your husband speak to you about an individual who had spoken to you or who wished to speak to you?"

She answered, "My husband is looking for pretexts for leaving us.

Every time I am pregnant, he always comes up with these arguments. The last time I was pregnant, he used to say that it wasn't his child that I was going to have. Anyway, he always throws those things up to me. Please Señor Presidente, summon Anatol so that he can tell what he knows, because I don't know anything. As I say, they are pure pretexts."

At the request of the wife, Anatol was summoned. Upon appearing he stated the following: "How can Horacio have said such a thing? Edmundo is my friend and neighbor. We are almost like family. It is not true. I did not say anything to him, much less to his wife. I have always gotten along very well with Edmundo. When I need his donkey, I borrow it, and now because of this I wouldn't dare. If people know something about me and if I fool around, it's with others, never with my neighbors, I can't be held accountable for things I have not done, much less thought about. That's why when my father told me that you had summoned me, I came immediately. . . ."

A date was set for the hearing with all present. The presidente addressed them.

"Now I am familiar with your statements and the reasons for this litigation.

"The mother-in-law swears that her son-in-law hit her and her daughter without her knowing why, and she requests that this abuse be corrected. The wife swears that her husband hit her without reason and asks that he be responsible for her condition, since she will soon give birth to a baby, and with the blows received she is being made ill. And the son-in-law reiterates that because of what they said to him, because they accused his mother of theft, he would like to separate once and for all. Horacio swears that what he said was true, and Anatol swears that it was not true."

The presidente continued: "Please try to calm down. Even as things stand, and with the gossip of others, we can still come to an amicable settlement so that you can return to your home again. I am afraid I do not have the power to bring about a separation. You would have to go to the head of the civil registry [in Villa Alta]. I am only in this office to settle litigations in the best way possible, resolving these conflicts so that they may not occur again. Now, Edmundo, since you were very violent when you hit your wife, knowing very well that she is pregnant, this could bring you very serious consequences. And, according to your mother-in-law's statement, you hit her too without her knowing why."

Edmundo reiterated that in any case, he was going to leave her, or better yet he wished the matter to be turned over to the sindico or to the alcalde to see how the matter would be resolved.

The wife responded, "If my husband turns the case to a higher jurisdiction, what am I going to do? I am ready to return to him in spite of what he did to me because he is my husband. But if he asks for it, where will I be? Because what's happening to me is his fault. He is the only one to blame."

After long discussion among the litigants, the presidente was not able to make them come to any agreement, and the defendant requested that the case be sent to the sindico and settled according to law. Since no agreement could be reached by the parties and because of the request of the defendant, the case was turned over to the sindico, as representative of the ministerio publico.

The issue of family reconciliation overshadowed the charge of physical abuse, and the defendant gained the upper hand for the moment by appealing his case. He avoided the physical abuse complaint by filing a countercomplaint—that his wife had called his mother a thief. Unfortunately, I do not know what happened in the sindico's court.

Although access to courts is immediate and although large families support their women, it is women who bear the consequences of assault and battery. In abuse cases Talean courts are essentially therapeutic or ameliorative. Although the courts do not turn their backs on physical abuse cases and although they do not allow private family law to regulate conjugal physical abuse, they do not have the ability to do anything structural about this widespread problem. In Talea, women's frequent use of the courts leads to individual solutions. Women are more likely to go to court to correct their man's behavior, or at least to shame him publicly. Men are more likely to use the court to simply end a relationship that has gone sour. As an individual proceeds through the life cycle, however, and as women reach the end of their childbearing years, their complaints about physical abuse diminish and questions relating to property become more important. In the younger years, conjugal problems seem to predominate, including issues of adultery and abandonment.

Adultery and Abandonment

Men commonly use adultery accusations to defend their physical abuse of their wife or to explain why they no longer support their family: "She has lost all the rights of a wife by committing adultery" or "The reason I hit her is because she engages in immoral acts." As we have seen in some of the earlier cases, Talean men are easily provoked to jealousy, and a word in the wrong place leads them to accuse a spouse of adulterous behavior. Sometimes their fears are based on reality, as in Case 56.

A woman came to the court and demanded support for her legitimate children. Her husband said that he wouldn't support them because she had lost all the rights of a wife by committing adultery and separating from him. This adultery and separation, he stated, was committed without his consent or the consent of any of his relatives, since they were working to earn a living for the family at the time. The husband and father recognized his children, and took them to his home to feed and educate and clothe them, and also to make them respect and obey their parents as well as their paternal grandmother, who lived in the same house with him. The children were ages 16, 14, and 6, and finally a nursing child born after the parents' separation and whom he therefore refused to recognize and refused to register. The husband refused to support the children unless they lived in his house. The children were visibly disturbed upon hearing this. Their godfather was thereupon summoned, and his opinion requested. He said he thought the children should either be with their father or be with the godparents if the father were not there, to avoid corruption by immoral acts of their mother.

The authority then, taking into account the gravity of the situation and realizing the damage to society that a lack of morals can inflict, decided the case thus: the three daughters, legitimate progeny of a marriage, who at this moment were living with their mother, were to live with their father from this moment on. He was exhorted to do his best by them. They were told to respect and obey their parents and elders and not to cause trouble of any kind.

Sometimes women run away with a lover and leave town. In one case, a man from a distant village near Ixtlán came to the Talean court in search of his wife. He told the court that when he was sick and not earning any money, his wife had abandoned him and their year-and-a-half-old child. The sindico in Talea told the man that if his wife were found, she would be jailed and sent back to her village. But some women who leave are never found, and it may be that the threat of punishment both in and out of court frightens them and discourages them from returning.

In Case 57, the extended family tried to pick up the pieces after a married woman abandoned her husband, home, and four children. The woman's mother took charge of two of the children when the father also abandoned them. The grandmother wrote the following letter to the municipal president.

I am writing you in the interests of my grandchildren, who have been abandoned by their father. Once more I come to you with the matter of the children, which was described last night, at which time it was suggested to me by the presidente that I return home with the children. Upon returning home, I was not allowed to enter my [bachelor] son's house, and I stayed in my neighbor's house with the children.

My son said to me, "I am obliged to look after you and support you and you alone, as I have told you, and not your grandchildren." For this reason the children were taken out of the house. Now that I returned with them, he put me out of his house, and I found myself in the street with the children and had to seek shelter in someone else's house. This is no way to live. The children are hungry, and where am I going to get food for them? My health does not permit me to work, since I am quite worn out and have no strength.

I am asking you for justice, Señor Presidente, since the father has the obligation for picking up his children. He is responsible for them and has the means of caring for them. As the father of a family, he should take care of his children, who are out in the street.

As for me, I release myself from any obligation for them. So I leave it to your judgment and hope you will bring justice to bear, and look forward to your cooperation.

A few days later there was a meeting in the court for the formal handing over of the two young grandchildren by the 68-year-old grandmother to her son-in-law, the father of the children. The grandmother appeared, accompanied by a 37-year-old daughter; the defendant, age 32, was accompanied by his 42-year-old brother. The claim against the father was abandonment of his children.

The presidente clarified the point that the sindico was not hearing the present case, which ordinarily would have been referred to him, because the sindico is the brother of the defendant.

When both parties were present, the letter written by the grandmother was read. . . . Her son refused to support the grandchildren, a year-and-a-half-old boy and a nine-year-old girl, whom she had taken in. He was agreeable to continue supporting her, since she was his mother, but not the two children. The grandmother asked that her son-in-law be made responsible for the children.

The presidente pulled out the earlier case in which it was noted that the defendant's wife had left her married home and gone to the house of her mother with her two small children earlier in the year. When her husband found this out, he went to see her to ask her to return home. Since she refused, he had to wait for the arrival of her mother, who at that time was absent from the town on a trip to some neighboring villages. Before her mother arrived, the young mother fled from her mother's house, leaving town for some unknown destination.

In order to care for the four abandoned children, the maternal and paternal grandmothers appeared before the municipal authority, and they were given charge of them. The earlier case record also stressed that abandonment by the mother and the harm to her children and her husband was proven, and that the crime will be investigated at a future time if the injured party requests it and it will be punished according to law.

In order to ascertain the truth or falseness of the maternal grandmother's letter, her son was called to appear. The son, a bachelor of 40 years, appeared and upon questioning answered that he was displeased with his mother because she had taken in the grandchildren, whom he felt he was not obliged to support because they have a father. He felt his only obligation was toward his mother. It is true that he put her out of his house, because he had ordered her to return the grandchildren and she didn't do it. If she tried to return to his house with the grandchildren against his will, then he would abandon the house and his mother and leave town. The authority heard the witness and his drastic and inconsiderate decision against his young nephew and niece and his mother.

The father was asked for his opinion, and he testified that since he and his brother had observed the bad treatment and lack of attention that the two young grandchildren had received, and having been convinced again of the scorn and hate that the uncle had for the youngsters, they had decided to take back the children, who from this date forward would remain under the care of the father. All parties signed an agreement to this effect.

Sometimes abandonment is equated with separation and comes early in a marriage when there are no children. In Case 58, a young woman age 18 lodged the following claim against her husband.

"I come to request that you make my husband appear before you to determine why he has abandoned the house. He divided all that we own and said that we are going to settle this right now because he has thought about leaving this house. Then I asked him, 'Why is it that you want to go?' and he said to me, 'Now that we are friendly, let's divide our things because when we are fighting, we can't do anything.' I answered that it was okay. What else can I add? So we divided the corn, the panela, the beans, the kindling; he even carried off my metate, the clothing trunk, the money that we have saved. And now, please your honor, call him and ask him why he has left me for no reason."

The presidente summoned the husband, who was told of the reason for the summons. The husband answered by saying: "Yes, it is true that my wife and I divided our things. I thought for a week about what I had to do, and I was ready to abandon her. I had it well thought out and with goodwill we accomplished the division and separation."

The presidente asked him what reasons he had for the sudden separation, or what difficulties had arisen. He answered: "The reason for the difficulty is my in-laws. We weren't on good terms for a week, but I stood it and didn't say anything, and then I thought it would be better to separate. Now things are just the way they were when she came to me; we have no obligations, and since her health is even better now than before, it's better to leave her before she or I make ourselves sick because of arguments. She is here, and let me tell you that I did not strike her while dividing our things, and when we had finished, I told her, 'Now you are free. I am not going to bother you, nor you me, from today on, and I give you the freedom to do whatever you wish. As for me, I don't want you to judge me. I know what I'm doing, since we proved that we couldn't get along during the time that we were married. I have a different personality from yours. I am violent, and so are you.' Now, Señor Presidente, I request that you draw up a documentation of separation from my wife because we are not compatible."

The presidente said that they should think about it because this was not a passing matter: "You are legally married, and when you got married, you thought about what you were doing. My authority doesn't allow me to give you a legal separation, and the only thing you can do is to return to your home. Try to examine and correct whoever is to blame and see who is right, in order not to continue with these difficulties. You are young, and perhaps due to lack of experience you fight. Both of you must accept things as they arise and try your best to avoid disputes."

At that moment a woman appeared in the court, stating: "I come to intervene in the case of my niece. She came to tell me of the difficulty she has with her husband, and asked me to accompany her since her parents refused to do so. I came here to appease matters. I don't want this niece and nephew to have these difficulties. I beg my nephew to give some thought to what he is doing and to return home. The parents of both should not allow them to separate simply because they feel like it. On the contrary, they should do everything possible to calm their children down. If the difficulty is with the mother-in-law, it would be better that she leave. If they wish, I will ask if they can go live at my mother's house while they work things out, or I am even ready to give them a little piece of land so they can build a house, without their giving me anything for it; as a gesture of goodwill I give it to them so that they will not separate. Now, I ask my nephew please, if his wife said something to him, to pardon her—we all have faults in this life—or even if his father-in-law said something to him that he forget the whole thing, and not pay attention to it."

The nephew answered that he was grateful for what she said and the goodwill of her intervention, but, he said, "You do not know how things started and what has been happening. I have thought it over and I cannot live with her."

Then the aunt answered, "It is not possible for these two to get together, and it is best, if they have thought this way, to draw up the document where they will sign their separation."

The presidente answered that he had no right to certify the separation. On the contrary, he noted that he must do everything possible to remedy the situation. The next day both parties would have to appear with their parents to discover the reason for this dispute, and the parents would have to discuss and resolve what their children were doing and to say if they themselves consented to the separation. The matter was left pending until the next day, when the parents of the couple were present. At that time the presidente told the parents that the couple had already divided what they had in the house.

The mother of the young man answered: "I didn't know. I thought they were going to the ranch, and for this reason he came to leave his things in my house. After he finished bringing his things in, he said to me, 'I'm telling you that I'm not going to live with my wife because I no longer can stand what's happening to me.'"

The presidente said to her, "Are you in agreement with this? Because as far as I can see, as parents you shouldn't permit them to separate." The young man's mother answered, "As far as we're concerned, there is no way to say that what they are doing is good. We would like for them to resolve their problems."

In response the presidente urged, "What must be done is that they go to live with you, so that you look after them. By law she is your daughter-in-law, you asked for her marriage to your son, and where else should she go, if not to your house?"

The wife answered that she was prepared to live with her in-laws, but her mother said that it would be better to leave them alone. To which the presidente responded, "Then you are the instigators of this case . . . whereas the parents of the young man say they are looking for a way to prevent the separation and you state the contrary. I don't know what to do."

The young man answered, "You have heard what my mother-in-law said, and you know that I don't lie." To which his father-in-law answered, "As the matter stands, if he wants to leave, let him see what he will do with his wife. We will not take her back, because she belongs to him."

The young husband answered, "I'm not going to leave her in the street. For this reason I have come to you so that you can offer her advice. I thought it best to leave her and then you would see what you would do with your daughter, because now we cannot live happily together."

His mother-in-law responded, "I didn't say that they should separate." The presidente answered, "Let's not play around. You just got through saying that they should be allowed to separate if they thought so, and as things stand I can't convince anyone."

The father-in-law then asked that the matter be turned over to the alcalde's office so that he might decide what to do. The presidente conceded to his wishes. The father-in-law added, "Nobody is turning his wife away; if I gave her to him, he should see what is to be done with her."

The young man's parents then added, "If he has already asked for this appeal, nothing can be done. Let's see how it is settled, because if it were up to me, I would not permit my son to do such a thing. I would take my daughter-in-law in, but if I do take her in, they will talk about me, and it isn't the same as if I were her husband."

After a lengthy discussion . . . the presidente ordered that the case be turned over to the alcalde.

There is an element of theater and formula in many of these cases, but especially in cases dealing with young married couples there is a sense of initiation into rights and responsibilities. In the preceding case much is made of the concept of "woman as property of her husband and her husband's family" in relation to the responsibility that they have for her care and welfare. None of the women in that courtroom carried the name of the man to whom they were married; they carried their father's name, and yet upon marriage the responsibility for the social welfare of the women shifted from their natal family to their conjugal networks.

The formulaic aspects of the case pivot around complainants' going to the court to formalize a separation and the court's response that separations do not fall within its jurisdiction but reconciliation does. Why, we might ask, do so many people ask the court for separation or divorce when they know full well that such action is not within the purview of the courts? In a few cases the intent is to appeal for separation all the way to the district court, but this process occurs in very few cases. What most litigants are doing is announcing their intentions publicly; so, too, the presidente publicizes the fact that he is acting in accordance with Mexican law, which permits him only to reconcile. If reconciliation does not work, then all three parties have fulfilled their obligations. In fact, what prevails in the absence of the state's forcing cohabitation is the law of the locale, which permits informal separation. In the preceding case, the responsibility for maintaining the marriage was placed squarely on the parents, and in particular the parents of the husband. Although the initial complaint was abandonment, abandonment was never pursued, and separation took center stage.

Adultery cases follow another pattern. They sometimes involve issues of abandonment and separation, but it is rare that the parents of the parties are brought into the case. Rather, adultery cases usually involve members of the same age set; they link people in horizontal relations rather than across generations. Case 59 involved a foursome, two couples who had been linked by adultery for over 15 years.

"I come to make a complaint against Señor Demetrio and his wife because they hit my husband, Señor Antonio. I cannot stand for this. What if they had killed him? Who else would be held responsible for it, but them? I request that the two of them be punished, and even more the wife of Demetrio, because my husband has been involved with her for the past 15 years. Many times my neighbors have told me that the two of them have gone out together collecting kindling. Now my husband is laid up because of the beating that they gave him. I cannot stand for this.

"Because of the crime of adultery he has been committing, I also accuse Señora Ana for going with him. She knows very well that we are married and that she is also. I am asking that justice be brought to bear and that you bring my husband in so that he can answer for what he did to make them beat him.

"A long time ago my husband worked with Demetrio during the planting season, but almost all the harvest ended up in her house. Maybe that was because they had already thought about what they were involved in. Also, when Señor Yagallo died, my husband came for three packages of sugar, and afterward I found out that he gave it to Ana so they could go to the wake, which also means that he is a pimp for Demetrio's wife, and he is not responsible for her.

"I have witnesses who saw how they hit my husband. The man who saw was Pedro. I found out, and he said to me that he fell out of the corridor into the road and that he was asking to be forgiven. My husband has been involved with this woman for a long time. They even had a child together. Many times I saw them, and I didn't dare to say anything to him for the sake of our children. . . . I request, Señor Presidente, that they be punished so that they know what they are doing."

When the presidente had heard the statement of the woman, Señor Demetrio was immediately summoned, and he appeared a few hours later. The presidente told him the complaint against him, and he answered, "Yes, it is true that I saw him in my house at that hour of the night when I arrived home. He was in the corridor, and when he saw me, he ran and he tripped over the kindling. I asked my wife why that man was in the corridor. I said to her, 'You don't understand; you're still involved with that man. Didn't you agree the time you had a child by him? And you went to jail.' Now, Your Honor, any man would do the same if he finds this man in his house. I don't even care if they go get her and put her in jail for betraying me. It's not the first time that they've done it. They have been betraying me for a while. Before, she used to come to the ranch with me, but now she doesn't want to go because that man doesn't leave her alone. I have been on the verge of calling him a coward, but I haven't done that. But look, Señor Presidente, I don't want to dirty my hands, and I am resigned. I thought that if I say it, they will get angry. Now I am resigned to leaving her for good. She'll see what happens if she goes on with that man, or if she goes off to look for some other men. Now she is not worthy to go to my house. We have older children. What kind of example can we give to our children, if they know that their mother is a whore? Now, I request, Señor Presidente, that she be called to testify because she and that man are to blame and because of them there is trouble in two families."

After hearing this statement, Señor Antonio was summoned, along with Señora Ana. When they were present, the presidente spoke to them and told them to tell the truth. They stated their names, age, and work. Then the beaten husband showed the bruises on his face, with part of the cheekbone swollen; he was limping and had scratches on his left arm. He stated the following: "Señor Demetrio struck me. It is not true that I was in his house. I was on the road. How can he say I was in the corridor? I can't walk. He is lying to say I was there."

The presidente asked him, "Then is it true that you went to Señora Ana's house?" He answered, "Yes, it is true. I went because I was drunk, and the truth is that I don't remember. You know how it is when one is drunk. He doesn't realize what he is doing. That is all I have to say."

Señora Ana was questioned and told to tell the truth. She stated the following, "Yes, it is true that Señor Antonio was in the corridor and that he fell into the road. He is very stubborn. He has always bothered me, but I did not tell my husband because my mother-in-law told me not to look for trouble. My neighbors always tell me that this man is standing behind my house, but I don't pay any attention to him. One time he even said to me, 'It doesn't matter if your husband isn't here, I've come for you.' Now, how am I going to go out when he says something like that? And if my husband leaves me, well, what would I do? I repeat that he is the guilty one in this matter. That is all I have to say."

The presidente told Señora Ana to present her witness. She answered saying that Señor Pedro had seen what happened. Upon hearing this, the presidente summoned Pedro to appear. When present, the latter answered that he was sleeping when he heard a very loud noise. "It was Señor Demetrio hitting Antonio and Antonio was asking for forgiveness, and I heard silence, and then Antonio was in the road." That is all he had to say, and he asked for permission to leave.

Having heard the statements of the plaintiffs and defendants, the court ordered that the matter be left to the following day, that Señor Antonio and Señora Ana spend that time in the public jail.

The next day the litigation was begun again. Spouses to the accused adulterers appeared, as did the accused. The presidente said to them, "This is a very serious matter, but if you work out a settlement to return to your homes, it will be granted to you because, as a fact, I cannot resolve this situation, since it is beyond my jurisdiction, since they have been married under civil law."

Demetrio said that it would be better if his wife left and went far away. He didn't want to see her. She would have a lot of nerve to return home after the way she had betrayed him, and it was not the first time: "Who knows what kind of affairs she has had with that damned man?"

His wife answered that she wasn't to blame, since it was Señor Antonio who came to look for her. The presidente responded, "You mean that you speak to him. Because no matter how good a woman is, if she gives the opportunity to be spoken to, then she is not a faithful wife. So you have the greater blame for committing that crime."

Antonio answered that it would be better if this matter could be settled amicably. He was ready to pay the corresponding punishment.

The presidente said to them: "This is how things stand in this case. Señora Ana is responsible for what happened to this man. Señor Antonio is responsible for having gone to Señor Demetrio's home in the middle of the night. I am here to resolve this with an agreement. You will recognize your blame and will pay the punishment. It can all be settled here. I will look for some means by which you can return to your homes again."

The parties said that they were prepared to pay, and the presidente told each one that he would impose a fine of 400 pesos in order that they understand and know what they are involved in, and he added, "If you do not pay and do not agree, I will send the case to Villa Alta, and there you can see what you can do."

The parties answered that they thought it was a lot of money; they were prepared to pay 300 pesos. The presidente said that was not possible and if they wanted to think about it, they could do so in jail. They then agreed to the fine, but because of their appeal the presidente set the fine at 300 pesos.

The presidente then asked the aggrieved if they agreed to the fine, and if they were prepared to return to the adulterers. They answered that they were, and that they did it for the sake of their grown children.

The aggrieved husband answered that he would take his wife back, on condition that she come into the fields to work as a man, as punishment, because she could not be at home as a wife should: "If she wants that, I will take her with me. If not, let her go where she pleases or go with her lover."

All accepted an amicable settlement, so this matter was terminated. All signed an agreement. The defendants admitted the crime of adultery. Also because of a previous settlement and since he had been held responsible for the child born to him and Señora Ana and the funeral expenses of the said child, who died, Señor Antonio had previously agreed to pay the sum of 250 pesos. The overdue payment of 250 pesos would be paid at this time. Señora Ana was fined the same sum of 300 pesos for adultery. She asked her husband's pardon and promised not to do it again and to do what he wished, without protest or excuses. Señor Antonio asked his wife's pardon and promised not to do it again and not to insult her when he was drunk, and agreed to live in the strictest harmony. . . . The document of settlement and agreement was drawn up with the agreement that these events will not be repeated. If the contrary occurs, this case would be immediately turned over to the proper authorities.

Liaisons between married people are not uncommon in Talea, or so it seems if one believes gossip, but only some of these are taken to the court as complaints of adultery. In such instances the complaint is associated, as in the previous case, with a dramatic action, such as having one's husband beaten up. In Case 60, a woman was notified that her sister-in-law was about to commit premeditated adultery and perhaps even abandonment. The woman placed herself in a position to spy on her sister-in-law and in particular to observe whether the couple intended to leave town by bus to Oaxaca. She hid under a coffee bush on a property neighboring that of her brother's home and witnessed the arrival of a man from the town of Solaga. He arrived with a young woman and, when he felt that it was safe, signaled to another man to come ahead. When her sister-in-law tried to open the door from the inside, she found it was locked. The man at the door tried to force it open, at which point the woman left for the court to formally accuse her sister-in-law. Immediately after the formal accusation, the sindico sent the police to apprehend the accused, who were picked up at the scene and held in the public jail. The sindico then passed the case to the alcalde's office. The next morning twelve people appeared in the court. The case was a complicated one involving several different families, accusations of adulterous relations between consenting adults, and an accusation of rape involving a minor, an unmarried girl. It moved from the presidente to the sindico to the alcalde.

The alcalde ordered the imprisonment of the four accused. When they appeared before the court, they were asked if it was correct that they had come to an amicable settlement and that they had requested that this matter be settled in this office. They were also asked if they as guilty parties had asked pardon from the persons they had offended and if these in turn had pardoned the offenders, to which the latter answered affirmatively.

The brother of the offended said that he and his mother pardoned the offenders under the condition that his brother and his wife leave the house in which they had been living and look for another room. . . .

As the meeting continued, the members of the court came to an agreement. In this case since all were pardoned, the claims were removed according to the article of the Penal Code, and since all were agreed to pay the sanctions imposed, it was determined that the adulterer and housebreaker would pay the sum of 500 pesos, the adulteress the sum of 150 pesos, the young 16-year-old who allowed herself to be raped and the sister of the adulterer 150 pesos each as principal accomplices in the crimes of adultery and housebreaking. The young man from Solaga also had to pay 150 pesos.

The alcalde informed all those present that the fines would be turned over to the municipal treasury to be used for construction and improvement of public works. Upon being informed of this decision, all agreed, immediately paying the fines. The meeting came to a close and the document drawn up was signed by those who took part in it.

In cases of adultery and even rape, nobody gains by appealing the case to Villa Alta, especially if there is a desire to continue a marriage or to begin a marriage that was initiated by a rape incident. Notice that the 16-year-old victim of rape was fined an amount equal to that of the rapist. The parties came together and worked out an accommodation that served the interests of harmony and community. The tone of such cases is distinctly different from that of cases dealing with abortion, as the following section indicates.

Abortion

The issue of abortion is a serious matter in Talea. The town is divided into sections headed by a chief, one of whose duties is to monitor and report possible abortion attempts. The influence of the

Catholic church is apparent when speaking to female believers about the manner in which abortion is dealt with in Talea, but conversations with men on the same subject indicate that control, not religion, is the central issue. When men report tracking a woman accused of abortion, there is a cat-and-mouse quality to the discussion. Case 61 is an example of how the Talean court investigates the crime of abortion.

A young woman who had had two children without being married became pregnant again, and when she realized this, she tried to abort the fetus. She went to a doctor who was in Talea to complete the social service duties required of Mexican physicians. Although the doctor said he would help her, his intentions were otherwise. He prescribed medication to keep her healthy, and her pregnancy continued until the fetus was about three months old. The woman did not return to the doctor, but managed to abort by herself with the aid of a *curandera*, a local curer. The curer was not a conscious accomplice. The young woman told her simply that she was not feeling well and wanted a bit of massage. With abortion in mind, she took two laxatives and some herb teas used for abortion. With these treatments she accomplished her objective.

Some days later the doctor noticed that she was unduly pale, and he suspected she had deliberately aborted. He reported his suspicions to the president so that he would investigate. The custom in Talea is for the section chiefs to be active vigilantes. The chief of her section summoned the young woman to the doctor's office to be examined, and it was proved that she had aborted because she had a continuing hemorrhage. After this examination, the court took charge of the affair and started to seek witnesses, among them the girl who had gone for the laxatives, the curer who had pressed the young woman's stomach, and finally a midwife who testified that she had passed close to the young woman's house and had smelled the characteristic odor of the herbs used for abortion.

While the authorities were investigating the case, the young woman was kept under surveillance but was not imprisoned or jailed; rather, she was left sitting in the corridor of the municipal building and watched by the police. At one point, she said she was going to eat lunch. As security she left her mother and one of her children with the police. Instead of coming back, however, she made the six-hour walk to Villa Alta, where she presented herself. At about six o'clock in the afternoon, a telegram arrived from the ministerio publico, saying that the woman had presented herself at his office. He ordered that the mother and child who had remained as prisoners be released. The town authorities had to comply, and on the following day the record was sent on to the district court. It was not possible to continue the case in Talea.

The following is part of the record of investigations conducted in Talea.

A woman was advised to answer to the charge of abortion. The 27-year-old woman answered that it was not true that she was pregnant; she reported that in the middle of the previous month she had gone to see the doctor in Social Service about pains she experienced at the time of her monthly period. Her suffering at this time was very severe, and she explained to the doctor that her last period, in the month of June, was not normal and that there was hardly any flow. At this time the doctor said, "You are probably pregnant," and he advised her to come by in a few days to know definitely. That was all that she got from the doctor, no medicines at all, and that was the end of the consultation.

The court asked her for how long she had been suffering from this malady, and she answered that it had been since the last time she had given birth; her baby was now 20 months old.

A few days later, she went to see another doctor (actually a traveling dentist), and she testified that the doctor said, "It is a menstrual upset." The defendant asked him if it could be a pregnancy, and he answered, "There are no facts to show this, because even by appearance it is known when a woman is pregnant." That was all she obtained at that consultation.

Very much disturbed by the rumors circulating about her honor, and upon hearing that the midwife had denounced her to the presidente, the woman went to the midwife's house to talk to her about the accusation she had made, and she asked the midwife to examine her, since that was her profession. The midwife examined her externally on her abdomen and did so thoroughly. Then she answered, "It's not as I thought. Perhaps the womb is out of place. The womb can't be felt, so we must wait a month to know definitely." She added that the midwife told her to come back in a few days.

Above all, the defendant denied the report of the doctor, insisting that it was a mistaken report, like the accusation of the midwife. The defendant said that she filed a grievance against the midwife for making false accusations against her. She insisted again that it was not true that she had been pregnant, and that she and her boyfriend were upset and offended because of the rumors circulating.

The declaration of the midwife occurred on the same date. The midwife is a widow of 73 years of age. She reported that over time she had noticed the pregnancy of the woman because of certain symptoms which appeared, such as paleness of the complexion, due to anemia caused by the pregnancy, and other telltale signs of her appearance. Citing her responsibilities as midwife, and in order not to be guilty of any crime herself, she denounced the woman before the section chief so that the authority would take note of and convey to the defendant the responsibilities she would have as a future mother. She reported that two days later the woman came and asked her to examine her because she was offended by the rumors circulating that she might be pregnant. The midwife testified that she examined the abdomen and found the following: there was no womb felt, the abdomen was completely soft, signs of abortion, pale complexion, loss of blood and sensation. The midwife declared that she questioned the woman as to why this was so, because as midwife she had noticed the pregnancy during a three-month lapse of time, and for that reason had denounced her. The woman answered that she had her last normal period in May, that in June it occurred but very lightly, and lasted only half a day, and the same again in July. In order to know the causes she had gone to see the doctor (the traveling dentist) so that he could examine her and give her a checkup, and after the examination of the abdomen and breasts, he had told her that she was not pregnant.

At this point the proceedings concerning the crime of abortion were turned over by the sindico to the alcalde in order that he might pursue the correct procedures and that he might call those necessary to discover who had been guilty of the crime committed.

I was never able to find out what happened in this case, but it is unusual for a woman to appeal an accusation of abortion to the district court. The woman had the support of her mother and possibly of her boyfriend, although he never appeared in the court, and she was 27 and experienced. She may have been pregnant or she may have suffered a menstrual disorder, but the presumption in such cases is always that the woman was pregnant and that her remedy was abortion. During my fieldwork many women asked me for medicine to prevent pregnancy. No one asked for help with abortion; the social environment was and is too antagonistic.

There are few avenues for a woman who has been wrongly accused of abortion, except the district court. The district court is, of course, governed by Mexican laws on abortion, which describe the penalties for abortion as well as the conditions that allow for a legal abortion (rape and health of the mother).

Discussion

In Talea the use of law augments personal power. Those intimates with less power use law to achieve more power, and for this reason the courts are a valuable resource for those who feel oppressed or frustrated. The cases presented in this chapter concern relations between men and women battling over issues of rank, intimacy, and control within the limits imposed by the broader sociopolitical realities. The predominance of cross-sex cases between intimates in Talea runs counter to what Donald Black predicted in 1976, when he argued that law is inactive between intimates, that "a person is less likely to sue a close kinsman than a friend, an acquaintance, a neighbor, a fellow tribesman," and so on (Black 1976: 46). In fact, litigation among intimates is alive and active in Talea.

Black (1976: 17, 22) also said that law varied directly with rank and that the lower ranks have less law than the higher ranks. Talean cases dealing with male-female relations do not seem to follow the pattern of more downward than upward complaints. Although the outcomes favor males over females, women use the courts against men (upward social control) in order to overcome the power differential between them. In cases against women, the power differential is heightened, as in cases of abortion where a woman has no right over her reproductive capacity. Backed by village law, abortion is dealt with in the most repressive manner, which violates women's privacy and rights over their own bodies. Such treatment is not found in any cross-sex complaints about men, as in paternity, physical abuse, abandonment, or adultery issues. In the issue of abortion, control exceeds punishment.

In *Drinking, Homicide, and Rebellion in Colonial Mexican Villages*, William Taylor (1979) stresses a pattern generally observed for Oaxaca, a pattern of violent households and relatively peaceful (although not conflict-free) communities. Taylor connects this pattern to the political setting: conflict restricted to relationships in the nuclear family was less likely to spread to factionalism at other levels of the community. Taylor found an unusually high proportion in the eighteenth century of female victims of physical abuse. He believes that in much of Indian Mexico at the end of the colonial period, the family was mainly a conjugal arrangement rather than the prime focus of allegiance, and he links this attitude to the Indian concept of the individual, which stressed the responsibility of individuals to the community and its primacy over them.

In Talea women plaintiffs evoke conciliatory and restitutive outcomes from court officials, whereas male plaintiffs evoke accusatory and threatening behavior from the judges. As long as cases brought by women dominate the Talean courts, the style they evoke will predominate. The behavior of law courts in the mountain Zapotec villages will drift in relation to changes in family structure, population mobility, and state initiative. I believe that state activity (and thereby downward social control as well) has been kept to a minimum by the high rate of female plaintiffs who present routine cases relating to female-male relations, and that this situation is possible only because of the free-landholding village structure.

With increasing contact with the state court, village solidarity is likely to decrease and the plaintiff role to atrophy as the state becomes the plaintiff in criminal matters. As women drop out of the male legal world, gender will be reflected most importantly in male predominance as defendants in criminal matters. The drift of law will then be in the direction of the extraordinary versus the routine case. Under such conditions, Donald Black's proposition about rank and intimacy will fit: under state law, law varies directly with rank, the lower ranks have less law than the higher ranks, and the law becomes inactive between intimates (Black 1976: 42).

The Talean court is characterized by upward social control; the Mexican state courts by downward social control. The state courts fit Black's proposition because the state restricts the plaintiff role and males monopolize the defendant role. As I have noted before, women leave their mark on the local judicial structure by using the courts, particularly as plaintiffs, and Talean courts are adept at borrowing the idiom of gender roles. When courts operate in a more active fashion that restricts women, the number of male users increases. Claim bringers set the courtroom agenda. As the case materials indicate, cross-sex encounters include female and male discourse. The predominantly conciliatory outcomes that result are products of this interaction. Indeed, as others have noticed, the control systems of the court are to some extent constituted in cultural categories of gender.

Chapter Eleven

Violence and Harmony in Same-sex Litigation

In this chapter I deal with violence between members of the same sex, predominantly violence between men, and with the process by which Taleans manage the contradictions between violence and harmony. Managing violence is an act of politics as well as one of law and justice for the Zapotecs of Talea, but not for all peoples. Among the Jalé of western New Guinea, for example, violence can escalate into war (Koch 1974). The Jalé have no political or judicial offices, and self-help is institutionalized as a method of conflict resolution when negotiation fails. Some villages near Talea also lack adequate braking mechanisms to prevent the escalation of conflict, and so it is doubly interesting to delineate the means by which disputes involving violence between members of the same sex are settled in Talea.

When Taleans say that Talea is a peaceful town, they do not mean that there is no physical violence. They mean that there is no factionalism, and little or no homicide—both kinds of behavior that would threaten the corporate village entity. The durability of village social structure depends first on respecting the municipal authorities' monopoly of power and second on keeping outsiders out of Talea's business. Taleans distance themselves from outside authority by prevention—by making sure that acts that would interest the state authorities, such as homicide and factionalism, are either controlled or prevented.

In Chapter 3, I described the ordering of social organization and discussed the function of structural mechanisms such as cross-linkage in preventing behavior seen as threatening to the village entity. I also discussed the value placed on respect, on vertical authority that ensures control from the center, be it the male head of a family or the men in the town hall. Although there are acts of physical violence in Talea, violence leading to or resulting from factionalism was minimal during the period under consideration (although not immediately before this period or in the 1970's, both of those periods being characterized by factionalism associated with Protestant missionary activity). With the exception of religious factionalism, the political realities of Talea have made it possible to settle violent conflict by peaceful means. As Taleans say, the difference between affairs of the house and those of the street is that the latter always come before the authorities.

Taleans frequently say that they value harmony and reconciliation, and even the most alienated Taleans stress this aspect of town life. How, then, does a society that values harmony and compromise, that stresses peacefulness, deal with incidents of physical violence? Some societies, such as the U.S. Southern Baptist community studied by Carol Greenhouse (1986), have a set of cultural injunctions against conflict. The people of Hopewell, Greenhouse tells us, not only avoid legal action but even try to refrain from voicing interpersonal disputes. In Talea the picture is a bit different. It is not so much that Taleans avoid conflict or indeed, as we already know, that they avoid using the courts, but rather that they seek harmony through procedural resolution, through remedies for conflict that has arisen. The Talean concern with harmony makes them not less but more litigious. Hopewell's Baptists pray for justice, but the Talean Zapotec primarily look to political rather than to religious authority for help. However, the manner in which conflict is resolved and harmony achieved for the people of both Hopewell and Talea has as its common purpose survival and maintenance of the community.

In this chapter the villagers themselves speak about offenses that we would call violence. Taleans are most alert to physical violence, especially when it occurs between unrelated males, because in the surrounding area (in Villa Alta, Yalalag, or in the Cajones area) such cases have escalated into wide-ranging factionalism involving further violence. Should the political process become part of the dispute, the municipality loses the neutrality essential for its authority and in the process cedes to the state the right to handle the dispute. Of course, such an outcome may be far from the litigants' minds; they are more likely to be caught up in the immediate action.

In his work on colonial Mexican villages, William Taylor (1979) found male peasant violence against the women they lived with and also against people from other towns and villages, but a pattern of relatively peaceful relations among male members of the same community. He commented on the "restriction of violent conflict to relationships from which it was least likely to spread to factionalism or new violence at other levels within the community" (ibid.: 107). However, inter-community violence was "tolerated, almost condoned, by the courts in their lenient sentences. . . . Violence was a widespread way of resolving differences that, within obvious limits, was permitted by the state as a legitimate expression of grievance" (ibid.: 169). As indicated in Chapter 10, Talean men aggress against women in a high proportion of family cases; on the other hand, there are also more cases of intra-community male/male violence than inter-community violence. The fact that the Talean court hears cross-sex assault cases and records them does indicate that to some degree violence against women by the men living with them is socially unacceptable. The town seeks to reconcile such cases, and, as I noted, rank and intimacy decide the outcome: the court and the husbands have greater power than the women.

In cases of violence between members of the same sex, especially between men, the ranking of the litigants relative to one another is less important. The central overriding issue between the litigants and the local court is the predominance of the authority of the court, the key to the independence of the landholding village. The issue for the court in relation to the litigants is harmony, and the ideology of harmony places high value on egalitarian relations and symmetry; "corrective sanctions" such as fines or jail are common.

Intra-village Violence Between Men

Physical violence is more prevalent between men than between women; it has a different character. The intensity ranges from raising hell while drunk, shoving, biting, or using an instrument of violence such as a rifle, a knife, or a machete. Although there is no simple relation between violence proneness and the amount and prevalence of alcohol consumption (see Taylor 1979: 28–73), most commonly men who become violent have been drinking, and violence between men usually takes place in public settings: the cantina, the store, or the streets. When women fight, violence is not usually associated with drinking or with instruments of violence; they usually bite or fight with their hands, and the relationships at stake are often extended and deep. Case 62, in which one man attacked another, illustrates the usual format: complaint, confrontation, a plea for pardon, and outcome.

After being kept in jail overnight, a 40-year-old Talean man was called before the court on the complaint of a 62-year-old bartender. The bartender complained that at about 11 o'clock the night before, several persons were still in his place drinking, and that when he refused to dispense the defendant's order on credit, the latter punched him and knocked him down, and then resorted to a machete that was on the bar and tried to kill him. With the aid of the others present, the defendant was disarmed and thrown out of the place. The plaintiff took advantage of a slight lull to call the police.

Confronted with this charge, the defendant declared that in fact he had acted indiscreetly, but that it was due to his being very drunk, and he assured the bartender that he never had any reason, any motive to fight with him. The plaintiff asked that he be fined.

In this case both parties were fined because the bartender and all cantinas in general have orders to close and stop all sales at 10:00 P.M. Because the act of violence took place after the stipulated closing hour, the bartender had violated the local ordinance. Hence, he was fined 25 pesos. The defendant was fined 100 pesos as a corrective sanction, so that he would not again break municipal law.

The presidente is often elaborate in his condemnation of people who do not respect local law, whether they be plaintiffs or defendants. And in male violence cases the responsibility of and to the authority is often cited in the proceedings, as in Case 63.

The police appeared before the presidente, saying that they were bringing before him two men who were fighting in front of a house off the square. One had a scratch on his face and a torn shirt. The other was in a state of drunkenness. The presidente asked them, "Why is it that you were fighting?" The first man said, "Señor Presidente, first I would like to know who made the complaint, because we are not complaining. That is, I did not complain, nor did he."

The presidente responded, "Of course, even though you don't complain, the duty of the police is to watch so that there will not be any fights in the street, because then if something serious happens, this authority finds itself in difficulties. So, why is it that you fought?"

"Look, Señor Presidente, this companion was drunk; I was sober. I was standing next to Domingo's house, and when he passed, without saying anything, he pulled me by the hand, and we fell. Now, it would have been different if the two of us had been drunk. Then the police would have had good reason to bring us. But since I was in my senses, it would have been much stupidity on my part to hit a drunk, knowing that he was drunk, which is something that I myself can settle very well with him." His companion added, "Please excuse, Señor Presidente. I am at fault, because I pulled him. But neither of us is making the complaint. He has wounded my hand, but I do not complain. So we do not need to argue any more. Please tell us what our fine is so that everything can be settled here."

The presidente said to him, "It cannot be done. You are both going to jail, you for putting out your hand and the other for being an insulter and drunk. You, Nino, should have notified this authority that he was insulting you. We have the obligation to correct. But not the way you did, you put out your hand. For that reason the authority exists. You cannot make justice by your own hand."

Nino answered, "Look, Señor Presidente, when was I going to come and report, if he had already grabbed me and had already given me a push?" The presidente answered, "When you see a drunk who is insulting you, leave and do not say anything. In the end he is drunk. More foolish is he who argues with a drunk, knowing that he is not in his five senses."

The defendants agreed with the presidente: "You are right. The two of us do not complain. Please tell us how much the fine is, and we will leave." The presidente answered: "That cannot be done. You are both going to jail" (and he rang the bell for the policía). Nino then argued: "Look, Presidente, I am not going to jail, so how much do I owe? I am willing to pay the fine for both of us, but do not take me to jail. Or tell me how much it is for bail." The two policía were present by then, intending to take the defendants to the jail, but Nino, still insisting, said, "But, Señor Presidente, understand me, understand me. I have a right to put up my bail." To which the presidente responded: "I have already said that it cannot be done. Police, carry out the order." The second defendant was taken to jail first because he was drunk. The regidor said to Nino, "Compa, do what the presidente says. You put out your hand, and you deserve your punishment. That is why the authority is here—to reclaim." Nino then said, "You are right. I committed a fault. Now I pay the penalty. I am willing to pay it. Or, if you do not want that, then a bail, so as not to go to jail, because I am not drunk. I am conscious of my acts." When the policía tried once more to take him out, Nino asked them to wait because he wanted to talk to the presidente once more, but the presidente repeated that he had given the order for the policía to take him: "Tomorrow we are going to settle this matter."

After the policía took Nino away, two hours passed, while some matters with the regidores were settled. Afterward the secretario intervened, saying to the presidente: "Look, Señor Presidente, I will tell you in my opinion how the matter with Nino was. It is correct that he pay the fine as he asked. The fine is his punishment. It is not that I want to take your rights as presidente, but why leave this matter to tomorrow if there is nothing to negotiate? Now he is in his senses and willing to pay his fine, or pay the bail as he said. The other man can stay in jail for being drunk and insulting."

The presidente answered, "You are right. I am going to order that he be let out." Then to Nino he said, "I had you brought so that you will pay your fine and go home." "Señor Presidente, it is as I told you a while ago. Neither of us complained, and now I am willing to pay if I committed a fault, but I am going to tell you the way the matter was. I was standing next to Edgar's house, when this friend came along drunk, and I didn't move because I know that I owe him nothing, and I have no reason to move. Upon passing, he insulted me and pulled me by my hand until he threw me over. And that is the way we both fell. I said to him, 'Look, compa, go, you are drunk. Go and sleep. It is better.' And he told me, 'You are not going to order me. I will go where I please. And it is my business if I drink. I am not drinking from your pocket.' And once again he pulled me, and then I became annoyed, and we fell because I hit him, and surely the police saw this, or I don't know what happened because I was surprised that they took me without a complaint."

The presidente said, "It is as I said a while ago. The duty of the policía is to watch out for public order, and if you were fighting, well, naturally, the policía have the right to intervene." "All right, all right," Nino said. "Tell me how much the fine is, and I shall leave." The presidente said, "I will sanction you with 15 pesos for each of you. I will let the other one out tomorrow so that he will be careful about insulting."

After paying his fine, Nino asked permission to leave. The same sanction would be imposed upon the second defendant, so this case was considered finished.

As soon as Nino had left, Edgar presented himself to the presidente, saying, "Excuse me, Señor Presidente. I appear before you with all respect and ask you the favor of freeing my compadre who is in jail. I don't know what he did. He had me called so that I would plead for him, so that I would come to ask you for his favor. He is my compadre, and I find myself obliged to intervene."

The presidente said, "Look, Edgar, your compadre insulted Nino and they struck each other. Your compadre is drunk, and for that reason he is detained, so that he will be punished." Edgar left for a few moments to speak to his compadre in jail, and upon returning said, "Look, Señor Presidente, my compadre says that he does recognize his faults and asks that you forgive him and says he is willing to pay the fine, but he wants to go home because tomorrow he has to go to work." The presidente responded, "He should have thought about his obligations before." Edgar said, "You are right, but for this time I earnestly beg you to give him his freedom. I will pay the fine and take him to his home so that he may rest." "All right," said the presidente, "but with the condition that you take him to rest. If he continues drinking or if the policía find him in a while in the cantinas when they make their rounds, then the punishment will be worse." Edgar answered, "That is good, Señor Presidente. I promise you that he will not leave his house."

The presidente ordered the defendant let out so that he could appear before him. In the presence of witnesses, the presidente said to him, "Only by petition of your compadre here do I give you liberty. Do you recognize your fault?" The defendant answered, "Yes, yes, Señor Presidente, I recognize my fault. Because I was drunk, I did that to my compa Nino. He was standing. I pulled him. And please tell me how much I will pay for my fault." The presidente said, "It is 15 pesos fine, on the condition that you go directly to your house to rest, because if you continue drinking the punishment will be worse." The defendant agreed; his compadre paid the fine, and they asked permission to leave. With this the case was considered finished.

Both of these defendants were repeat offenders in this court, but the real offense in the case had to do with Nino's taking authority into his own hands: "You put out your hand," and "You cannot make justice by your own hand." Nino had a reputation for bucking authority, especially the village authority. He was a well-to-do man who runs a business in Talea but is seemingly always found on the street where the action is, where he was all too often making justice by his own hand. Self-help is disapproved of in Talea, because it is correctly perceived as a threat to village autonomy. Actually some years later Nino damaged the corporate entity by actively participating in a religious cleavage between traditional Catholics and newly converted Protestants. As I look back on the cases in which Nino appeared, the building toward a break with municipal authority was clearer than any simple reading of individual recorded cases might have indicated. The right to exercise ultimate authority belongs only to the town officials. Even in cases of self-defense, litigants are told not to take authority into their own hands. This case also illustrates that from the point of view of the litigants, the use of supporters to soften a judgment may have an effect, although not always.

In Case 64, involving one of the principals, a local merchant who in a state of drunkenness threatened the life of another, the pressure of supporters was formidable; so was the resistance to pressure. The issue was physical assault on the sindico. The defendant was a well-to-do citizen from a good family who, even though he drank a good deal, had been able to accumulate a large amount of capital. He was a generous and well-liked person who was seen as a good citizen.

This case was taken from observations recorded during the summer of 1965. The defendant had been drinking all afternoon and was quite drunk. He arrived at a cantina where the sindico had stopped to buy some cigarettes. The defendant was brandishing a 22-caliber rifle. He got into an argument with the sindico and finally assaulted him. The sindico ordered the policía to put the defendant in jail.

The sequence of events that followed was colored by the fact of drunkenness; both the sindico and the defendant were drunk, although the defendant was more drunk. As soon as the presidente arrived, he took charge of the case. But supporters also arrived to intercede on behalf of the defendant. The sindico kept insisting that the defendant had to stay in jail until the next day, but his supporters argued that their friend was *gente*—a gentleman—and therefore too important to be jailed. The defendant was brought in, still drunk. He slapped the sindico on the back, and everybody laughed.

In the end he was released and taken home. After the defendant and his supporters left, the presidente, the sindico, and the *tesorero* [treasurer] continued to talk about the *gran delito* [the serious crime].

The next day the case was brought before the alcalde. Since the sindico
was involved, he could not hear the case. The woman who owned the cantina where the action had occurred gave testimony. The defendant was
placed back in jail with a whole array of supporters talking to him. The supporters came into the alcalde's office led by a schoolteacher. The teacher
tried unsuccessfully to intimidate the alcalde. Then he tried to explain
away the actions of the defendant by saying that the defendant was drunk,
that he was really a sensitive person and a good citizen, and then once again
he tried to use drinking as an excuse. The alcalde said, "For whatever reason
he did it, the fact remains, and it is a big problem."

Two more supporters came in and argued with the sindico, while two
others came in to speak with the alcalde; one was a relative of the defendant,
the other a ritual kinsman. They seemed to be protective of the defendant's
reputation and urged that things be held in confidence. The defendant was
allowed out of jail to have lunch. The policía showed esteem for the man.
The relationship between the defendant and the sindico was made clear by
the defendant; the defendant's father's sister was the sindico's mother. The
sindico was described by the defendant, his cousin, as a rustic type who
took things too seriously. As the day progressed, supporters and the sindico
went in and out to speak with the alcalde.

At 3:00 P.M. the defendant entered with the teacher to see the alcalde.
The alcalde asked the teacher to leave, though the teacher objected, saying
that he was a friend and wanted to help the defendant with the agreement
that was to be drawn up. When the teacher had left, the alcalde read the
testimony to the defendant and asked him to identify the gun, which the
defendant did. The alcalde then began to talk about the seriousness of
the crime, saying that for four years after a serious crime like this one the
defendant could not take on any civic duties. "One does not have the rights
of a citizen," he said. "When a person like you gets into trouble, it is really
different." The defendant asked, "How much is my fine?" After some back
and forth, the alcalde said 500 pesos. When the defendant objected, the alcalde said, "If you give us 500 pesos, we will be able to write another proceeding [*acta*] that will say that the 500 pesos was a voluntary contribution." The defendant went out to get the money and upon his return began
once again to argue with the sindico in Zapotec. The teacher returned and
joined in also. The main defense now was that there was no intention to
harm and that therefore there was no case. The defendant paid the fine, and
the record did not incriminate him.

Clearly the defendant was not only a man with many supporters but a
good citizen in the town, a principal, after all. This case took all day to hear.

In this case of violence, a bargain was struck to protect the defendant's reputation, but the large fine and the brief jailing served as
punishment. The plaintiff's failure to raise cries of lack of respect for

authority is not surprising because, as a principal, the defendant was part of the village authority. Protecting the defendant's reputation in this case meant protecting the integrity of municipal powerholders.

One feature of cases of serious physical violence, such as when a man wounds another man, is the search for motive. In fact, this search for motive is one of the common requests that plaintiffs make when presenting their complaint—"que se busca motivo"— and such a request often directs the pattern of court confrontation. In Case 65, the alcalde's court went to great lengths to find out if there was a motive involved in the street fight between two brothers-in-law.

The sindico passed on to the alcalde the results of the investigations relative to a crime that had occurred the afternoon before, when Tino cut his brother-in-law Beto's left hand with a machete. The injured party was receiving medical attention from the doctor, and the accused was in jail. The sindico also handed over the instrument, a machete. The case was brought to the attention of the sindico by Beto's mother-in-law. The following testimonies were collected by the sindico.

Beto testified before witnesses. He was warned to tell the truth and was asked why he was attacked. He answered that yesterday was the fiesta of San Pedro. He was passing by the office of the tesorero at 6:00 P.M. when he encountered his brother-in-law Tino, who was inebriated. Tino requested that Beto take him home, since he was drunk. Beto accompanied his brother-in-law, and while chatting on the road they argued, and so Beto took leave of Tino before reaching Tino's house. He had only gone a few steps when his brother-in-law overtook him and without a word attacked him with a machete. Trying to defend himself, Beto reached out and his left hand was cut. Tino, being drunk, fell to the ground. At this moment a neighbor was passing by, and he took Beto to his house and put alcohol and a bandage on his wound and from there took Beto to his own house. When the family heard what had happened, the mother-in-law immediately went to the municipio with the complaint.

Beto was exhorted to tell the truth and was warned of the punishment incurred by false testimony in court. He was again asked to inform the court what was the cause of his brother-in-law's aggression with the machete. Beto answered that he didn't know the cause, that he accompanied his brother-in-law so that Tino would not commit some disorder, since he was drunk, because if he neglected him he would be going against his sister [Tino's wife]. Beto had asked Tino whether he could get work from him, and Tino had answered that it would be better to give him work in July and August, as do the wealthy. Beto then said that he should not offend him because he was poor, and seeing his brother-in-law's treatment of him, he turned before reaching his brother-in-law's house. Beto was asked if Tino was very drunk, to which he answered only a little. He was asked if they had argued before, and he said no.

Beto's mother-in-law was asked if her son-in-law had some difficulty or quarrel with Tino, to which she replied that there had never been trouble between them.

Beto's mother was also asked if her son had trouble with Tino, to which she replied that she didn't have anything to declare pro or con.

The sister of the plaintiff and wife of the defendant, Tino, appeared to give testimony and was asked in what condition her husband was when he arrived home the night of the assault. She answered that she wasn't home because she had gone to the mill. When asked if her husband had some quarrel with her brother, she answered that there never had been trouble. When asked if she found her husband at home when she returned from the mill, she said yes, and that she had found him in the corridor of the house but that she didn't know if he were sleeping because he had his face to the floor, and she did not speak to him because she knew he was very drunk. When she arrived home from the mill, various [neighborhood] children told her that her husband had fought with her brother. She asked a neighbor whether it was true and then went to see her mother. But since she did not find her mother at home, she returned to her own home, but on the way she ran into her husband, who was being hauled to jail by a group of policemen. He was taken away without shoes or a hat. She said that when her husband was drunk, he didn't know what he was doing because he lost his judgment. She added that until then her husband had not had anything to eat and had only sent her a request for vinegar.

The wife of the plaintiff, Beto, was asked why her brother-in-law should have come to blows with her husband. She answered that they had had no trouble and that they had always worked together happily. When asked if her husband arrived home with his senses or inebriated on the night of the fight, she replied that he was sober and that he had trembled only because he said he was in such pain. When questioned if her husband had told her why he was attacked, she said that her husband had informed her only that her brother-in-law had wounded him with a machete while he was taking him home.

A cousin of the plaintiff was interrogated and asked what he knew about the quarrel that Beto and Tino had. The cousin answered that he knew nothing, only that he had found Beto with a bleeding left arm and when he asked what had happened, Beto replied that Tino had wounded him without saying what his motive was. Tino was lying in a slight ditch along the road. The cousin immediately took Beto to his house to help him.

Testimony of a neighbor was that the neighbor was on his way to get water at the well when he saw Beto and Tino. On his return from the well, Tino asked him if he had seen Beto, and he replied that Beto was standing a little further up the road. Tino continued until he reached his brother-in-law, but the neighbor did not notice whether Tino carried a machete or not. On his second trip to the well, the neighbor saw Beto and Tino together, Beto with a bloody hand, fighting with Tino, saying, "Look what you've done to me, and you have no right!" The neighbor also saw a machete lying on the ground, and upon meeting Tino's daughter he told her to pick up the machete, which had been thrown near the road, and take it home. Then he went home.

In his testimony the defendant said that he did not remember anything about a quarrel with his brother-in-law, nor if he left him at his house. When he was asked if they had had some difficulty before, he replied no, that they had always worked together and sustained complete harmony. When asked if he did not remember that while drunk he had offended his brother-in-law, providing the motive for their fight, he answered that he did not remember that they fought because he was inebriated; only his brother-in-law, who was sober, would remember. Tino said he recalled seeing Beto with a completely bloody face from the hair to jaw, with blood running down his shirt in front and the right shoulder, dripping down his right pant leg. . . .

Five days later an agreement was signed with the alcalde and sindico present. A *convenio amistoso*—a friendly agreement—was signed, without coercion because they are family. Tino and his family begged Beto to pardon the defendant for the offense and injury caused, being willing to pay him for the days he could not work and for medical expenses. Beto said that he understood that they were family, and it surprised him that Tino attacked and did what he did, because they had never quarreled before. He regretted that his brother-in-law had caused this *fracaso* [disaster], but realized that his brother-in-law was unconscious and not in his right senses when he injured him. He was willing to forgive him for his serious fault if Tino agreed to pay him for the two weeks it would take him to recuperate and for medical expenses. Tino replied that he agreed to Beto's conditions and that his and his family's desire was to eradicate their difficulties with the forgiveness of Beto and his family. Both parties showed and proposed to resolve the case with this friendly agreement with the alcalde's specified sanctions.

Beto signed the agreement forgiving his brother-in-law. Tino signed a request for forgiveness. The medical doctor listed the injuries plus the results of his examination: (1) the wounds would take more than two weeks to heal; (2) the injured party's life was not in danger; and (3) he expected complete recuperation of the left hand.

The alcalde and sindico concluded the following: by virtue of the fact that the two parties and their families had celebrated a friendly agreement, in which the defendant asked forgiveness from the plaintiff, and since Beto had granted Tino pardon and both families had agreed, and furthermore, since both parties were related and requested that the case terminate before the alcalde [and not be referred to Villa Alta], the alcalde agreed to close the case. However, the alcalde fined Tino 60 pesos as a sanction and in addition fined Beto 40 pesos for having hit his brother-in-law while sober [as the testimony maintained].

Even in self-defense Beto should not have taken the law into his own hands, another instance of a strict line on self-help. But in this case the questioning did not focus on taking the law into one's own hands. The issue was motive: Was there any? Should the court have been alerted to any evidence that might have prompted the violence? If the authorities had found evidence of motive, they would then have dealt with the root causes in the relationships and not merely addressed the current instance of violence. It is motive, rather than guilt, that is the issue. When no motive is found, both parties are usually penalized, the plaintiff is compensated, and the case ends in Talea. If a motive is found, the case would be opened up to issues beyond the original complaint in search of harmony.

In Case 66, two men appeared before the presidente. The first was drunk, and the second was completely sober. The first man opened:

"I went to collect a debt that my stepfather has had pending with me since last year, a loan in the amount of 200 pesos. I come here to speak against my stepfather because when I went to his house because I was in need of money, he looked for excuses not to pay me. He said that because of other debts that I had with him he couldn't pay me. . . . I answered him, 'It's all right if you say that I also owe you, and everything can remain in that manner. Don't pay me anything, but I want you to vacate the house that belonged to my father, and to leave my father's house.' When I said this, he became disturbed and tried to hit me. I ran to avoid an argument because he is my stepfather. Then he followed me until he reached me, at a distance of about 10 meters, and we were fighting. He grabbed an object and tried to hit me with it. I have a witness who saw everything that happened—the woman who is in Miasa. She saw."

Once the presidente had heard what the plaintiff said, the stepfather immediately said, "It's not that I wanted to hit him. I only owe him 200 pesos, and I am going to pay it. But he is very violent when he is collecting a debt and wants it to be done immediately. I even said, 'Look, on Monday I will pay you everything you say that I owe you. At this time my coffee hasn't dried, and it isn't ready for sale. It isn't much that I have,' I told him, 'four or five little trees, but I am going to pay you.' He says that I wanted to hit him. It is true that I grabbed a piece of rock, and I wanted to hit him. But I didn't hit him. When one is really going to strike, one does it quickly, but he is exaggerating. And besides, he was rather drunk. Now he wants me to move out of his house. . . . I will leave this house. I will see where I can stay. I told him I have my little piece of land in the east of this village. So I will go to my house, but he must replace it, because he had it torn down."

The stepson then answered that Elías [the former presidente] ordered him to do it, and the plaintiff asked that the former presidente appear so that he could tell what had been ordered of him. Immediately the presidente ordered that Elías be summoned. Since he was not home, the hearings were postponed until the following day. In the meantime, however, they called the woman who was witness to the event. The young woman was summoned and gave her testimony: "I was coming from the market, and when I arrived home, I saw that the plaintiff was grabbing a man with a blue shirt. I don't know who the man is; I only know the owner of the house. But I don't know what thing he picked up off the ground when bending over. And that is all I can say, and all that I saw." She asked permission to leave, and the matter was left for the morning.

When they met again, the presidente said to the litigants: "Once again we are going to settle this matter." He asked the stepfather the reason for the fights with his stepson. He answered: "When my wife died, the mother of my stepson, I said to him, 'Look, Miguel, don't get upset; some friends of mine are coming to take some of the things I have in this house, so that I can go to my house next to my son Raymundo.' Upon returning after leaving the cross for my wife, my two compadres came to the house where we all lived, and said in the presence of my stepson, 'We have come to make arrangements for our godson Raymundo, since unfortunately his mother has died, and we wish to have certain matters settled.' I answered them that I was grateful for their being concerned for my son, but that I could not say because what my stepson says is what is always done." The stepson said [at that time] that he could not dispose of matters because "one of his brothers went away to study and the rest of the brothers had died and I am the only one, and I have no one except for my stepfather and some day I will need him and he needs me, and I can't let my [step]brother and stepfather leave my house." The stepfather continued, saying, "All of this was just left in words because we were family and had no arguments. But now my stepson is always drunk, and I don't pay attention to him when he does these things. Now I know that the mezcal is what makes him become that way with me. And now I am ready to leave the house when he replaces my house and land, because he ordered that it be torn down. I don't even know what he did with the roof tiles. The motive that he has now is because I owe him some money, and I haven't been able to serve him more. That is why he takes that attitude. . . . Now let us not argue anymore, and let the authority resolve what is to be done."

The stepson said, "I ask and request what I said before. What he did I cannot stand, and I ask that he leave my house. I didn't think that he would do this. That is why I ask that he leave the house of my father, because it belonged to my father."

The presidente, increasingly aware of the motives of the two parties, said to the stepson: "Look, Miguel, what you are doing is not correct. Remember that he is your stepfather and that you have a little brother. Someday your conscience is going to bother you for what you are doing to them." Miguel answered, "I have already done that which I was supposed to do, and I already have it well thought out, that the two leave. It is no longer my obligation to look after the two. I have already helped them very much." The stepfather said, "Look, Señor Presidente, here I bring a letter from Miguel's brother, Father Martín, in which he says, 'We must all be united,' that he and Miguel are going to do everything possible, that there are no difficulties."

"But look, Señor Presidente," said Miguel, "that has already passed, and my brother doesn't know how that man has treated us. I bring here some documents which are copies of what happened before. We have it all written down. Here are his antecedents of how he treated my mother and my brothers." The stepfather responded, "Well, you may say what you like, but your mother in the end brought me back to your house, and she insisted that I return." The stepson said, "Look, Señor Presidente, why are we going to argue? I am willing to pay him the cost of what he says is his. I will see how I do it. Thank God that I have the satisfaction that I am not armless and unable to work and have money; I can. But I want you to say, Señor Presidente, how much it is, so that in your presence I can bring the money. . . . Before, he did what he pleased with us, but now things have changed." The stepfather said, "I don't want money. I want him to replace the house that was torn down."

The presidente then called Elías, the former presidente who Miguel had said ordered him to tear down the walls of his stepfather's house. When Elías arrived he gave unwilling testimony, saying that he could not remember if he had given such an order, but that if he had, it was only to avoid possible accidents. They had cleared out a number of places in town as safety measures.

What followed was an offer on the part of the stepson to pay his stepfather for what had been a house in ruins and the refusal of the stepfather to take money rather than a replacement of his house. The presidente then gave up, suggesting that they pass the case to the sindico and that Miguel think about it again, adding, "You must think that he is your relative, and I will give you a period of time so that you can think it over." "All right," answered Miguel. "I don't say that I don't respect him, for I do. Please, I ask a time of three hours to consult whether my wife wants me to communicate with Father Martín, or if we should wait until he arrives."

The next day the two men were back in the presidente's office. Miguel was now saying that his stepfather had to vacate the house because the roof was dangerous and needed fixing and suggested that his stepfather stay with him while he fixed the roof. The stepfather agreed that the roof was dangerous, but he was willing to move out until Father Martín arrived. Then once again Miguel asked about the money his stepfather owed him, and the stepfather once again said, "I have already told you that when my coffee is dry, I will sell it and pay you. I do not deny that I have to pay you." They all agreed to leave the case unfinished until Father Martín returned the following month.

In disputes that deal with members of the same family, when something is festering that causes an eruption of physical violence, it is not the fighting that is central, but rather the reason for the fighting that takes center stage. This is also true in same-sex cases between unrelated persons. Taleans are not concerned so much with an act of violence as they are with the context in which it occurs: Will it escalate? Is it due to loss of the senses? Is it related to a series of events leading up to violence? Can further violence be prevented? How best can the victims be compensated? Is it possible to make harmony? Case 67 is an example of Talean pragmatism in violence cases.

The sindico heard evidence pertaining to acts of aggression and lesion committed by an employee of an agency against another employee of that same agency as a result of a blow on the side of the face. The defendant was jailed and the head of the agency notified to appear and testify as to what he saw. . . . The defendant recognized his fault and was most willing to accept and pay for the medical attention of the wounded man and to pay the corresponding fine. The wounded man agreed and wished to have the case settled as soon as possible, too, and asked that there be no more legal proceedings. The wounded man was paid the salary of two days' work, and his medical bill was also paid. The sindico fined the defendant 50 pesos, which was immediately paid.

Case 68 exhibits the same perfunctory quality.

Fino stabbed Lucian with a knife during a brawl in a bar belonging to Zenon. The wound was a head wound. Fino was found guilty and fined 30 pesos and was pushed roughly out of the courtroom toward the street. He was told to take care not to offend the wounded man again, either by words or action. He was told to practice more self-discipline and to respect his elders.

In Case 69, a policeman encountered a driver of the Transportes Oaxaca out late at night. The policeman told the driver that it was time for him to go to his lodging because it was late. At this the driver answered that no one was going to tell him what to do. Insults began to fly, and the driver became violent, took out his pistol, and hit the policeman on the head and face with it. The policeman then hit the driver on the head with his flashlight, and immediately the driver fired twice. One bullet hit the policeman "in the region of the fossa iliaca on the left side." Shortly thereafter the driver was captured by the police and taken to jail. When the case was heard, the wounded man requested that the case be handled in a friendly manner. The defendant was removed from jail. According to the sindico's records:

The defendant admitted all that had happened and asked to be judged and to have the case settled. He was told that the obligation of this authority is to follow legal channels unless an agreement is reached spontaneously, in accord with the authority.

The case was settled by an agreement [*acta de convenio*] under the following terms: first, the wounded plaintiff pardoned his offender if he was willing to pay the medical bills and compensate him for five days of lost work. The offender agreed to make these payments. Then, the authority informed both parties that it could recognize the agreement only if the delinquent was willing to pay a fine that took into account the gravity of the crime committed and to agree to confiscation of his pistol. The offender agreed, whereby he submitted voluntarily to the conditions and amounts he would have to pay.

In Case 70, the physical violence was serious. The defendant inflicted serious wounds on the plaintiff, a younger man. Yet, as we see in this lengthy case, the difficulties between the parties were brought to the surface piece by piece, so that the court was able to reach a balanced judgment, "an agreement between both parties," as one petitioner said, which would not have the effect of "disorganizing the group."

In August, Fidel, a 74-year-old father and his interpreter brought a complaint against Tino for crimes of aggression and injuries perpetrated against his young son Paco. The case was heard by the sindico, and then, along with one blanket, one outer shirt, and an undershirt with signs of blood that proved the wounds inflicted on the young man, was turned over to the alcalde. The presumed guilty party was also turned over to the alcalde along with the testimony from the sindico's record.

Paco was assaulted and wounded by Tino when the young man was en route home to rest. As he passed by the house of his aggressor, according to the plaintiffs, he [the aggressor] shone a flashlight into his eyes and, having identified him as Paco, without weighing the responsibility, attacked him furiously in a furtive and tricky manner. They didn't know what type of weapon was used by the older man Tino, but the wounds were on the face by the left eyebrow and by the ear on the same side. As proof they presented Paco's clothing, which proved the wounds, since they were all bloody. The son, Paco, was in bed, and the two plaintiffs asked the authority to go to his bedside to take down his testimony.

The sindico gave the order to the police for the apprehension and detention of the defendant. He was to be incarcerated in the public jail and be at the disposition of the authority. In the meantime the investigations of the case proceeded. Two men from the town presented a written request for the release of the prisoner under personal bond. This request was granted, since it came under legal terms, and the prisoner Tino was freed on the condition that he present himself to the court the next day so that the investigation could continue. . . .

The sindico and his personnel went to the house of the wounded person, since he was unable to come to the offices to give testimony because of the wounds he had suffered. He was asked to tell the truth. He stated that he was 27 years old, single, a sandal maker. He was asked whether he knew of the complaint registered by his father and the interpreter against Tino, and he answered in the affirmative. He further declared . . . that the day before, having finished his work, he retired to his own home, ate dinner, and afterward went toward the building where the members of the town orchestra practice. After being with some companions there, he and they headed home separately. As Paco went toward his house, at the crossroads of the main street, he encountered a subject who shone a light in his eyes and, being very close to him, uttered an obscenity, and without further preamble struck him very hard over the left eyebrow, which immediately started to bleed. The wounded man said he was able to identify the aggressor by his voice. The only thing he said at the time was "Tino," and that he had not thought to call him any bad word, nor had he intended to offend him. He saw that his aggressor immediately went inside his house and closed the door. Paco then decided to go back to the center of town for some alcohol with which to wash out his wound. He covered his wound with his blanket until he got to Zenon's store, where he obtained some alcohol. He lost his hat when he was wounded. Zenon applied Band-Aids to the wounds, since he had not been able to get medical attention. Zenon then accompanied him to the authorities, but, it being very late, they found the offices closed.

From there Paco went to the house of his friend who had been with him earlier that evening and told him what had happened. The friend then accompanied him to the home of his [Paco's] parents in order to get a blanket before going to bed at the house of his cousin. As they passed the place where he had been assaulted, they saw that his hat was no longer there. He added that he told his parents nothing of what had happened.

He was asked about possible motives for the assault and answered that, approximately one month before, the wife of Tino had gone by the house of the victim to investigate whether he had had amorous relations with her niece, Josefina. And when the wife of Tino was ill, she pronounced the name of Paco, and because of this her husband had decided to leave her or to deliver her back to her parents. Later the brother of the aggressor's wife spoke to him of this same thing, informing him that because of these reasons Tino hated him. He said that he himself was not sure about the truth of these matters and that Tino had not mentioned them to him, but he supposed that they must have motivated the violence against him.

After this testimony, the sindico witnessed the fact that the wounds were located on the left eyebrow, nose, and ear, and he took Paco immediately to the doctor in the village for medical care.

Testimony was taken from the defendant, who was married, 38 years old, and a miller by occupation. He was informed why he had been detained. Tino answered that he had indeed assaulted and wounded Paco. He was asked to give the reasons for his action, and he answered the following. On July 10 his wife had been ill. He questioned her because her relatives and other people said it was fright [susto]. His wife told him that she had had a terrible fright with the disaster of the roof, which had caved in the previous year. She said she had also received a serious fright from Paco on a night in May of this year, when she was asleep in her house, in bed in the upstairs living room of the house. (Tino had had to go out that night because he was a musician and had to play on the day of San Isidro. He said he didn't notice when Paco left the group in order to go and commit the abuses against him.) Anyway, his wife told him that a few minutes after saying her prayers for the night, the doors being closed but not locked on the lower floor of the house, Paco made his way to where she was. When she awoke, she saw Paco lifting her blanket, and seeing so suddenly that he was there, she was very frightened, but recognized him as Paco. He fled rapidly, without saying a single word.

The defendant said he did not take Paco to task for this because he was a friend whom he had always respected and had confidence in. Also he said that he never showed Paco any hatred because he didn't believe the story to be true. However, on July 11 a woman came to the door of his mill and in a very direct manner asked him if he was having marital difficulties with his wife. Tino replied by asking her why she asked such a question, and she said that Paco had told her that it was because of himself that Tino and his wife were having problems. It was because of this that he [Tino] decided to commit this act of violence. He would never have dared to do this had he not been in possession of such information, since he was entirely sane when he assaulted Paco. The young woman, Rosa, had said that Paco had told her, "We have better relations." This, coupled with the fact that Paco had entered his house with suspicious intent and because his wife had had a fright that resulted in a prolonged illness, furnished the reason for the assault.

Now the giver of testimony said that with this proof of the offenses committed by Paco, he was asking that legal procedures be taken against him. If Paco had not done anything on that night in May, why should he be telling people about it without any reason? Tino said he felt justified in beating up Paco. He was then asked for the details of the encounter he had with the plaintiff, and he answered that on that night he encountered Paco at the center of town, in front of his house. As Paco drew nearer, he said he asked him what he had been telling on the streets. Paco didn't answer and was surprised. It was to be supposed that since he was guilty, he didn't have an answer. When Paco began to run away, Tino hit him over the head with an empty bottle he had with him.

Rosa was then called to testify. She was accompanied by her mother because she was a minor, 16 years old. She was informed why she had been asked to appear and was asked to tell what she knew. She said that she was going into the mill when she saw Tino at the doorway. He caressed her with his eyes and a smile, and when she came nearer, she asked him why he was smiling. He answered that he wished her to go to his house and live with him. She asked if he was quarreling with his wife, and he answered that he was. She then said that that was what Paco had spoken to her about, that they had been having trouble. Then she went into the mill, and he went toward his home. Later that day Tino asked her why and how Paco had spoken to her about Tino, and she answered that on July 11, as she was in the patio of her house, Paco came up the road. Paco, upon seeing Rosa with a baby in her arms, said, "How would it be to have a baby of my blood?" to which Rosa replied, "I would have to be drunk." Then Paco added, "So that you could then have fights and unpleasantness as in the house of Tino." This was all. He had continued on down the road and she had gone inside.

At this point the case was consigned to the office of the alcalde, so that he might proceed through legal channels if necessary [i.e., to Villa Alta]. The alcalde and the sindico, along with the defendant and the wounded man and the original plaintiffs, conferred. The following document was presented for ratification.

The undersigned, Tino and Paco, wish to make known the following:

First, I, Paco, registered a complaint on July 15 before the sindico municipal through my representatives against Tino for having beaten and wounded me on the left eyebrow. After I put forth this complaint, the sindico initiated preliminary investigations and then consigned the case to the alcalde.

Second, I, Tino, when required by the sindico municipal to state my reasons for asaulting Paco, declared that he had come into my home, taking advantage of my absence, as I was performing my duties as a musician in the orchestra. On this occasion he attempted to abuse my wife, who received a serious fright, especially since she was already in bed with our children. As already stated, she was frightened by his entrance and as a consequence became gravely ill, which justifies my aggression.

Third, because we have both thought of the mutual convenience of reaching an amicable settlement of our quarrel, we have decided to mutually pardon each other for the offenses we have committed and ask this authority to cancel or negate all complaints.

Fourth, we have decided that the cost of medical care shall be paid by the wounded one.

Fifth, as already stated, we beg you, with all due respect, to take note of this agreement that we have arrived at, which we found based on Article 106 of the Penal Code, extinguishing thus all penal action. We inform you that we submit to your judgment on what sanctions we have incurred through our actions in the present case. . . .

There follows [another] statement, which says the following:

Before you, in a respectful manner, I wish to state the following: I have some knowledge of the quarrel between Tino and Paco. . . . The results are that the young man Paco has been gravely injured at the hands of Tino. They are both members of the Recreation and Labor Orchestra, and I wish to bring before this court a petition as director of the aforementioned group, that there be a unanimous transaction, that is to say, an agreement between both parties, that they will not permit the furthering of this quarrel, which could have the effect of disorganizing said group. . . . The orchestra uses the house of Tino F. as a rehearsal hall, so for all this I do not want a motive of displeasure to exist on the part of the owner of the house, or any difficulties for or against this particular quarrel. For all the above reasons, Señor Presidente, I beg you to accept with amiability this humble petition. . . .

Signed by the Director of the Orchestra

The alcalde ratified the document of agreement between the plaintiff and the defendant and inserted it in this brief as was ordered. Because of the petitions of the plaintiff and defendant and the director of the orchestra, and because the quarrel might affect the orchestra of which they were both members, the quarrel was now passed over. However, in relation to the disciplinary sanctions, the court determined that they should each be fined 30 pesos, to be paid in cash to the municipal treasury for public works.

Over and over again, the concern is with social relationships and with the causes of disruptions in relationships. The driving force in the proceedings is the maintenance of harmony. In this context, what at first appeared to be a unilateral act of physical violence recedes into the background. In searching out the complex motives, the court officials transform the case from an examination of unilateral to one of bilateral action. The officials in the court make the balance by searching for and giving weight to the motive for physical violence. The plaintiff was not even compensated for his medical costs. If the plaintiff had asked the defendant for compensation, the defendant could have retaliated by asking the plaintiff to cover the cost of curing his wife's fright. What made this a serious case was not the violence per se, but the fact that it was violence inflicted while the aggressor was sober, with the potential for escalation. As the director of the orchestra said, this quarrel "could have the effect of disorganizing the group," since both plaintiff and defendant were members of the orchestra and factionalism could result. Bringing out the motive results in seeing the defendant's action as evening out the relationship. Two wrongs make for an agreement (convenio). If there had been no strong motive and no special circumstances as in Case 65, the defendant would have been accused of self-help, or taking the law into his own hands. In this case the fear of factionalism or escalation was greater than the threat arising from self-help.

Case 71 resulted from a drunken brawl that involved a large number of men, not all of them drunk.

The sindico began investigation of the complaint registered with the police of Talea last night by Berto. According to the police, the complaint was followed by the arrest of young Raymundo as well as Agosto and young Cipriano.

Berto was summoned to clarify his complaint, and he said that about 10 o'clock last night he had gone to Agosto's bar with Cipriano. Both were already drunk. Once there, Cipriano invited him to have a drink together with some other friends, among them Raymundo. Within a short time Cipriano provoked a fight, and they were obliged to go outside into the public street. Raymundo separated them, and they continued in peace.

At this time the plaintiff, Berto, was embarrassed that the others were watching them from the door of the bar, watching the *escándalo*, and he said to them, "You are watching the dance, and if you want to watch the dance, why don't you go to Solaga?" At this instance young Raymundo gave him a strong blow, in a sneaky way, which struck him on the face and upper cheek. Berto said he did not tangle with his aggressor, but continued on his way toward his home. In front of the home of Tiburcio, his enemy caught up with him, hit him, and knocked him to the ground, where he continued to hit him in the face with his hands, while he kicked other parts of his body with his feet. Berto said he made an effort to get up and went to inform the police.

Cipriano was present and before being released from jail, he was asked how much of what had happened he could account for, and he answered that Raymundo had indeed struck Berto, and he said that he himself was drunk when he tried to intervene to stop the fight. A young man did not let him, and even held him to keep him from doing so *because he was suspicious of the intentions of Raymundo because he had observed that he was sober when he hit* [my emphasis].

Agosto was summoned as owner of the establishment that sold mezcal late at night. Upon being questioned, he said that Berto and Cipriano had come to his bar already drunk and had invited their friends to join them. Young Berto had offended him with obscene words, which were insupportable. *He did not wish to strike him because he was not drunk* [my emphasis], and because he was the owner of the establishment, but he had gotten quite indignant.

Another witness, Emiliano, was summoned and questioned. He said he knew nothing because he was drunk also, and just happened to notice there was a fight going on, but didn't even know who it was that was fighting, but he did admit to having held Raymundo in order to avoid more disorder.

Then Raymundo was ordered released from jail, where he was being held because of the accusation of hitting Berto. Raymundo admitted to hitting him in the face, and said that it was due to the offensive manner in which he and his friends had conducted themselves. He said that Berto was out of his head.

It appeared that both sides were at fault. They requested the sindico to settle the case and stated that they were willing to accept sanctions. The sindico determined that since there were no serious wounds on the body of the plaintiff, Raymundo was fined the sum of 30 pesos, which had to be paid in cash to the treasury on the same day. The owner of the bar was fined 15 pesos for having permitted the sale of liquor late at night, thus violating the ordinance passed by the court at the beginning of the year. For having been the prime mover of this disturbance, young Cipriano was fined the sum of 15 pesos. Emiliano, for not having declared all he knew about the disturbance, and in whose very testimony one could deduce that he had obstructed the police the night before when they searched for Raymundo, was fined 15 pesos.

In these kinds of brawls, everyone is liable. In trying to figure out who did what to whom, the court is careful to hear everybody out and to impose punishment in the form of fines. In this case the plaintiff did not get fined for the use of provocative language because he had already had justice meted out to him—he had been beaten up. Again the original complaint is transformed. The issues in the case are expanded beyond the physical violence that motivated the action of complaint in order to include the violation of a village ordinance and the withholding of information from the court. Physical violence is considered more worthy of court time if the violence is committed when the actor is sober. Violence committed while sober is a serious matter that merits a fine relative to the situation.

Intra-village Violence Between Women

Violence between women occurs infrequently; the cases are brief and not as extensive as those we have seen between men. Most important, violence between women is unlikely to lead to village factionalism. Case 72 involving recidivists was recorded in 1961 in the alcalde's office.

Having been called by the police, Nonfa testified that Carmen had insulted her with obscenities, for which she hit her on the street. Nonfa reported that an agreement was made the previous year that both of them should get along, or the court would proceed against them.

Hearing this, the alcalde ordered the secretary to find the case in the archives and found that it was true. There had been an agreement signed by the litigants and their husbands. For contempt of court, the alcalde fined each one 30 pesos and reopened investigations.

The husbands pleaded with the alcalde to stop further investigations in order not to waste time. The alcalde then said that if the wives were agreed to the punishment that he imposed for having offended public morals and using violence, he would fine them each 15 pesos, which, added to the earlier 30 pesos, made a total fine of 45 pesos that each would have paid to the treasury for public works. The alcalde warned them that if their differences continued, he would be obliged to invoke the Penal Code against them, and told them that from this day on they should act like rational people and forget their disagreements. They promised not to violate the present agreement.

Case 73, is much the same: one woman complaining that another had inflicted physical harm, and the alcalde finding that the action was reciprocal and fining both litigants.

Juana appeared in court to sue Andrea for bodily injuries inflicted on her by the latter. When cited, the defendant in turn showed marks on her right arm from a bite inflicted by the plaintiff. When investigations were pursued, the court concluded that neither party had sufficient reason to injure the other, and that the whole affair was due to the rashness of both. Each woman was fined 25 pesos, and they signed a document in agreement with the court.

In Case 74, we never fully learned the outcome of a conflict. The hearing of this case was casual—the officials entered late and inter-rupted the case to carry on other business.

A woman between the ages of 25 and 30 appeared in the court and presented her complaint to the presidente. The woman, Angela, came in with her baby. A few minutes later another woman, Felicity, entered. They had to wait for the presidente, who had already been informed that Felicity had hit Angela. The two women were neighbors, and a third woman, also a neigh-bor, appeared as witness.

Felicity was questioned by the presidente and corrected by the witness. Then the plaintiff spoke, and immediately all three women began speaking in Zapotec at the same time. Other witnesses appeared. The case was se-rious because Felicity had gone to Angela's house with a complaint and *had struck her in her own house* [my emphasis]. Felicity denied that she did this. At any rate the presidente said that if there had been a man at home and he had intervened, this conflict in the house would probably have been settled without coming to his office. Felicity was put in jail as punishment, and the case was to be continued in the morning.

Case 75 dealt with two women who had come to the Talean mar-ket from the neighboring village of Juquila. Juquilan women drink in public, unlike Talean women, and when they drink, they usually act sentimental or happy rather than contentious, but occasionally a fight breaks out.

Cristina presented herself before the presidente with the complaint that Teresa, who was from her same village of Juquila, had hit her.

Immediately the presidente ordered the police to find the accused, in order to discover the motive for the fight. The police arrived with Teresa, who was interrogated. The accused answered, "It is true that we fought, but she hit me first, and I had to defend myself. Cristina always does this to me.

She is always fighting. This is not the first time that we have come before this authority."

The presidente asked them what the motive for the fight had been. Teresa answered, "It was just because she had been drinking that she began to insult me and hit me. Now, why did she put in a complaint against me if she started the fight?" Cristina answered, "That is not true. I said nothing to her. Now why did she run, when she says that she did nothing to me?" Teresa responded, "I did not run. Rather, I headed for my ranch house because it was already late, but the police caught up with me when I got to the capilla of San Antonio. Why should I have run if I had not committed a crime?"

Cristina answered, "Now, if my little boy gets sick from fright [susto], you will be responsible because he became very frightened." Again, they began to argue because they were in a state of inebriety. The presidente ordered that they be detained in jail, as a punishment to both of them for provoking scandals in public areas and for having fought because of drinking. Minutes later, Felix, Cristina's husband, appeared and asked that he be punished in his wife's place because she had to go to her ranch house with the child. The presidente agreed, and he was detained in jail instead of his wife.

The next morning Felix and Teresa were brought before the court along with Felix's wife, Cristina. They asked how much the fine was. The presidente said, "I will fine each of you 10 pesos for being so scandalous." Cristina answered, "I will give 5 pesos." The presidente did not accept that, and finally both parties paid their fines. Cristina said, "It is all right now I have paid, but if my little boy becomes ill, the only responsible one is this Teresa. And I will come here to place the complaint." Both parties were then free to leave.

Fright (susto) is something from which women and children suffer most. It can be caused by anything that frightens a person—a snake, a rat, or another person. The symptoms are diarrhea, headache, sometimes vomiting, fever, and loss of appetite. When a child gets diarrhea and a fever or any of the other symptoms, the mother will say her child has susto. The consequence of Case 75 lies in not so much the repeated drunkenness of the two women, but in whether the fight that ensued can be said to be the cause of the child's susto. If it can, then the person who started the fight is liable for the child's medical expenses. Men do not usually complain that someone caused them to have susto, especially in a court of law. But little was made of the actual act of fighting in this case. More is said about noise-making, and once again the interest is to see if there is a deeper motive than whatever may have been situational and thus provoked by alcoholic consumption at the Monday market.

Aggression is an act against the community. In the majority of cases, violence is dealt with by a "corrective sanction" rather than by restitution to the injured party. In Case 76, two women were on their way to the Talean market from Tabaa and Yoxobe, respectively, when they got into a fight. Señora Rufina G., the woman from Yoxobe, complained to the Talean authorities that Señora Trinidad S. from Tabaa had started a fight with her en route to market and that this same woman had bitten her on the left hand. The accused was apprehended and put in jail. Later, when presenting testimony, the defendant admitted her aggressiveness and said that she had attacked Rufina for trivial reasons. The presidente levied a corrective sanction in the amount of 25 pesos, which she paid immediately.

In yet another case, number 77, a young woman who was a resident of Talea but who came from another town in the region was sent on an errand by her employer, also a woman. When she did not return immediately, the employer and her sister went to find her and encountered her strolling back to the house. A fight ensued, and the young woman freed herself and ran to the municipio to lodge a complaint. Again the sanction of 20 pesos imposed on the two sisters was a "corrective," once it was concluded that the fight did not have any deep or serious roots. In the heat of the moment, however, the case was appealed from the presidente's office to the sindico and then to the alcalde.

Discussion

The meaning of violence in Talea depends on the situation; violence per se is not a problem. In fact, the use of violence as a category that is important by itself is more a Western concept than a Zapotec one. For the Talean Zapotec the issues are community, relationships, motive. Violence associated with drunkenness is different from aggression committed when sober. Violence between men is more threatening than violence between women because it has more potential for escalation. In addition, the root causes of aggressive behavior are more important than the symptomatic behavior reflected in acts of violence because these mountain people are wary that an act might "disorganize the group." The Zapotec think sociologically about harmony and violence.

In their theory of behavior, aggressive acts by the individual are to be understood by reference to the wider social environment. In settling particulars, they seek to balance relationships by searching out all the motives of the concerned parties. The decisions of the court can then be more symmetrical to the parties, particularly if the parties are of the same sex.

There is a difference between same-sex violence and cross-sex violence in respect to symmetry and balance because the issues reflected in cross-sex violence cases have less potential to escalate. Unlike men in other geographic regions of the world, such as the Mediterranean, a Zapotec man who abuses a woman is not thought to be abusing the honor of her family. Thus, in cross-sex cases the court conciliates and applies corrective sanctions, but may not bring into balance the asymmetrical power relations between men and women.

The cases of violence that end up in the alcalde's court make clear the political relation between the villages and its citizens and between Talea and the district court. There is a general agreement that citizens should settle cases locally, for some of the reasons enumerated earlier: it's cheaper, it's less bureaucratic, and the corrective sanctions help the town pay for public works. In addition, values of harmony and balance are maintained and nourished. By contrast, at the district court the outcomes are, at least theoretically, less negotiable between litigants. This difference places local court officials in a position to bargain, the threat being that it would be worse for the litigants in the district court. On the other hand, when citizens are cognizant of the discrepancy between the law of the village and that of the state and believe they are better off at the district court, the community loses its bargaining power. Whichever court holds the greater attraction for litigation puts that court and its constituency in a position of greater power because to use a court is to recognize its authority.

As local court officials have told me, "affairs of the street" always find their way to the village courts, not only because the police are on watch for public disturbances but also because Taleans themselves recognize their need for the third-party services of the court officials—"to hear their problems, to remind them of their duties and obligations, to 'correct' them, and thereby erase any errors they might have committed." When Taleans stop using their courts, it will signal a transfer of authority elsewhere, for example, to the state or to the family unit. Nonuse of the court might also signal the disorganization of the community, but at least during the 1960's the village was able to manage the contradictions between violence and harmony by contextualizing violence and focusing on attaining harmony. The Talean concept of justice interweaves with the concept of harmony as attainable through litigation, through confrontation in the court (careo) and through paying one's dues either by compensating the injured party or more frequently by paying fines to the court. The preponderance of fines over restitutive devices indicates the frequency of assertion of authority by the community. Indeed (and Durkheim would agree), violence is not only, as Taylor (1979: 169) says, "a widespread way of resolving differences," but also the trigger that activates the legitimate expression of village authority.

Chapter Twelve

Individual and Community Interest in Property Cases

Property is an idiom of social relationships, and disagreements over property illuminate certain fundamental values. To understand the social meaning of property among the Talean Zapotec is to understand how they think about property in relation to the individual and how they relate to one another and to their community. In a farming community land and water are central to survival, and other property such as poultry is central to networking. A position of power is crucial for access to agricultural resources, and the contest over power lies at the heart of disputes over scarce resources. The context gives disputes their meaning.

With the exception of brief periods of surplus wealth, such as that created by the simultaneous harvesting of corn, beans, sugarcane, and coffee, the Talean economy is oriented toward subsistence needs. This colors people's ideas and perspectives about property. Land is respected because it has the power to give life and because it can lash back if not treated well. Each plot has its own name and a spirit that needs to be recognized and placated. If not placated, plots become bad lands (*malos terrenos*). In the realm of poultry and livestock, the same is also true. The meaning of property derives from its social and cultural context. Turkeys are identified as the property of particular families, and since they are used to pay a brideprice, they may be designated in advance as intended for a son's marriage. Pigs are raised by women to provide them with an independent cash income, social security in time of need. The investment in pigs is akin to an investment in young coffee plants. The cash returns can pay off a debt or serve as a down payment on a piece of land. A mule carries you where you need to go or hauls your produce to market. Horses are a luxury item that can be rented out. And the produce from the land, corn and beans, gives daily nourishment. The relationships between these property rights of a subsistence nature and the social and cultural structure delineate a vision of the world that recognizes both individual and collective interests.

In addition to subsistence, there are market concerns, especially in relation to movable property; the products of the land—corn, beans, sugarcane, and coffee—and livestock are sold for cash. The value of movable property differs from that of land and water. The affection for things produced is implied in the diminutives used to refer to them, such as *cafecito* or *frijolito*, an indication of how much of the person is invested in the product being sold. The possessive that usually precedes a reference to these products—*mi frijolito* or *mi cafecito*—underscores the private ownership of the products of individual labor. The relationships between these property rights (which are of a market rather than a subsistence nature) and social and cultural structure reveals a world in which individual interests predominate.

Max Gluckman (1965: 116–17) once argued that the social function of movable property differed from that of immovable property. Immovable property provides the framework for social continuity, whereas movables "establish links between individuals occupying different immovable properties." It is probably true that these two kinds of function merit differentiation, with one representing the maintenance of historical linkages and the other representing a distribution system creating horizontal social linkages. In reviewing Talean clashes over property, however, I prefer to distinguish between individual rights and community obligations and between individual rights and dyadic contracts (between two people) in order to see whether individual interests are more likely to clash with collective interests in immovable property disputes over land and water rather than in disputes over fungible or movable property.

Disputes over both movable and immovable property are frequent in Talea. They range from conflicts over the disposition of inherited family property to boundary problems, landownership, trespass, theft, arson, and fraud. Since harmony and the prevention of conflict are deeply embedded in the Talean worldview, it is worth summarizing what techniques the villagers use as prevention. Disputes that involve collectivities are often managed and avoided by various watchdog committees such as the water committees that spring up around wells used for washing clothes and supplying households with needed water. But there are other, more indirect techniques, such as gossip about stingy people or the threat of witchcraft or prevention by means of legal document.

Taleans are most attentive to the making of wills so as to prevent disputes after they die. The following will was made by a man who had bad relations with his brother and did not wish the brother to inherit from him. The will makes clear his wishes and also gives some indication of how these mountain people think about land when distributing it. The court records state:

A woman presented herself in the office of the alcalde, declaring that she had come in the name of Pablo to request that the court come to hear his last will and testament because he was ill and advanced in age.

The alcalde immediately ordered the transfer of personnel of the associated court of the sindico, representatives of the ministerio publico in Villa Alta, they being present in the house where the spouses Señor Fidel and his wife, Señora María, lived. The witnesses were also present when Señor Pablo was questioned.

Señor Fidel's words were listened to . . . and without coercion of any kind . . . he decided the following:

First, he disposes of a plot of cultivated land for the planting of corn of a capacity of 5 liters, known by the Zapotec term of "Yubuela," situated in the southern section of this village and at approximately a distance of 500 meters, to the Señora María.

Second, he disposes of a house with its respective corridor, which lacks a patio, in the eastern section of this municipality and at a distance of two blocks from the municipal buildings, to the Señora María.

Third, the *testador* [person making the will] disposes of a plot of land in the country to the Señora María known in Zapotec by the name of "Rayahingulag," situated to the east of this village and at a distance of 2 kilometers from the municipal buildings, with a capacity of 1.5 liters for the planting of corn.

Fourth, [he] disposes to his niece Paula of one plot planted with young coffee trees in the eastern section of this municipality, with a capacity of one-quarter of an almud of planting of corn [about 1.5 liters].

Fifth, [he] disposes to his niece Paula of a plot of land in the country known in Zapotec as "Loma Radoo," situated on the eastern side of this village at a distance of approximately 2 kilometers. This plot is composed partly of oak trees and partly of cultivatable land, the capacity of which is 4 almudes for hand planting of corn.

Sixth, [he] disposes of another plot to Señora Paula with the name of "Lachilungunn" in Zapotec, situated to the east of the municipal buildings of this village, with a capacity of 5 liters of corn.

Seventh, the last disposition is a plot of agricultural land known by the Zapotec name of "Raageva" located in the section east of the municipal buildings of this village, with a capacity of 6 almudes of corn. Said real estate may be disposed of by selling, as convenient to the desires or interests of the testador.

Eighth, the testador has a carnal brother who bears the name of Sotero, and in view of the fact that he doesn't get along well with Pablo and shows his indifference, he determines to leave the aforementioned real estate to his nieces. . . .

Ninth, Señora María in union with her husband, Señor Fidel, is in charge of administering him food, lodging, clean clothes, and all that is necessary for his personal use; to these same conditions his niece Paula freely agrees . . . and the parties state that they will comply with the promise.

Tenth, this act is verified in the presence of the alcalde and the witnesses [who were named and described].

Eleventh, Pablo also states that he has no debts to pay or to collect.

Twelfth, in reference to the funeral costs in case they shall exist because of death, they will be paid for by Señores Fidel, María, and Paula, nieces of Pablo.

Signed and/or thumbprinted on the day and year and hour noted.

But it is not always possible to prevent conflicts. Disputes over property predominate in all three Talean courts. In each complaint the issues may be framed in terms of what is legally correct (legal justice); what is socially correct (equity or social justice); and what is likely to keep the peace (harmony). The type of property under dispute indicates the likelihood of a conflict being dyadic—a complaint phrased between two people—or one that involves larger numbers of people, a collective complaint. Boundary disputes or debts usually involve a pair, whereas access to land and water may involve larger numbers of people.

There are different types of ownership in Talea. An individual may be the single owner of a piece of property or a joint owner, as when two people share the ownership of a house. In addition, there is collective ownership, such as property purchased by a barrio or the village band collectively to ensure the continuity of their collectivity. Finally, there is communal ownership, whereby, for example, the village as an entity owns land that is legally recognized as communally held. The type of ownership (individual, joint, collective, or communal), the type of property (movable or immovable), and the type of interest (individual, dyadic, or collective-communal) are the major variables that interrelate in any given case.

Individual Rights and the Community Interest

Case 78 illustrates a clash between collective interests and individual ownership.

The following people appeared before the presidente: Señores Polonio, Felipe, Lorenzo, Filomeno, Isauro, Fausto, Marcelino, Teotulo, Miguel, and Ventura. All were neighbors and natives of this village and lived in the southern section. They came to place the following complaint against Señor Zenon. They said, "Excuse us, Señor Presidente, but we have come here to settle a matter and to complain of what Señor Zenon has done to us. All of us cannot settle this matter, and it is because of that that we have come to this authority, so that you with your authority can resolve what we should do. We come to prevent his saying that we are mistreating him or that we are spreading falsehoods. We come to tell you that he doesn't want us to drink water from a river that is on his property. We need the water for washing clothes; our women need it. And Señor Zenon took away the rocks upon which the clothes were washed. He also took the railing away. And we are all certain that those rocks and that railing were there before Señor Zenon bought that land. And it is not just that he treats us thus, because from before, that spring of water was there, with all the rocks, to wash. Now, we come before you to complain because that man refuses us the water and the place so that our families can go to wash or take water for our houses."

Once informed by the group of citizens, the presidente said to them, "That is good. I am going to call in Señor Zenon to settle this matter because it is not just that he takes the water from you and that he takes your rocks for washing. As you say, the rocks were already there, so why did he take them away? Do not worry. I am going to call him, and you be ready when I call you. I shall see how I can settle this with him. So you may leave," he told them.

Immediately the presidente ordered that Señor Zenon be summoned. The same day Señor Zenon presented himself before the presidente, who said to him, "I have called you to settle a matter. Several neighbors came to complain before this authority about what you have done to the spring of water that is on your land. They say that you took away the rocks where their women go to wash. You also took the railing."

Señor Zenon responded, "It is true that I took them away because they are mine. I put them there. I put the rocks there. I fetched them from my ranch. I fixed that, but these people are too much. That place is very dirty and smells very bad. They leave everything in such a way that it is disgusting. They don't wash there. They just throw junk in that place."

The presidente then said to him, "But they say that the rocks were already there and so was the railing before you bought the land, and why is it, they ask, that you took them away?" Zenon answered, "Let them show me where it says that on the land the rocks must be used to wash. Let us see where it is confirmed. For my part there is no permission that they occupy my land because I pay the tax. Those people are abusing private property. And I said that there was no permission. I took away the rocks because I am going to plant coffee trees in that place, because it is mine. They can complain where they wish, and the case can be consigned so that they see what they are doing."

The presidente said to him, "Why are you denying them the right to get water, since you know that is something which cannot be denied? They need that for their homes." Señor Zenon answered, "That is true, Señor Presidente, that is what God has us do, and if they want water, I will not deny them that water. They may take all they want. But if they want to wash, they must take the water to their homes and wash there. They can't wash on my land because I am going to occupy it. Saying this, let us not talk more. There is no permission for them to wash. I do give them permission to take the water to their homes, but there is no permission for them to wash." Saying this, Señor Zenon left the court.

Then the presidente summoned the citizens who had complained to tell them what Señor Zenon had said. Immediately, the citizens presented themselves, and the presidente reported that Señor Zenon had said that "the place is very dirty, that there is always garbage there, and that you don't clean it up, that he put that railing and the rocks there, but took them away because he says he is going to plant coffee trees."

Then the men said, "Look, Señor Presidente, what he is saying is an excuse. We don't have the same manner of thinking that he does. That man is abusing us, and he pays no attention to our request. And we are certain that before he bought the land, the rocks were there already, as was the water. Now why does this man tear down the railing and throw away the rocks that we had? He went to throw them in the little stream which is next to the spring. Now the banana trees that we planted—he harvested the fruit, and we don't complain about that because it is on his land. Now out of meanness he cut down the banana trees and let them fall in the stream and doesn't take them away even after having harvested the crop. Now he has told our women and us, 'I will not give you permission to come and wash because you don't go to cut my coffee when I need you. I give guarantees to those that work for me, but you don't come when I need you.' He also says that it smells bad. That is true, but that is the water which comes from the toilets of the town. That dirty water comes near to where they go to wash clothes, and with the heat it always gives off a bad odor. Also, we with our money constructed wooden boxes to have water wherever it is needed. He went to uncover them on purpose without our knowing it. Now, it wasn't our whim to fix up that place. He himself invited us to name a chief of the spring so that he and his aides would be aware of whatever was needed. Also the wooden boxes that gather water, he sold us the wood to make them. Also, the place there is not level or in good condition as a washing place. It was an ugly ravine, in fact, and only with a great deal of work were we able to make a level place so that it would be somewhat good. It even got to the point where he said, 'It would have been better if the little stream dried up, so that you would not come to bother me.' For these reasons, Señor Presidente, please, we want you to arrange this matter. What are we going to do without water, since it is indispensable to life?"

Once informed of all that was put forth, the presidente said to them, "Gentlemen, tomorrow we are going to settle this problem because today is unsuitable. Tomorrow, Monday, present yourselves here to see if Señor Zenon can be made to understand what he is doing."

On the following morning nine men were present on one side, and Señor Zenon on the other. The rest of the declarations began. The presidente said to Señor Zenon, "Since the matter could not be resolved yesterday, the gentlemen who are complaining about what you did are present today." Zenon answered, "Have them tell you how many years they have made use of that spring and those washing places." They answered, "About ten years." "These men," Zenon said, "tell lies because before, the water was in a different place. I myself put it in the place that they say they fixed up." The gentlemen answered, "That is a lie; the spring has been there for a long time." Then Señor Zenon said, "Why do you want to order my property? Why did you dig without my consent? There is the water, which is federal, but there is no permission for you to occupy my land without my consent."

The presidente said, "Look, Zenon, what you are doing is bad. When one no longer exists, one cannot take the water. It all stays in this world. Why are you doing this with these people?" Zenon answered, "It's out of the law. You cannot oblige me. Now, I fixed the road because it was very slippery. I, with my hands, fixed it. They have not been worried about fixing it." The men answered, "That is a lie. We fixed the road because he ordered it of us. He wasn't there. We are always concerned with the stream of water so that it will remain regular."

"It is as I said," said Zenon to the presidente. "There is no right; there is no permission. I did not buy the place for them, so why do they occupy it? I have already arranged a place further down with some rocks for my workers, those who are in my service. I didn't arrange it for others." The presidente said to him, "Then I understand that you only give permission to the women who are in your service and who work for you, and the ones who don't do you harm?" Changing once again, Zenon said, "It smells very bad. That place stinks." The gentlemen said, "That is true that it smells, but it isn't the water from there, it is that from the toilets which come out of this village. And you know well that it passes near that place." Señor Zenon said, "A regidor can go and see if what they are saying is true." Then one of the men present said to him, "Look, Zenon, you yourself said to my wife that it is because she doesn't cut your coffee that there is no permission for her to wash." Zenon answered, "I have already said that there is no permission for them to go to wash. I don't deny them the water whenever they want it, but they cannot put up wash places. There is no permission, and they are abusing private property."

The presidente, upon seeing that the cited Zenon was not willing to have the water used for washing, said "I will not be able to settle this matter. I will have to assign the case to the sindico."

Zenon responded, "It is well that this matter be assigned. We shall see if they have the right because it is they who want to take my right from me. You can consign the case, Señor Presidente, so that we will know how we stand, or if they will present a written statement saying that the land belongs to them. I have already said they can complain where they please, but there is no permission."

The plaintiffs replied, "Señor Presidente, you have already heard Señor Zenon say that he has put rocks for his workers to wash, and we who don't want to work for him don't have the right to use the water. None of us are taking a piece of land from him. Rather, right there, where the rocks are, we want to put other, better ones, without taking anything away from him. On the contrary, we planned to put up a railing so that his coffee trees wouldn't be damaged. But this man doesn't think. If he asks that it be consigned, we are ready. What else are we going to do? We need that spring so that our women can go to wash our clothes."

Declarations on both sides were finished. The presidente wanted Señor Zenon to make a friendly agreement in order to settle the case and have the water continue to be taken to wash clothes. He tried to make Señor Zenon see that in conscience he should give the place because it was there before he bought the land. But the defendant paid no attention and roundly denied giving consent for continuing to wash and for improving the washing place at the spring. Zenon said it would be better to have the matter consigned, since the authority could not resolve this matter because the accused party was not in agreement. The case was consigned to the sindico.

Taken at face value, this case is best understood as a subsistence issue: access to water needed for survival. But there is also an indication of a nonmaterialistic basis for the dispute, revolving around the individualistic character of Western property law, which is not to be mediated by traditional conceptions of need and equity—a conflict of laws. In addition, there is raw power: "You work for me, and I will make water and washing space available." In the domain of power, the dispute may be explained as a metaphor of social relationships in which the dispute over water is incidental to the dynamic of social relations. In this light, the dispute becomes a code in which power relations are being thrashed out or ceremonially reinforced. It was reference to God-given substances (water) and recognition that water was federally controlled that enabled the presidente to persuade the accused to give access to the water. But that was as far as he was able to move Zenon. The accused refused to open access to the land for washing clothes. What had to be resolved was the reason for this action, the motive: Was he refusing access as a way to defend his individual ownership rights, or was he using his rights to the land as a way to force his opponents to work for him? Or both?

Landownership is the basis of power and privilege. Water ownership is conceived of as separate from the land, and although water may be perceived locally as belonging to the community, federal control over water marks the ascendancy of the central government over the community. Individuals, however, do not remain passive observers as the structuring of property changes around them. They exercise power and control as best they can to enhance their personal situations. It is by means of village courts that the traditional conceptions of collective rights are upheld or destroyed in disputes between group interests and those who adhere to the principle of private ownership. Sometimes, as in Case 79, the property owner comes to see that the public good is the more important and accedes.

Manuel appeared before the authority to complain of damage done to his land located in the jurisdiction of Yatoni. Manuel is a resident and native of Talea. He claimed the damage was done by the residents and the authority of Yatoni on the third Sunday of this month. The damage was to a certain number of coffee-bearing plants, for which the municipal agent should have advised the owner so that he could protect the coffee plants, which were unjustly destroyed by the opening of a road. A visual inspection was carried out by the sindico on the land called "Lachilido." Upon the request of Señor Manuel, the authority inspected said property to prove and affirm the damage that Manuel had claimed. A witness had gone to said location . . . accompanying the sindico.

Then, Manuel was notified and asked to define his complaint. After a few minutes of thought, he said that he did not wish to make the complaint or submit the case to further investigation, nor did he wish to press charges of any sort, nor exact justice for the damage done to his property because he had arrived at an understanding that this damage had to happen to his property because it was a public works project, done for the benefit of the public by the people of Yatoni. This authority questioned the plaintiff to ascertain whether he would ratify this resolution, and he said that he was not willing to have the matter go any further.

When the complaint is one against private citizens, rather than against a village government, the participants are more stubborn. In Case 80, the issue is access to land. When landholdings are small plots distributed over the countryside, it is sometimes difficult to get to one's land without crossing over the land of another, which is usually done by a network of paths.

Señora Petrona brought a complaint before the presidente: "I come to inform you and to file a complaint against Señora Dolores because of what she said to me. The workers of Señor Vicente were carrying adobes, and they passed over Señora Dolores's land, which had a road on it before, but she says that it is her land. That is, she is in charge of this land because the owner gave her a letter entrusting her with caring for his interests. And now that Señora Dolores has arrived [from Tlacolula], she has closed the passage. I said to her, 'Why did you close it?' And Señora Dolores answered, 'It's not yours.' And I said to her, 'Stand up on the rock wall where we border with Señor Olivo [the owner], and you will see that it is my land that you are trying to command.' My brothers Vicente and Delfino took away the obstacle

Señora Dolores had placed since they could not pass with their adobes. I had asked her before, 'Why do you close off that which is not yours? Leave that little path because many people live in these places.' But she paid no attention to me and closed it again. And I have documents to protect me. And this is why I come to complain because for a year these things have been happening."

Once the presidente was informed of the complaint, Señora Dolores was summoned in order to respond to the complaint. She presented herself minutes later. The presidente said to her, "Señora Petrona complains that you have closed the path, putting garbage and obstacles so that no one can pass." Dolores responded, "That is a lie. Since last year we have been agreed that that place be closed. And Señora Alta, the neighbor who lives below, says that before there was no passage in that place. That her land borders— how can Señora Petrona justify that the landmark rock is placed where it is? Señora Petrona came and insulted me. That is why I am closing off that passageway. She said that I am an outsider, that no one has the right to block passage. I have the documents of ownership, and no one has the right to pass through again. It had just been closed when she came like a beast and said that I had taken up the landmark rocks. I have a letter from the owner where he tells me not to let anyone pass by because there was no road before. I did not ask the workers why they passed by. I just went to the place and closed the passage. Señora Petrona has no place there. We were just able to close it, and now they go and open it. We border with Alta and Josefa. Señora Petrona wants to go where she does not belong."

Once informed by both declarations, the presidente cited both of them for the confrontation [careo]. The presidente said to them, "How is this matter? Señora Dolores said that you insulted her and that you went to open a road which had not been there before." Petrona answered, "There is a stone. Dolores wants to get to where it is not hers. Salomon and Juan can come; they were authorities when I sold the land for the orchestra. They can tell how it was arranged before Rosa died. Rosa had consented that there be a little road for the people who were living below her. She was an understanding person. Now this woman—it isn't even hers. They only have her caring for this place. Señora Dolores does not even know how it was arranged. And now she comes along closing the passage. That is much egoism on her part. What would she think if I closed all the roads that she uses to get to the house of Olivo?"

Dolores answered, "What ignorance of this woman! The documents are those that speak." Petrona responded, "This is how we arranged it with the late Rosa. She and I were in agreement to leave this little passage. So was Alta. I want to emphasize that the road is not for me. I do not even pass below. It is for the neighbors. And since they pass through my land, I do not tell them not to pass. I am not an egoist."

Dolores said, "I wish that Alta would come, Señor Presidente. She says that there was no road, and that she is willing to have it closed." Petrona answered "Have Lino and Juan come too, so that they can state how it was."

Dolores then said, "I have a letter where I am authorized to care for the interests of Señor Raúl, and I want you authorities to come and see this problem."

Señora Petrona said, "Look, Señor Presidente, the ex-presidente also received this problem, but he did not resolve it because he was leaving office."

The presidente then said to them, "Look, señoras, about these roads. It is indispensable that they remain. There are many people who need them, perhaps because they give them access, or bring them closer to the Camino Real. But if you will enter a friendly agreement, so that both will give a little land for a road, you will avoid difficulties. And it is a simple matter for each of you just to stick to your landmark rocks."

"All right," answered Señora Petrona, "but have those who were in the orchestra come and state where it was that I sold them land. Because I did sell them land." Señora Dolores answered again, "Why are we going to argue more? The documents are what can say best." Señora Petrona said, "All right, since Dolores is not the legitimate owner, we cannot settle anything with her. If you as authorities would do the favor of communicating with Señor Raúl, please ask that he come here to settle." "It is well," said Dolores. "If the right is not given to me, then we will have to postpone this complaint while I write Raúl."

Both parties were in agreement that the matter be postponed until the legitimate owner arrived.

The confrontation sharpened the argument between what is in the interest of the public, and what is the right of a private owner. Señora Dolores was an outsider. How could she be expected to know the custom? Every time Señora Petrona pointed out the custom, Señora Dolores made reference to written legal documents.

Eventually Señor Raúl wrote to the presidente recounting what Señora Dolores had written him and chastising the presidente for not giving due importance to her argument. He said, "As you know, Señor Presidente, property should be respected . . . but when Señora Dolores went to you to prevent further problems, she was far from receiving justice. Rather, you chose to ignore the fact that she had a letter of attorney as my proxy. . . . QUE EL RESPETO AL DERECHO AJENO ES LA PAZ [respecting the rights of others is the peace]." The presidente responded with a polite note asking Raúl to return to Talea so that a friendly settlement could be made.

Disputes over rights of passage are common in Talea and although they may start in the presidente's office, they generally find their way through the appeal process. The tenacity with which litigants stick to their positions and the difficulty in coming to a friendly agreement suggest that these cases are arenas of personal contest, even though frequent mention is made of community interests. In

Case 81, a woman accused a man of trespassing on her land with his mules, damaging the land and trampling the coffee plants that lay in the way. She complained that when she spoke to him and asked him not to repeat the trespass, he made fun of her.

When Tomás appeared to respond to María's accusation, he claimed that he was not trespassing but passing on his own land, using a path that had been there since long before. He asked how María could now deny him the right to pass. He said that she had accused him of trespassing during a previous year, saying that he had cut her fruit trees. He had told her, he said, who it was that was cutting her avocados and who had trespassed, but she continued to point the finger at him. When they had their confrontation in court, the two litigants stuck to their positions.

The presidente then said, "Because you are neighbors in land, let us make a friendly agreement. The señora is right in wishing to reclaim damages for her plants because there is much labor involved in growing plants, particularly coffee plants. On the other hand, the señor is right in wanting to pass there because it is the only path that exists for him to get to his land, and it is not possible to open another. So let us agree that the señor will not pass with his animals so that crops are destroyed, and if he has to pass through, he will carry the wood out on his shoulders rather than bring his mules in over the path." The presidente then asked the litigants if they were in agreement. The woman agreed and accepted as long as he didn't bring in his mules. And the man also agreed not to pass with his animals, saying that he would take his wood and coffee out without the aid of his mules. They both signed the agreement.

Then two weeks later, María returned to the municipio with the complaint that Tomás had violated the agreement and that she herself had seen him come in with his mules to move wood. The accused was called, and since there were other witnesses who had seen him take his mules in, the case was now serious. The presidente asked the sindico to investigate. Tomás asked if the sindico would examine whether it was right to close this path because there were many people who needed to use it. María claimed that her rights as property owner had been violated because whenever she went to Mexico City, people took advantage and did harm to her property. Since the presidente was not able to deal with the case, he consigned it to the sindico.

Early the next month three people appeared in the presidente's office: the two previous litigants, whose land bordered on each other's, and a third person, Ignacio, who also shared a boundary with María, whose property was called in Zapotec "Blog-Lo'c." The presidente again suggested a friendly agreement so as to avoid more difficulty. María was ready to make an agreement with her neighbors if they paid for the damage to her property, which, according to her estimate, added up to 500 pesos. The presidente stated that in his judgment the damage amounted to 300 pesos. Ignacio now spoke up, saying that the señora had no right to claim what belonged to his family and not to her. Further, he asked her to produce witnesses to prove that he was responsible for the damage and asked her to present papers proving her ownership of the land. Besides, he had given his land to his son-in-law and had not set foot on it for years. Ignacio concluded that the documents would tell the story of who owned what. Tomás also refused to pay because there were many other people who used this path and she shouldn't be blaming him alone. He also asked for witnesses and offered to buy María's land from her so that they wouldn't have further difficulties, and because he had no other recourse. But if she insisted on receiving damages, Tomás continued, "Present your witnesses who saw me damage your property." Again, the presidente declared that he was unable to solve this problem, and he passed the now expanded case to the sindico.

The same contentiousness can be observed in Case 82, a dispute over water running into a communal washing area from the *chorros* (waterspouts) of the Tres Marías. The problem began when Señora Petra wanted to fix the tank in which the water from a chorro was collected. This she did, ignoring the fact that this chorro was not her property, but rather had been deeded to the community in 1914 by a relative of the people who live near the chorros.

When Señora Petra tried to fix the chorro, the neighbors objected because Señora Petra considered it her property. Some of the neighbors tried to impede the work, and there was violence. Then Señora Petra denounced one of the neighbors to the presidente, asking at the same time for an order from the district court in Villa Alta. Villa Alta did issue an order that the work should continue under the supervision of the sindico.

When the job was finished, Señora Petra wanted to charge the neighbors for the job, but they refused to pay. She reported this matter to the sindico, giving him a list of the people who used the place. The authority nominated Señor Juan to be the representative of the neighbors so that he could make a budget or estimate of the costs of this job. Since the neighbors did not accept this arrangement, Señora Petra asked the sindico to summon all the neighbors of the chorro to persuade them to share the expenses in a fair way. When the neighbors gathered, the sindico explained why they should cooperate. At this point the floor was taken by a haughty neighbor who directed herself personally to the sindico, saying, "Salomón, you and Juan are sold on Petra." She started to insult Salomón, who in his capacity as sindico ordered her to be incarcerated. Her son-in-law offered to substitute for her, but the haughty woman was not allowed to speak. The case could not be settled by the sindico. It was sent on to the alcalde, who did manage to settle the conflict, whereby Señora Petra ceded the job, which had been done for the common good of the neighbors, without any restitution whatever for the expenses she had had. Later this agreement was ratified by the decision of a federal land agent, who came to Villa Alta to deal specifically with this case.

But this was not the end. A few months later the same antagonists appeared before the sindico again. This time the neighbors brought the complaint against Petra. According to the court records:

Señora Petra got into the spring with the pretext of cleaning the water tank. She opened the tank's drainage valve, thus making it impossible for people to do their laundry.

The sindico asked Señora Petra what aim she was pursuing when she harmed the users of the spring. Señora Petra protested that it was all a lie and that she had not been offending anyone, nor they her, by which means she expected to avoid a sanction for disobeying the earlier agreement. She added, in relation to the filthy storage tank, that she had been cleaning it but late at night or in the early morning. The opposing parties protested that what she said was false.

The sindico decided to issue both sides a warning because they had mutually offended each other without having in reality any powerful motive to do so. In addition, the authority determined that from this date on and with the purpose of avoiding any more friction between the parties, the cleaning of the spring would be taken care of by the town. With the exception of Señora Petra, all were in agreement. Señora Petra said she did not think that the town should clean the spring. The investigation was concluded, and the case forwarded to the agency of the ministerio publico in the judicial district of Villa Alta.

The parties were then summoned to Villa Alta, and Señora Petra was denounced in the following manner:

"Señora Petra, a well-to-do person, has attempted to have exclusive use of a water jet that serves to satisfy the needs of the community. It is not known in what way she acquired the domain of the property, constructing her house in such a manner that the water jet is under her porch. Since the persons in the community saw a threat to their interests, they protested to the local authorities, and later to the district court. Things calmed down for a little while, but for months and despite orders by the court to keep free the use of the water jet, Señora Petra has obstinately bothered every person who comes close to the water. The plaintiffs beg to have the problem solved once and for all so that peace and tranquillity might return to this little community and its people."

The court in Villa Alta then ordered the Talean court to investigate the facts, the necessary documents of ownership, and any other information pertinent to the case. Once again the case was investigated, and statements recorded of the difficulties encountered with Señora Petra. This case had been going on for several years and was essentially a war between families expressed in a fight over water and the relative power of the litigants with local authorities and with the Villa Alta judiciary. Señora Petra's influence was with the local authorities, her opponents' with the Villa Alta court. Each party pulled in the direction of its greatest personal power.

Conflict between jurisdictions is not uncommon. Case 83 involved a man from Yatoni, a small village under Talean jurisdiction. Apparently the defendant thought he had more clout at the district level.

A fire began in the lands of Yatoni in the pasture called "Yalagu Belgr," which was the property of a man called Secundo who was burning his *rosa* [brush]. This fire spread to the jurisdiction of Talea due to wind, burning plants, coffee bushes, and a ranch house. Since Felix of Talea saw that his rancho was in danger, he came to advise the authorities, and while they gathered the villagers to fight the fire, others of Talea were already fighting it, people whose land was also being threatened. In the meantime the people of Yatoni came down to put out the fire.

The Talean authorities summoned Secundo of Yatoni to question him about the origin of the fire. He denied having been the cause. He argued that two people of Talea who were working close by were the ones who had started the fire. They were summoned also and in their defense said that the land they had been working was not of rosa, but was instead arable land, and for that reason they had not made any fire to burn.

The authorities went to make a visual inspection and affirmed that on the land belonging to the men of Talea there was no sign of fire. In the meantime the man from Yatoni was imprisoned until further inquiries could be made. Since it was Holy Week, the prisoner begged permission to return to his village in order to celebrate. The presidente gave permission on condition that he could provide a person who would be responsible for him and for his return on Saturday. Ignacio was his bailsman. The prisoner was released, but instead of going home, he went to the court of Villa Alta, where he obtained a document. With this paper the prisoner returned to the Talean court on Monday, and by means of it both the case and the prisoner were given over to Villa Alta. The prisoner was taken, with his hands tied, to the district center, thereby closing the case in Talea and passing it over to Villa Alta.

In cases where there is a serious threat to the public good, the villagers are stringent in their manner of dealing, unbought and unbuyable. When two systems of law coexist, conflict of laws is bound to be recognized as a problem of some magnitude for the village. Conflict is dealt with explicitly at times and in a more disguised manner at other times. State and village law often disagree over what is more important—the public good or the individual. Individuals, such as the man from Yatoni, have a keen understanding of which jurisdiction is more favorable to their plight or where their situation is more negotiable.

Individual Rights and the Dyadic Contract

Disputes over boundaries or over partitioning of a harvest are usually between a pair of people. People who share boundaries are of approximate socioeconomic positions in that they are both landowners. People who are partitioning a harvest may be of equal or unequal position, but both have implicit contractual obligations characterized by either symmetrical or asymmetrical patterns, both of which are distinguished by an exchange of obligations. These forms of exchange, or reciprocal obligation, can be examined in detail for the manner in which complaints are expressed and resolved in courts intent on making the balance or restoring harmony to a disturbed dyadic relation. As George Foster (1961, 1963) has shown in another context, the dyadic contract is particularly important in defining social relations in the sphere of everyday subsistence activity, a sphere that is not defined by group interaction.

In Case 84, a woman complained about a boundary problem.

Señora Cipriana appeared before this court with a complaint against Señor Alberto. She was from Talea, and he was a native and resident of Yatoni. The complaint was that Alberto had been damaging her land called "Racin" (or Xaca) because he rerouted the water that had served as a boundary between their lands in such a way as to damage her interests. He also invaded that part of the land with sugarcane plants [*mata de cana*], which he actually planted there.

Alberto was questioned as to whether he knew of any previous agreement about the land that he might have had with the deceased father of the plaintiff, and he testified that he did not. He was asked if he had any documents that accredited him with the land under question, and he answered that he had no title of property.

Señora Cipriana then presented an acta de convenio [an agreement] written in the municipio before the presidente, dated January 1947, on which appeared the signatures of both parties, the plaintiff's father and Alberto, in which their quarrel was resolved in legal form and in which the present defendant agreed to recognize the boundary in a conscientious manner. Said boundary was fixed as an *arroyo de agua* [the stream] and was to be respected by both neighbors. Señor Alberto had committed a grave fault, in that there existed an agreement signed before the authority that he had violated without legal motive.

For this reason the sindico fined him 50 pesos, which he had to pay in cash to the municipal treasury. In relation to the actual abuse of land that he was accused of, he admitted this abuse, but promised not to repeat such action before an agreement was arrived at with Cipriana. The case was closed, and the sindico ordered him to put the water back where it belonged, where it had existed, and to gather the sugarcane plants that he had planted on the property of Cipriana, in order to avoid difficulties. He promised to comply.

Both parties agreed, and the sindico told the plaintiff to report to him if the defendant did not follow the agreement by removing the damage and threat to her property. The agreement reinstated the obligations inherent in boundary relations.

In the next two cases it is the relationship that is at stake. In Case 85, the plaintiff complained to the sindico against a neighbor for preempting part of the land known by the name of "Lluuaz," which had small coffee trees on it.

In answer to the complaint, the defendant said that he was ready to make a friendly, mutual agreement with the plaintiff about the land in question. The plaintiff was informed that the defendant wished to settle in a friendly way with the aim of continuing to live in harmony and as good neighbors and sharers of a common boundary. The sindico allowed them the liberty of arriving at a friendly agreement, and after a short discussion they both agreed that the affair did not merit continuance of legal procedure. The defendant had not touched a grain of coffee on the trees in question, nor had the plaintiff since the date of his complaint. The plaintiff would continue to recognize as his property up to where his mother and the deceased aunt had owned, and where there was a boundary of stones placed by the sindico in 1959. This boundary had been recognized by both parties until for unimportant reasons they came to this authority. Both parties were reconciled, arriving at an agreement that caused the plaintiff to withdraw his complaint, which had been nullified by virtue of this document. The accused said that he would abide by the existing boundary, thereby avoiding all kinds of trouble and leaving the plants he claimed, by his own free will and consent.

"Until for unimportant reasons they came to this authority" suggests that there is some recurrent antagonism between the parties, but it is not written into the record. The property as defined comes to symbolize the state of the social relationship. In Case 86, the resolution is easier on the parties because there are discrepancies in the legal documents. A man complained to the sindico about his sister and her husband, whose land bordered on his and who were damaging his property. He showed documents proving his ownership of the property in question. The sister and her husband were notified of the case, and they also showed documents proving their ownership. Both sets of documents agreed with the legal register's records and with those in the land records office in Villa Alta. The sindico suggested to both parties that they try to reach a friendly agreement.

This authority, upon seeing the impossibility of their arriving at a mutual agreement due to the differences in dimensions apparent in their documents, proceeded to the site accompanied by the personnel of the sindico's office, as well as the parties in question, in order to settle the case.

First, they ratified the dimensions of the site according to the documents of the plaintiff, which indicate 23 meters vertically on the part in question. Subsequently they ratified the dimensions according to the documents of the sister and her husband, which indicate a dimension of 12.25 meters vertically. The sindico then tried to divide by half so that in the middle there would be placed a stone to mark it, but opportunely the plaintiff said voluntarily that he would cede and recognize the dimensions stipulated in the documents of his sister, with the object of not causing any difficulty. Then the sindico ordered the placing of a border stone, subject to 12.25 [meters], thus accepting the documentation of his sister. The sindico questioned the plaintiff as to whether it [his offer] was of his volition and he answered affirmatively, so the stone was hammered in. Thus the affair was settled, firmly, irrevocably, and recognizedly, both parties promising to respect their properties according to determinations arrived at with the present setting of the boundary.

Case 86 dealt with more than a dyadic relation since three family members were involved. Unlike the two preceding cases, here the plaintiff took the initiative in making an agreement by withdrawing his original complaint. After all, the documents were contradictory, and he was dealing with his sister and her husband.

Boundary cases that deal with boundaries between houses in this densely packed town are more sensitive in terms of dyadic relations. In Case 87, a man denounced his neighbor because when he began construction on his property, he left absolutely no space between the houses and built right on the border line. In the process of clearing away the rubble, old boundary markers were destroyed. The sindico had to investigate and to "examine the motives for removing the boundary markers." In other cases, house construction may damage property on adjoining lots. If such cases get to court, they usually signal violation of unspoken reciprocal agreements with some history. But, in general, boundary cases are between people of relatively equal homeowner status.

Some relationships in Talea are not considered equal although they may be characterized by cooperation, for example, the relationship between a landowner and a sharecropper. In Case 88, the dyad is not grounded in immovable property such as land; it is impermanent. A complaint was brought to court by a landowner against his sharecropper in the early 1960's. The case first appeared in the presidente's office; as a result of the hearing, the defendant was jailed, and the case consigned to the alcalde. The issue dealt with a verbal agreement over the partitioning of land owned by the plaintiff but sharecropped by the defendant and planted in corn. The two men had marked their partitioning agreement with stakes, but upon reflection the sharecropper was unhappy with the division. A third party had tried to work out the disagreement in a friendly way so as to keep the problem out of the hands of the authorities, but none of these propositions and verbal arguments satisfied the sharecropper. The alcalde was able to reach the following written agreement.

The sharecropper presented an estimate of the expenses he had had in connection with the work already done on the property of the landowner. The estimate was discussed so as to be able to fix wages in accordance with the season in which these jobs were done, and the authorities worked out an agreement to which the plaintiff and defendant agreed. (1) The sharecropper was to be given, in cash, 300 pesos, which he requested and which was the estimated value of the work done; (2) the same sharecropper of his own free will returned to the owner the property, work, and planting already done; (3) the owner agreed to make the payment of 300 pesos, and upon this payment the landowner was absolutely free to claim the whole crop produced by his land and all that it might produce; (4) this was agreed upon [by both parties], and the document was signed.

The agreement redefined the relationship between landowner and sharecropper as a relationship between landowner and day worker; this redefinition allowed the alcalde to translate an issue of movables into a question of cash return for daily labor. Unlike many of the preceding cases, this solution involved not bonding but separation. When officials deal with boundary complaints, separation is not usually an option. The technique of translating immovables into fungibles or cash as a means of resolving problems is, however, often used in inheritance cases, such as those in which a parent has left one house to several children. The house is sold cheaply to one of the children, and the money paid is then distributed among the rest of the children. The parent, in such situations, was searching for avenues that would increase the likelihood of bonding rather than separating siblings who might have had difficulties with rights in common property.

Dyadic relations of a continuing sort may also result from mortgaging land, from lending money for interest, or from the very agreements that are made in court to settle disagreements. In Case 89, a woman had mortgaged a piece of land to a man for 700 pesos, but he had never paid anything on this land. She asked that he make a payment on her loan of seven years, and he asked for a two-month extension. Meanwhile he also asked that he be allowed to continue to work the land and to harvest the sugarcane crop, from which he would give the plaintiff a portion. The plaintiff agreed, and the case was postponed, pending a cash payment.

In Case 90, a dispute between two people had supposedly been settled by an agreement that the defendant would pay the plaintiff in sugarcane for the damage his bulls had done to the property of the complainant. The agreement was violated, and the two were back in the presidente's court. It was a long and heated case about abuses and insults and broken promises and about how much sugarcane constituted a proper payment of reparations, with frequent accusations of lying. As with many of these personal cases, there is much repetition in the declarations. The plaintiff had an agreement but the defendant wouldn't pay, and the presidente was challenged to do something about it because threats were flying from the plaintiff if the defendant didn't keep his word this time. The defendant argued that he was poor and was being taken advantage of by the plaintiff. The presidente arrived at a compromise: the defendant would pay the debt in two weeks; if he didn't, he would be punished for contempt of court. Furthermore, the presidente said, "If the plaintiff continues to insult you, keep your hands to yourself. It is the job of the authorities to deal with such matters."

Collective interests are not defined as such in cases dealing with dyadic relations connected by movable property. Movable property cases involving dyads focus on "friendly agreements," which are needed because the principle of reciprocity has been violated. It is in the violation, when goods and services are not exchanged as expected, that the dyad is reinforced by the authorities. Ties between neighbors are defined by the very violation of neighborliness that causes redefinition of the implicit contract between the two.

The same bonding behavior is common in complaints between debtors and creditors, often in spite of the substantial time between promise and payment. In Case 91, Nora came to the alcalde with the following problem.

Aurora (now deceased) together with her daughter Delfina made a contract with Nora as creditor and the others as debtors, as was demonstrated by the IOU Nora showed to the court. This was for 240 pesos, which Aurora and Delfina received, and which the contract stated was to be repaid within the year, this loan having been secured by a mortgage on the house of Delfina, signer of the IOU in question.

To this date the debt had never been paid, and Nora was obliged to bring the matter to court so that a solution might be found.

Delfina was asked to recognize her debt. She testified that she did so and said that she was willing to pay this debt within 60 days from that date in

75-peso payments every 15 days until she had paid the 300 pesos she admitted was the amount owed [including interest].

Nora was asked for her feelings on the subject. She said that ten years had passed, and Delfina didn't take into account the fact that she had been living in the mortgaged house all this time. However, not finding any other way in which to settle the case, Nora said she would pardon the time that the debtors had lived in the house.

Delfina was exhorted to comply with this disposition of payments. If she did not do so, she would be punished with the penalty the case merited.

Sometimes debt cases lend themselves to separation rather than bonding. In Case 92, Héctor mortgaged a field planted with sugarcane for a term of three years to Pedro. With rights over the mortgaged land, Pedro leased the field to José to cultivate and harvest the cane. Héctor didn't agree that José should work the field, and so he was willing to repay Pedro the amount of the mortgage and terminate the contract.

Although the term of the mortgage was not completed, Pedro agreed to take Héctor's money and terminate the contract, provided José was repaid for his work, for cleaning the sugarcane, and other expenses. A few days later Héctor went to Pedro's house and paid the mortgage to Pedro's wife. When Pedro arrived home, he accepted the money but refused to consider the mortgage contract terminated until Héctor recompensed José for his work. José claimed 35 pesos for his work, and Pedro 45 pesos for rent he had paid. Héctor refused to pay the total amount of 80 pesos. Since it was impossible to convince Héctor to repay this obligation, the sindico passed the case to the alcalde to resolve. The alcalde made an agreement: Pedro received 45 pesos from Héctor and José received 20 pesos from Héctor.

Property cases that involve theft range from those referred to as *robo* (robbery) to those that are described as *abuso de confianza* (abuse of confidence). They also involve dyads, although sometimes serially, as when one steals regularly from one person after another. In Case 93, a Talean woman complained about another woman from the town of Zoogocho. The accusation was theft. The police went in search of the accused and arrested her.

She confessed that she had indeed stolen a pillow slip from the plaintiff. She was urged to return to her home with a policeman to fetch the stolen object. . . . The object was identified as being of some use and worth approximately 30 pesos. . . . On the other hand, it was proved that the defendant had robbed before and that she had tried to sell stolen things.

These crimes having been proved, crimes committed in the very heart of this village, and this court recognizing its responsibility for theft and sale of stolen objects, decided that the defendant be punished corporally and monetarily. Having first punished the plaintiff [by jailing her] and she being unable to pay a fine, the alcalde together with the sindico examined the case again and after a long discussion decreed that the defendant be freed immediately and be banned from the village to return to her place of origin.

Relationships are closest between members of the same family, next closest between members of a neighborhood, then between members of the same village, and finally between people of different villages. Compare the theft of the pillow slip with a series of cases in 1961 in which people stole coffee from neighbors. In Case 94 a man accused a woman whose land bordered his. She cut coffee on his land and responded to the complaint by admitting she took the coffee. She promised to replace the amount taken or to pay 15 pesos, the value of the green coffee in question. She asked for a week in which to cover payment, and both sides agreed to open a clearing along the border in order to make the dividing line clear. The defendant also paid a fine of 15 pesos and was told she must not commit such offenses again.

In Case 95, a woman accused a man of abuse of confidence in cutting coffee on her land. They had had troubles before, and the defendant admitted that this time he had cut such coffee and had promised to pay 2 kilos of dry coffee to the plaintiff but had not done so. He was fined 25 pesos for contempt of the agreement between them.

In Case 96, the woman who complained was from Talea, and the defendant was from Yatoni. Here the accusation was the crime of coffee robbery, not abuse of confidence. Upon investigation, it turned out that the woman was already in litigation with the man over questions of landownership and boundaries. The accusation of robbery was a harassment, for which she was punished.

At other times people borrow property without permission, but the word "robbery" does not enter. In Case 97, the sindico heard such a case in which one man accused another of taking his wooden plow without permission.

The defendant took this object without advising or getting the consent of the owner. He went onto the property and took it to use in his work. Investigations continued, and the defendant confessed to the abuses. Because he needed the farming implement, he had gone to the house of the plaintiff and taken it.

The plaintiff testified that he noticed the wooden plow was misplaced, and so immediately he and his sons started a search for it, finding it two days later on the ranch of the defendant.

The sindico suggested the following settlement. The plaintiff should be reimbursed the estimated value of the plow and the days lost in the search.

The plow was estimated at 12 pesos, and for the two days lost in the search for the plow at 12 pesos a day, or 24 pesos. Once the case was settled between the two men, the sindico fined the defendant 40 pesos in accordance with the crime as described in Article 352 of the Penal Code.

In Case 98, we have a situation of out-and-out robbery.

A woman presented her complaint to the presidente: "I come to place a complaint against my neighbor because he stole my turkey, and at this very moment he is eating it. I went to see and I recognized the feathers. Besides, this man does not have a turkey or the money to buy one. It is not the first time that turkeys have been lost in our barrio. The other neighbors are always complaining, but until today we did not know who was doing these bad things. Please go and bring this man here and send somebody to bring the pot so you can see the turkey."

The police were sent to fetch the man. They came back with him and his pot. He was put in jail for the night, and the case was heard the next day, on the charge of robbery. The chief of police gave his declaration: "I went with five policemen to the house of the accused, and there he was, sitting eating a plate of pure meat, which appeared to be chicken or turkey. I told him to come with me, and he told me to wait until he finished eating. At this minute, the plaintiff arrived, entered, and went to the pot where there was still half a turkey and said, 'Look, here is my turkey.'" The police were ordered to take the pot to the municipio.

The plaintiff declared the following: "Here I am again. I would have liked the police to make him carry the pot so that everyone could see how shameless he is to have eaten my turkey. It cost me three days of looking to find it, and I had to work hard to raise enough money to buy it [in the first place]. And one of the times I was passing his house, I saw my turkey's feathers and a bone. I entered his house, and he was very cynical and said nothing. I put my hand in the pot and saw that my turkey was cooked. Then I realized the harm, and I decided to lodge a complaint against this man to make him pay me for this animal."

The presidente asked her how much the turkey had cost, and she responded 28 pesos. He told her to return the next day, "Vamos a hacer justicia [We are going to make justice]. In the meantime the defendant will be punished in jail so that he can think a bit about what he did. He isn't a child; he is an old man, and he goes around doing these stupid things. So don't worry, we will do everything possible so that he pays you what he owes you."

The next day the presidente started investigations by asking the accused how it was that he came to rob the woman of her turkey, and the accused said, "What happened is that this woman came to accuse me." The presidente said, "She made a complaint against you because you stole her turkey, and it is not the first time. You have been doing this in the section where you live; people have been losing their animals. This is just the first time that you have been caught."

The defendant responded that it was not true that he stole; he had purchased the turkey. The plaintiff then said, "How can you say this when I recognized the feathers of my turkey in your yard?" The defendant then argued, how could they think that he would rob her when she was his neighbor? The presidente then said to the defendant, "Well, tell me, you who do not work, who gave you the money to buy a turkey? There is proof that you did this bad thing." At this point the defendant admitted that he stole the turkey and promised never to do it again, and asked for the plaintiff's forgiveness. The presidente said that it was not in the plaintiff's hands to forgive, that that was the court's authority, and that he was going to sanction him for the crime he had committed of eating an animal which was not his.

The defendant continued, "How much does the woman want for her turkey?" The señora answered, "Twenty-eight pesos, because it was fat." The accused said, "I'm not going to argue, and you, Señor Presidente?" The presidente responded, "So that you are more careful and don't do this anymore you have to pay the cost of the turkey, which is 28 pesos, and a fine of 50 pesos for the robbery and abuse you have committed."

The defendant agreed and asked permission to go borrow the money. The presidente let him go with two police accompanying him so that he wouldn't escape. The defendant returned several hours later, saying that no one wanted to lend him money. The presidente ordered him back in jail so that he could notify his family, who might respond for him. One of his relatives arrived and was directed to the jail to speak to the defendant, who told him he was in jail because he had been drunk. The relative said he would pay his fine for drunkenness, but the presidente said, "This man is a liar; he stole a turkey. . . ." The relative then thanked the presidente and said if that was so, he would not pay his fine. "When one has a desire to eat meat, he has to work to buy it, but unfortunately my relative is lazy and a drunk, and I am not going to sacrifice myself to help him. Let him stay where he is a bit to think about what he has done." And with that the man left.

Once again the defendant asked permission to go with the police to find a loan. He returned some hours later with the money and said to the presidente, "Now I come to pay for the turkey and to pay my fine." Before the presidente let him free, he said to him, "Now you are free. Don't repeat this act because it is bad and they are your neighbors. What if you need them one day? The way you are, nobody would help you. They have to work hard to buy their *animalitos*, and you go and steal them to eat." The defendant answered, "It is all right, Señor Presidente. Now that I am free and I have paid what I owe, please give me back my pot with the turkey so that I can finish eating it. I paid for it, so I might as well enjoy it." The presidente ordered the pot returned to him.

Later that same afternoon, the man who had loaned the defendant the money, Alberto, appeared before the presidente: "It is I who lent the defendant money to pay his fine and the rest, but as security I [made him] mortgage a piece of coffee land located near his house. I gave him 80 pesos, and now I find out that the coffee land is not his, but belongs to his grand-children. I come to you in anticipation of a problem. If I go to this land to cut coffee, the mother of the children could place a complaint against me. Please call the mother of the owners so that she can say whether she would let me cut coffee or, better yet, have the defendant give me back my money so I don't get involved in a mess. If I had known it wasn't his land, I would not have gotten involved."

The presidente asked Alberto if he wanted to remain in the deal, and he responded no, because the land didn't belong to the debtor. The mother of the children who owned the land was sent for, and the presidente said he would try to get the money back for the lender.

The mother was questioned: "Is it true that when your mother-in-law died, she left such and such land to your children and are there witnesses?" The mother answered that it was true and there were witnesses, and she asked that the father-in-law be called to testify to the truth. Once again they sent for the accused.

When the accused arrived, the presidente said to him: "I have called you to testify if it is true that your deceased wife left for your grandchildren the piece of land that you mortgaged with Alberto." The accused then said that it was true that his wife had left that land to her grandchildren. [In Talea married women hold property in their own names and may bequeath it to their descendants even though their husbands are still living.] The presidente continued, "If your wife left the land to the grandchildren, then why did you mortgage this land with Alberto?" Since there was no answer, the presidente turned to the daughter-in-law: "And now that your father-in-law has mortgaged your children's land, do you give Alberto permission to cut coffee?" The daughter-in-law answered that it would be better to give Alberto his money back and cut the coffee herself. She had been asked by her father-in-law, who came accompanied by the police, to lend him some money to pay a fine, and she had refused because she was sick of his drunkenness, but now she understood. She asked that the land documents be returned to her and said she would pay the money back to Alberto because the land was not hers; it was her children's property. The father-in-law thanked her and said he would see that she got the documents. The exchange was carried out.

When Alberto had left, the presidente said to the accused, "Your daughter-in-law has paid the money for you. Please present the [house] documents [as well] so that your daughter-in-law may fix the house up before it falls down." The father-in-law said that he would as long as when the house was fixed, she would allow him to live in it. She agreed and said that she wanted to fix the roof before it was too late. The accused turned over the documents. The case was closed.

In the end the man's family was forced to come to the rescue of a chronic alcoholic, and the offender was not punished for mortgaging family lands that did not belong to him. Robbery is a very serious matter, more serious than physical violence if the amounts of fines and the stigma attached to repeat thievery are indications.

Between dyads who are related or who know each other well, the action of thievery is sometimes softened by the use of terms such as *abuso de confianza*. In Case 99, the accused was thought to be a habitual thief. If the relationship were dispensable, the charge would have been robbery, as in Case 100, when a contractor accused his *mozo de confianza* (trusted laborer) of robbery. But in the settlement of Case 99, the presidente told the worker that he was punishing him with a fine for abuso de confianza, a term that has an emotional quality that the English legal term "embezzlement" lacks.

Because robbery is a serious accusation, people are punished when they accuse someone wrongfully of robbery. In Case 101, a woman accused a man of gathering wood on her land without permission, and she used the word *robo*. When, upon investigation, it was found that she had wrongfully accused the man, she was sanctioned with a fine of 30 pesos "because of the falsities which you have stated before this authority, and 15 pesos for accusing an innocent person of being a thief. And to you, Tomás [the defendant], I give the sanction of 15 pesos for having told the plaintiff that her son-in-law is also a thief." When the plaintiff complained that the defendant had been charged too little, the presidente said, "You made false declarations, and if you are not in agreement, you can spend a day in jail so that you can think about what you have done."

In Case 102, a man accused another of stealing a wooden plow beam. It, too, was a wrongful accusation, and the defendant asked compensation for his damaged honor: "I ask for my honor, and for punishment so that another time he will not go about saying things which are not true." The presidente said, "I will never be able to settle this matter, because this man asks for his honor." The plaintiff begged that the case be settled in a friendly way and not consigned to the sindico, and the man accused of robbery finally agreed as long as an acta was drawn up stating that "nothing was confirmed of which this man accuses me." The presidente fined the plaintiff 25 pesos for leveling false accusations and for not verifying his accusation.

Discussion

Contractual ties and relations of dependence cut across social groups in Talea, and conflict over property, whether movable or immovable, indicates an ordered and structured world, if not always a just one. Ownership, tenancy, the credit system, the market system—all embody obligations and commitments between individuals, and property is the medium for expressing the meaning of these relationships. A lender does expect to be paid, a landowner hopes for a return from a sharecropper, and so on.

The interplay of property rights and social structure is well illustrated by a focus on interests. When a dispute is between people who share a dyadic contract, control over the relationship dominates over substance. In other words, the individual's interest is embedded in the relationship. By contrast, collective interest disputes focus on the substance, such as land and water, and involve numbers of people rather than dyads.

In dyadic disputes, the court is a stabilizing force, which, when it enjoys trust and respect, enables court officials to conclude mutually acceptable settlements reached by friendly agreement. However, the court's unilateral rulings on fines, which act as "corrective punishment," force those who are unable to pay to become clients of the moneylenders. And thus, the system of fines redistributes property, albeit in the shadow of the court, in the form of cash impounded by the municipio and of interest paid to the moneylender. Two systems, then, operate side by side: a system of compromise and mutual agreement, and a system of monetary penalty that redistributes property. This is true whether the issue is a property complaint or some other type of complaint.

The people of Talea have methods for protecting their possessions and their investments. Property is regulated by the courts as well as by public opinion and conceptions of absolute rights, such as the right of all human beings to water. The multiplicity of cases tells a good deal about the mental frame of the villagers, who strain their ingenuity to create more resources for themselves. It also testifies to the power and organization of the village to ensure and keep watch over questions of ownership; the court is a respected regulator of property rights.

The users of the court, both men and women, are enterprising participants, and many of them use property to improve their leverage in society. Distinctions in wealth are asserted and maintained through the court system of dispute handling. Ultimate responsibility for the poor, the alcoholic, the elderly, or the orphaned, however, is shared by the town and their family.

In conflicts over property, harmony may be sought through bonding mechanisms (such as compensation) or through separation (dissolution of a contractual relation). Dyads are at the heart of many disputes over property, but groups are an important part of the court cases. Disputes over contracts delineate the character of social relations, and disputes over collective interests establish the definition of community in relation to state control. Ideas of individual property ownership are compatible with present-day state control and state penetration, although the degree of fit between traditional collective or communal interests and the Mexican state has fluctuated over time.

Chapter Thirteen

Contests About Governance

The idea that cross-cutting alliances or conflicting loyalties and cultural mechanisms such as harmony ideology influence the expression and management of discord has been accepted in anthropology, although not without critique (Starr and Yngvesson 1975; Dillon 1980). The observation that cross-linkage and cultural ideals about harmony and negotiation may be insufficient to inhibit conflict is also generally accepted. In this chapter, I use cases of controversy over and about governance to indicate the dynamic between forces of harmony and controversy.

As has been noticed, respect for authority is inextricably linked to village autonomy. Court proceedings indicate the Talean ability to create and reward conformity and build consensus. Yet, discord and disagreement are also prominent within the village. Taleans have much to disagree about and exhibit simultaneous tendencies toward consensus and harmony and toward controversy and litigiousness. What happens in cases of disagreement over the rights of authorities or the responsibilities of citizens as citizens? Do the Taleans as citizens govern their authorities in the municipio? Do they discipline them, or are they intimidated by authority? Is defiance expressed? Are there boundaries to the tolerance Taleans have for their elected officials, and how are these boundaries controlled by a need for harmony and autonomy? To what degree is this village justice system controlled by its citizens, and to what degree is a locally controlled justice system able to discipline those who flout authority?

The Nature of Respect, Responsibility, Authority, and Autonomy

The prevalence of rituals of respect among the Zapotec of the Sierra Juárez is one indication of their attitudes about authority and

responsibility. Those who hold offices (cargos) with assigned responsibilities are also assigned authority and respect, which terminate
immediately on leaving office. The same pattern of respect and responsibility is found in human relations with the supernaturals. Responsibility, authority, and respect define attitudes toward human
and nonhuman authority. At the same time the Zapotec are aware
that position does not guarantee performance. If assigned responsibilities are not executed or not executed properly, then respect for
authority is replaced by a challenge to authority.

The Talean Zapotec and their neighbors observe rituals of respect.
Men tip their hats and women bow as they enter and exit the courtroom; they refer to the presidente as Mr. President; or, as I mentioned earlier, in villages like Juquila they bring to court a bit of
mezcal as a ritual drink of respect. At the same time the mountain
Zapotec feel they have a right to challenge authority if it is abused.
One avenue of challenge is gossip. Another is refusal to serve when
elected. Still another is open discussion at the town meeting. But on
occasion the authorities are challenged in court.

I have included a chapter on problems of governance because
ideas about public authority are best revealed in such cases, and because perceptions that appear in contests of governance are indicative of ideas about how a community ought to function publicly.
Unlike their Mixe neighbors who have evolved more authoritarian
structures and who in recent times have frequently resorted to caciques (political bosses), the Zapotec are intensely egalitarian about
governance. That is, they believe that people in public roles are accountable and must upon occasion be brought to a public accounting. Refusal to give service, the rendering of arbitrary judgments,
the imbibing of alcoholic beverages while performing public service, theft of property, or incompetence are complaints bound to
enter the courtroom. Indeed, aggrieved men and women seldom
hesitate to charge the town authorities, for after all, "they are men
like us," not immune to charges and not immune to harassment
when they are irresponsible, a view not uncommon to American
Indians elsewhere.

In "Two Concepts of Authority," Walter Miller (1955) encapsu-
lated the differences between how authority is conceptualized and
operationalized among the Central Algonkian Indians of the North
American Great Lakes region and among the European newcomers.
What Miller observes applies in part to the differences in conceptions of authority among the Talean Zapotec and the Mexican state,
which is after all European. "In the European cultural tradition a
rather remarkable phenomenon can be noted: authority, or 'power,'

is conceptually equated with height or elevation . . . authority is reified, quantified, elevated and pictured as flowing downward . . . The Central Algonkian conceives of authority as the resultant of ongoing interaction between individuals" (ibid.: 276–78). Miller speaks of an "aversion to vertical authority" among the Algonkian Fox and notes that they are quoted as saying: "Since all men are made of the same clay, there should be no distinction or superiority among them" (Thwaitess 1905: 2. 499; quoted in ibid.). Miller goes on to say: "The vertical authority relationship is a fundamental building block of European society. Without it the phenomenon of 'ranked' authority—where given individuals are permanently empowered to direct others—would be impossible, and ranked authority is an indispensable feature of European organizational systems." In a society where authority is conceptualized as horizontal, different principles are used to deal with the authority in question. In Talea the authority to govern is temporary, something you have only while you are in office, and as with the Fox, no permanent relationship of superordination-subordination results from officeholding if one does not observe the rules of office. Officials, after all, are carrying burdens (cargos).

As noted in Chapter 4, town officials are elected by men of voting age and serve for one year without pay. The office work is sedentary (in comparison with fieldwork), and when the men become bored, they are often moved to drink to enliven the dullness. Alcoholism that follows or accompanies public office is also a product of stress, a stress caused by a feeling of vulnerability. As I mentioned before, service as a town official does not attract power seekers—townsmen are drafted. They are not "winners" in the sense of being victorious. Their feelings of vulnerability often stem from the ease with which they can be called to account. A legal charge against an official can result in loss of esteem, time, and money, for if he is not backed by the town as a whole, his life as well as the lives of his family, is affected. As one presidente noted, the hunter becomes the hunted. Understanding the vulnerability of officials further explains the Talean style of dispute handling. In Talea, compromise and give a little, get a little serve as "tranquility for the decision-maker" (Colson 1973). This Talean style contrasts with another mode of authority; in the district court the style is more hierarchical and follows a model that separates authority from the right to charge or challenge the actual performance of officials by those lower in the hierarchy (Parnell 1978a, 1989).

Disciplining Public Officials

The rationalization for disciplining public officials is often discussed in terms of shame. Feelings of shame over what public officials have done require disciplining of the officials. In Case 103, inebriation, unauthorized use of funds, and physical violence resulted in the jailing of two Talean officials.

The presidente was somewhat drunk, as was the alcalde. Some days before, the presidente had told the alcalde to turn in the accounts of the alcalde's office, and now he repeated his request for the alcalde to turn in the accounts to the municipal treasury because the alcalde has no authorization to use the fines collected by the court. The alcalde refused, saying he would not be ordered around by the presidente. Whereupon the presidente responded that at the town meeting about to be held he would announce that the alcalde didn't want to turn in the money. The alcalde responded that he was not refusing, only waiting for his secretary's father to pay him the 30 pesos his secretary took. The presidente reminded him that the money he was asking for is not for lending; from the moment the fine is received, it should be deposited in the treasury. The alcalde answered that the presidente might collect the money from his secretary's father. The presidente responded that he had not lent the money, so why should he collect it, and if someone is going to be punished, the alcalde should go to jail too for lending money that is not his and without authorization.

The two officials went on arguing heatedly about this. The alcalde pushed the presidente and, when the latter fell to the floor, gave him a kick. Seeing the incident, the regidor intervened and the policía came in and took both of them to jail, leaving the first regidor in the presidency. The first regidor gathered the other regidores and discussed the act they had witnessed. One regidor said, "It's shameful that they did this in the town hall, and even more shameful because they were drunk. Who doesn't drink mezcal—we all drink—but with the positions they hold, they shouldn't do this. They are the first ones who should set the example. Now they have done the opposite—they fight in the town hall and get drunk." A second regidor said, "It's shameful that this thing has happened, now that it is market day. What will the people who saw the presidente fight with the alcalde say? Both of them must be punished. And we won't take them out of jail until tomorrow so they can think about what they are doing. Also, they must be fined for the offenses committed."

The second regidor agreed, but on the same day at 7:00 P.M. the regidores met to resolve a pending matter. The presidente was to meet with the new director of the band who was taking over the responsibilities of office. The first regidor thought that they should let the presidente out of jail so that he could meet with the band, arguing that his presence was necessary because if the presidente were not there and afterward something happened, he could make the regidores responsible: "He should go to that meeting even if he is a drunk." The others agreed, but there was a general consensus that the presidente had failed the village. However, yet another regidor argued that if they let the presidente out, they would have to let the alcalde out of jail too.

If we don't let the alcalde out too, he will complain, and he won't want to pay the fine. He'll say they weren't punished equally, and for these things not to happen, we must agree to take them both out even if we tell the alcalde about the presidente's engagement with the band. If they agree to appear early tomorrow before the regidor, we will let them out; if they don't want to, then we don't have to let them out. That is the only compromise there is, and if this compromise doesn't come about, then let them stay there so they are punished.

Everyone thought the suggestion a good one, and the regidor then moved to call the police chief to explain why they wanted to let the presidente out of jail. When the regidores and other officers were present, the police chief was informed of what was happening.

Things are getting complicated. We don't want you to think that the regidores are taking away your rights or that the principles of authority are being disrespected. You know that any person who goes to jail is presented before the authorities at nine o'clock on the next day. The police have to see that such abuses are not committed. The presidente and the alcalde have committed offenses, but the situation is this. The regidores see themselves as obligated to let the presidente out of jail so he can witness the taking of office of the new band leader. If this were not the case, we would not intercede for him.

To which the chief of police answered:

Well, not all of us policemen are in agreement as to what happened. Where has one ever seen presidentes fighting with the alcalde? We are not about to let him out. We'll let him loose only because of the obligation, but once the deal is over, we'll put him in jail again so that he will be disciplined.

But the presidente and the alcalde were let out of jail after they agreed to appear before the authorities in the morning. In the morning the first regidor turned the case over to the sindico, informing him what had happened the previous day and noting that the incident had embarrassed the town because a lot of people had come to market. He also told the sindico that he would know what sanction to give them to ensure that such things did not happen again in the municipio.

It would be another matter if it were a bar or in the street; if they have some problem between them, let them settle it, but unfortunately they didn't think about what they were doing and it happened here.

The sindico admonished the litigants:

Well, it's not correct that these difficulties exist between you. We each have our own responsibilities, and besides those of us appointed to serve should not argue. If some matter crops up it is all right to argue as long as we're in full use of our faculties and not drunk. So that the regidores are satisfied that you have been punished for offenses and lack of respect for the authority, I fine you with the sum of 20 pesos apiece.

The presidente responded:

Well, you will excuse me, but I don't recall what happened. After all, all I did was to demand from the alcalde his accounts. He got mad and told me, "You can't order me around" and gave me a blow, and I fell. But I have the right to demand the money. But most likely he already spent the money, and that's why he got upset.

The sindico explained to him:

Nobody is taking away from your authority. But make sure you are in full possession of your faculties and not drunk. An inebriated person cannot do justice. So you got violent under the effects of a few drinks, and you see the results.

The alcalde then spoke his part.

I guess I have no option but to recant if I pay the fine. I already told the presidente that if I am to turn in my accounts, he should wait a little more while I recover the money. But since he is stubborn and I am violent, I got mad. And since we were both drunk, I gave him one so he would get mad at me once and for all. So I will pay the fine, please, in the afternoon, and ask that you please wait a little more for me to give you the sum for the treasury.

The sindico said that that was a matter between the alcalde and the presidente and recommended that the money be turned over as soon as possible to avoid difficulties. The presidente said he would only pay his fine when the alcalde paid because if not, "He'll play the fool and not pay." The regidores were stern in their responses, threatening to put them both back in jail if they did not pay their fines by the afternoon. Both parties agreed.

What is interesting about this case is the attention paid to the brawling rather than to the initial accusation of the presidente that the alcalde was lending treasury monies without authorization. The latter was a problem between the two officials. Their public behavior was the business of the remaining authorities. The lines of authority were clear in each part of the case—who should put them in jail, who had the right to let them out of jail, who had the right to question the lending of treasury monies without authorization, and so on. The issue was conflict behavior. Notice that both officials were fined equally, although one had initiated the assault. Both had violated harmony values that embody the town authorities' mode of resistance to incursion of outside forces attempting to control them, values that incorporate their manner of self-regulation.

In some instances of inappropriate behavior by officials, the result is removal from office—a more drastic response than fining. For example, one sindico was dismissed by a decision of the town meeting because he was "arbitrary and drastic in his decisions." I know of no example of officials removed from office because of drinking. Usually they are reprimanded, put in jail, and/or fined, but not removed from office.

At times an ex-presidente may be called to explain inadequate accounting, as in Case 104.

Señor Felipe, the ex-presidente, had refused to participate in communal work projects and, as a result, had been called to the municipio. Once there, he refused to answer the presidente's question and instead insulted him and threatened to go to the district court. The ex-presidente then brought a case against the presidente to the sindico. What began as an argument over whether the ex-presidente should have been excused from tequio because of the sacrifices he suffered during his year of service escalated into an argument over the charge of fraud brought against him by the presidente. Apparently, the ex-presidente did not want to show the village the accounts of a bill he had charged various coffee merchants (to the amount of 300 pesos per person), an accounting he never made clear while in office.

Felipe said he did not want to deal with the sindico; he wanted to deal with the agent of the ministerio publico in Villa Alta. He said that the accounting was placed on the table in the municipio in early January after he left office. The sindico informed Felipe that the villagers wanted to know whether the amount he had gathered (to pay a state tax) had been enough or if there were money left over; they wanted to know what he had done with the money. Felipe answered that they could go over the account he had placed on the table (unacknowledged by anyone else). Felipe was informed that due to the menaces and rebelliousness he had exhibited to the presidente, and for the falsehoods about the accounting, the sindico decided to fine him 25 pesos and in addition 5 pesos he has to pay to the municipal authority for his part in the repair of the road, which motivated this case in the first place.

The accused then laughed and ridiculed the officials; he stated flatly that he did not have to pay anything to this authority, that he expected the case to be forwarded to the district court, where he would talk to the municipal authority. He also refused to sign transmission papers. While the papers were being drawn up, the sindico told him he would remain a prisoner in the corridor of the municipio. Felipe refused this and said that he would prefer to be in jail and not outside, and without it being so ordered he went into the jail, and there he remained without the order or consent of the sindico. After several hours he was taken from the jail, where he was of his own free will, and asked whether he had decided to pay the fine imposed on him. The ex-presidente insisted that the case be consigned to Villa Alta, but once again refused to sign the testimony.

The sindico forwarded the following document to Villa Alta.

In the office of the undersigned sindico and his witnesses: Thus Felipe was responsible for crimes of rebelliousness, threats, and opposition before the municipal authority of this village. During investigations into the crime of fraud, the suspect was found responsible during his office of municipal presidente. The present investigations are sent to the agent of the ministerio publico in Villa Alta so he may determine the settlement.

I never learned how this case turned out, but it did not escalate into a village division. Possibly Felipe was called to financial accounting in Villa Alta far removed from Talea and further publicly embarrassed should he have been found guilty as charged; alternatively Felipe might have been called to account at a town meeting, where room for negotiation between officials would have been less possible than in Villa Alta. Indeed, it is possible that Felipe might have been subjected to both the district court and the town meeting. The attitude of newly elected officials underscores my earlier observation that they do not feel like or act like "winners"; indeed they act more like losers in a roulette game. In Case 105, a newly elected official felt desperate enough to ignore his duties.

The mayor of Otatitlan was brought to Talea by the police of Otatitlan for acts of indiscipline and dereliction of duties. According to the records transferred from Otatitlan, the defendant indicated that his acts of indiscipline were due to a misunderstanding between him and the previous official regarding how to administer a municipality. The Talean presidente suggested a meeting of Talean officials in Otatitlan with the officials of Otatitlan, the defendant, and his father. The defendant claimed he could not be there because he had business pertaining to farming. In answer to the accusation that he had fled from the town jail, he admitted this was true, but the Otatitlan authorities had detained him once more until his transfer to the Talean court.

Having heard the declarations of the defendant the presidente imposed on him a fine of 40 pesos for offenses committed, saying that this was only a disciplinary sanction so that in the future he would adequately fulfill the duties he had been charged with in the governing of his town. At the same time the presidente explained to the mayor's father that he should advise his son to faithfully carry out his farming responsibilities in a manner subordinate to his official duties. Maybe in the future he would not be responsible for his son's abuses against authority.

An agreement was drawn up and signed with copies for all the present parties and one to be forwarded to the offices of the agent of the ministerio publico in Villa Alta.

Sometimes the official in question simply flees the area so that he cannot be called to account. In Case 106, an official resigned.

The citizens of Yatoni held a town meeting in order to deal with the problem of a substitute *agente municipal* [the equivalent in an agencia to the presidente in a municipio]. The agente municipal had resigned from his position. The presidente of Talea had gone to Yatoni to resolve the problem of transfer of authority. The previous agente had left his post without just cause. He wrote a letter in which he set forth his resignation, but the town did not accept it because it lacked a legal and justifiable basis. He was advised by the Talean presidente that there was no legal basis for him to leave the agencia abandoned and that he must return to carry out the cargo that the town had conferred upon him.

On the following day the Talean presidente was informed that the agente from Yatoni had abandoned his job and that it was urgent that the case be resolved. The presidente wired a letter to the next in charge to substitute in order that he proceed immediately to locate the agente and summon him with speed to avoid disorder in official activities and public works.

On the fourth day the substitute agente and his regidores presented themselves, saying that they had followed orders but that the agente was no longer in the jurisdiction and they had been informed by well-informed channels that he had left for the city of Oaxaca. The Talean presidente went with his officials to the Yatoni town meeting, where he said: "At the petition of the substitute agente and the rest of the regidores, we come to this agencia to settle this matter. First I want to know, now that all the men of the village are together, what are the reasons that motivated the agente to leave this agencia?"

The people responded: "Because of his violent temperament. The reasons he sets forth are excuses—saying that some citizens are attacking him. That is why he left—and without motive he left, because we are building two schoolrooms. He told some of the people, 'I no longer want to be here. I am tired of working.'" They continued: "This man left without a just reason. And now, Señor Presidente, we leave to your charge our problem in order that by means of your authority you dictate that which is necessary so that the head of this position be named, since we are confused [*descontrolados*] and without direction. Today we planned to work, because we are working for the benefit of our village. But not having someone in charge or a chief, we cannot work." One of the principales from the village said, "Those of us who have already given our services think that if the agente left his position in this way, then by right the position belongs to the substitute agente. So on our behalf we ask as a favor that Señor Jerónomo remain with the charge of this agencia so that the public works which have been begun will not fall to disorder, since the village is disposed to carry out the work of constructing the mentioned classrooms."

Once proposed, the presidente said to Jerónomo, "By virtue of this village petition I ask you, Señor Jerónomo, to be in charge [*encargado*] of this agencia." Señor Jerónomo answered: "I cannot take this position because the work that he has left is too much responsibility, and perhaps they [the citizens] are going to do to me what they did to him. There are many who do not respect the authority. They make fun of them, and I do not want these things. If I were to take charge, it would only be for the official matters of the agencia. But I do not want to make a commitment to the work because of my economic situation. Furthermore, if I did make the commitment, the townsfolk always say many things while working. They have already told me that it is because of my wishes that I am serving as encargado. By not taking the position, I protect myself from these sayings. I could do what the other agente did, abandon my position, but I do not have that intention because I respect . . . I am willing to remain in charge of official matters."

On the one hand, without someone in the role of agente, we were told, the people are "confused and without direction," and without someone in charge of public works they "cannot work." On the other hand, the official should not want the position, he should be "encargado," burdened with it.

After a long silence the townspeople pleaded with Señor Jerónomo to be in charge of official matters and public works and said they were prepared to obey him. At this point the presidente added: "As has been noted by the incumbent, the authorities have not been respected here, and for this reason this man does not want to take any responsibilities, because of your poor conduct. Because of the nature of this problem, I want you to be in agreement [*de conformidad*, or in conformity] that Señor Jerónomo remain in charge of this agencia."

Everyone unanimously claimed to be in agreement, asking the favor of the substitute agente.

. . . Then directing himself to Señor Jerónomo, the presidente said, "You have heard the petition that they are making you. Asking the favor that you remain in charge of the entire agencia, and of the works and that they are disposed to obey and respect you. As for me, I give wide powers to you that you know that my office respects and backs you in the problems which might arise from this new settlement."

Señor Jerónomo responded: "If this is the will and petition of my village that I take charge, I am in agreement, but I will need the presidente of the school committee to help me so that both of us can agree on the classrooms being built." All of the townfolk agreed it could be done and hoped that the presidente of the school committee agreed.

The presidente of Talea then said to the school committee chair that his help was indispensable, the school committee chair said he could not commit himself because people do the same thing to him as to the agente. They do not obey, they make fun, and they gossip. The townsmen responded that from today on they would obey and that he should be designated [as holding] an official capacity. Under these conditions the school committeee chair agreed to serve.

Once all the problems were discussed and solutions were agreed upon, the Talean presidente once more exhorted the people to cooperate, and an act of the agreement was drawn up and signed.

The power to govern was negotiated by establishing that the people delegated power to the office and that the service of the official was a favor the official did for the people. Without an agreement there could be no delegation. Without delegation there could be no public works. The model was one of interdependence, not of subordination-superordination. And it is not only over the positions at the top of the ladder that cases are generated. Policemen can be brought to court because of failing to fulfill obligations. As in case 107, threats to quit service are not uncommon.

One day the sindico was drunk, and he made rude remarks to the presidente and also said he was going to quit because he could not stand the municipio any longer. The presidente said that he knew what he was doing and that he would not accept any renunciation of office; if the sindico wanted to quit, he could do so directly in the offices of the ministerio publico in Villa Alta.

The sindico left the office, and the presidente told his secretary to notify the alcalde that the sindico had abandoned his duties. The regidor said to ignore him because the sindico was drunk. The presidente responded that whatever state he is in, the sindico has no excuse to tell him anything. The next day the alcalde heard the case between the sindico and the presidente, which had been prompted by the handling of drunks who had been brought in by the police. The alcalde lectured both officials on the seriousness of disintegration of a municipal corporation, which results in harm to society and the general public. Both the sindico and presidente were given a moment of silence so they could measure the consequences of the present action. The parties agreed to a reconciliation, and the alcalde exhorted them to help each other *in the services that the town has conferred upon them* [my emphasis] and to respect in the same manner the faculties of each individual. Tempers were quieted, and the officials returned to their obligations.

Suddenly we were in another world. The presidente received an emissary from the town of Tabaa indicating that Talea should send to Tabaa for the school breakfasts the first lady of the republic was donating to all the schools in the republic. An official note was drawn up for the presidente of Tabaa telling him that it was not possible to collect the breakfasts because of the expensive bus fares and asking him to send the shipment for Talea back to the charity in Oaxaca. The Talean authorities explained that if the first lady wished to donate breakfasts to Talea, she could do so directly since Talea was now served by bus. As with the Central Algonkians, the Talean Zapotec were not impressed by superordinate authority, although they recognized that external authority could not be ignored, anymore than could internal obligations.

Challenging Court Actions

There were instances of citizen challenge of municipio authority: schoolteachers who thought "they knew more," ex-presidentes who thought they should be immune, or just plain people who either thought they had been wronged or who out of anger wished to harass the municipio. The following case was selected to illustrate a challenge of court action; it involved a woman of about fifty. This case, as with others chronicled in a less legalistic and more narrative style, was reported to me by the town secretary, whose duty it was to make a legal record of cases; it shows, as the secretary said, just how "the hunter ended by being hunted."

In 1963 court officials received an urgent summons from Villa Alta demanding that the Talean officials present themselves in Villa Alta for a matter of a penal nature. The court officials left immediately. The secretary accompanied the presidente because that official could not express himself well in Spanish. They presented themselves before the ministerio publico, who told them they faced the serious charges of dispossession and robbery. Case 108 started like this.

About January 15, a Talean woman who lived in Mexico City sent a letter asking the authorities to intervene by helping her remove a woman occupying her house. She wanted the house vacated because she had had complaints about the tenant's bad reputation. Moreover, the woman continued, she had asked her tenant to vacate a year ago, and the tenant had not obeyed. She asked the municipio to evict her tenant because it was difficult for her to come all the way from Mexico City to evict her.

The presidente sent to the tenant and explained the reason for the summons. She said she would vacate the house but asked for a period of eight days to vacate. Her request was accepted. Once this period was over, she was summoned again and this time ridiculed the authority. She came in very drunk and said, "Take me out if you can." Finally she left, but was subsequently apprehended by the police, who took her to jail by order of the presidente. The next day she appeared and of her own will, apologized and asked that she be given another grace period of a few more days. The presidente told her she would have 24 hours, and if she did not obey, she would be evicted for disobedience. She did not obey the order. At this time, by order of the sindico, a regidor was sent with a warrant ordering her to vacate the house, and the police went with the regidor to evict her. Afterward, the tenant spread a rumor saying the authorities had forced her from her house, robbing her of 3,000 pesos she had in her chest. She went around saying this on the streets; it is telling that she never complained at the presidente's office.

At this point in his report, the secretary added that the woman sold things in the plaza—things like spices or pots from Oaxaca— things of little value. It was really a lie to say she had money that could be stolen in her house. Moreover, he said, this woman was going around with nobody to watch over her; her husband had left her for being an adulteress, and she had a terrible record in Talea.

The ex-tenant went on a trip to Oaxaca, and one of her friends advised her to complain before a lawyer and to present a brief to the public prosecutor's office. The complaint accusing the authorities of dispossession and robbery was well argued because it was made by an Oaxacan lawyer. From Oaxaca it was remitted to Villa Alta, and for that reason the Talean presidente was summoned to appear there.

Upon arriving in Villa Alta, it was obvious that the ex-tenant was not there. Since the agent was in charge only of investigating and submitting what he found to Oaxaca, he suggested that the presidente go to Oaxaca and talk with a lawyer who could deal with the matter, because the accusation came directly from Oaxaca. Since the agent of the ministerio publico had strict orders to apprehend the presidente and since he was well acquainted with the people of Talea, he said, "I will tell the State Attorney's office that you did not show up here, and because you had to go to Oaxaca on official business and knew from well-informed sources that the accuser was bragging about accusing you before the public prosecutor's office, you will take advantage of the trip to see what it was all about."

The Talean officials set out for Oaxaca immediately on Friday morning, and in Oaxaca arranged matters with the lawyer, a friend from Talea who has much influence in the government. They let it be known that they were interested less in fighting the woman than in disproving her savage accusation that the authorities were guilty of robbery. The lawyer promised he would deal with the matter, and the presidente and his secretary returned to

Talea on Monday. As the secretary noted, they had a lot of work pending in the municipio and, because of this woman, were losing time and accumulating work. The lawyer was informed about the accuser's record, of her having been to jail several times over the years and having gone to Villa Alta as well.

The owner of the house was informed about what was going on and offered to pay the expenses incurred. According to the secretary [and noteworthy for brevity] the case was settled simply, and the woman has remained in Oaxaca for the time being.

Jane Collier (1973) explored the forces that simultaneously undermine and reinforce the system of "customary law" in the Mayan community of Zinacantan in Chiapas, Mexico. She noted the increased use of village courts and their increasing incorporation of Mexican law. Although the competition between two systems of justice may produce legal involution and a greater use of local courts in Oaxaca as well, a few, usually people on the periphery in one way or another, will move out of the local courts and favor use of the Mexican system. If citizens challenge the local courts in the state system, local officials will be moved to use the services of legal professionals to fix their problems with the state. If those who challenge the court are central rather than peripheral town figures, the local courts will decline in prestige and legitimacy. Talean law offers the advantages of traditional procedures within the selected substance of Mexican law, an accommodation of centuries.

Part IV ❦ Connections

Chapter Fourteen

Harmony in Comparative Perspective

Anthropologists are working to develop a theory of culture that distinguishes an organic and consensual culture from a hegemonic culture. A hegemonic culture is constructed at a point and reaches out to permeate the whole; it is a culture constructed by groups and interests. The culture of harmony, for example, is constructed as part of the development of Christianity as a messianic religion associated with particular political economies (see Comaroff and Comaroff 1986; see also Beidelman 1982).

It has taken social scientists decades to abandon the idea of culture as an integral entity separate from reality, which is a less perfectly bounded phenomenon. In addition, we must distinguish the use of the concept of culture as an instrumental strategy of institutions or organizations from its use as an analytical tool. The original view of culture, which is in question today due to the admixture of cultures on a grand scale, was instrumental. When Taleans practically or ideologically construct their culture as a harmonious one, they are using culture as an instrument. So, too, when social scientists describe the Talean Zapotec as harmonious, they are participating in that larger hegemonic force, constructing a picture of other peoples for a variety of purposes apart from analytical, scholarly ones. What is needed in the present instance is an unpacking of ideas of harmony (and controversy), particularly as they relate to disputing processes. Harmony ideologies may be used to suppress peoples by socializing them toward conformity in colonial contexts, or they may be used to resist external control, as the Talean Zapotec do. Harmony must be broken down into its various components in order to understand its meaning and controlling power (Rose 1988).

Harmony in Non-Western Societies

In what follows I concentrate on harmony ideologies in the Western colonial and Christian missionizing contexts, selecting examples principally from classic monographs on law in former British colonies in Africa and from ethnographies on the Pacific regions of Polynesia and Micronesia. They turn our attention to the role of Christian missionaries in reconstructing local disputing processes. Elizabeth Colson (1974: 86–87) pointed to a first-step analysis, noting that African societies maintained local autonomy in the face of colonial incursion by using local law; she did not emphasize the role of missionaries as influencing that local law, but neither did others. Indeed, an examination of a few dozen monographs in legal anthropology indicates a fairly general lack of interest in what the missionaries were doing, a neglect reflecting the writer's interest in indigenous cultures. Beidelman (1974) refers to missionaries as the most ambitious of all colonialists in their desire to penetrate every facet of cultural life, and Shapiro (1981) points out that anthropologists treat missionaries as part of the setting, much like rainfall and elevation—peripheral to the real objectives of anthropological research. Although there are exceptions, most of the anthropological materials reveal connections that inspire one to pursue the relations between the Christian imperative and the dissemination of harmony ideology at the local level.

In his monograph on the Barotse of Zambia (also called the Lozi), Max Gluckman (1955) noted in his case analyses that the Catholic missionary fathers go on tour asking for complaints. He reports that the Barotse have a right to complain to their chiefs, the district commissioners, and the missionaries (ibid.: 74), but gives no further explication in regard to missionary justice. The Barotse have absorbed the beliefs and ideology of Christianity, although few are practicing members of the mission sects. Gluckman notes that "litigious consensus breaks down when judges and litigants have different norms as where a Catholic husband might deny the kuta's [the tribal court's] power to divorce his wife" and that "the divergence between general and sectional ethics and the established law has increased since the [beginning of the] British protectorate [1924], and . . . this divergence is likely to grow" (ibid.: 157, 223). He refers here to the breakup of the homogeneity of Barotse society.

In an incident entitled "The Case of the Watchtower Pacifists," Gluckman (1955: 158) indicates how Christian values enter the courts. Six members of the Watchtower sect refused on pacifist grounds to pay a tax for war funds, saying (among other things) that they would flee from hostile enemies and that only God could order them to fight. Others accused them of not respecting traditional authority. Gluckman reports that although such cases were still rare in Barotse kutas, "quotations from the Bible were bandied about by pagans as well as Christians." He concludes his discussion of Christian missionaries by noting, "On many of these points Lozi public opinion is united. Indigenous standards of ethics are being threatened, and the demand is for the law to be amended to protect these standards" (ibid.: 222). Gluckman never studied the missionary courts.

Nadel's work on the Nuba (1947) of the Sudan is truly rich in details of the complexities of the interrelations within which "customary" law operates. He speaks of the change from the old, negotiated settlement to the new, authoritative system "in which the court dictates sentences and pronounces verdicts" and observes:

These neat, well-planned arrangements are belied by the court proceedings. There is little conscious procedure. The court sessions are confused, without plan or order. Always there will be several people talking simultaneously. Chiefs and sub-chiefs converse together or shout at each other across the room. Parties left sitting from a previous case will heartily join in the next, though it concerns them not at all. The audience overflows into the court chamber, and the court chamber invites the cooperation of the audience. Constantly side-tracked, and side-tracking each other, in impromptu arguments, plaintiffs, defendants, and judges seem parties, not to a planful legal investigation, but to a disturbed and often indecisive controversy.

These are not merely externals. They reflect an uncertainty inherent in the whole attitude of the people towards judicial decisions. This attitude is still in large measure dominanted by the traditional conception of legal actions, as decentralized, group-to-group settlements of disputes. The very large number of Sheikhs and Wakils [deputies] who sit on the court shows the desire of even small localities to be represented. The families of litigants invariably turn up in a body to take part in the discussions—as they would take part in the quarrels or fights of their individual members. Often the negotiations are carried on between the opposing groups rather than through court and chief, and the court members act, not as impartial judges, but as partisans, tied to plaintiff or defendant by clan or kinship. [1947: 161]

Nadel obviously understands only too well the role that missionaries play in relation to change in general and to law as a means of change, in addition to the influence of the British colonial government. Although Nadel is able to outline the procedural and substantive changes in law wrought by the British, such as the outlawing of raids and wars, the widening of the orbit of the law beyond old political units, the disappearance of self-help, and the narrowing of legal responsibility to the individual, when he comes to missionaries, he speaks of moral education rather than direct influence on the legal code.

Often religious education leads to a blind, superficial adoption of the forms of religion rather than of its ethical essence. It contains, too, so many elements which clash with the life as these tribes know it, and will ever know it, that their beneficial effects must appear dubious. Indeed, Islam as taught by narrow-minded zealots, and Christianity as taught by many missions, clash as much with the life as we . . . know it, and with the fruits of our long evolution which we now desire to share with the backward races of the world. . . . Religious education uproots first, and rebuilds afterwards. Christianity, even more than Islam, plans to build a new society. . . . Christianity—the rigid, orthodox persuasion of missions—is an uncompromisingly alien creed. It cannot be satisfied with underlining the universal moral tenets—the evilness of murder, respect for property or marital rights. It ignores traditional [east African] marital rights in preaching monogamy; it breaks up the family system; it bans dances as bad, or beer-drinking as immoral, and thus denies vital features of social integration. It aims at changes so radical that they demand . . . the protection of *ad hoc* created laws rather than lend strength to a slowly emerging new morality. [1947: 512]

The outside influences on "law," the colonial civil servants and missionaries, did not always agree, but they did share the underlying goal of "securing the continued harmony of law and social development" (ibid.: 510).

Schapera (1959) orients his work more along substantive law, and his comments on changes wrought by Christian missionaries and their converts in Botswana focus on the moral position against plural marriage, beer drinking, and the like. Under the influence of Christianity, "the ritual aspect of the Chieftanship has considerably decayed, and with it one of the most powerful sanctions underlying the chief's authority" (ibid.: 71). Schapera was referring to the role the chief played as tribal priest. Under British rule his powers in regard to external policy were taken from him, and the right to appeal his verdicts was instituted. Schapera also noted: "in almost every tribe the Chiefs, inspired either by conversion to Christianity or by the desire to keep pace with modern tendencies, have abolished old usages and imposed various new laws. Tswana law at the present time is therefore by no means the same as it was, say, in the middle of the nineteenth century" (ibid.: 43). The change in the substance of the law is more clearly acknowledged by Schapera than is the manner of dealing with controversial issues of law.

Gulliver's (1971) study of the Ndendeuli of Tanzania also contains sparse information on the role of missionary activity. He does inform us that most of the eastern Ndendeuli had accepted Islam but practiced it superficially. He also tells us that in the second half of the nineteenth century the Ngoni (mainly Christians) governed the Ndendeuli, who were harshly treated by the German authorities but largely left alone by the British colonial administration. Catholic Benedictine missionaries worked in the area but, according to Gulliver, did not have a significant impact on the Moslem Ndendeuli. It is not clear from Gulliver's account what it means to be "largely left alone," but the pattern of dispute settlement within the local community is clear. There was no intervention by or appeal to a superordinate external authority. The official institutions were controlled by non-Ndendeuli and represented an alien authority. External authority was viewed as arbitrary and able to deal only with part of a dispute. And as Gulliver (1963) noted for the Arusha, a Masai group in Tanzania, the desire to preserve a distinct way of life and opposition to external influences led people to emphasize norms that would accomplish these goals.

In discussing the administration of justice among the Shona of Zimbabwe, Holleman (1974) describes the politics of the group or wider collectivity in much the same manner as Gulliver speaks of the Ndendeuli.

Justice aims at *solving* the conflict between the parties rather than *deciding* its legal aspects in terms of law. Justice . . . then becomes a process of persuasion with the accent on the reasonable behavior of all concerned in a spirit of give and take. . . . The successful end of a tribal process is a judgement which both parties formally agree to accept and observe. [1974: 18]

This quotation comes from a book that deals with African law as it faces changes in personal and group aspirations and in obligations and loyalties. As Holleman notes, much more is at stake than

a personal search for suitable compromises between the conflicting values of a new and complex world. The legal basis of marriage and legitimate offspring, the respective responsibilities of husband and wife, of parent and child, the nature and strength of their wider kinship affiliations and obligations, in short, the very structure and coherence of corporate kin-groupings, are being affected in the groping search for new norms. [1974: 148]

Swaziland has been described as a unique case of the "triumph of indigenous authority and a substantial subordination and/or containment of alien legal norms" (Takirambudde 1983). Recent field-work in Swaziland provides the clearest formulation of the uses of harmony in land controversies. Laurel Rose (1988) indicates the con-tradiction between Swazi ideology and practice and examines how harmony ideology is used at different points in the disputing pro-cess, predominantly by the chiefs as they walk a tightrope between new elites, foreign developers, and commoners. Commoners and new elites are challenging old formulations about land, and the chief's use of harmony rhetoric is said to be a strategy for indigenous hierar-chical control. Harmony ideology is found in the speeches made at customary legal proceedings and national meetings and rituals. Church rhetoric states that respect for authority and peaceful social relations ensures continuation of Swazi culture.

Swazi statements about harmony suggest its multidimensional nature. Rose notes the following aspects: unity, consensus, coopera-tion, compliance, passivity, and docility. And although all Swazis de-fine harmony as social unity and cultural integrity, the manner of use differs by class. She reports that the traditional elites use har-mony ideologies to legitimate their administrative roles and validate the continuance of the traditional land tenure system. The new elites use harmony to legitimate their positions; although they may create an illusion of unity that accords with their individual and class interests, they are often responsible for internal social conflict. Both traditional and new elites use harmony ideologies to justify control. In court cases Swazi commoners strategically respond to harmony ideologies in presenting their case. Commoners do resist harmony ideologies when they feel that the social good has been violated or when they, as individuals, will suffer severe consequences. Although Rose and others indicate that Swazi law practices are indigenous in origin, there is evidence to the contrary. Rose herself has pointed out (pers. comm.) that chiefs recite a Christian prayer before each law case is to begin.

There are differing constellations; examples from Africa indicate the double impact of Christian missions and colonial courts on Af-rican law and the consequent ubiquitousness of harmony ideology. According to Martin Chanock (1985) and others, an idealization of African dispute processes has evolved from the colonial situation: "a way of settling personal disputes and conflicts of interest by try-ing to find a solution acceptable to both parties" (ibid.: 5). Chanock goes on to note that legal writers concurred with the idealized view held by anthropologists.

African law was a system of keeping the balance . . . geared . . . not to decisions imposed but to acceptable solutions. In the traditional African community there was no polarization of needs, of taste, or of values, and once the facts were established the same solutions will appeal to all and ways to achieve them will seem obvious. . . . The feeling of balance will be something spontaneous and self-evident. [Ibid.: 6]

In Chanock's sensitive exposition of the myths and images of African "customary" law, the processes of reconciliation, and the egalitarianism of precolonial societies, he points to the contradiction between African ideology and practice in the pre- and postcolonial periods. For example, among the Chewa of Malawi the precolonial period was a time of harsh punishment for sorcery, theft, and adultery, a contrast to later Chewa notions that judicial institutions functioned to remove hatred by patient examination and persuasion. Chanock also quotes Canter (1978) on the Lenje of Zambia, noting the contradiction in values that the Lenje offer when speaking of reconciliation that is harmony with force. Chanock notes that "maintaining harmony (with 'forcefulness') loses its patina of egalitarian warmth."

For my purposes Chanock's synthesis of the data on the missionary presence from the 1830's onward is revealing of the early connection between local law and Christian missions and goes far beyond anything anthropologists were able to write about. Chanock uses the term "missionary justice" (1985: 79) to call attention to the fact that from the early 1800's missionaries were heavily involved in the settlement of disputes according to a Victorian interpretation of the biblical law they had brought with them, which they generally fitted with English procedures as they knew them. Chanock mentions several early missions notorious for their zeal and violent punishments. He notes that these early excesses in punishment led to a change in policies, but that the missions continued to be active as conciliators in disputes. Although there was variation between regions and between different mission groups, Chanock notes the contradictions in mission justice. On the one hand the hearing between disputants was to be a "discussion," but on the other hand the missionaries felt the need to punish miscreants. They found it difficult to respect the separation of religion from law that is so much a part of the current Western system. They found this separation especially difficult to maintain in relation to the laws of marriage and divorce, which they saw through the lens of mid-Victorian Christian law; indeed, some missionaries promulgated the Ten Commandments as the law. According to Chanock, the missionaries were glad to be peacemakers and hand down Christian judgment, and the colonial courts evolved the whole into something we call customary law, a law emphasizing conciliation and compromise operating on the principles of Christian harmony ideology.

Chanock's work richly covers the origin, use, and modern consequences of harmony ideology. From the point of view of local law, compromise is the politics of adjustment. But more important, compromise becomes a politics of survival when indigenous communities try to restore a lost social solidarity as they learn to cope with threats from more powerful societies. Community courts become the places where people engage in discourses that establish and reinforce common beliefs and values and that are conscious political strategies for those societies where the colonial administration imposed indirect rule with its features of relative local autonomy. Groups that support a harmony ideology often share the belief that the forces of disorder lie outside their group. In fact, the recognition of external threat sometimes mobilizes beliefs with a religious basis. African peoples at different points in their contact experiences—when war and raiding are being put down, when sophisticated African native courts are dealing with colonization of the governing and missionizing kind, or when agriculturalists in scattered settlements seek to avoid contact whenever possible—are making use of compromise strategies to survive as collectivities in forums that flow from the colonial governmental and missionizing period.

The plot thickens as I move to materials from the Pacific. The arrival of Wesleyan missionaries in Tonga in 1826 began a process of Westernizing indigenous institutions. The legal framework for the new order has lasted for over a hundred years. The Tongans are said to have enthusiastically accepted Christianity, and missionaries of various stripes have since worked in Tonga. Still, anthropologists have evinced scant interest in the influence of evangelical behavior on dispute resolution strategies.

George Marcus (1979) describes the litigation of disputes in court as an alternative mode of conflict management among the Tongans of Polynesia, for whom social avoidance and ready conciliation are more characteristic of parties in dispute. The Tongans frequently use the European-derived court system but, Marcus notes, through the use of lawyers are able to resume friendly relations following litigation. There are contradictions because litigation is considered shameful, and yet they litigate in a manner that allows the resumption of calm, polite relations among disputants. It would be useful to know what the missionaries have been telling the natives about the morality of disputing. For example, there are Mormon missionaries in Tonga presently, and Mormon leaders have been vocal about courts and litigious behavior. Brigham Young did not mince words in describing courts as "a cage of unclean birds, a den and kitchen of the devil, prepared for hell" (quoted in Dredge 1979: 199). The introduction of Western government and the dismantling of the former system of social stratification occurred simultaneously with the introduction of Christian beliefs. The contradictory elements that Marcus notices may be the contradictions of Western courts and Western Christianity, respectively symbolized by controversy and harmony. The ideas he records about when and how to get angry, how to ask forgiveness, and how to express residual resentment are reminiscent of the Georgia Baptists so well described by Carol Greenhouse (1986).

In another article in the same volume as Marcus's article, Letitia Hickson (1979) zeros in on the relationship between a hierarchial social structure—a common feature in Polynesia—and harmony as control. The author never mentions the religion of the Fijians she studied; nor does she mention missions. Hickson argues that harmony in Fiji is maintained through a hierarchial order defining the relationships between rights and duties that must not be challenged if traditionally sanctioned social and economic processes of exchange are to continue. The ideology is supported by both religious belief and a secular ritual. Offending a person of superior rank incurs illness or death by supernatural forces such as spirit ancestors. Ceremonial apology provides a way of averting such dangers as well as symbolic reinforcement of the structure. Hickson concludes by reporting that the adjudicated settlement is not favored because it is inadequate to the job of providing complementary forms of deferential behavior between unequals.

The New Guinea materials offer clearer insights on how the introduction of Christian morality affects the disputing process. In New Guinea, both the spread of Christianity and the absence of colonial courts with their indirect rule determine the manner in which indigenous communities handle contention and disputes in contact situations. Marie Reay explicitly refers to the impact of religion.

With the spread of Christianity, a greater proportion of councillors and *komisis* [men who helped the councillors] were now directly affiliated with some mission or other—usually Catholic, Lutheran, or Swiss Evangelical Brotherhood, more rarely Nazarene or Seventh Day Adventist. These introduced a new style of court hearing. Often the councillor would walk away and say a silent prayer before returning to take his place cross-legged in the middle of the roughly semi-circular group. He would rebuke people who spoke angrily, saying that anger belonged to Satan and that God was watching. He placed more emphasis on the restoration of friendly relations than on the allocation of *kumap* [reparations], on the principle that all men were brothers in the eyes of God and traditionally *kumap* was not required of actual brothers. He was usually satisfied that friendly relations had been re-established by the disputants' willingness to shake hands as he commanded. In introducing the court and examining witnesses he would speak very gently, without the forceful authority of the "strong" councillor. He had no rules to follow to bring the case to a successful conclusion, apart from praying that people's anger would "die" and trying to make them shake hands. He could either imitate the practice of "strong" councillors he had observed or *luluais* and *tultuls* [headmen appointed by the administration] he had known, by summing up and pronouncing a judgment involving the transfer of money and valuables, or continue to preside over a dispute that drifted along until it petered out. Mission-influenced councillors were not alone in choosing the latter course. The councillor's court was not simply a vehicle for settling disputes; it was also an instrument people could use to ensure a public hearing of grievances. . . .

Disputes between men and their wives, which formerly the men themselves had to settle, had now become the province of councillor or *komisi*. With the status-raising activities of the Administration and the influence of the missions (one of which had been systematically concentrating on female conversions), men had lost much of the authority they had traditionally had over their wives; and dispute settlers knew that if they did not take the women's complaints seriously they were accountable to the *kiap* [administrative officers]. Many of the disputes between men and their wives were chronic disagreements that dragged on for years and blew up periodically over some trifling issue. [1974: 219–20]

Reay also describes the role of missions in settling disputes between clans and in prohibiting other violence. The missionary presence is strong, and once again missionaries are the advance guard.

The missions had also been playing a part in pacifying the warlike clans and prohibiting violence in inter-personal relations. They claimed some success in reducing the incidence of female infanticide, of suicide, and of people being killed in the heat of anger. People credited them with policing the Administration's ban on both killing witches and mutilating adulterers and pig-stealers. The missionaries were concerned that the clans adhered to their traditional enmities and still looked forward to an eventual resumption of warfare. In 1958 the missionary anthropologist Aufenanger (1959) made a study of war magic and destroyed the war magic houses (*obo kundje nggar*) belonging to a number of groups on the northern side of the Wahgi River and also around Kup, east of Minj. In 1961 the Catholic Mission resumed this work and accounted for the war magic of a few more clans, but those of the Minj area resisted firmly. [1974: 209–10]

In the same volume, Ann Chowning (1974: 152–53) questions the emphasis that anthropologists have sometimes placed on restoring peace and harmony in disturbed social relations. In speaking of the days before pacification, she observes that few serious disputes were amicably settled among the Sengseng. Chowning notes that some Melanesian societies tolerate and even enjoy quarreling, provided it does not lead to killing within the community; some people do not feel the need to live in harmony.

On this same point, A. L. Epstein, the editor of the volume, remarks that living in amity is a social value and different societies attach different weight to it.

Amity as an ideal is likely to be more strongly emphasized where people find it important, for whatever reasons, to remain together in relatively stable residence. This situation does not obtain in Sengseng where the traditional settlement pattern, associated with a bilateral system of kinship which does not tie people to particular localities, tends to isolate each nuclear family. Far from invoking the values of village unity, the Sengseng hold to the ideal of peaceful separation. [1974: 32]

He goes on to say that accounting for different attitudes toward quarreling and the means of control may profitably be approached by looking at village networks of social relationships. Furthermore, Epstein tells us, the colonial policies of the Australian administration prevented the development of either village autonomy or village courts. The Australian administration "has consistently refused to . . . set up 'native courts' on the African model. . . . Reluctance to accord legal recognition to the work of indigenous dispute settlers has rested on the assumed incapacity of New Guineans to handle disputes with the required degree of impartiality" (ibid.: 35–36). The Epstein volume raises important issues connected with the idea of culture as an unbounded phenomenon, and the few observations on the systematic connection between missions and disputing processes are sketchy; one can feel the power of the missions from the observations of Reay and Chowning.

In searching through the ethnographic data, I became more sympathetic to the problems that ethnographers in the field for a short time might have in documenting an influence taking place in people's minds over a long period of time. In the excellent article "Evangelical Rhetoric and the Transformation of Traditional Culture in Papua New Guinea" (1981), Edward Schieffelin was able to penetrate the drama and rhetoric of the evangelical process as it relates to disputing processes. Schieffelin illustrates how the church motivated the Kaluli of New Guinea to accept Christianity. He points to the key symbols of Judgment Day and the Second Coming of Christ as used by the pastors, parts of which paralleled and confirmed elements in the Kalulis' own mythological and religious tradition. Judgment Day not only made sense to the Kaluli as revenge, but also altered the relations between people. Traditionally relations between individuals were regulated by those involved, guided by the canons of reciprocity and sanctioned by the threat of retaliation or revenge. With Judgment Day, conduct toward others is no longer a matter between two persons but between each individual and God: "The fundamental direction of moral reciprocity was moved from the horizontal plane between people to the vertical between man and God mediated by pastor and church organization" (ibid.: 155). Pastors used the rhetoric of Judgment Day to undercut the traditional means of social harmony or social solidarity in order to install new ones. They suggested, for example, that if one killed a pig, the meat should be given not to just one person, but to everybody. This injunction destroyed the meaning of prestation. In traditional times the unreciprocated gift or unavenged wrong presented the protagonists with the urgent need to take steps to attain resolution. Now Judgment Day is replacing this process, not only between individuals, but in general.

Although Schieffelin does not deal directly with justice, it is apparent that the transformation of social relations also changed the Kaluli sense of justice in such a manner as to repress the urgency for conflict resolution through reciprocation or compensation. Another contribution of Schieffelin's report is his emphasis on the function of rhetoric as "the vehicle by which the message is rendered into a social construction upon reality" (1981: 156).

Citing Kidder's (1979) distinction between the "command model of law" and the interactional model for understanding the complex relationship between local-level law and imposed law, George Westermark (1986, 1987) presents an interesting case of Christian influences from the village of Agarabi in the highlands of Papua New Guinea. The Agarabis were the earliest converts to Adventism in the Highlands. Adventists perceive themselves as the followers of the *true* Christian faith. As such, they employ several church-related activities in dispute management, such as taking oaths on the Bible, the communion service, rituals of confession, and intervention by church elders. Interestingly, Westermark observes that Adventists use village courts as often as non-Adventists, even though the courts emphasize adjudication rather than mediation. This use occurs despite the church elders' attitude toward litigation, which they characterize as "not good . . . like shooting a man with an arrow, it is like killing him" (Westermark 1986: 133; 1987: 118–19). But Adventists, says Westermark, use the courts to obtain a sympathetic hearing for their beliefs. At times, these beliefs are given precedence by equating Adventist rules with the laws of the government.

Adventist beliefs only partially limit followers in their use of secular methods, and judicial hearings are utilized even though church officials disparage them. However, dispute outcomes are shaped by the Adventist desire for group harmony and religious merit (Westermark 1987: 131). Westermark identifies one use of the court as a forum for proselytizing *because* "court proceedings do not encourage a proper Christian attitude of conciliation" (ibid.: 142). Yet, in spite of his recognition of the role of religious ideology, Westermark concludes with a quote from Worsley (1984: 59) to the effect that we must not forget that people have the ability to select bits and pieces of the systems that intellectuals build and to recombine them for their own purposes. It seems that because the links between the national and the local level were not drawn taut in New Guinea, alien religious groups have been able to make significant contributions to the pool of bits and pieces that people use to build their own dispute-processing systems.

In another context, Norman Forer (1979) examines the historical roots of the imposition of Western law on American Indians and concludes that any understanding of this process needs to be broad-gauged.

The United States, early in its political life, supported church missionaries in their task of persuading the Indian to accept private enterpreneurship and resettlement. Four interested parties—commercial, clerical, agricultural, and governmental—initially banded together to decide how federal Indian policy could best be turned to their own advantage. Later, Indian intratribal solidarity had to be fractured in order to create a faction amenable to these interests, and hence a fifth collusive partner. This relationship has remained to the present day, with the government gradually, but by no means completely, removing the resocialization process from the churches to its own educational and welfare institutions.

Although Forer's views may be too simplistic or too conspiratorial for the tastes of some readers, his five interested parties are found in many situations of culture contact. The most powerful force in introducing harmony ideology need not be the missionaries. Note, for

example, the state-sponsored informalism in parts of the Indian sub-
continent in the nineteenth and twentieth centuries. The "state"
in the guise of the British East India Company, imperial India, or
modern India has promoted "arbitration" and "compromise," ideals
most persistently expressed as *"panchayat* justice." The history of
the rise and spread of the idea of "panchayat justice" is still being
written, but it is generally conceded that its political intent is pacification, a quieting of the population. Following in the tradition of indirect rule, the East India Company courts in rural southern India mo-
bilized to decentralize and reorganize local self-government, using
the institutional forms of panchayats (Meschievitz and Galanter
1982; Meschievitz pers. comm.).

Enlarging the Context in the West

Although twelve years of observations of Talean court activity
yielded a harmony law model, changes from harmony to confrontational or adversarial law models and back have been documented by
historians for a number of societies, usually from the point of view
of the third party rather than the litigants. Richard Kagan's (1981)
history of Castilian litigation between 1500 and 1700 is one of legal
evolution, revolution, and devolution. With rapid changes—demographic, social, legal, and political—following the Spanish incur-
sions in the New World, the courts came to be linked to increased
adversarial legal behavior and presumably to declining religious fervor. According to Kagan, the medieval tradition, which allowed a
magistrate to base his decisions not on the law but on his own es-
timation of what was correct, was altered to a more formal legal
system that allowed one litigant to defeat the other (ibid.: 22–23).
Kagan suggests an interesting although not altogether convincing
hypothesis based mainly on economic variables.

I am suggesting . . . that the changes set into motion by economic expansion and population growth were the fundamental cause of much of the increase in litigation recorded in Castile's courts. . . . Peasants in England
and France experienced similar tensions . . . and in these countries the evidence also suggests that litigation in the sixteenth century was on the rise.
[Ibid.: 136]

Kagan argues that with geographic mobility and fragmentation of the
primary group came an increase in the number and types of disputes,
which could not adequately be resolved by the informal mechanisms of conciliation and compromise. The adversary process and a

confrontational style were henceforth used as a political and economic legal strategy. The compromise model, however, was ex-
ported to Mexico along with Christian evangelism, where it took
root at the village level for local disputes.

The use of conciliation was widespread in Spanish America, as
was the belief that litigation was to be avoided at all costs. David
Langum (1987) describes the local-level system of dispute resolution
in Mexican California as a community-based legal system whose
goals included conciliation of the parties and the use of community
pressures rather than force to compel dispute resolution, a style that
differed from the regular Mexican trial courts or the courts of first
instance.

> The thesis here is that the primary social function of the Mexican process of
> civil litigation was to heal the breach in the community and between the
> parties caused by the dispute. Resolving the lawsuit itself, in the sense of
> determining disputed facts, declaring who was right and who wrong, or
> compensating victims for harms suffered, all this was secondary. Concilia-
> tion was an effort to utilize a paternalistic process that involved . . . "father-
> figures" to assert gentle pressures upon the disputants to reconcile them-
> selves and accept a face-saving settlement without the necessity of formal
> adjudication. This form of dispute resolution, it was believed, would heal
> the breach in society and in the community. . . . The thesis implies, then,
> that the primary function of the Mexican California courts was to prevent
> litigation, a startling reversal of our normal expectations. [1987: 131–32]

Langum traces this tradition to the late Middle Ages in Spain and
notes that the paternalism of the system was overwhelmingly approved in the Spanish colonies. He quotes other sources from Mexico
indicating widespread and overwhelming support for this harmony
tradition in the practical treatises of Mexican legal publications.
Langum's book describes legal values in collision on the Mexican
California frontier between 1821 and 1846. The Anglo-American ex-
patriates who came to Mexican California held a different set of
legal values, ideas based on the common-law system that looked for
certainty, and they abhorred the particularistic manner of the Mexi-
cans. Values of individualism and acquisitiveness provided the necessary context for a growth of litigation in Spain and Anglo America.
"What does individualism imply for a legal system? . . . First is the
decision to define a disputant as an adversary, and to struggle until
there is a clear winner and loser [instead of making attempts] to resolve conflict. . . . The harsh common law judgment accomplishes
this adversarial definition by reducing a controversy to a clearly defined winner" (1987: 134). According to Langum, legal values in col-

lision were embodied in the conflict between an individualistic law on the one hand and paternalism, communalism, and the spirit of conciliation on the other hand.

Interestingly, similar legal values collided in seventeenth-century New England. Unanimity was carried to an extreme as New England villages strove to maintain internal harmony in order to remain independent from Boston (Lockridge 1970; Zuckerman 1970). These villages used power "to serve the common interest at the expense of competing individual claims" (Auerbach 1983: 16). Yet with the rise in commerce and trade, the courts played an increasing role in managing disputes. With the rise of economic and social stratification, industrialization, and new immigration, and with the decline in church membership, legislation accelerated. And as communities disintegrated, legal tradition replaced the countertradition expressed in mediation and arbitration.

Auerbach argues for the appearance of alternatives to courts during different periods of American history and in the process pinpoints the post–Civil War period as a time when the state began to organize alternative dispute settlement processes in order to allay fears of class warfare and racial discord. A century later a similar pattern appeared. During the 1960's adversarial law was highly valued in the United States as a means for attaining civil rights and civil remedies in issues of race and sex and in consumer and environmental questions. However, there was a backlash. A variety of strange bedfellows with mixed motives—businessmen, lawyers, judges, psychologists, and religious people and laymen—marshaled their allies and moved with surprising speed to introduce a policy embodying harmony ideology in the form of alternative dispute resolution (ADR). Over a ten-year period they translated that ideology into action and institution building (Abel 1982; Goldberg et al. 1985; Nader 1989b), a result that cannot be explained by any single variable.

The point of calling attention to the use of harmony or adversarial modes in both the Spanish-Mexican and Anglo-American legal traditions is to seek to explain why fluctuations in legal ideologies associated with a tolerance for controversy or a search for harmony surface from time to time and to examine the consequences. The Talean uses of harmony and the collision of legal values between the Talean Zapotec village courts and the Villa Alta state courts have different meanings for the villagers and for the village. At issue is not individualism versus community, for both concepts are known and valued by the mountain Zapotec. At issue are resistance and repression in the context of religion and the political economy of the wider polity.

Watching the current ADR movement in the United States, I wonder whether the simultaneous increase in Protestant fundamentalist beliefs about handling conflict (Greenhouse 1986), particularly among the Baptists and the Mormons, and the popularity of psychological therapy models of conflict resolution centering about consensus (see Abel 1982; Gibbs 1963; and Baumgartner 1988) are clues to the global melding of ideologies that are useful to systems of control. Is the story of the people "without history" linked to our story? Is harmony ideology linked to both control and freedom? I was inspired to examine the ethnographic record for the spread of European Christianity (both Catholic and Protestant) and colonialism as one source of the harmony ideology that anthropologists often attribute to "the natives." Although the materials are by no means exhaustive or definitive, the comparative perspective is vital to any understanding of the transformations of dispute resolution and indicates that the case of the Talean Zapotec is by no means unique. If the bounded village is a fiction or at least a conscious and instrumental product of both the external and internal polity, so, too, is the concept of harmony.

Harmony ideology is most likely part of the hegemonic control system that entered Middle America by means of Spanish law and Catholic missionaries. Talean Zapotec use of harmony, both in its cultural and in its social-organizational form, is counter-hegemonic. Harmony and controversy are different poles of the same system of control: the disputants bring controversy, and third parties apply the rhetoric and practices of harmony. The ethnographic connections between disputing processes, political colonization, and missionization constitute the empirical base for testing the hypothesis that the harmony model of law and associated ideologies are used to restrict the encroachment of external, superordinate power and are components of a political ideology that is counter-hegemonic.

The theoretical issues raised by this preliminary survey pivot around the origin, use, and consequences of the concept of harmony. The limitations of the ethnographic data should be acknowledged. The data are uneven and range from implicit to explicit connections between religious proselytizing and disputing processes. The ethnographic writings are better as we approach the contemporary period. By now social science has established the collaboration between institutions of power and influence (Mills 1963). Prior to such findings, a number of anthropologists saw a connection between colonial governments and local law, but they were less inclined to recognize the connection between religious colonialism and local law.

The example of the Talean Zapotec is suggestive of a theory of cultural control that merges harmony and conflict as part of the same control system. Harmony and conflict are not antithetical, as previous theories have suggested. We Westerners may have difficulty grasping the idea of an ideology that values harmony or controversy neutrally unless we understand that any morality regarding harmony and conflict is as contrived as the construction of a social organization that mirrors either ideology. Those of us who attend Christian churches in the United States can attest that Sunday sermons are still filled with the rhetoric of harmony ideology. One characteristic feature of disputing processes and their basis in morality is their attractiveness as forums for an ideological marketplace.

Chapter Fifteen

Ethnography and the Construction of Theory

The Talean Zapotec have created a set of premises that together form a "harmony ideology." This set of premises, derived
partly from indigenous beliefs and partly from Christian missionaries, has allowed them to combat the vandalizing aspects of colonialism and to form the basis for their peaceful utopia. What resulted
is a peace at any price culture that is a social success, sometimes at a
cost to individual Zapotec. Harmony comes at a price. Defense may
turn into oppression, not only among the Zapotec but among other
peoples as well.

The principles that govern an ordered Talean social life are deeply
embedded in social activity and neither coterminous with any sphere
of social activity nor stable through time. Social organization is
based on hierarchy (command), symmetry, and cross-linkage, which
in the daily round serve to stratify, level or equalize, and integrate
the village. The dimensions are integrative (or controlling) because
they are not stable across settings such as religious ritual, work practices, or leisure activity. All three dimensions are found in every domain of village social organization, although over time and for different events, each dimension carries a different weight.

In Talea all groups, whether governmental, religious, or kin, are
organized along command-model hierarchical lines. In the civil and
religious organizations, in work relations, in the family, hierarchy is
based mainly on generation, sex, and age. The leveling dimension, or
the value placed on egalitarian relations, may be contradictory or
complementary and operates in many of the contexts where hierarchy is found, such as the family. Cross-linkage embodies ties of association that result from membership in multiple groups.

Stresses, strains, and fissive activity end up in court because the principles of social organization are not sufficient to control behavior; harmony ideology reinforces organization. The court deals with behavior that slips between social fields where the processes mentioned above operate to restrain conduct. Standards are not homogeneous or universally shared, and as is illustrated in the case materials, the court becomes an important institution for reaffirming and renegotiating, among other beliefs, the ideology of order and harmony, the morality of disputing behavior.

The Spanish Crown created the semiautonomy that both grows out of and supports Talean values of mutual aid, social order, equity, prevention, and village solidarity. Many indigenous communities like Talea utilized the separation of jurisdiction, which was partly motivated by the desire to break up the pre-Conquest apparatus of power, to promote village autonomy. The cost of village autonomy was individual conformity, which was fine as long as Taleans put community before persons.

Maintaining the facade of the bounded community has served the Zapotec well. It has produced in Talea a social organization in which order is not solely law nor even solely a result of law and the enforcement of law. Community courts and community organizations are interdependent. In this book I have analyzed how and why interdependence works. Varying structural poses that adapt to changing situations, Talea has interacted with world systems, in the economics of cash cropping, in the periods of bouts with evangelicals, or in political opposition to government penetration.

The comparison of intra-village mechanisms of disputing reveals opening and closing reactions to external forces, the contraction and expansion of village reliance on the outside that I mentioned in Chapter 1. When external forces impinge on the family, the court becomes the "father"; when outsiders threaten the autonomy of the court, the town meeting supports Talean autonomy; and when these more visible and public institutions fail, there is the supernatural. Fail-safe systems are good insurance. And the powerless console themselves with the thought that in the end it all comes out even. Changes occur over time, but the ideology of a bounded system is elastic and there are plugs to cover each hole in the dike, that is, as long as the system is bounded or is *perceived* as such. Division destroys the bounded community, and once factionalism is pervasive, the elastic use of hierarchy, leveling, and cross-linkage cannot maintain collectivity.

Even before the rapid changes that followed the opening of communications and increasing evangelical activities during the 1960's,

1970's, and 1980's, one could see a shift in Talean social organization of the daily round. In the family, the increasing absence of egalitarian relations is most striking in husband-wife relations and is attributed to Westernization more generally. Male dominance is noticeable in Talea among those who have had regular contact with Western culture. It is also noticeable because it contrasts with neighboring monolingual Zapotec villages, where spouses share authority more equally. On the other hand, relations between parents and children are becoming increasingly egalitarian—also something attributed to recent contact with the outside. In the realm of symmetry, there were signs of transformation as early as the second or third decade of this century. Through the creation of the savings and loan associations called barrios, and the discarding of traditional leveling devices, such as loading the heaviest religious cargos on the richest men, the economic burden has shifted from the individual with a surplus to the group and to people of middle economic status who are upwardly mobile. Ritual kinship also operated as a leveling device, and the rich still care for more godchildren than do the poorer families. But there are indications that this pattern of social leveling and linkage, too, is beginning to change; there is a growing preference for godparents from within the family or the same economic class.

In Talea, leveling devices have given way to stratifying devices, and the social order maintained through the technique of ensuring that citizens share multiple memberships in a variety of organizations is being eroded by out-migration and village exogamy and by a concern for custom-tailoring a personal life. As Taleans have felt outside forces (religious, political, economic, and personal) impinging on and weakening village unity and autonomy, they have increased the number of cross-linking committees and commissions and developed regional organizations. They cannot, however, control the pull of personal life by such means entirely.

A dominant motif in Talea is that the court should hear any dispute brought to it. Individuals initiate complaints that are both caused by and result in patterns of organization and structure at the societal level. In this sense the participants are the movers of law. The actors' sense of power and their knowledge of court organization provide them with guidelines for arguing about how humans should behave if social well-being is the goal. The actors are not merely strategizing to win in the sense of personal gain; they are participating in the internal workings of this system of conflict handling, which appears so intent on settling people's problems and designing agreements to maintain the status quo. Yet, ideas about how to address wrongdoing are molded by social and political ideologies and may originate in places far removed from Talea. Emerging patriarchal values are creating gender conflict and schooling a generational conflict. Whether citizens actively mobilize their efforts to cause change or decide to leave well enough alone depends on whether they see themselves as empowered, active agents or as passive ones. They can step in to right a wrong, or they can give clemency should the situation warrant. Personal relations that are by their nature defined as potentially long-term, such as lender-debtor relationships, usually become part of a well-conceived, long-term strategy for recouping a debt. Fights die, but debts do not. In Talea, citizens not only are able to activate remedies for their own cases, but are consulted by town officials in cases dealing with sensitive matters such as contact with other villages that might involve the district court. Group responsibility for decision-making is stressed in all actions that involve the state.

In a community court operated by lay people, judicial thinking is bound to reflect community values and consciously recognize social utility as the basis for decisions. Although litigants play an important role in deciding cases, town officials have been delegated the authority to decide cases *with the social good in mind.* This delegation of authority is most important in cases involving political oppositions: the authorities in opposition to the police, to the schoolteachers, to members of sects, to the officials in the district court and beyond. With good reason Talean court officials feel concern about cases involving political opposition because they may directly threaten village court authority. Harmony is not usually a goal of these groups.

The discourse that runs through the materials from the Talean courts is one of harmony and balance between the principals. Taleans say theirs is a peaceful town, a place with no factionalism and little or no homicide. There is physical violence, but their depiction of self refers only to behavior that would threaten the corporate village entity. Real violence is that leading to or resulting from factionalism. The Talean concern for harmony makes them more litigious because "you should not take authority into your own hands." In cases of violence, it is not the fighting that is central but rather the reasons for the fighting. Taleans are concerned with the social context in which violence occurs. Will it disorganize the group? In cases that could escalate—"the dangerous cases"—the solution to two wrongs is an agreement, and often the original complaint is trans-

formed beyond the complaint of physical violence to include a violation against the court or against the community by the accused. Aggression against the community requires corrective sanctions, not
restitution. To correct is to erase, and the process of correction
makes it apparant that managing the contradictions between violence and harmony, between balance and controversy, is more an act
of politics than one of law and justice.

In cross-sex cases harmony is pursued through confrontations
that motivate a village official to wax eloquent on harmony and the
importance of role and obligation. Cross-sex violence has little potential to escalate. Such cases activate the village authority as con-
ciliator. The frequency of cross-sex violence gives the courts their
predominantly conciliatory slant. Female plaintiffs evoke suasion
and restitution from court officials, whereas male plaintiffs evoke
accusations and threats. Harmony ideology accommodates both
styles when the final purpose is control.

In the interplay of the property rights of individuals and social
structure, control over relationships rather than over the object dominates. But in clashes between collective interests, the locus is on the
importance of the object itself in settling disputes. In cases of disputes over substance, there is competition with the Villa Alta courts.
In the end, the pattern is the same: local court officials are vigilant
in disputes that threaten the whole. Their tolerance for contentiousness and litigiousness is wide as long as the bounded community is protected. For this reason the communities are peaceful
though not conflict free, an observation especially relevant in cases
involving women. There is nothing harmonious about the way in
which an accusation of abortion is handled, and violent households
are not seen as incompatible with harmony writ large.

The pattern of violent households and relatively peaceful (though
not conflict-free) communities is not universal for rural communities; rather, it is a product of a particular type of political arrangement. People affected by broad processes that disrupt their lives usually deal with the most immediate manifestations rather than with
abstract forces like evangelism. As noted earlier, in *Drinking, Homicide, and Rebellion in Colonial Mexican Villages*, William Taylor
(1979) observes that in much of Indian Mexico at the end of the colonial period the family was mainly a conjugal arrangement—a productive and reproductive unit—rather than the prime focus of allegiance. Taylor links this attitude with the Indian concept of the
individual, which stressed responsibility to the community and the
primacy of community.

One need not romanticize—village solidarity means group survival, and village courts that deal with the minutiae of village life mean local control over village life. In this instance courts become an instrument to defend the social order because they legalize processes of internal order by means of harmony ideologies. The litigants use the courts to shape the boundaries of that order. In Mitla, also in Oaxaca, Elsie Clews Parsons (1936) noticed village solidarity in the face of outsiders. In a later study of Mitla, Charles Leslie (1960) attributed village solidarity to the desire to feel "civilized"; violence was said to be uncommon, and peacefulness and a unified community were supreme social values. The pattern of litigiousness has also been observed in villages in the Valley of Oaxaca. As Henry Selby notes, "The Indians were never slow to defend themselves and their community. They were litigious and effective" (1974: 135–36).

Connecting Ethnography and High-Level Theory

The recent resurgence of anthropological interest in the temporal dimension has been accompanied by disparagement of earlier ethnographic approaches as static or antihistorical, or too localized. Criticism is directed especially at structural-functional theorists who saw law as important to social order and who described society as composed of a set of enduring and relatively harmonious relations in which law is part of a larger system of social control, though perhaps not the most important part. In such constructs reciprocity, interdependence, cultural consensus about obligation, and other mechanisms serve to minimize the role of law or to make the law function as an institution that works to integrate society by clarifying values and behaviors and by ensuring that disputes do not continue to arise. The structural-functionalist theorists were and are internalists for the most part; they describe societies as if they were bounded.

If the early functionalists were internalist in their analyses and focused on tradition—its structure, its enduring nature, its stage of equilibrium—then contemporary anthropologists seem more interested in transformation. World systems theorists (Wallerstein 1974), dependency theorists (Frank 1967), and the Euro-development theorists (Wolf 1982) examine the effect of external forces, of macro-structures, on traditional micro-structures. Both the interest in tradition and the interest in cultural diffusion are standard fare in the anthropological menu, with one usually coming after the other. However, in the present work I illustrate how enduring relations, cultural structures, and world systems interact in ways that result in legal styles of conciliation and in structures of equilibrium—factors to be found where colonialism and Christianity have moved together. Today, by virtue of the speed of social and cultural change, we are able to better recognize the relationship between local cultures and external social forces such as religious and political colonialism, an observation that earlier functionalist studies with internalist perspectives neglected. This awareness forces us to reflect on grossly unequal power structures that overlap in interesting ways, resulting at times in conciliatory legal styles.

What is exhilarating about contemporary anthropology is the growing critique of intellectual paradigms and the "truths" that anthropologists construct from particular paradigms. This is all to the good; however, there is a danger that we might conclude that everything we write about is constructed and therefore "unreal." I argue in this book that the enduring structures described by anthropologists are part of reality and part of the presentation of self of natives to outsiders, part of their adaptation to systems of domination, and that in this context indigenous legal systems appear in equilibrium, or in balance or in harmony.

In ethnography, the realization that the social and cultural fields were broader that the small community under scrutiny made us change the domain of study, made us move out of the community (as Malinowski must have when he realized that an understanding of the *kula* trading ring involved tracing transactions between many Trobriand islands) to include forces that played on and affected community contours (Asad 1973; Wolf 1982). The longitudinal method has seldom been used in ethnographies of law based on particular peoples. Llewellyn and Hoebel (1941) took cases spanning a seventy-year period of rapid change in Cheyenne history and compressed them into an ethnographic present while ignoring external forces of change. In the 1980's the development of ethnohistorical models of law that combine the historical with social-organizational and cultural approaches within the framework of power structures enables us to understand the dynamics of legal change caused by shifting political, economic, or religious alliances (Attia 1985; Hammoudi 1985; Greenhouse 1986; Moore 1986; Nader 1989a) while remaining conscious of our role in constructing anthropological theory.

As I mentioned in the Preface, I combine social and cultural analyses in this book with historical, comparative, and introspective approaches (see also Nader 1972, 1976). Decades of refining and elaborating ethnographies added new dimensions of analysis, but the particular took center stage and both the comparison and the study of the spread of institutions and ideas were pushed to the margins. Comparison became part of the internal analysis of variations, and cross-cultural comparisons were considered methodologically difficult and prone to the ethnocentrism inherent in positivist models. Yet, studies of particular societies could be perceived as a result of circumstances unique to the local scene when there might be evidence to the contrary. We have followed the travels of tobacco from the New World to the Old World and on around the globe, a spread that impacted small- and large-scale systems. We know that religious systems and economic systems, or even subsystems contained in these larger entities—Christianity and Islam, or capitalism and communism, or colonialism and neocolonialism—spread about the world, and we know these external ideologies have an impact on smaller systems. Yet, for the most part we have not integrated our knowledge of traveling ideologies into our understanding of the law in particular societies.

In *The Behavior of Law*, Donald Black (1976: 4) observes that the style of law varies across the world, across relations, from one legal setting to another, from court to court, and from case to case. Legal styles vary with the stratification of social life, its morphology, culture, organization, and social control, and I would add with the diffusion of legal cultures, by imposition or otherwise. Anthropologists concerned with law as social control have consistently underestimated the extent to which Western political and religious traditions have structured the meaning of conflict and harmony. What the anthropologist records is pre-coded with a long historical experience of hierarchy, hegemony, and resistance that survives into the contemporary world of non-Western peoples.

In a seminal paper written by Starr and Yngvesson (1975) entitled "Scarcity and Disputing: Zeroing-in on Compromise Decisions," the authors suggested that anthropologists of law have carried their own harmony ideology to the field and as a result have exaggerated the argument that disputants with multiple ties try to compromise their differences. According to the authors, the published data of Gluckman, Gulliver, and myself made more of the argument that disputants with multiple ties compromise their differences than the data warranted.

Gluckman in *The Judicial Process among the Barotse* (1955), Gulliver in *Social Control in an African Society* (1963), and Nader in "Styles of Court Procedure: To Make the Balance" (1969b) emphasized the compromise or reconciliatory nature of the processes they studied among people in multiplex relations. . . . However, some of their case outcomes cannot be described as compromises between competing claims, some settlements to disputes did not reconcile the disputants, and when an outcome of a reconciliatory process was not to the disputant's liking, he frequently took his complaint elsewhere, sometimes to several different dispute handling forums in order to seek a decision in his favor. (Ibid.: 562)

As partial explanation they observed:

The literature . . . reflects a bias. . . . A Durkheimian emphasis on harmony of interests and shared goals has heavily influenced our thinking and seems to have shaped the ways in which anthropologists have perceived the handling of disputes. . . . It is important to separate the objectives of the disputants from those of the third party, whose interests most frequently will be in maintaining the status quo. (Ibid.: 559–60)

Starr and Yngvesson raised important issues—the degree to which scientific observers are caught by the thought systems of their own cultures and the way that different disciplinary lenses in legal studies screen out data. It is certainly true that anthropologists of law had read Durkheim, an eminent French sociologist often associated with equilibrium theory. It is also true that the literature on courts reflects different disciplinary interests: political science focuses on judicial decision-making; sociology and criminology on the defendant and the legal profession. More recently, other actors such as court clerks and plaintiffs have been studied. An interactive, processual approach looks at all these participants in the courtroom or in the disputing encounter simultaneously. But in addition we need to look at culture.

In my article "Styles of Court Procedure" (Nader 1969b), to which Starr and Yngvesson refer, I described the main feature of Talean court style as one that values achieving a balance between the principals in a case. I also completed a documentary film entitled "To Make the Balance" (1966a). Specifically in Talea the aim of compromise arrived at by adjudication or in some cases adjudication based on compromise: "is to rectify the situation by achieving or reinstating a balance between the parties involved in a dispute" (1969b: 69). After presenting cases taken from the 1966 documentary, I commented: "The judge is a warden of order and fair play among peers. He resolves conflict by minimizing the sense of injustice and outrage felt by parties to a case. . . . He is expected to render a verbal and written agreement for each case—an agreement that *consensus would label equitable*" (ibid.: 85; my emphasis). In this same paper I tried to separate the specifics of the cases from the continuous features that permeated court activities and gave the proceedings their style. Outcome rather than decision was the important dimension for style. Outcome centered attention on the desired result, harmony.

Both parties had to agree on the decision, but "compromise" was not always a result of mutual concessions. It was the judge, rather than the litigants, who, after listening to the parties, decided where consensus lay or how to press the litigants into making their own agreement. In many cases the decision is the judge's understanding of what is best for the social good—which generally means the restoration of relations to a former condition *or* to a condition where conflict is made absent. From the point of view of the users, "making the balance" may look different. In cross-sex cases, for example, female plaintiffs rarely come to court seeking compromise for complaints of physical abuse, lack of support, or abandonment. Yet they are usually awarded conciliatory decisions that are ameliorative at best.

In other cases, when the judge is not a warden of order and fair play minimizing the sense of injustice and outrage, he should be. Taleans distinguish judging well from not judging or fining, and they distinguish good justice from bad justice and finding resolution from finding guilt. But when we look at the whole picture, Talea appears to be a highly ordered village. Taleans are active in asserting themselves to find remedies for wrongs, and their judges are active in articulating a harmony model for dispute resolution. The Taleans litigate because they do not like problems to grow, fester, or escalate. For court officials, the core of harmony style and the associated ideology facilitate internal governance and serve to manage problems stemming from conquest and domination.

Theories explaining legal models or dominant tendencies in disputing processes have been concerned with single variables, like the nature of relations between litigants (Gluckman 1955), or with situations where scarce resources form the basis of a dispute (Pound 1959: 70; Starr and Yngvesson 1975). Such theories are generally limited to an internal perspective. Disputing styles are a component of political ideology, however, and often the result of diffusion. Enlarging the context allows us to come closer to understanding the wider meaning of a conciliatory style and how it effects individuals and collectivities.

The Anthropological Circle

Ambiguities surrounding the study of the cultural components of law have been plentiful even among anthropologists, in whose discipline culture plays a central role. The nature of the societies that anthropologists studied was always implicitly compared with the anthropologist's culture of origin, especially when he or she was dealing with justice or questions of right and wrong because the values in these cultural realms are part of the deep structure of consciousness. Assumptions held among anthropologists by virtue of their cultural upbringing are rarely questioned systematically. The linguist Edward Sapir (1924) referred to consistent, harmonious, balanced cultures as "genuine" rather than "spurious." Configurationalists such as Sapir and Ruth Benedict were interested in discovering the themes or values that hold a culture together and in distinguishing it from other cultures. For the users of an equilibrium model—anthropologist or native—conflict was discord, its opposite was order or harmony. On the other hand, Max Gluckman even found "peace in the feud" (Gluckman 1959). Like Sapir, those anthropologists who could not find peace in the feud equated conflict with anomie (in good Durkheimian tradition) and with deviant, abnormal behavior (and sometimes excluded such behavior from their publications); harmony they equated with adherence to cultural elements, something normal. Dahrendorf (1967) noted that the functionalists' stress on common values and equilibrium may have stemmed from a concern with normative behavior or nostalgia for synthesis. The point here is to recognize that the negative and positive valuations assigned to conflict and harmony may be seen as products of a cultural construction to which Western or European social scientists belong. Try asking Americans, or Japanese for that matter, if they can imagine harm stemming from harmony. Harmony and conflict models are cultural constructs, grids through which we view the behavior of others, components others use to control or to protect themselves from control.

This book espouses a view that neither conflict nor harmony activity is inherently more "genuine" or more "spurious" or that one is somehow better than the other. As much "evil" may result from harmony ideology as "good" may result from conflict ideology, or vice versa. The need to indicate that the conflict and harmony models may both be examined for their social value suggests the difficulties that lay persons and social scientists have had in examining these behaviors in a detached manner. By virtue of entrapment in culturally constructed and preferred models, theoretical discussions of harmony and conflict hide values and confuse the analysis, ignore the data, or manipulate publics.

I have worked in three different field sites: in the south of Mexico, in the south of Lebanon, and among dispersed people in the United

States. Most of this book has featured the nature of harmony ideology as an aspect of Talea's social and cultural process, as part of its political balancing act. The discourse of harmony among the Talean Zapotec is undoubtedly connected to the spread of Christianity and colonial policies, as it was among the other people that I mention in the preceding chapter. In south Lebanon the conflict ideology was most apparent. For the Shia Moslems of Libaya, the conflict model was reflected in a social organization characterized by endogamous duality. In the United States we have three clusters of ideology: the adversary, controversial, or confrontational model; the consensus, therapeutic, or harmony model; and the efficiency model. What informants say in all three fieldwork sites is indicative of the construction of cultures of disputing processes. The Zapotec claimed that there were no disputes, although they litigated in high proportion. The Shia Moslem easily admitted there were conflicts. In the United States the expressions of cultural ideas are contradictory; some say Americans are too litigious, others say they are not litigious enough, still others that the system of dispute management is not efficient enough—all responses reflective of dispute-processing cultures.

Anthropologists of an earlier day setting out to understand other cultures used the concept of culture to describe shared traditions passed from one generation to another and the products of that shared tradition. We can no longer speak about culture solely as the organic notion of earlier anthropologists. Now theorists speak about hegemony as a form of cultural control. Ideas such as harmony and behavior such as confrontation (or even legal efficiency) may originate locally and spread, be imposed, be recombined and used to control or to resist control, and result in distributing power by means of the remedy generated.

Anthropologists of law and legal historians are now observing that with the spread of political and religious colonialism harmony replaced feuds and wars, and that later in new nation-states the harmony model, commonly associated with small communities, was being replaced by the adversary model (Nader 1978; Nader and Todd 1978). The old nation-states appeared to be moving in the opposite direction. Such observations indicate that cultural values underlying disputing processes change over time and circumstance and are profoundly political. Both harmony and controversy have different meanings to different peoples and classes, but they may be used for similar purposes. Sally Merry (1982) has made a similar point in relation to mediation. The key differences between harmony ideologies revolve around harmony as means or as goal, or simply as justification. For the Zapotec disputing may be a means to harmony and to autonomy and self-determination; for the Shia Moslems conflict is part of the struggle in life, normative behavior. For those spearheading commercial or colonialist policies, harmony is an ideology of pacification and a way to "civilize" populations, a tool to create different cultural forms.

How harmony is perceived by the folk fits with the prevalent social science theories: in equilibrium theory, as in Zapotec beliefs, social relations must be kept in balance; in liberal theory, law responds to social need, and harmony is seen as social justice; in Marxist theories, law is a product of the capitalist ruling class, as it is in the colonial context; and in conflict theory, in which disputing is normative behavior, it is part of the struggle between groups. A theory of harmony requires that finer distinctions be made between control over and remedies for individuals and the social order. Social scientists who have looked at cultural components of dispute resolution without drawing distinctions between levels of activity find it difficult to develop a theory of harmony that encompasses more than particular dispute resolution styles. In the article "Styles of Court Procedure: To Make the Balance" (Nader 1969b), I contrasted the harmony model in disputing processes with a zero-sum game model in terms of the impact on individual litigants. The analysis was set in the example of particular cases, and the meaning of harmony or zero-sum models for the construction of law and the social order was implied: the impact on the wider social order was the impact on the individual writ large. I missed the meaning of harmony as an internal accommodation to conquest and domination. Black (1976) describes the conciliatory style as having a standard of harmony and of solution through resolution. To the Zapotec or the Tongans, conciliation, harmony, and resolution have quite different meanings even though they share a common history of Christian missionizing and colonialism. The differences may be explained by social-structural variables. But typologies are not useful for understanding the diffusion of global ideologies.

Conciliation, harmony, and resolution have such different uses and consequences as to merit different labels (see Rothschild 1986). Harmony that leads to autonomy is different from harmony that leads to control or oppression or pacification; conciliation may lead to conflict as well as to peace; and resolution may lead to injustice as well as justice. Disputing processes cannot be explained solely as a reflection of some predetermined set of social conditions. Rather, they reflect the processes of an evolving cultural construction, that may be a response to demand, a product of ruling interests, a result of class conflict or accommodation. Harmony as a general conception for life should be scrutinized in relation to the construction of law, much as conflict and controversy have been examined in relation to the development of law (Nader 1989b).

We have given recognition to conflict because it is exemplified in behavior. Harmony on the other hand is housed in the mind. Anthropologists have made strong advances in demonstrating that law and politics are not isolatable, and we are now reaching the understanding that religion and law are not separable. The morality of disputing processes is now everywhere heavily influenced by ideologies of a religious nature. Law and religion may have been officially separated in Western legal systems, but in former colonies of the Western world they are not. It follows from these observations that a new range of questions will center on contemporary disputing as an epiphenomenon of controlling processes that will continue to cycle into the next century.

Reference Matter

References Cited

Abel, R. L.
    1979   Western Courts in Non-Western Settings: Patterns of Court Use in Colonial and Neo-colonial Africa. *In* The Imposition of Law, S. Burman and B. Harrell-Bond, eds. New York, Academic Press, pp. 167–200.
    1982   ed., The Politics of Informal Justice. Vol. 1: The American Experience; Vol. 2: Comparative Studies. New York, Academic Press.

Asad, T., ed.
    1973   Anthropology and the Colonial Encounter. New York, Humanities Press.

Attia, H.
    1985   Water Sharing Rights in the Jerid Oases of Tunisia. *In* Property, Social Structure, and Law in the Modern Middle East, A. Mayer, ed. Albany, State University of New York Press.

Aubert, V.
    1966   Some Notes After the Burg Wartenstein Conference on the Ethnography of Law. Memo to L. Nader.
    1969   Law as a Way of Resolving Conflicts: The Case of a Small Industrialized Society. *In* Law in Culture and Society, L. Nader, ed. Chicago, Aldine Publishing Company, 282–303.

Auerbach, J.
    1983   Justice Without Law? New York, Oxford University Press.

Aufenanger, H.
    1959   The War-Magic Houses in the Wahgi Valley and Adjacent Areas (New Guinea). Anthropos 54: 1–26.

Baumgartner, M. P.
    1988   The Moral Order of a Suburb. New York, Oxford University Press.

Beidelman, T. O.
    1974   Social Theory and the Study of Christian Missions. Africa 44 (3): 235–49.

1982   Colonial Evangelism: A Socio-historical Study of an East African Mission at the Grassroots. Bloomington, Indiana University Press.

Berg, P.
1974   The Zoogocho Plaza System in the Sierra Zapoteca of Villa Alta. *In* Markets in Oaxaca, S. Cook and M. Diskin, eds. Austin, University of Texas Press.

Best, A., and A. R. Andreason
1977   Consumer Response to Unsatisfactory Purchases: A Survey of Perceiving Defects, Voicing Complaints, and Obtaining Redress. Law and Society Review 11: 701–42.

Black, D.
1973   The Mobilization of Law. Journal of Legal Studies 2: 125–49.
1976   The Behavior of Law. New York, Academic Press.

Bohannan, P.
1957   Justice and Judgment Among the Tiv. London, Oxford University Press for the International African Institute.

Borah, W. W.
1951   New Spain's Century of Depression. Ibero-Americana, no. 35. Berkeley, University of California Press.
1983   Justice by Insurance: The General Indian Court of Colonial Mexico and the Legal Aides of the Half-Real. Berkeley, University of California Press.

Boyum, K. O., and L. Mather, eds.
1983   Empirical Theories About Courts. New York, Longman.

Canter, R.
1978   Dispute Settlement and Dispute Processing in Zambia: Individual Choice Versus Societal Constraints. *In* The Disputing Process: Law in Ten Societies, L. Nader and H. F. Todd, eds. New York, Columbia University Press, pp. 247–80.

Chance, J. K.
1978   Indice del Archivo del Juzgado de Villa Alta, Oaxaca: Epoca Colonial. Publications in Anthropology 21. Nashville, Tenn., Vanderbilt University Press.

Chanock, M.
1985   Law, Custom, and Social Order: The Colonial Experience in Malawi and Zambia. Cambridge, Cambridge University Press.

Chinas, B.
1973   The Isthmus Zapotecs: Women's Roles in Cultural Context. New York, Holt, Rinehart and Winston.

Chowning, A.
1974   Disputing in Two West New Britain Societies: Similarities and Differences. *In* Contention and Dispute: Aspects of Law and Social Control in Melanesia, A. L. Epstein, ed. Canberra, Australian National University Press, pp. 152–97.

Cohn, B. S.
1959   Some Notes on Law and Change in North India. Economic Development and Cultural Change 8: 79–93.
Collier, J. F.
1973   Law and Social Change in Zinacantan. Stanford, Calif., Stanford University Press.
Colson, E.
1953   Social Control and Vengeance in Plateau Tonga Society. Africa 23: 199–212.
1973   Tranquility for the Decision-maker. In Cultural Illness and Health, L. Nader and T. W. Maretzki, eds. Washington D.C., American Anthropological Association, pp. 89–96.
1974   Tradition and Contract: The Problem of Order. Chicago, Aldine Publishing Company.
Comaroff, J., and J. Comaroff
1986   Christianity and Colonialism in South Africa. American Ethnologist 13: 1–22.
Dahrendorf, R.
1967   Society and Democracy in Germany. New York, W. W. Norton and Company.
de la Fuente, J.
1949   Yalalag: Una Villa Zapoteca Serrana. Serie Científica. Mexico City, Museo Nacional de Antropología.
Dennis, P. A.
1987   Inter-village Conflict in Oaxaca. New Brunswick, N.J., Rutgers University Press.
Dillon, R.
1980   Violent Conflict in Meta' Society. American Ethnologist 7 (4): 658–73.
Dredge, C. P.
1979   Dispute Settlement in the Mormon Community: The Operation of Ecclesiastical Courts in Utah. In Access to Justice, vol. 4, The Anthropological Perspective: Patterns of Conflict Management. Essays in the Ethnography of Law, K.-F. Koch, ed. Milan, A. Giuffrè, pp. 191–215.
El Guindi, F.
1973   The Internal Structure of the Zapotec Conceptual System. Journal of Symbolic Anthropology 1: 15–34.
Epstein, A. L., ed.
1974   Contention and Dispute: Aspects of Law and Social Control in Melanesia. Canberra, Australian National University Press.
Fallers, L. F.
1969   Law Without Precedent: Legal Ideas in Action in the Courts of Colonial Busoga. Chicago, University of Chicago Press.
Forer, N.
1979   The Imposed Wardship of American Indian Tribes: A Case Study

of the Prairie Band Potawatomi. *In* The Imposition of Law, S. Burman and B. Harrell-Bond, eds. New York, Academic Press.

Foster, G.
1961   The Dyadic Contract: A Model for the Social Structure of a Mexican Peasant Village. American Anthropologist 63: 1173–92.
1963   The Dyadic Contract in Tzintzuntzan, II: Patron-Client Relationship. American Anthropologist 65: 1280–84.
1967   Tzintzuntzan Mexican Peasants in a Changing World. Boston, Little, Brown and Company.

Frank, A. G.
1967   Capitalism and Underdevelopment in Latin America. New York, Monthly Review Press.

Friedman, L. M.
1983   Courts over Time: A Survey of Theories and Research. *In* Empirical Theories About Courts, K. O. Boyum and L. Mather, eds. New York, Longman, pp. 9–50.

Gay, J. A.
1881   Historia de Oaxaca. 2 vols. Mexico.

Gerhard, P.
1972   A Guide to the Historical Geography of New Spain. Cambridge, Cambridge University Press.

Gibbs, J. L.
1963   The Kpelle Moot: A Therapeutic Model for the Informal Settlement of Disputes. Africa 33: 1–11.

Gluckman, M.
1955   The Judicial Process Among the Barotse of Northern Rhodesia. Manchester, Eng., Manchester University Press.
1959   Custom and Conflict in Africa. Glencoe, Ill., Free Press.
1965   The Ideas of Barotse Jurisprudence. New Haven, Yale University Press.

Goldberg, S. B., et al.
1985   Dispute Resolution. Boston, Little, Brown and Company.

Gordon, R. W.
1982   New Developments in Legal Theory. *In* The Politics of Law, D. Kairys, ed. New York, Pantheon Books, pp. 281–93.

Greenhouse, C.
1986   Praying for Justice: Faith, Order and Community in an American Town. Ithaca, N.Y., Cornell University Press.

Gulliver, P. H.
1963   Social Control in an African Society: A Study of the Arusha, Agricultural Masai of Northern Tanganyika. Boston, Boston University Press.
1969   Dispute Settlement Without Courts: The Ndendeuli of Southern Tanzania. *In* Law in Culture and Society, L. Nader, ed. Chicago, Aldine Publishing Company, 24–68.

1971   Neighbours and Networks: The Idiom of Kinship in Social Action Among the Ndendeuli of Tanzania. Berkeley, University of California Press.

1979   Disputes and Negotiations: A Cross-cultural Perspective. New York, Academic Press.

Hahm, P-C.
1967   The Korean Political Tradition and Law. Seoul, Hollym.
1968   Korea's Initial Encounter with Western Law, 1865–1910. Korea Observer 1: 80–93.

Hammoudi, A.
1985   Substance and Relation: Water Rights and Water Distribution in the Dora Valley. *In* Property, Social Structure, and Law in the Modern Middle East, A. Mayer, ed. Albany, State University of New York Press, pp. 27–57.

Hamnett, B. R.
1971   Politics and Trade in Southern Mexico, 1750–1821. Cambridge, Cambridge University Press.

Hickson, L.
1979   Hierarchy, Conflict, and Apology in Fiji. *In* Access to Justice, vol. 4, The Anthropological Perspective: Patterns of Conflict Management. Essays in the Ethnography of Law, K.-F. Koch, ed. Milan, A. Giuffrè, pp. 17–39.

Hirabayashi, L.
1980   Migration, Mutual Aid and Association: Mountain Zapotec in Mexico City. Ph.D. Dissertation, Department of Anthropology, University of California, Berkeley.

1986   The Migrant Village Association in Latin America. Latin American Research Review 21 (3): 7–29.

Holleman, J. F.
1974   Issues in African Law. The Hague, Mouton Publishers.

Hunt, E. R., and E. Hunt
1967   The Role of Courts in Rural Mexico. *In* Peasants in the Modern World, P. Bock, ed. Albuquerque, University of New Mexico Press, pp. 109–39.

Hurst, W.
1981   The Functions of Courts in the United States, 1950–1980. Law and Society Review 15: 401–72.

Kagan, R.
1981   Lawsuits and Litigants in Castile, 1500–1700. Chapel Hill, University of North Carolina Press.

Kearney, M.
1972   The Winds of Ixtepji: World View and Society in a Zapotec Town. New York, Holt, Rinehart and Winston.

Kennett, A.
1968   Bedouin Justice: Law and Customs Among the Egyptian Bedouin. London, Frank Cass.

Kidder, R.
    1979   Toward an Integrated Theory of Imposed Law. *In* The Imposi-
            tion of Law, S. Burman and B. Harrell-Bond, eds. New York, Aca-
            demic Press, pp. 289–306.
Koch, K.-F.
    1967   Conflict and Its Management Among the Jalé People of West New
            Guinea. Ph.D. Dissertation, University of California, Berkeley.
    1974   War and Peace in Jalemo: The Management of Conflict in High-
            land New Guinea. Cambridge, Harvard University Press.
Krislov, S.
    1983   Theoretical Perspectives on Case Load Studies: A Critique. *In*
            Empirical Theories About Courts, K. O. Boyum and L. Mather,
            eds. New York, Longman, pp. 161–87.
Kroeber, A. L.
    1917   Zuni Kin and Clan. Anthropological Papers of the American Mu-
            seum of Natural History, 18, pt. 2, pp. 39–205.
    1957   Style and Civilizations. Ithaca, N.Y., Cornell University Press.
Langum, D.
    1987   Law and Community on the Mexican California Frontier: Anglo-
            American Expatriates and the Clash of Legal Traditions, 1821–
            1846. Norman, University of Oklahoma Press.
Laviada, I.
    1978   Los Caciques de la Sierra. Mexico City, Editorial Jus.
Lemoine, V. E.
    1966   Algunos Datos Históricos-Geográficos Acerca de Villa Alta y su
            Comarca. *In* Summa Anthropologica: En Homenaje a Roberto J.
            Weitlaner. Mexico City, Instituto Nacional de Antropología e
            Historia, Secretaría de Educación Pública, pp. 193–202.
Leslie, C.
    1960   Now We Are Civilized: A Study of the World View of the Zapo-
            tec Indians of Mitla, Oaxaca. Detroit, Wayne State University.
Llewellyn, K. N., and E. A. Hoebel
    1941   The Cheyenne Way: Conflict and Case Law in Primitive Juris-
            prudence. Norman, University of Oklahoma Press.
Lockridge, K.
    1970   A New England Town: The First Hundred Years. New York,
            W. W. Norton and Company.
Maine, H. S.
    1861   Ancient Law, Its Connection with the Early History of Society
            and Its Relation to Modern Ideas. London, John Murray. Paper-
            back edition: Boston, Beacon Press, 1963.
Malinowski, B.
    1926   Crime and Custom in Savage Society. London, Kegan, Paul,
            Trench, Trubner and Company.
Malinowski, B., and J. de la Fuente
    1982   Malinowski in Mexico: The Economics of a Mexican Market

System. Edited and with an introduction by Susan Drucker-Brown. London, Routledge and Kegan Paul.

Marcus, G.
1979   Litigation, Interpersonal Conflict, and Noble Succession Disputes in the Friendly Islands. *In* Access to Justice, vol. 4, The Anthropological Perspective: Patterns of Conflict Management. Essays in the Ethnography of Law, K.-F. Koch, ed. Milan, A. Giuffrè, pp. 69–104.

Mather, L., and B. Yngvesson
1980–81   Language, Audience, and the Transformation of Disputes. Law and Society Review 15 (3–4): 775–821.

Mauss, M., and M. H. Beuchat
1906   Les Variations Saisonnières des Sociétés Esquimaux; Etude de Morphologie Social. Année Sociologique 9: 39–132.

Merry, S.
1982   The Social Organization of Mediation in Nonindustrial Societies: Implications for Informal Community Justice in America. *In* The Politics of Informal Justice, R. L. Abel, ed. New York, Academic Press, vol. 2, pp. 17–45.

Meschievitz, C. S., and M. Galanter
1982   In Search of Nyaya Panchayats: The Politics of a Moribund Institution. *In* The Politics of Informal Justice, R. L. Abel, ed. New York, Academic Press, vol. 2, pp. 47–77.

Metzger, D.
1960   Conflict in Chulsanto: A Village in Chiapas. Alpha Kappa Delta 30: 35–48.

Miller, W.
1955   Two Concepts of Authority. American Anthropologist 57 (2/1): 271–89.

Mills, C. W.
1963   Power, Politics, and People: The Collected Essays of C. Wright Mills, I. L. Horowitz, ed. New York, Oxford University Press.

Moore, S. F.
1958   Power and Property in Inca Peru. New York, Columbia University Press.
1986   Social Facts and Fabrications: Customary Law on Kilimanjaro, 1880–1980. New York, Cambridge University Press.

Nadel, S.
1942   A Black Byzantium. London, Oxford University Press.
1947   The Nuba. London, Oxford University Press.

Nader, L.
1964a   Talea and Juquila: A Comparison of Zapotec Social Organization. University of California Publications in American Archaeology and Ethnology 48 (3): 195–296.
1964b   An Analysis of Zapotec Law Cases. Ethnology 3 (6): 404–19.

1965a   Choices in Legal Procedure: Shia Moslem and Mexican Zapotec. American Anthropologist 167: 394–99.

1965b   The Anthropological Study of Law. American Anthropologist, Special Issue: The Ethnology of Law, Laura Nader, ed., 67 (6): 3–32.

1966a   To Make the Balance. Film Distribution: University of California Extension Media Center.

1966b   Variations in Zapotec Legal Procedures. *In* Summa Anthropologica: En Homenaje a Roberto J. Weitlaner. Mexico City, Instituto Nacional de Antropología e Historia, Secretaría de Educación Pública, pp. 375–83.

1969a   Law in Culture and Society: An Introduction. *In* Law in Culture and Society, L. Nader, ed. Chicago, Aldine Publishing Company, pp. 1–10.

1969b   Styles of Court Procedure: To Make the Balance. *In* Law in Culture and Society, L. Nader, ed. Chicago, Aldine Publishing Company, pp. 69–91.

1969c   The Zapotec of Oaxaca. *In* Handbook of Middle American Indians, R. Wauchope, general ed. Austin, University of Texas Press, vol. 7, pt. 1: 329–59.

1972   Up the Anthropologist: Perspectives Gained from Studying Up. *In* Reinventing Anthropology, D. Hymes, ed. New York, Pantheon Press, pp. 285–311. Reprinted in Anthropology for the 1980's, J. B. Cole, ed. Glencoe, Ill., Free Press.

1976   Professional Standards and What We Study. *In* Ethics and Anthropology: Dilemmas in Fieldwork, M. Rynkiewich and J. P. Spradley, eds. New York, John Wiley and Sons, pp. 167–81.

1978   The Direction of Law and the Development of Extra-judicial Processes in Nation-State Societies. *In* Cross-examinations: Essays in Memory of Max Gluckman, P. H. Gulliver, ed. Leiden, E. J. Brill, pp. 78–95.

1979   Central vs. Peripheral Problems in Disciplinary Science. Paper presented in a Plenary Session on the Emergence of Global Society, American Anthropological Association Meetings. Cincinnati, Ohio, November 29, 1979.

1980   ed., No Access to Law: Alternatives to the American Judicial System. New York, Academic Press.

1981   Little Injustices: Laura Nader Looks at the Law. Odyssey Series PBS film, first shown November 3, 1981.

1983   A Comparative Perspective on Legal Evolution, Revolution, and Devolution. Michigan Law Review, pp. 993–1005.

1984a   From Disputing to Complaining. *In* Toward a General Theory of Social Control, D. Black, ed. New York, Academic Press, pp. 71–94.

1984b   The Recurrent Dialectic Between Legality and Its Alternatives: The Limitations of Binary Thinking. University of Pennsylvania Law Review 132 (3): 621–45.

1985   A User Theory of Legal Change as Applied to Gender. *In* The Nebraska Symposium on Motivation: The Law as a Behavioral Instrument, G. B. Melton, ed. Lincoln, University of Nebraska Press, vol. 2, pp. 1–33.

1986   Some Notes on Alternative Dispute Resolution: A Bifurcate Perspective on the Making of an Ideology. Lecture delivered at the University of Florida Law School.

1989a   The Crown, the Colonists and the Course of Village Law. *In* History and Power in the Study of Law, J. Starr and J. Collier, eds. Ithaca, N.Y., Cornell University Press, pp. 320–44.

1989b   The ADR Explosion: The Implications of Rhetoric in Legal Reform. *In* Windsor Yearbook of Access to Justice, Spring.

Nader, L., and D. Metzger
1963   Conflict Resolution in Two Mexican Communities. American Anthropologist 65 (3): 584–94.

Nader, L., and H. Todd, eds.
1978   The Disputing Process: Law in Ten Societies. New York, Columbia University Press.

Paddock, J.
1975   Studies on Antiviolent and "Normal" Communities. Aggressive Behavior 1: 217–33.

Parnell, P. C.
1978a   Conflict and Competition in a Mexican Judicial District. Ph.D. Dissertation, Department of Anthropology, University of California, Berkeley.

1978b   Village or State: Comparative Legal Systems in a Mexican Judicial District. *In* The Disputing Process: Law in Ten Societies, L. Nader and H. Todd, eds. New York, Columbia University Press, pp. 315–50.

1989   Escalating Disputes: Social Participation and Change in the Oaxacan Highlands. Tucson, University of Arizona Press.

Parsons, E. C.
1936   Mitla, Town of the Souls, and Other Zapotec-Speaking Pueblos of Oaxaca, Mexico. Chicago, University of Chicago Press.

Pérez-García, R.
1956   La Sierra Juárez. 2 vols. Mexico City: Gráfica Cervantina.

Pospisil, L.
1958   Kapauku Papuans and Their Law. Yale University Publications in Anthropology 54. New Haven.

Pound, R.
1959   An Introduction to the Philosophy of Law. New Haven, Yale University Press.

Radcliffe-Brown, A. R.
    1952   Structure and Function in Primitive Society: Essays and Ad-
            dresses. Glencoe, Ill.: Free Press.
Reay, M.
    1974   Changing Conventions of Dispute Settlement in Minjarea. *In*
            Contention and Dispute: Aspects of Law and Social Control in
            Melanesia, A. L. Epstein, ed. Canberra, Australian National
            University Press, pp. 198–239.
Ricard, R.
    1966   The Spiritual Conquest of Mexico: An Essay on the Apostolate
            and the Evangelizing Methods of the Mendicant Orders in New
            Spain, 1523–1572, translated by L. B. Simpson. Berkeley, Uni-
            versity of California Press.
Richardson, J.
    1940   Law and Status Among the Kiowa Indians. Monographs of the
            American Ethnological Society, no. 1. Seattle, University of
            Washington Press.
Rose, L.
    1988   The Politics of Harmony: Land Dispute Strategies in Swaziland.
            Ph.D. Dissertation, Department of Anthropology, University of
            California, Berkeley.
Rosen, L.
    1984   Bargaining for Reality. Chicago: University of Chicago Press.
Rothschild, J.
    1986   Mediation as Social Control. Ph.D. Dissertation, Department of
            Sociology, University of California, Berkeley.
Royce, A. P.
    1974   Prestige and Affiliation in an Urban Community: Juchitan,
            Oaxaca. Ph.D. Dissertation, Department of Anthropology, Uni-
            versity of California, Berkeley.
Salzman, P. C.
    1988   Fads and Fashions in Anthropology. Anthropology Newsletter
            29 (5): 1.
Sapir, E.
    1921   Language: An Introduction to the Study of Speech. New York,
            Harcourt, Brace and Company.
    1924   Culture, Genuine and Spurious. American Journal of Sociology
            29: 401–29.
Schapera, I.
    1959   A Handbook of Tswana Law and Custom. New York, Oxford
            University Press.
Schieffelin, E. L.
    1981   Evangelical Rhetoric and the Transformation of Traditional Cul-
            ture in Papua New Guinea. Comparative Studies in Society and
            History 23 (1): 150–57.

Schmieder, O.
1930   The Settlements of the Tzapotec and Mije Indians, State of Oaxaca, Mexico. University of California Publications in Geography, vol. 4. Berkeley.

Schneider, D. M.
1957   Political Organization, Supernatural Sanctions and the Punishment for Incest on Yap. American Anthropologist 59 (5): 791–800.

Selby, H.
1974   Zapotec Deviance: The Convergence of Folk and Modern Sociology. Austin, University of Texas Press.

Shapiro, J.
1981   Ideologies of Catholic Missionary Practice in a Postcolonial Era. Comparative Studies in Society and History 23 (1): 130–49.

Spradley, J.
1970   You Owe Yourself a Drunk: An Ethnography of Urban Nomads. Boston, Little, Brown and Company.

Starr, J. O.
1978   Dispute and Settlement in Rural Turkey: An Ethnography of Law. Leiden, E. J. Brill.

Starr, J. O., and B. Yngvesson.
1975   Scarcity and Disputing: Zeroing-in on Compromise Decisions. American Ethnologist 2 (3): 553–66.

Swadesh, M.
1949   El Idioma de los Zapotecos. In Los Zapotecos, by Lucio Mendieta y Núñez et al. Mexico City, Universidad Nacional de México, Instituto de Investigaciones Sociales.

Takirambudde, P.
1983   External Law and Social Structure in an African Context: An Essay About Normative Imposition and Survival in Swaziland. Comparative and International Law Journal of Southern Africa 16: 209–28.

Taylor, W.
1979   Drinking, Homicide, and Rebellion in Colonial Mexican Villages. Stanford, Calif., Stanford University Press.

Van Velson, J.
1969   Procedural Informality, Reconciliation and False Comparisons. In Ideas and Procedures in African Customary Law, M. Gluckman, ed. London, Oxford University Press, pp. 137–52.

Vélez-Ibañez, C.
1983   Bonds of Mortal Trust: The Cultural Systems of Rotating Credit Associations Among Urban Mexican Chicanos. New Brunswick, N.J., Rutgers University Press.

Wallerstein, I.
1974   The Modern World System: Capitalist Agriculture and the Ori-

gins of the European World Economy in the Sixteenth Century. New York, Academic Press.

Westermark, G. D.

1986   Court Is an Arrow: Legal Pluralism in Papua New Guinea. Ethnology 25 (2): 131–49.

1987   Church Law, Court Law, Competing Forums in a Highlands Village. *In* Anthropology in the High Valleys: Essays on the New Guinea Highlands in Honor of Kenneth E. Read, L. L. Langness and T. E. Hays, eds. Novato, Calif., Chandler and Sharp Publications, pp. 109–35.

Whitecotton, J. W.

1977   The Zapotecs: Princes, Priests, and Peasants. Norman, University of Oklahoma Press.

Williams, N.

1987   Two Laws: Managing Disputes in a Contemporary Aboriginal Community. Canberra, Australian Institutes of Aboriginal Studies.

Wolf, E.

1959   Sons of the Shaking Earth. The People of Mexico and Guatemala: Their Land, History and Culture. Chicago, University of Chicago Press.

1982   Europe and the People Without History. Berkeley, University of California Press.

Worsley, P.

1984   The Three Worlds: Culture and World Development. Chicago, University of Chicago Press.

Young, C. M.

1976   The Social Setting of Migration: Factors Affecting Migration from a Sierra Zapotec Village in Oaxaca, Mexico. Ph.D. Dissertation, University of London.

Zuckerman, M.

1970   Peaceable Kingdoms: New England Towns in the Eighteenth Century. New York, Alfred A. Knopf.

Index

In this index an "f" after a number indicates a separate reference on the next page, and an "ff" indicates separate references on the next two pages. A continuous discussion over two or more pages is indicated by a span of numbers, e.g., "57–59." *Passim* is used for a cluster of references in close but not consecutive sequence.